Urban Microclimate

Urban Microclimate

Designing the Spaces Between Buildings

Evyatar Erell, David Pearlmutter and Terry Williamson

earthscan
from Routledge

First published by Earthscan in the UK and USA in 2011

For a full list of publications please contact:
Earthscan
2 Park Square, Milton Park, Abingdon, Oxfordshire OX14 4RN
711 Third Avenue, New York, NY 10017

First issued in paperback 2015

Earthscan is an imprint of the Taylor & Francis Group, an informa business

Copyright © Evyatar Erell, David Pearlmutter and Terry Williamson, 2011.
Published by Taylor & Francis.

All rights reserved. No part of this publication may be reproduced, stored in a retrieval system, or transmitted, in any form or by any means, electronic, mechanical, photocopying, recording or otherwise, except as expressly permitted by law, without the prior, written permission of the publisher.

Notices
Practitioners and researchers must always rely on their own experience and knowledge in evaluating and using any information, methods, compounds, or experiments described herein. In using such information or methods they should be mindful of their own safety and the safety of others, including parties for whom they have a professional responsibility.

Product or corporate names may be trademarks or registered trademarks, and are used only for identification and explanation without intent to infringe.

ISBN 13: 978-1-138-99398-3 (pbk)
ISBN 13: 978-1-84407-467-9 (hbk)

Typeset by Domex e-Data, India
Cover design by Rob Watts

A catalogue record for this book is available from the British Library

Library of Congress Cataloging-in-Publication Data

Erell, Evyatar.
  Urban microclimate : designing the spaces between buildings / Evyatar Erell, David Pearlmutter, and Terry Williamson. – 1st ed.
      p. cm.
  Includes bibliographical references and index.
  ISBN 978-1-84407-467-9 (hardback)
  1. Architecture–Environmental aspects. 2. City planning–Climatic factors. 3. Architecture–Environmental aspects–Case studies. I. Pearlmutter, David. II. Williamson, T. J. (Terry J.) III. Title. IV. Title: Designing the spaces between buildings.
  NA2542.35.E82 2010
  720'.47–dc22
                                                            2010013892

Contents

List of Figures, Tables and Boxes   *vii*
Preface   *xv*
List of Abbreviations   *xvii*

Introduction   1

1   Scales of Climatic Study   15

2   The Urban Energy Balance   27

3   The Urban Heat Island   67

4   Urban Air-Flow   85

5   The Energy Balance of a Human Being in an Urban Space   109

6   Thermal Preferences   125

7   Application of Climatology in Urban Planning and Design   141

8   Microclimate Design Strategies in Urban Space   145

9   Vegetation   165

10   Linear Space   189

11   Modelling the Urban Microclimate   209

12   Case Study 1: Neve Zin   231

13   Case Study 2: Clarke Quay   239

14   Glossary   251

Index   *259*

List of Figures, Tables and Boxes

Figures

A	Aerial photographs of Peterborough, taken from altitudes of 658m and of 5.08km	4
B	Change in population density with increasing distance from city centre for several Australian cities	5
1.1	Schematic section of the urban atmosphere, showing the development of the urban boundary-layer (UBL) relative to the urban canopy-layer (UCL)	16
1.2	(a) Schematic view of a symmetrical urban canyon and its geometric descriptors, and (b) sky view factor (SVF) as a function of canyon aspect ratio (H/W)	19
1.3	Geometric parameters for calculating the sky view factor from a point on the ground in a plaza-type space (a) at a given distance from one continuous wall and (b) at the centre point of a circular space	21
1.4	(a) Schematic view of a rectangular courtyard-type space showing its geometric descriptors and (b) approximated SVFs as a function of both H/W and L/W	22
1.5	Examples of urban SVF estimation using 3D urban models with GIS analysis software	23
1.6	Upward-looking fish-eye lens photograph for estimation of SVF in an urban space	23
2.1	Schematic section showing urban surface energy balance components	28
2.2	Generic effects of urban surface geometry on the penetration, absorption and reflection of solar radiation, and on the emission of long-wave radiation	31
2.3	Measured convective heat transfer coefficient h_c for horizontal building roofs at various wind speeds U	39
2.4	Measured convective heat transfer coefficient of vertical walls on buildings at various wind speeds	39
2.5	Schematic section showing the removal of sensible heat from a built-up urban surface by wind turbulence	41
2.6	Relationship between average evapotranspiration at a site and fraction of the surface cover vegetated	48
2.7	Energy fluxes over an open-air scaled urban array, for different configurations of 3D geometry and water availability	49
2.8	Daily progression of energy flux components over two dry open-air scaled urban surfaces, showing the signature pattern common to urban environments: the peak in net storage heat flux ΔQ_S precedes that of net radiation Q^*, which in turn precedes Q_H. In the late afternoon ΔQ_S becomes negative, with heat dissipating throughout the night.	52

2.9	Correlation between the net storage heat flux ΔQ_S and net radiation Q^* for the two open-air scaled urban surface arrays depicted in Figure 2.8	53
3.1	Isotherms showing the mean minimum temperature for November 1981 in Mexico City, demonstrating the existence of a nocturnal urban heat island (UHI) in the city	68
3.2	Generalized cross-section of a typical urban heat island (UHI)	68
3.3	The surface heat island of Kuwait city	70
3.4	Typical diurnal variation of urban and rural air temperature (top) and the resulting nocturnal UHI intensity (bottom)	71
3.5	Relation between maximum observed heat island intensity and the population of North American and European cities	71
3.6	Relation between maximum observed heat island intensity and the height-to-width ratio of a sample of street canyons at the centre of 31 cities	72
3.7	Hourly values of the temperature difference between an average of two urban street canyons and an open reference site in Adelaide, Australia during May, June, January and March of 2000–2001	76
3.8	Correlation between the diurnal temperature range recorded at a street canyon site and concurrent records from a standard station in a nearby suburb of Adelaide, Australia	78
4.1	Schematic section showing typical pattern of air-flow over an isolated building, depicted as streamlines (top) and general flow zones (bottom)	86
4.2	Air-flow pattern around a tall slab building	87
4.3	Flow pattern around a sharp-edged building	87
4.4	Flow regimes associated with different urban geometries	88
4.5	Threshold lines dividing flow regimes as a function of building and canyon geometry	90
4.6	Correlation between wind speed attenuation and angle of attack for street canyons of varying aspect ratio	91
4.7	An idealized representation of the lee vortex formed in an urban street canyon by above-roof wind blowing at normal incidence to the canyon axis	92
4.8	An idealized representation of the flow in an urban street canyon generated by above-roof wind blowing parallel to the canyon axis	92
4.9	An idealized representation of the lee vortex formed in an urban street canyon by above-roof wind blowing at an angle to the canyon axis	93
4.10	An idealized representation of two counter-rotating vortices formed in a deep street canyon by above-roof wind blowing perpendicular to the canyon axis	93
4.11	Effect of differential heating of canyon surfaces on the lee vortex generated by relatively weak above-roof wind	94
4.12	An idealized representation of the vertical profile of the mean wind speed above an urban area	96
4.13	Definition of surface dimensions used in morphometric analysis, for describing the frontal area density (A_F/A_T) and plan area density (A_P/A_T)	99
4.14	Conceptual representation of the relation between height-normalized roughness parameters (zero-plane displacement d/H and roughness length z_0/H) and the packing density of roughness elements, using (a) the plan area index A_P/A_T and (b) the frontal area density A_F/A_T	100

5.1	Schematic depiction of radiation exchanges between a pedestrian and the surrounding urban environment	111
5.2	Schematic section showing components in the calculation of direct radiation on a pedestrian body, looking perpendicular to the solar rays	112
5.3	The relation between the diffuse component of global radiation and the cloudiness index	114
5.4	The variation of sky emissivity with air temperature and relative humidity under clear-sky conditions (left), and the percentage increase in long-wave radiation as a function of cloud or fog cover (right)	116
5.5	Schematic depiction of convective heat exchange between the standing body and urban environment, as a function of the skin–air temperature difference and horizontal wind speed	120
6.1	An example of the Olgyay Bioclimatic Chart	127
6.2	Object means: shade covering a children's playground in Yeroham, Israel (top) and in Darling Harbour, Sydney, Australia (bottom)	133
6.3	Passengers waiting for a train stand around radiant heaters when the temperature is close to zero (Gare du Nord, Paris)	135
6.4	A family party under a tree in a park, Adelaide, Australia (ambient temperature 34°C)	136
8.1	The flat-plate solar collectors installed on the roof of the terrace building are shaded by the taller building on higher ground to the south	146
8.2	A simple 'solar envelope' guaranteeing solar access to a building, defined by an imaginary inclined plane, above which no part of the adjacent building may project	147
8.3	Solar gain indicator for a vertical, south-facing window in Manchester, UK	148
8.4	Pedestrian arcades protecting the pavement from the sun (or rain) may be constructed as an integral part of the building (left) or a light-weight add-on to it (right)	149
8.5	Solar envelope developed for a commercial redevelopment in Tel Aviv, Israel	150
8.6	Horizontal profiles of normalized wind speed at $z = 0.1H$ for various approach wind incidence angles for a shelterbelt with $W = 0.5H$ and a porosity of 75 per cent (top) and 43 per cent (bottom)	152
8.7	Simplified flow field and fundamental vortex structures in a street canyon with aspect ratios of $H/W = 1$ and $L/W = 10$ for flow perpendicular to the canyon axis	154
8.8	Wind field (a) and pollutant dispersion (b) as computed by the MIMO computer code for a square canyon (symmetric case)	156
8.9	Wind field (a) and pollutant dispersion (b) as computed by the MIMO computer code for a deep symmetrical street canyon	156
8.10	Wind field (a) and pollutant dispersion (b) as computed by the MIMO computer code for a deep asymmetric street canyon (step-up notch)	157
8.11	Wind field (a) and pollutant dispersion (b) as computed by the MIMO computer code for a deep asymmetrical street canyon (step-down notch)	157
9.1	The development of an internal boundary-layer as air flows from a smooth, hot, dry, bare surface to a rougher, cooler and moister vegetated surface	166

9.2	Moisture advection from a dry to a wet surface: (a) evaporation rates and the vapour balance of a surface air layer; (b) surface evaporation rate E_0, and mean water vapour concentration of the air layer; (c) vertical profile of water vapour in relation to the developing boundary-layer	167
9.3	The trees in this liman provide a welcome relief from the desert sun, but have no measurable effect on air temperature beneath them	172
9.4	This *Prosopis juliflora* tree loses its foliage for only several weeks each year, beginning in late February. Even when entirely bare, it still casts a substantial shadow, as seen on the wall behind it	173
9.5	The jacaranda trees are expected to provide most of the shade in the future	173
9.6	Maximum and minimum permeability of different tree species may vary by as much as two months	174
9.7	The trees lining the broad suburban street (top) provide almost complete shade, but buildings are set back and flushing of air at street level is not a problem. In the avenue (bottom) the row of trees adjacent to the buildings on the left is too close to the facade, and when they are fully grown will cut off air-flow near the wall.	179
9.8	Generic location in plan view of shaded areas relative to a broad-canopy tree, by time of day and season (for mid-latitude regions in the northern hemisphere)	181
9.9	This parking lot is almost always shaded through the combined effect of the trees and the whitewashed wall	181
9.10	Diners in this outdoor restaurant are shaded by the trees as well as by the fabric canopy	182
9.11	The effect of vegetation on normalized values of the Index of Thermal Stress (ITS) at the courtyard spaces during summer daytime hours (Local Standard Time) with corresponding levels of subjective thermal sensation; (a) non-shaded spaces (left) and (b) courtyard configurations with overhead shading by either trees or mesh (right)	184
10.1	Linear urban spaces of different aspect ratio and different character: (a) a low-rise residential street in North America; (b) a well-defined traditional European street; and (c) a pedestrian street in the dense urban fabric of a Middle-Eastern city	190
10.2	Schematic section of symmetrical urban canyon with pedestrian at its centre, showing parameters for calculation of the shading coefficient	192
10.3	Shading patterns for street canyons of varying height–width (H/W) ratio, at different hours on (a) a summer day and (b) a winter day. Shadows are calculated for a location at 30°N latitude.	193
10.4	(a) Diagrammatic canyon section showing parameters for the calculation of view factors to the sky (SVF), walls (WVF) and floor (FVF) from the point of view of a pedestrian at the canyon centre; and (b) variation of these view factors, as a function of canyon H/W, for H = 6m	195
10.5	Hourly Index of Thermal Stress by H/W ratio for canyons with axis orientations of north–south, east–west and two diagonal rotations (parallel and perpendicular to the prevailing northwest wind)	201

10.6	Summary of thermal sensation by canyon H/W ratio and axis orientation in terms of the total hours of discomfort on a summer day (top), and a Discomfort Index (bottom) accounting for both the duration and severity of overall discomfort	203
10.7	Shading patterns for a 'selective' urban grid at different hours on a summer day (21 June) and a winter day (21 Dec)	204
10.8	Examples of urban canyon cross-sections, looking north along a north–south axis (top) and west along an east–west axis (bottom), illustrating climatic response in terms of basic geometry and secondary shading treatments	205
10.9	Examples of detailed shading treatments in urban streets: (a) shade trees and building façade projections, and (b) shading canopies across the full width of a pedestrian market street	206
11.1	OASUS model: (a) view looking north; (b) layout of array; (c) detailed plan of measurement area and (d) schematic canyon sections with location of measurements	213
11.2	Part of geometry and computational grid for CFD study of pedestrian-level wind conditions around the Amsterdam 'ArenA' football stadium in The Netherlands	215
11.3	Comparison of measured air temperature at urban street canyon with temperature predicted by CAT from Bureau of Meteorology (BoM) data for a ten-day period in May 2000	217
11.4	Comparison of the cumulative frequency distribution of the CCP at the reference meteorological station for Glasgow, Adelaide and Sde Boqer	221
11.5	Effect of canyon aspect ratio on the *relative* change in the CCP of Glasgow, Adelaide and Sde Boqer for the three-month summer period, based on air temperature predicted by CAT with anthropogenic heat input set to zero (a) and with variable heat input (b)	222
11.6	Effect of canyon aspect ratio on the *absolute* change in the CCP of Glasgow, Adelaide and Sde Boqer for the three-month summer period, based on air temperature predicted by CAT with anthropogenic heat input set to zero (a) and with variable heat input (b)	222
11.7	Computer rendering of the case study building	223
11.8	Effect of urban density on the simulated peak heating and cooling loads for Glasgow and Sde Boqer	224
11.9	Change in annual budget for heating the generic office building (top) and cooling it (bottom), as a result of urban modification of air temperature and with mutual shading, as predicted by EnerWin for three locations in different climate zones	226
12.1	Monthly average values of air temperature at Sde Boqer	232
12.2	Total monthly insolation at Sde Boqer	232
12.3	Monthly water balance for Sde Boqer, showing difference between precipitation and potential evapotranspiration (PET)	232
12.4	Thermal comfort analysis for Sde Boqer	233
12.5	Two circulation systems at Neve Zin	234
12.6	Driving speed in the woonerfs is restricted by the landscaping	234

12.7	North–south alleys with pergolas provide shade and protection from wind and dust	235
12.8	Building lots at the Neve Zin neighbourhood are clustered in groups of four. Building envelopes must overlie a 'P-point' at the extremity of the cluster. Drawing (a) shows location of P-points in two neighbouring clusters, while photo (b) shows a model of actual buildings constructed in the respective lots. Shadows in photo correspond to 9.00am on the winter solstice.	236
13.1	Monthly average values of air temperature at Singapore	240
13.2	Total monthly insolation at Singapore	240
13.3	Monthly water balance for Singapore, showing difference between precipitation and potential evapotranspiration (PET)	240
13.4	Thermal comfort analysis for Singapore	241
13.5	Overall conceptual approach to microclimate modification at Clarke Quay	241
13.6	Shade canopies in the Clarke Quay development	243
13.7	Plan view showing arrangement of the canopies in the Clarke Quay development	244
13.8	Section through street showing shade canopies projecting above roof height	244
13.9	View of air vents and ventilation fans installed to supplement natural air-flow at street level by mechanical means	245
13.10	Trees provide natural shading, in addition to artificial canopies	245
13.11	View of central plaza with sprayers operating	246
13.12	Predicted thermal comfort results for street level: with no canopy or fans (top); with shade canopy installed and assisted ventilation (below)	247

Tables

1.1	Differentiation of spatial scales for climatic study, with characteristic dimensions and phenomena as suggested by Oke (1987)	18
2.1	The albedo and thermal emissivity of typical natural and man-made materials	30
2.2	Sample of albedo values assigned to various land use classifications by several researchers	33
2.3	Formulae to calculate the atmospheric emissivity of clear skies e_a	35
2.4	Values of the coefficients used in Equations 2.12 and 2.13 above to compensate for the effect of clouds on long-wave radiation in the atmosphere	36
2.5	Empirical relationships for estimating the magnitude of the surface heat transfer coefficient for convection, h_c	38
2.6	Values of the α and β parameters	47
2.7	Average β W m^{-2} and α for several urban areas investigated by Grimmond and Oke (2002)	47
2.8	The thermal properties of typical natural and man-made materials	50
2.9	Values of the coefficients used in the objective hysteresis model (OHM) to describe storage heat flux in several classes of surface types	53

2.10	Average annual anthropogenic heat flux densities	55
2.11	Diurnal and seasonal variations in anthropogenic heat flux of several cities	59
4.1	Vertical wind profile parameters for different terrain types	96
4.2	Typical roughness length (z_0) of homogeneous surfaces	98
4.3	Typical roughness properties of homogeneous zones in urban areas	99
4.4	Roughness parameters as a proportion of the urban canopy height, determined through (a) measurements above scale-modelled urban arrays (Pearlmutter et al 2005) and (b) morphometric models surveyed by Grimmond and Oke (1999)	101
4.5	Terrain Factors	102
6.1	Indicative metabolic rates of adults engaged in various activities	129
6.2	Typical insulation value of clothing	129
9.1	Characterization of Park Cool Islands (PCIs)	169
9.2	Shading effect of selected trees found in North America	175
9.3	Summary of the results of modelling studies on the effect of increasing the vegetated area of cities	178
11.1	Average monthly maximum canyon heat island (K) predicted by CAT for different canyon aspect ratios during the hottest three months of the year	218
11.2	Average monthly maximum canyon cool island (K) predicted by CAT for different canyon aspect ratios during the hottest three months of the year	219
11.3	Annual energy budget for heating and cooling the test building in the three test locations for different street canyon configurations, using air temperature modified by CAT but assuming no mutual shading	225
11.4	Annual energy budget for heating and cooling in the three test locations, for different street canyon configurations, as predicted by CAT – with mutual shading	226

Boxes

5.1	Sol-air temperature	118
5.2	Mean radiant temperature (MRT)	119
9.1	Vegetative landscape treatments and thermal stress	184
11.1	The COSMO model	211
11.2	The OASUS model	212
11.3	ENVI-met	216
11.4	Case study: The effect of urban modification of air temperature on the potential for cooling buildings by ventilation	220
11.5	Case study: Effect of accounting for urban air temperature on the simulated energy performance of a fully air-conditioned office building	223

Preface

The quality of life of millions of people living in cities can be improved if the factors that affect the urban microclimate are understood and the form of the built environment responds to them in an appropriate way. Underlying this belief is the notion that climatically responsive urban design is fundamental to sustainability. When the design of spaces between buildings is informed by the opportunities and constraints of the local climate, pedestrian comfort will be enhanced – encouraging city dwellers to conduct more activity outdoors, and in turn to moderate their dependence on air-conditioned buildings and private vehicles. Integrated design at the urban scale will also enable individual buildings to make better use of 'natural' energy, improving the comfort of occupants and lessening their reliance on fossil fuels for heating and cooling.

While building climatology focuses on indoor climate to satisfy the needs of the occupants, urban climatology is mainly concerned with the overall urban area and its effects on the lower atmosphere. This book seeks to address an intermediate physical scale. It answers the question 'how can the design of significant places and spaces between buildings be informed by knowledge of the microclimate?'

The book, which is based on recent advances in climatological research and reflects a thorough understanding of the physical processes involved, bridges the gap between the scientific state-of-the-art and its application in urban design. It was written by architects, who have carried out extensive research on urban microclimate, in addition to their practical knowledge in architecture and town planning and their experience in teaching. It is thus based both on sound understanding of the interaction between buildings and the open space surrounding them, and on the issues that face architects and planners in the process of designing the urban environment.

The book is divided into four sections:

The first section provides an overview of the processes that characterize the urban microclimate, and which differentiate it from the climate of the Earth's boundary-layer in rural locations. It is based on an extensive review of published academic research by climatologists and geographers. This body of work, although available to researchers at universities, is generally not accessible to architects and planners. It is presented in a systematic and rigorous manner, but with the intention of making it easily understood by readers lacking any prior knowledge of the field.

The second section of the book is devoted to an exploration of human thermal comfort in outdoor spaces. It begins with an analysis of the energy balance of a pedestrian in the street, which differs from that of a person in an indoor environment because radiant exchange is often the dominant mechanism affecting comfort, and because air-flow is typically much faster. It then proceeds to question whether comfort standards developed for controlled indoor conditions may provide useful guidance in the design of outdoor spaces, and suggests that the perception of thermal comfort outdoors may depend on context to a much greater extent.

The third section discusses the application of climatology as part of the process of planning the urban environment. It is devoted to practical issues such as building density, street orientation and the extent of landscaped areas with respect to their effect on building energy performance and on pedestrian thermal comfort outdoors. Architects and planners may find this section especially relevant, but climatologists will also find it a useful guide to the issues that are of most concern in the practical world.

The fourth and final section describes case studies of two urban projects, the construction of which was driven primarily by concern for microclimatic conditions. The projects differ both in the climatic characteristics of the respective locations and in the type of intervention required:

- The first of the two studies describes the design of the Neve Zin neighbourhood in the Negev desert of Israel. Unlike many projects where a single architect is responsible for the design of both the overall scheme and the individual houses, the planners of Neve Zin were required to create a set of regulations and guidelines to provide a framework within which individual houses could be designed by other architects – while still attaining certain objectives relating to the microclimate of the public space and the degree of exposure of the houses to sun and wind.
- The second study describes a project carried out as part of an urban renewal scheme in Clarke Quay, in tropical Singapore. This project sought to modify the microclimate of several streets, and to promote pedestrian comfort without actually enclosing the space and fully air-conditioning it. Although the expense was substantial, the project is instructive because the design is driven largely by an analysis of the climatic factors affecting outdoor thermal comfort.

We hope that this book will prove to be a useful reference for professionals in the fields of architecture, landscape architecture and urban design, for policy makers involved in urban planning and for geographers and climatologists concerned with urban processes.

List of Abbreviations

ASV	actual sensation vote
ASHRAE	American Society of Heating, Refrigerating and Air-Conditioning Engineers
AHI	atmospheric heat island
BLHI	boundary-layer heat island
CLHI	canopy-layer heat island
CBD	central business district
CCP	climatic cooling potential
CFD	computational fluid dynamics
CAD	computer-aided design
EWA	energy weighted albedo
ECI	Equatorial Comfort Index
ETFE	ethylene tetrafluoroethylene
ET	evapotranspiration
FVF	floor view factor
HVAC	Heating, Ventilation and Air-Conditioning
H/W	height-to-width ratio
IA	incidence angle
ITS	Index of Thermal Stress
IBL	internal boundary-layer
IUTB	intra-urban thermal breeze
LAI	Leaf Area Index
L/W	length to width ratio (of a street canyon)
LST	local standard time
MRT	mean radiant temperature
MOST	Monin-Obukhov similarity theory
MEMI	Munich Energy-balance Model for Individuals
NVA	nadir view albedo
OHM	objective hysteresis model
PCI	park cool island
PNC	particle number concentrations
PM	particulate matter
PET	physiological equivalent temperature
PBL	planetary boundary-layer
PMV	predicted mean vote
PPD	predicted percentage dissatisfied
PV	photovoltaic
RUROS	Rediscovering the Urban Realm of Open Spaces
STBS	Singapore Tropical Building Submission
SVF	sky view factor
SET	standard effective temperature
SEB	surface energy balance
SHI	surface heat island
UV	ultraviolet
UBL	urban boundary-layer

UCL	urban canopy-layer
UHI	urban heat island
WVF	wall view factor
WBGT	wet bulb globe temperature
USGBC	United States Green Building Council
W	watt
WBCSD	World Business Council for Sustainable Development
WEB	Wind Energy for the Built Environment
wwr	window : wall ratio

Introduction

People often drift into the square to act out their dramas. Clearly a street won't do. Passions need room, the attentive spaciousness of a theatre ... Last Sunday there was a boy striding up and down the square for two hours, shouting into his phone, his voice fading each time he marched off south, and swelling in the afternoon gloom as he returned. Next morning, on his way to work, Perowne saw a woman snatch her husband's phone and shatter it on the pavement. In the same month there was a fellow in a dark suit on his knees, umbrella at his side, apparently with his head stuck between the garden railings. In fact he was clinging to the bars and sobbing. The old lady with the whisky would never get away with her shouts and squawks in the narrowness of a street, not for three hours at a stretch. Couples come to talk or cry quietly on the benches. Emerging from small rooms in council flats or terraced houses, and from cramped side streets, into a wider view of generous sky and a tall stand of plane trees on the green, of space and growth, people remember their essential needs and how they're not being met.
(Ian McEwan, *Saturday*, 2006)

All of us who have lived for any time in a city will relate to the description above. It is a small example of what Jan Gehl describes as the *Life Between Buildings* (Gehl, 1986). We often think of people living their life inside buildings and we may not see that in fact for one reason or another we spend much of our time outside – between the buildings.

It is between the buildings that much social interaction takes place. Pedestrians passing in the street; people sitting on park seats, observing; a group waiting for a bus; a busker entertaining the shoppers; a couple sipping coffee on a café terrace; a fair with dodgem cars or a music festival: all are scenes that take place *outside*. The spaces and places of these, and many other everyday activities, have a special social, cultural and even economic significance.

Urban climatology is one feature of the design of these spaces between buildings: we need to understand their microclimate so that we may manipulate the spaces to create better environments for humans. At the same time, understanding and especially being able to predict these microclimates may also help us design these spaces to improve aspects of the performance of the adjacent buildings. If the environmental quality of the outside spaces is enhanced there will be more opportunity for people to stay outdoors, with beneficial effects on health and with a positive contribution to the local economy.

What makes a space successful from a climate point of view? William Whyte used time-lapse photography to study how people used outside spaces in New York. He documented the comings and goings, the rituals, the rhythms of encounters and basically what made some spaces 'work' and others not. He found that significant elements in the success of places related to the effects of sun, wind, trees and water. However, he found that in general such effects are almost wholly inadvertent. Sun studies and the like made for new buildings tend to be defensive in nature, aimed at gaining planning permission rather than investigations of what benefits there might be, to whom and when. (Whyte, 1980, p43). This trial and error approach to urban design is explained by Peter Bosselmann, who studied the climate in Vancouver, when he observed 'although the relationship between a city's form and its climate has been intuitively understood, intuition cannot predict how specific future buildings will affect climate conditions' (Bosselmann, 1998, p140). While there is still no single comprehensive model that can predict pedestrian comfort in public open spaces, recent advances in urban microclimatology that combine experimental and computational techniques make evaluation of this aspect of a person's interaction with the environment more accessible and realistic.

The urban environment and design

Heath (1966, p59) points out that the interaction and perception of space is partly cultural, partly social and partly physiological: 'Man's relationship to his [sic] environment is a function of his sensory apparatus plus how this apparatus is conditioned to respond.' The sensory apparatus includes visual, auditory and olfactory messages received via eyes, ears and nose, and thermal and tactile sensations through the receptor systems in skin and nerves.

While this book concentrates on what we might call 'climate-sensitive urban design', it must be seen as part of a larger picture. To make this clear some definitions and discussion will be helpful.

The term 'urban design' came into being about 50 years ago as design professionals realized that there were design issues which fell between and across the individual fields of architecture, landscape design and planning. Urban design became shorthand for the composition of architectural form and open space in a community context. But what is 'design' and what is 'urban'? David Yencken, then Professor of Landscape Architecture and Environmental Planning at the University of Melbourne, suggested that:

> If Design is understood to mean the shaping and fashioning of the physical world for a conscious human purpose, then there are very few environments in which we live and work which have not been influenced by Design and all human artefacts are by definition designed. Although this is not a common meaning given to Design, it is useful to begin with such a definition because it helps make clear that Design is not an esoteric activity ... but an activity with which all humans are actively involved and which fundamentally influences every person's life. (Yencken, 1995, p30)

The notion of the 'conscious human purpose' differentiates designing from other forms of making. In this urban design draws together purposes from many ideas of place-making – environmental responsibility, issues of social/cultural meaning, equity and economic viability, for example – into the creation of places of beauty, function and distinct identity. Later we will argue that purpose(s) in urban environment design must be thought of as context-dependent in time and space.

The term 'urban' is derived from the Latin *urbānus* ('city'), meaning:

1   Of, relating to, or located in a city.
2   Characteristic of the city or city life. (Williamson and Coldicutt, 1986, p332)

For demographic data the definition of urban areas varies according to the national census definition, which is different in almost every country (United Nations, 2006). For example:

- *France*: all communes containing an agglomeration of more than 2000 inhabitants living in contiguous houses or with not more than 200 metres between houses; also communes of which the major portion of the population is part of a multi-communal agglomeration of this nature.
- *Israel*: all settlements of more than 2000 inhabitants, except those where at least one-third of households participating in the civilian labour force earn their living from agriculture.
- *Australia*: all cities and townships with a population of 1000 or more.
- *Peru*: populated centres with 100 or more dwellings.

If we want to think about the spaces between buildings in a general way then it is obvious that these definitions are not satisfactory for our task, so let's tease out the meaning in a different way.

For a start we could probably accept that the opposite of 'urban' is 'rural' or 'country'. In popular culture 'urban street wear', 'urban music' (rhythm and blues music that involves electronic instruments) and 'country music' are accepted distinctions. The terms rural, country or countryside conjure up pictures of farms, of sheep and wheat, vineyards or orchards; maybe even a forest, a scene approaching a desert or perhaps a coast with mangroves.

We don't usually associate a dwelling or a small group of buildings in a rural environment with the term 'urban'. Yet this small group of buildings will have adjacent spaces that may be the subject of design consideration in the same way that we might tackle the climate design aspects of a city square. As Baruch Givoni tells us:

> The climatic conditions in a man-made urban environment may differ appreciably from those in the surrounding natural or rural environs ... each urban man-made element: buildings, roads, parking area, factories, etc., creates around and above it a modified climate with which it interacts. (Givoni, 1989, pp1–2)

So perhaps the term 'urban' relates, for example, to size, density, physical character of buildings or the built environment, economic functions, societal functions, the character of the social life or even the degree of climate modification? But as communities increase in size from hamlet to village to town to city to metropolis, where does 'rural' stop and 'urban' begin? Even in 'remote' Australian locations, human-constructed facilities still modify the climate, even in a small way. Perhaps the term 'urban' has an administrative meaning, in the way that we understand 'city', 'council', 'borough', 'municipality', 'shire', 'commune', 'department' or 'metropolitan area'. Perhaps 'urban' should be associated with (or contrasted with) 'suburban' or 'suburbia'? Examining the aerial photographs of Peterborough (Figure A), a township of around 2000

Figure A Aerial photographs of Peterborough, taken from altitudes of 658m and of 5.08km

Source: Google Earth (http://maps.google.com/maps?ll=-32.973293,138.83796&z=14&t=h&hl=en, accessed February 2010).

people in the mid-north of South Australia, we can probably make out a general distinction between urban and rural areas. But would a development on the rural land be excluded from urban design considerations on the basis of its location? If so, charges of arbitrariness and even elitism in the practice could be levelled against such a decision.

Population density as an indicator of the urban–rural divide raises the problem of where precisely to draw the boundary between them. As Figure B

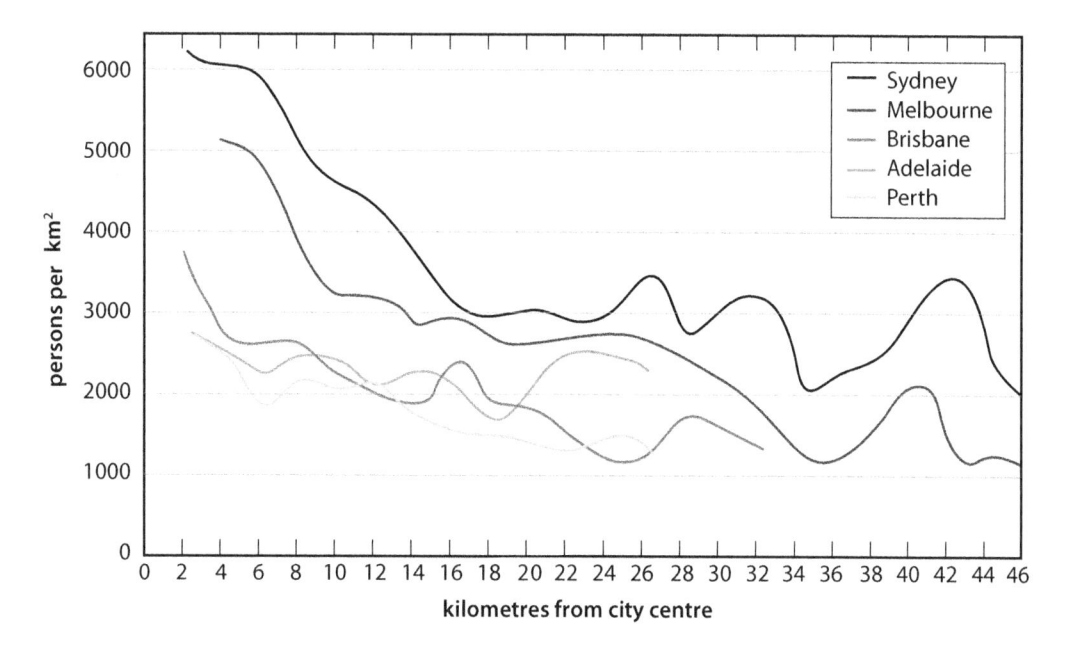

Figure B Change in population density with increasing distance from city centre for several Australian cities

Source: Baker et al (2000).

shows, a density profile is often a continuum that might have one or more distinct peaks, but may not necessarily indicate a well-defined cut-off point.

The lack of any objective definition of the term 'urban' led the American sociologist Dewey, examining the discipline of urban sociology in the 1960s, to write, 'if the objective referents for the terms "urban" and "rural" cannot be established it is reasonable to argue that they be abandoned' (Dewey, 1960).

The difficulty, however, is to find a satisfactory alternative description. Nomenclatures such as 'site design' or 'place-making' fail to capture the total sense of what we are trying to convey with this book.

Therefore in this book 'urban design' should be understood in the widest sense as applying to any situation where facilities constructed by humans modify the prevailing microclimate. As such it can extend from a consideration of the structure of a city, to neighbourhoods and streets, and to spaces around buildings including courtyards. If we see urban climatology and building climatology as components of a spectrum, then urban climatology can conveniently be thought of as all aspects of the climate outside the building.

Climate and urban environments

The climate of a location is usually understood as comprising a number of physical aspects and includes temperature, moisture content of the air, rain, wind, fog, snow, insolation, cloudiness and general air quality (as determined by various pollutants and particulate matter). Humans by various means are able to inhabit almost all of the climate conditions on Earth – the tropics, arid climates and even the harsh Arctic environment.

Much of the literature dealing with climate and design focuses on the effect of climate on the built environment and in particular on creating comfortable indoor conditions. Most authors offer the observation that throughout history one purpose of building houses has been to provide shelter from the often hostile conditions occurring outside, caused by a combination of temperature, wind, rain and sun. As Olgyay and Olgyay write:

> House design has reflected, throughout history, the different solutions advanced by each period to the continuing problem of securing a small controlled environment within large-scale natural setting – too often beset by adverse forces of cold, heat, wind, water and sun. (Olgyay, 1963, pV)

The relationship between climate and the outside or urban environment has been a topic of some study and discussion for at least one hundred years, but only in recent years has systematic research been undertaken in the area. Perhaps the first scientific study of the urban climate as such was conducted by Luke Howard, who identified an urban heat island (UHI) in London (Howard, 1818). The climate of London served as the basis for another landmark study of urban climatology bearing the same title, which incorporated meteorological data from 18 standard meteorological stations in the Greater London area, supplemented by data from more limited stations and from mobile (vehicle) traverses (Chandler, 1965). The wide-ranging study found substantial variations not only in air temperature but also in humidity, occurrence of fog and duration of sunshine, which were attributed to anthropogenic sources of heat and air pollution.

The design of outdoor spaces requires an understanding of the local environment. This has traditionally been the role of architects, who have relied on intuition, personal experience and the example of others. For instance, a study of the indigenous architecture of the cold desert of Leh and hot desert of Jaisalmer (Krishan, 1996) included numerous observations regarding appropriate design strategies for such climates. A study of the indigenous towns of Algeria combined with an analysis of solar angles led to the recommendation that solar access be restricted to elevations of 60 to 70 degrees or more, by means of controlling the street width and the use of cantilevered balconies (Mazouz and Zerouala, 1998; 1999). The ancient town planners of the Middle East have often been credited with a superior understanding of the environment, suggesting that there were lessons to be learned for modern planners (Rahamimoff and Bornstein, 1981; Potchter, 1990–1991).

The discipline has since evolved into a distinct branch of meteorology. Lowry (1967) gave a popularized description of the mechanisms leading to the creation of a distinct urban climate, and a decade later enough research had accumulated on the subject to produce an extensive book (Landsberg, 1981).

Urban climatologists have also attempted to apply theoretical insights in order to influence real-world planning. Oke (1984) found a number of shortcomings in microclimate research that prevented it from becoming an applied science, including a lack of quantitative techniques and relationships; lack of standardization, generality and transferability; and the absence of clear guidelines for those wishing to learn and use climatological principles in settlement planning. He identified several research topics that could help bridge the gap, and later carried out an analysis of the effect of street aspect ratio on various meteorological parameters, coming to the conclusion that a height to width ratio (H/W) of 0.4 was an appropriate geometrical guideline for the design of mid-latitude cities (Oke, 1988).

An attempt to synthesize generalized rules and guidelines that may be of value to urban designers in different climates was carried out at the behest of the World Meteorological Organization (Givoni, 1989). It contains a broad overview of the state of the art of published research by planners and microclimatologists, and prescriptions for urban design in a variety of climates, but lacks generalized quantitative tools to assist in the resolution of real-world design problems in specific conditions.

Contemporary issues

The world is undergoing the largest wave of urban growth in history. Since 2008, for the first time more than half the world's population is living in towns and cities. By 2030 this number will swell to almost five billion, or an estimated 61 per cent of global population. At present the United States is the most highly urbanized large country in the world with 87 per cent of its population living in cities. However the new urban growth areas will be concentrated in Africa and Asia. While mega-cities have captured much public attention, most of the new growth will occur in smaller towns and cities with a population less than 500,000 people. In principle, cities offer a more favourable setting for the resolution of social and environmental problems than rural areas, but reduced availability of resources means responding to the magnitude of the change will be fraught with considerable difficulties.

Access to safe and healthy shelter is essential to a person's physical, psychological, social and economic well-being and should be a fundamental part of national and international action. The right to adequate housing as a basic human right is enshrined in the Universal Declaration of Human Rights and the International Covenant on Economic, Social and Cultural Rights. In 2000, 192 United Nations member states and at least 23 international organizations agreed upon Millennium Development Goals that aim to reduce extreme poverty and child mortality rates, to fight disease and epidemics such as AIDS, and to develop a global partnership for development by the year 2015.

One main goal is to address issues of sustainability such as reversing the loss of environmental resources, reducing biodiversity loss, providing access to safe drinking water and basic sanitation, and overall, creating a significant improvement in the lives of at least 100 million slum dwellers. Nothing, however, is said about the urban development necessary to promote human health and well-being. Yet as Mills suggests:

> There are clear links between the climate of a settlement and its potential sustainability. Its opportunities for gathering energy, its need for energy conservation and its ability to dispose of airborne wastes are largely controlled by the climate it experiences. Moreover, urban design decisions will create microclimates that

either accentuate or moderate the properties of the background climate. Thus, there is a clear role for an applied urban climatology in the planning of sustainable settlements. (Mills, 2006, p70)

Design by objectives

Many authors have proposed the idea that throughout the world peoples have adopted building solutions and outdoor spaces that correspond to the prevailing climate to achieve desirable living conditions. This idea of climatic determinism is not a recent phenomenon. Some of the earliest known writings on architecture and town planning deal with climate as a principal factor governing design.[1] But as Amos Rapoport points out:

> Climatic determinism has been widely accepted in architecture as well as in cultural geography, although in the latter it has recently found rather less favour. One need not deny the importance of climate to question its determining role in the creation of built form ... In architecture the climatic determinist view, still rather commonly held, states that primitive man is concerned primarily with shelter, and consequently the imperatives of climate determine form.
> (Rapoport, 1969, p18)

It is very doubtful that ancient architects and town planners designed specifically to achieve comfortable conditions, at least in the sense of the word 'design' as we use it. The present day notion of comfort as a set of expectations, physical conditions and personal imperatives is a relatively recent 20th century invention, as is the concept that buildings and spaces should perform in response to environmental factors. Rather, older buildings and town planning traditions resulted from a complementary process of evolution driven by the physical environment, resources and climate mediated by social needs, institutional arrangements, taboos and a good deal of trial and error, rather than conscious decision-making. In his treatise on town planning in the Greek and Roman civilizations dating from the fourth and fifth centuries BC, Haverfield (1913) found almost no references to climatological aspects being considered to inform town plans.

Climate, science and design

> Where science is the collected body of theoretical knowledge based upon observation, measurement, hypothesis and test ... design is the collected body of practical knowledge based upon sensibility, invention, validation and implementation. (Archer, 1979, p18)

Urban microclimatology as a branch of science can have conceptual 'applications' as well as instrumental applications: it can change our understandings of the way things are, or it can inform us concerning a specific end, for example, ensuring that an area is shaded at a particular time.

Scientific understandings of, for example, the urban heat island (UHI) effect, give us a complex and subtle understanding of the topic – an understanding which could not easily be achieved otherwise. This conceptual application of science enables us to understand the heat flows in a space in order to think about its design, and thereby to apply science in a way that does not necessarily involve any calculations. Aside from conceptual applications of this kind, there are the 'problem-definition' applications, which can help to explore ends for particular design problems or groups of problems. Context-specific field studies, such as studies of thermal preferences in areas of a particular city, are an example that can be employed directly in design decision-making.

Science can also be defined as the application of a method, rather than as being coincident with any substantive topic such as thermal performance of buildings. It is thereby recognized that one might design for good environmental performance by basing one's design on precedents of spaces which are accepted as working well or – for example in the case of a particular climate aspect wind – design might be based on careful observation of existing spaces.

Employing knowledge of climate in a design must not only be seen as the (or even a) basic determinant of design. The problem of integrating scientific knowledge and design knowledge was highlighted by Hillier and Penn:

> Buildings and built environments must satisfy a range of functional criteria – structural, environmental, economic, social, organizational, visual, and so on. These functional criteria are independent, in that they are nothing like each other but are interactive in that when you change a building to get one right you may make something else go wrong. This creates two knowledge problems in the making and managing of buildings [built environments]. One is integrating knowledge of the product and its functioning into a better understanding of the buildings [built environments] as a complex whole. The other is integrating the process to create the virtuous circle of progressive product improvement through feedback from user experience. ... these are aspects of the same problem, and have a common solution. The solution starts from a very simple observation: that the different functional criteria affect each other only through the building [built environment]. It follows that to see how they relate, we must therefore take a building centred rather than a discipline centred view of buildings and how they function. (Hillier and Penn, 1994, p332)

Design decisions are quicker if made from experience

There is a growing tendency to assume that instrumental applications to design decision-making are the most appropriate approach. However, instrumental or tool-like applications of climate science should be limited only to cases where, for the particular design problem (in its particular context with its particular stakeholders), there is:

- clarity regarding the ends which are to be addressed by this science; i.e. ends should be adequately defined and agreed upon by relevant stakeholders;[2]
- an authoritative scientific means available to address those ends;
- an understanding that the costs, monetary or other, of using this approach are justified in the light of alternative approaches to addressing those ends, and of alternative use of resources.

This argument ties the question of applicability of instrumental approaches to each particular design problem. Concepts such as 'adequate' and 'justified' can only be understood in relation to particular problems. Since design problems do not come fully predefined, but rather need to be explored, applicability can best be determined by an iterative approach in which initial understandings of the problem and the means of addressing it are refined. If groups of similar design problems are to be identified so that scientific means of addressing them can be developed, these design problems must be tested for similarity to each other, and for relevance to the scientific means, by considering ends and costs. One means of achieving this iterative approach is the problem-focused approach developed in response to concerns of the kind raised by Hillier and Penn regarding inter-relatedness of ends, means and contexts.

The need for clarity in defining ends might be taken to imply that building scientists and designers should agree on some standard generalized ways of defining all main building-related ends. The CIB Committee W60 (Performance Concept in Building) is one group seeking to provide universal design criteria (CIB, 1982). On the other hand, as Hillier and Penn suggest, because of the need to understand these ends as an inter-related whole, in relation to each particular, prospective building, it might be difficult or impossible to arrive at general definitions of ends, as the main issue is not the general definition but the definition of ends in the particular case.

Another way of approaching this dilemma is to consider whether ends should be defined in abstract terms, such as the human 'requirement' for thermal comfort, or in more concrete, building-related terms such as 'maximize area of paving'. Though these two examples can be inter-related, they are not inter-related by any invariant or general connection, such as a causal link between increased south-facing glazing and increased comfort, but are only inter-related in the context of the particular design example. Therefore, at least for these ends, the question of whether to define ends in abstract or concrete terms cannot be answered by opting for both, and specifying predefined connections between the abstract and concrete ends.

Both the 'abstract' and the 'concrete' definitions of ends can be useful to designers, and both have limitations. A concrete definition such as 'maximize area of paving' has the advantage of being very easy to apply in practice, but has the disadvantage that it gives no clue to intelligent application. For instance, does it apply in the example above if there is a multi-storey building immediately to the south that restricts solar access? An abstract definition has the advantage of showing fundamental reasons for particular design decisions, but it needs to be interpreted in order to be applicable. If ends are too abstract, the designer can lack adequate guidance on *how* to realize them in practice; if ends are too concrete, the designer can lose sight of *why* that particular building design feature might be applicable, and therefore of why it might not be applicable for some designs and in some contexts.

Possible concrete climate-related urban design ends that may apply to particular projects include shading of pedestrian areas (in a hot climate) or planting wind breaks (in a cold and windy location). Examples of abstract climate-related urban design ends that may apply to particular projects include ensuring pedestrian thermal comfort, maintaining air quality levels, providing daylight to all buildings and guaranteeing solar access for building-integrated solar energy applications, such as photovoltaic (PV) cells or solar water heaters.

Considering theory and practice

Most (if not all) literature on climate and built environment design assumes climate to be central or even the starting point for urban design. Olgyay and Olgyay (1963, p11) for example suggest as a first step 'a survey of climatic elements at a given location' and as a second step 'to evaluate each climate impact in physiological terms'. They suggest that the climate data relating to temperature, relative humidity, radiation and wind should be analysed to extract the yearly characteristics. While such a recommendation may seem logical, the obvious lack of climatic information in real-world planning and design practice points to a mismatch between this recommendation and the requirements of the urban design process. The procedures for applying theory-based information suggested in the literature – a 'correct' design approach, often linear and obligatory – does not fit well with what is possible in practice. In real-world practice design decisions are negotiated between the various stakeholders and interest groups with all of the power relationships that play out in such negotiations. Page (1968) described this liaison as the 'chicken-and-egg' nature of the urban design problem. Because urban design displays all the properties of a 'wicked problem'[3] the process is complex and fragmented.

While we know from case studies that early framing of a problem strongly affects the direction of the entire design process further down the track, we also know that in real-world urban design projects time and financial constraints rarely allow extensive pre-design investigations related to specific requirements. Because there are few design projects where professionals from disciplines such as meteorology or biology are involved, the urban designer will in practice make the major decisions. With pressures to integrate the multitude of requirements into a working design, the time- and money-consuming approaching of gathering and analysing the detailed site-specific climate data is simply not possible.

As the design process moves on and the concept designs are subjected to validation, the potential benefits of discretionary climate-sensitive design features will be subjected to consideration and possibly even detailed economic analysis to assess the financial implications. Market driven imperatives of marketability and longevity will often ultimately determine what is acceptable and what is not, leaving little place for design initiatives that come solely from an environmental agenda. Climate-sensitive design issues will only come to the fore if there is an obvious reason to do so.

Conclusion

> Traditionally, environmental research and design is characterized by the separation of research and designer. The 'givers' and 'receivers' of research information are essentially remote. (Kernohan, 1990, p175)

The application gap created by this dualism should be considered if, as is our intention, the purpose of the knowledge presented in this book is to inform designing. The challenge we face in this book is to present valid scientific information that can readily be integrated into the real-world process of designing.

Notes

1. For example the Greek scribe Xenophon writing on the teachings of Socrates around 400BC says:

    > 'When one means to have the right sort of house, must he contrive to make it as pleasant to live in and as useful as can be?'

    > And this being admitted, 'Is it pleasant,' he asked, 'to have it cool in summer and warm in winter?'

    > And when they agreed with this also, 'Now in houses with a south aspect, the sun's rays penetrate in to the porticoes in winter, but in summer the path of the sun is right over our heads and above the roof, so that there is shade. If, then, this is the best arrangement, we should build the south side loftier to get the winter sun and the north side lower to keep out the cold winds. To put it shortly, the house in which the owner can find a pleasant retreat at all seasons and can store his belongings safely is presumably at once the pleasantest and the most beautiful.' (Xenophon, 1923)

    Similarly house design advice given by Vitruvius (1960) in the first century AD for the far-flung Roman Empire was influenced by an awareness of the climate:

    > If our designs for private houses are to be correct ... it is obvious that designs for houses ought similarly to conform to the nature of the country and to diversities of climate.

2. This point is not intended to preclude 'what if ...' applications, in which one asks, for example, 'If I increased the street width, what effects would this have on air-conditioning loads?' Here it is clear that the issue in question is air-conditioning loads.

3. First postulated by Horst Rittel (quoted in Buchanan, 1992, p15) wicked problems have ramifications that make them difficult to solve. A wicked problem meets the following criteria:

- The problem is an evolving set of interlocking issues and constraints. Indeed, there is no definitive statement of the problem. You don't understand the problem until you have developed a solution.

- There are many stakeholders (people who care about or have something at stake in how the problem is resolved). This makes the problem-solving process fundamentally social. Getting the right answer is not as important as having stakeholders accept whatever solution emerges.
- The constraints on the solution, such as limited resources and political ramifications, change over time. The constraints change, ultimately, because we live in a rapidly changing world. Operationally, they change because many are generated by the stakeholders, who come and go, change their minds, fail to communicate, or otherwise change the rules by which the problem must be solved.
- Since there is no definitive problem, there is no definitive solution. The problem-solving process ends when you run out of time, money, energy, or some other resource, not when some perfect solution emerges.

References

Archer, L. B. (1979) 'The three R's', *Design Studies*, vol 1, no 1, pp17–20

Baker, E., Coffee, N. and Hugo, G. (2000) 'Suburbanisation vs Reurbanisation: Population Distribution Changes in Australian Cities', in *Australia: State of the Environment Second Technical Paper Series (Human Settlements)*, Series 2, Department of the Environment and Heritage, www.environment.gov.au/soe/2001/publications/technical/suburbanisation/index.html#issue, accessed February 2010

Bosselmann, P. (1998) *Representation of Places: Reality and Realism in City Design*, University of California Press, Berkeley

Buchanan, R. (1992) 'Wicked problems in design thinking', *Design Issues*, VIII(2), pp5–22.

Chandler, T. J. (1965) *The Climate of London*, Hutchinson, London

CIB (1982) *Working with the Performance Approach in Building*, International Council for Research and Innovation in Building and Construction (CIB), Rotterdam, The Netherlands

Dewey, R. (1960) 'The Rural–Urban Dichotomy: Real but relatively unimportant', *American Journal of Sociology*, vol 66, pp60–66

Gehl, J. (1986) *Life Between Buildings*, Van Nostrand Reinhold, New York

Givoni, B. (1989) *Urban Design in Different Climates*, WCAP–10, World Meteorological Organization, Geneva

Haverfield, F. (1913) *Ancient Town Planning*, Oxford University Press, Oxford

Heath, E. T. (1966) *The Hidden Dimension*, Doubleday, New York

Hillier, B. and Penn, A. (1994) 'Virtuous circles, building sciences and the science of buildings: Using computers to integrate product and process in the built environment', *Design Studies*, vol 15, no 3, pp332–365

Howard, L. (1818) *The Climate of London Deduced from Meteorological Observations*, W. Phillips, London

Kernohan, D. (1990) 'Architectural science and design in harmony: Avoiding the Application Gap', in Plume, J. (ed) *Proceedings of the Joint ANZAScA/ADTRA Conference*, Sydney, University of New South Wales, pp175–182

Krishan, A. (1996) 'The habitat of two deserts in India: Hot-dry desert of Jaisalmer (Rajasthan) and the cold-dry high altitude mountainous desert of Leh (Ladakh)', *Energy and Buildings*, vol 23, no 3, pp217–229

Landsberg, H. E. (1981) *The Urban Climate*, Academic Press, New York

Lowry, W. P. (1967) 'The climate of cities', *Scientific American*, 217, pp15–23

Mazouz, S. and Zerouala, M. S. (1998) 'Shading as a modulator for the design of urban layouts based on vernacular experiences', *Energy and Buildings*, vol 29, pp11–15

Mazouz, S. and Zerouala, M. S. (1999) 'The derivation and re-use of vernacular urban space concepts', *Architectural Science Review*, vol 42, no 1, pp3–13

McEwan, I. (2006) *Saturday*, Vintage, London

Mills, G. (2006) 'Progress toward sustainable settlements: A role for urban climatology', *Theoretical and Applied Climatology*, vol 84, pp69–76

Oke, T. R. (1988) 'Street design and urban canopy layer climate', *Energy & Buildings*, vol 11, pp103–113

Oke, T. R. (1984) 'Towards a prescription for the greater use of climatic principles in settlement planning', *Energy and Buildings*, vol 7, pp1–10

Olgyay, V. and Olgyay, A. (1963) *Design with Climate*, Princeton University Press, Princeton

Page, J. K. (1968) 'The fundamental problems of building climatology considered from the point of view of decision-making by the architect and urban designer', *WMO Technical Note No. 109*, World Meteorological Organization, Geneva

Potchter, O. (1990–1991) 'Climatic aspects in the building of ancient urban settlements in Israel', *Energy and Buildings*, vols 15–16, pp93–104

Rahamimoff, A. and Bornstein, N. (1981) 'Edge conditions – climatic considerations in the design of buildings and settlements', *Energy and Buildings*, vol 4, pp43–49

Rapoport, A. (1969) *House Form and Culture*, Prentice-Hall, Englewood Cliffs, NJ

Rittel, H. and Webber, M. (1973) 'Dilemmas in a general theory of planning', *Policy Sciences*, vol 4, pp155–169

United Nations (2006) 'Notes to Table 6 – Urban and Total Population: 1997–2006', Demographic Yearbook, www.unstats.un.org/unsd/demographic/products/dyb/dyb2006.htm, accessed March 2010

Vitruvius (1960) *Vitruvius: The Ten Books on Architecture*, Dover Publications, New York.

Whyte, W. H. (1980) *The Social Life of Small Urban Spaces*, Project for Public Spaces, New York

Williamson, T. J. and Coldicutt, S. (1986) *Comparison of Evaporative Cooling and Refrigerative Air-Conditioning for Dwellings in South Australia*, Department of Architecture, The University of Adelaide, Adelaide

Xenophon (1923) *Memorabilia and Oeconomicus*, William Heinemann, London

Yencken, D. (1993) 'Design in Australia', quoted in Competing by Design: The National Design Review Report (1995), National Design Review Steering Committee, The Australian Academy of Design, Sydney

1
Scales of Climatic Study

The very existence of a city has significant modifying effects on the local climate – both within the built-up area, and in the atmosphere above and beyond its boundaries. The nature of these modifications depends on a wide range of physical variables, which can be observed and evaluated at distinctly different spatial scales.

Relative to the Earth's diameter (about 12,700km), the layer of atmosphere blanketing it is extremely thin. The portion of the atmosphere which is directly affected by the terrestrial surface, known as the 'troposphere', reaches a height of no more than 10km, and on a short time scale of several days, this affected portion is limited to an even shallower layer known as the planetary or atmospheric 'boundary-layer'.

In an urbanized area, this lowest part of the atmosphere – known as the *urban boundary-layer* (UBL) – is decisively affected by the nature of the built-up terrain. The UBL may be further divided into a number of sub-layers, and the distinction between them is fundamental to urban climate.

- As depicted in Figure 1.1, the complete UBL is defined as the entire volume of air above the city that is influenced by its surface characteristics and by the activities within it. From the upwind edge of the city, the UBL grows in height as air passes over the built-up terrain (Figure 1.1, top). It generally extends upward to about ten times the height of the buildings in the urban area, and it also extends beyond the urban area in the downwind direction.
- The upper part of the UBL, and the bulk of its volume, is considered a 'mixed layer'. Within this layer the atmosphere is influenced by the presence of the urban surface, but is not fully adapted to it: in other words, the impact of the non-urban upwind terrain is felt as well. The height of the mixed layer varies according to atmospheric stability and the magnitude of the urban effects.
- Up to a height of about four to five times that of the average building, a *surface layer* may develop that is entirely conditioned by the 3D geometry and other attributes of the buildings and ground cover below (Figure 1.1, bottom). This surface layer forms when the air has passed over a sufficient length of ground that has urban attributes, including the roughness created by sharp-edged structures and the heat that is generated within the city. Due to the turbulent mixing of air, however, the properties of this layer are not affected by individual urban elements such as single buildings and streets. Rather, they are conditioned by the texture of the urban surface as a whole.

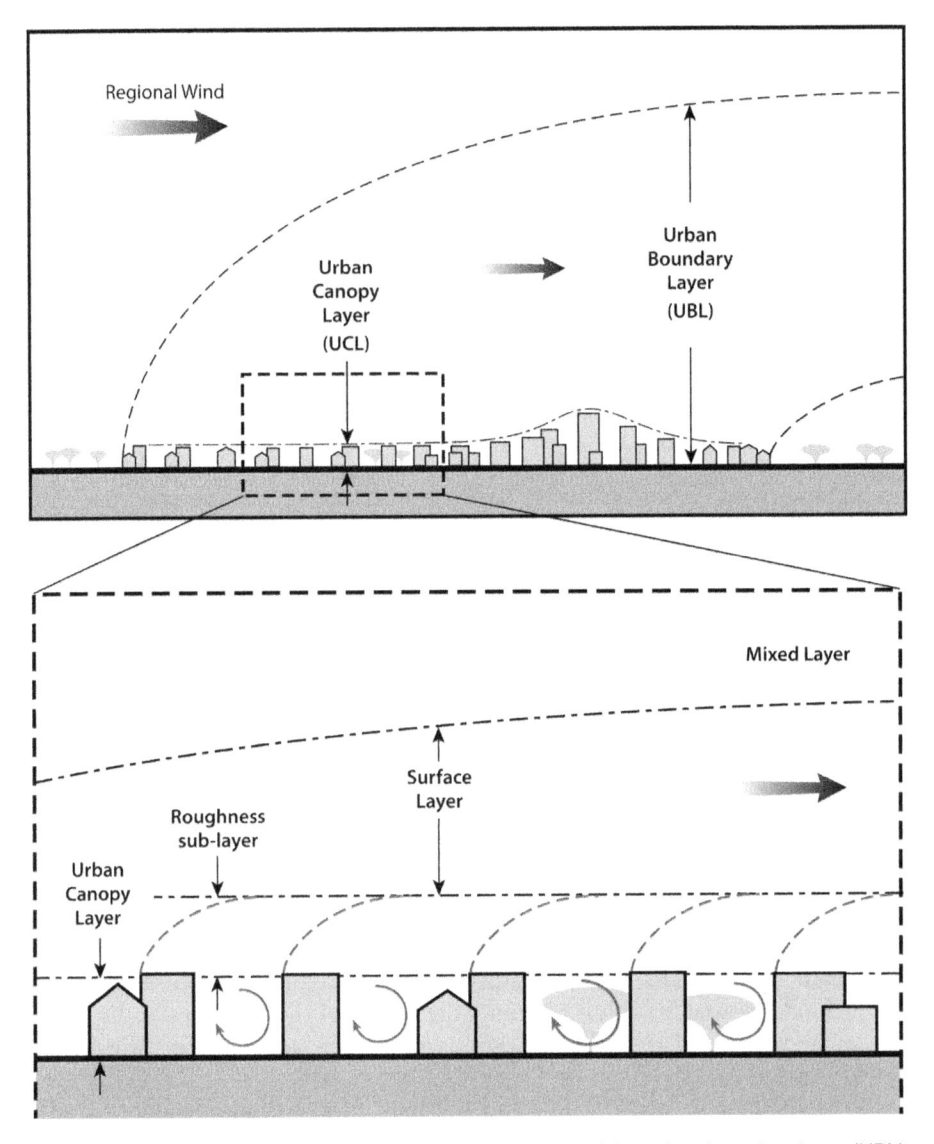

Figure 1.1 Schematic section of the urban atmosphere, showing the development of the urban boundary-layer (UBL) relative to the urban canopy-layer (UCL), which reaches the average building height (top), and the distinction between the homogeneous surface layer above the city and the heterogeneous urban canopy (bottom). The mixed layer and roughness sub-layer are transition zones above and below the surface layer, respectively.

This is an extremely important feature, since it is only within this layer that (a) the vertical profile of wind speed follows a systematic logarithmic curve (see Chapter 4) and (b) the vertical exchange of energy between the urban surface and the atmosphere is homogeneous, allowing turbulent fluxes of heat (and pollutants) to be measured at any point above the surface (see Chapter 2). For this reason, the surface layer is also known as a *constant flux layer*, or alternately as the *inertial sub-layer*.

- The blending of effects from individual surface features that characterizes the surface layer does not occur immediately above the roofs of buildings, and therefore that layer's lower boundary is typically found at a height of at least twice the average building height. Below this level is a highly variable *roughness sub-layer*, in which the air-flow consists of interacting wakes and plumes introduced by individual roughness elements. This zone is also known as a layer of transition between the homogeneous surface layer above, and the highly variegated urban surface itself – which is typically comprised of buildings of different heights, vegetation and open spaces of various dimensions.
- The very lowest part of the urban atmosphere is the *urban canopy-layer* (UCL), which extends from ground level to the height of buildings, trees and other objects. In sharp distinction to the surface layer above, the UCL is characterized by a high level of heterogeneity, since conditions vary widely from point to point within the canopy volume (see Figure 1.1).

Due to the inherent heterogeneity of the UCL, a unique microclimate is established within any given urban space, with air temperature, wind flow, radiation balance and other climatic indicators being determined by the physical nature of the immediate surroundings as well as by the urban and regional environment. The proportions of the space, the thermal and optical qualities of its finish materials and the use of landscape vegetation are all design parameters that modify climate at this scale. Because urban design may have localized impacts such as these on outdoor thermal comfort and building energy loads, the microclimate of urban spaces is rightfully considered an architectural issue.

If the term microclimate is in fact defined as 'the climate that prevails at the micro-scale level', it is important to quantify the range of spatial scales that fits this definition. In Table 1.1 the idea of micro-scale climate is placed within a geographical context, showing the characteristic dimensions and atmospheric processes that apply to different levels of scale. Note that there is considerable overlap between the dimensional ranges given for different scales, since the scale at which different phenomena occur will inevitably vary according to the specific terrain.

The *macro-scale* is appropriate for describing air masses and pressure systems related to weather – phenomena which are viewed on a scale of hundreds of kilometres. While large urban areas may influence such weather patterns, this level of scale does not resolve detailed features of cities. However at the *meso-scale*, which describes terrain on the order of magnitude of tens of kilometres, urban areas and their internal climatic effects are clearly identifiable. At the *local scale*, a resolution of single kilometres or less can clearly reflect man-made objects such as buildings, which – in the context of a city or town – make up the urban fabric. This scale, also known as the urban scale, is of primary interest in the study of urban climatology.

Still, architectural decisions are typically made at a smaller scale than this, with buildings or groups of buildings in a single design project rarely covering an area that is more than several hundred metres wide. The micro-scale refers to this smallest realm, where individual structures and trees cast shadows and

Table 1.1 Differentiation of spatial scales for climatic study, with characteristic dimensions and phenomena as suggested by Oke (1987)

	Scale	Approximate limits	Characteristic climatic phenomena
	Macro-scale	>100km	Jet stream, hurricanes
	Meso-scale	10km–200km	Local winds, thunderstorms, large cumulus clouds
	Local/urban scale	100m–50km	Tornados, small cumulus clouds
	Micro-scale	1cm–1km	Dust devils, small scale turbulence

divert the flow of wind, and where built elements as fine as balconies and textured wall cladding modify the reflection of sunlight and the radiant temperatures to which people are most directly exposed.

Geometric descriptors of the urban fabric

Despite the heterogeneity of the urban canopy in almost any real city, it is useful to describe the fabric of buildings and open spaces in terms of quantifiable measures that express its density or other physical properties that influence the micro-scale climate.

The urban canyon

One of the most widely used models for making such a description is the *urban canyon* – which, as its name would suggest, refers to a linear space such as a street which is bounded on both sides by vertical elements such as the walls of adjacent buildings. As a model, the urban canyon may represent both a recurring module from which the textured urban surface is composed, and an individual space that is inhabited at ground level by people and urban activity.

The geometry of the urban canyon may be described by three principal descriptors (see Figure 1.2):

- The *height–width (H/W) ratio*, also known as the aspect ratio, describes the sectional proportions of the urban canyon. It is defined as the ratio between the average height of adjacent vertical elements (such as building facades) and the average width of the space (i.e. the wall-to-wall distance across the street). While the aspect ratio applies most directly to symmetrical canyons

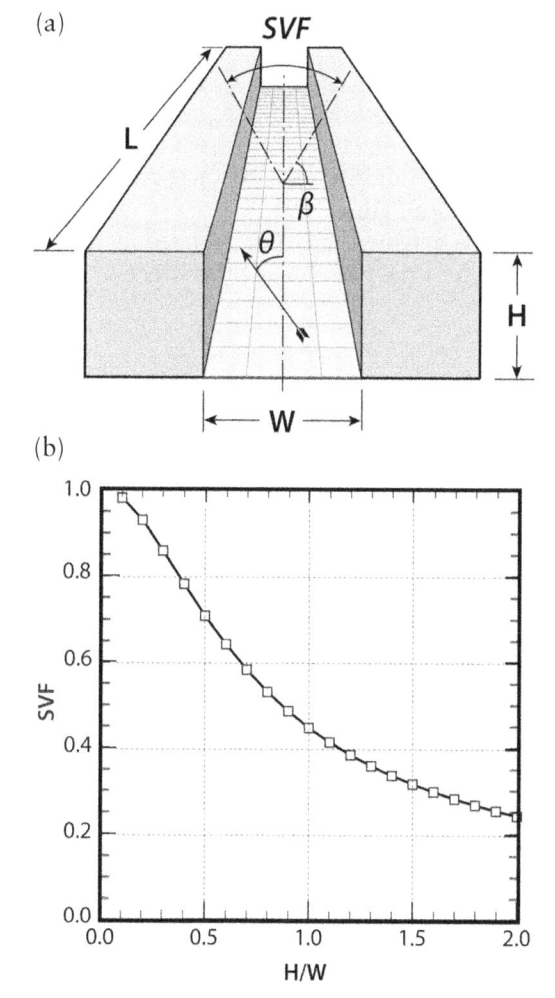

Figure 1.2 (a) Schematic view of a symmetrical urban canyon and its geometric descriptors and (b) sky view factor (SVF) as a function of canyon aspect ratio (H/W)

Note: SVF is measured from the centre line on the ground plane of a canyon whose length is considered semi-infinite.

whose adjacent buildings are of continuous height and have a common setback, the averaging of both height and width allows for a general categorization of real-world streets which are almost always irregular to one degree or another. An additional measure, which is sometimes used together with H/W, is the canyon length L, though in many cases L is much larger than either H or W and the street may be treated as semi-infinite.

- The canyon *axis orientation* (θ) represents the direction of the elongated space, measured (in degrees) as the angle between a line running north–south and the main axis running the length of the street or other linear space, measured in a clockwise direction. Often the canyon axis orientation is simply described by the closest cardinal direction (e.g. N–S, E–W) or diagonal (NW–SE, NE–SW).
- The *Sky View Factor (SVF)* of an urban canyon is closely related to its aspect (H/W) ratio, as it also describes the cross-sectional proportions of the canyon. The SVF is the proportion of the sky dome that is 'seen' by a surface, either from a particular point on that surface or integrated over its entire area.

When measured from the centre line on the ground plane of a symmetrical canyon of semi-infinite length, the SVF is given by:

$$SVF = \cos \beta \qquad (1.1)$$

where $\beta = \tan^{-1}(H/0.5W)$ and where H and W describe respectively the average height and width of the canyon (see Figure 1.2).

For an asymmetrical canyon, the SVF may be similarly calculated by simply averaging the values obtained from each of the two sides of the street:

$$SVF = (\cos \beta_1 + \cos \beta_2)/2 \qquad (1.2)$$

where $\beta_1 = \tan^{-1}(H_1/0.5W)$, $\beta_2 = \tan^{-1}(H_2/0.5W)$ and H_1 and H_2 are the average heights of the buildings on the two sides of the canyon.

The geometric descriptors of urban canyons have been found to correlate in a useful way with a number of climatic effects. Both the aspect ratio and SVF of central-city street canyons have a direct relationship with the urban heat island effect (see Chapter 3), and the SVF is an essential parameter when quantifying the cooling of a space by long-wave radiation emitted from the ground to the sky or the exposure to diffuse solar radiation from the sky (see Chapters 2 and 5). Different threshold values of H/W have been shown to divide between different *wind regimes*, or general patterns of air-flow over the urban surface (see Chapter 4), and the canyon proportions also play a role in direct solar shading and in the modification of urban albedo. The influence of building elements on either air-flow or direct sunlight varies, however, not only with urban density (as expressed by H/W or SVF) but also with direction to the extent that the canyon's axis orientation must also be considered with respect to the prevailing wind direction and sun angles.

Non-canyon urban spaces

The SVF may also be estimated for other types of space, whose geometry differs from a linear-type street canyon. Some of these spaces may be described, in simplified form, by a single cross-section – as with the canyon, which is assumed to be semi-infinite in length. For example, the SVF at a given point in a space such as a large plaza, which is bounded on only one side by a sufficiently long wall and is effectively open in all other directions, is estimated as $SVF = (1 + \cos\beta)/2$, where $\beta = \tan^{-1}(H/D)$ and D is the distance from the point of measurement to the wall (see Figure 1.3a). Similarly a circular plaza would have, at its centre point, $SVF = \cos^2\beta$ where $\beta = \tan^{-1}(H/r)$ and r is the radius of the circle (see Figure 1.3b).

There are other types of urban spaces that cannot be described by a single cross-section, but which have a relatively simple and regular geometry. A rectangular courtyard, for instance, has its view to the sky obstructed not by two walls (as in the canyon) but by a total of four walls, two in each direction. An approximation of SVF which accounts for walls of finite length and regular geometry in three dimensions (described by H, W and L, as seen in Figure 1.4) is then given by the product of the SVFs in each of these two different directions:

$$SVF \approx \cos\beta_W \cos\beta_L \tag{1.3}$$

where $\beta_W = \tan^{-1}(H/0.5W)$ and $\beta_L = \tan^{-1}(H/0.5L)$.

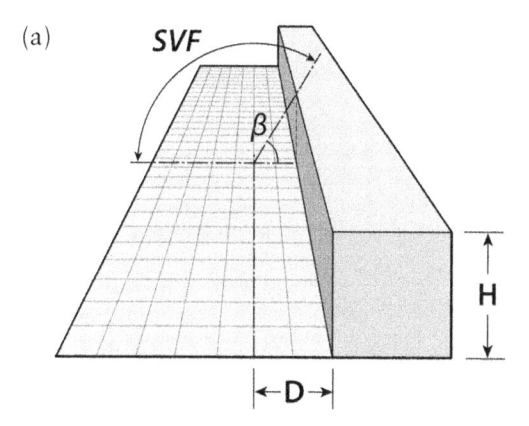

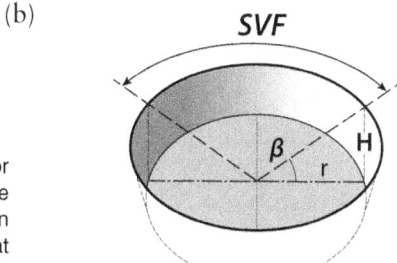

Figure 1.3 Geometric parameters for calculating the SVF from a point on the ground in a plaza-type space (a) at a given distance from one continuous wall and (b) at the centre point of a circular space

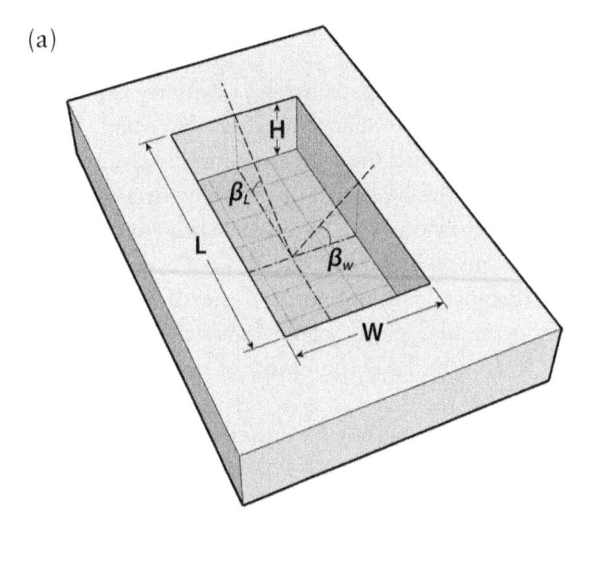

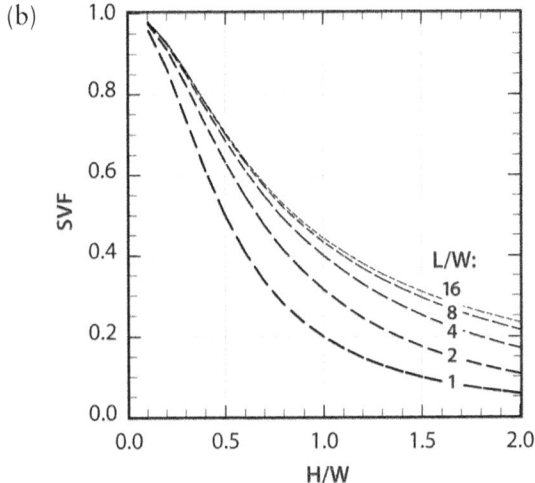

Figure 1.4 (a) Schematic view of a rectangular courtyard-type space showing its geometric descriptors and (b) approximated SVFs as a function of both H/W and L/W

For more complex and irregular geometries, which are characteristic of most real urban settings, a variety of tools may be used to estimate the SVF. Some of these tools are computational, and have been integrated with solid modelling software so that the urban geometry can be built in three dimensions and the view factors may be obtained at selected points within the model (see Figure 1.5).

Another, more traditional, method utilizes fish-eye lens photography to provide a full-sky view in an actual (or physically modelled) urban setting (see Figure 1.6). Refinements have been made to such techniques to allow highly accurate estimates of SVF even for complex arrangements including fine building details, trees and other irregular urban features.

SVF Field Data	3DSky View SVF	Actual Urban Geometry	3DSkyView 2D Stereographic Scene
0.59	0.62		
0.24	0.28		

Figure 1.5 Examples of urban SVF estimation using 3D urban models with Geographic Information System (GIS) analysis software

Source: Based on Souza et al (2003) (top) and Gál et al (2007) (bottom).

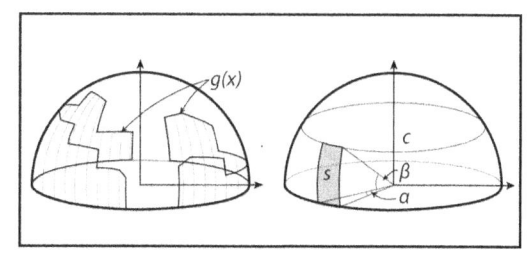

Figure 1.6 Upward-looking fish-eye lens photograph for estimation of SVF in an urban space

Photograph: W. Motzafi-Haller.

Additional descriptors

Several other quantitative measures of the urban surface may be mentioned, each of which has been utilized in climate studies that seek to correlate either the overall energy balance or specific energetic processes with the physical design of the city:

- *Frontal area density* is a three-dimensional measure of urban density, defined as the ratio between the vertical surface area of all building facades facing the prevailing wind direction and the overall horizontal plan area (as detailed in Chapter 4). This descriptor has been correlated closely with aerodynamic roughness of the textured urban surface.
- *Plan area density* defines the density of building coverage on the ground as the simple ratio between the horizontal area of buildings and the total horizontal area (see Chapter 4).
- *Vegetated fraction* is a measure of green space in the city, quantifying the ratio of horizontal area covered by vegetation to total horizontal area.

It is worth mentioning that all the above descriptors are essentially geometric measures, and as such are differentiated from other commonly used metrics of urban density such as the size of population or number of dwelling units per unit area. City size and density in this more traditional sense have also been shown to correlate with climatic effects such as the UHI (see Chapter 3), but it is important to stress that these are indirect relationships, which embody not only the effects of physical design but also the effects of human activity (expressed through such processes as building construction and ongoing fuel consumption) on the urban climate.

References

Gál, T., Rzepa, M., Gromek, B. and Unger, J. (2007) 'Comparison between Sky View Factor values computed by two different methods in an urban environment', *Acta Climatologica et Chorologica*, Universitatis Szegediensis, Tomus 40–41, pp17–26

Oke, T. R. (1987) *Boundary Layer Climates*, 2nd edition, Methuen & Co., London

Souza, L. C. L., Rodrigues, D. S. and Mendes, J. F. G. (2003) 'Sky view factors estimation using a 3D-GIS extension', *Proceedings of the Eighth International IBPSA Conference*, Eindhoven, The Netherlands, 11–14 August 2003

Additional reading

Arnfield, J. A. (2003) 'Two decades of urban climate research: A review of turbulence, exchanges of energy and water, and the urban heat island', *International Journal of Climatology*, vol 23, no 1, pp1–26

Arnfield, J. A. and Mills, G. (1994) 'An analysis of the circulation characteristics and energy budget of a dry, asymmetric east–west urban canyon. II. Energy budget', *International Journal of Climatology*, vol 14, no 3, pp239–261

Grimmond, C. S. B. and Oke, T. R. (1999) 'Aerodynamic properties of urban areas derived from analysis of surface form', *Journal of Applied Meteorology*, vol 38, pp1262–1292

Grimmond, C. S. B., Cleugh, H. A. and Oke, T. R. (1991) 'An objective urban heat storage model and its comparison with other schemes', *Atmospheric Environment*, vol 25B, pp311–326

Grimmond, C. S. B., Potter, S. K., Zuttner, H. N. and Souch, C. (2001) 'Rapid methods to estimate sky view factors applied to urban areas', *International Journal of Climatology*, vol 21, pp903–913

Johnson, G. T. and Hunter, L. J. (1999) 'Some insights into typical urban canyon airflows', *Atmospheric Environment*, vol 33, nos 24–25, pp3991–3999

Kondo, A., Ueno, M., Kaga, A. and Yamaguchi, K. (2001) 'The influence of urban canopy configuration on urban albedo', *Boundary-Layer Meteorology*, vol 100, no 2, pp225–242

Mills, G. (1997) 'An urban canopy-layer climate model', *Theoretical and Applied Climatology*, vol 57, nos 3–4, pp229–244

Nakamura, Y. and Oke, T. R. (1988) 'Wind, temperature and stability conditions in an east–west oriented urban canyon', *Atmospheric Environment*, vol 22, no 12, pp2691–2700

Nunez, M. and Oke, T. R. (1977) 'The energy balance of an urban canyon', *Journal of Applied Meteorology*, vol 16, pp11–19

Oke, T. R. (1988) 'Street design and urban canopy layer climate', *Energy and Buildings*, vol 11, nos 1–3, pp103–113

Oke, T. R., Johnson, G. T., Steyn, D. G. and Watson, I. D. (1991) 'Simulation of surface urban heat islands under ideal conditions at night. Part 2: diagnosis of causation', *Boundary-Layer Meteorology*, vol 56, pp339–358

Pearlmutter, D., Berliner, P. and Shaviv, E. (2005) 'Evaluation of urban surface energy fluxes using an open-air scale model', *Journal of Applied Meteorology*, vol 44, no 4, pp532–545

Schmid, H. P., Cleugh, H., Grimmond, C. S. B. and Oke, T. R. (1991) 'Spatial variability of energy fluxes in suburban terrain', *Boundary-Layer Meteorology*, vol 54, pp249–276

Steyn, D. G. (1980) 'The calculation of view factors from fisheye-lens photographs', *Atmosphere-Ocean*, vol 18, no 3, pp254–258

Voogt, J. A. and Oke, T. R. (1991) 'Validation of an urban canyon radiation model for nocturnal long-wave fluxes', *Boundary-Layer Meteorology*, vol 54, no 4, pp347–361

Watson, I. D. and Johnson, G. T. (1987) 'Graphical estimation of sky view-factors in urban environments', *Journal of Climatology*, vol 7, no 2, pp193–197

Yoshida, A., Tominaga, K. and Watatani, S. (1991) 'Field measurements on energy balance of an urban canyon in the summer season', *Energy and Buildings*, vol 15, nos 3–4, pp417–423

2
The Urban Energy Balance

Any attempt to understand how the microclimate of the built environment differs from that of the rural surroundings must start with an analysis of differences in their surface energy balance (SEB). This chapter introduces the basic equation describing the energy exchange that takes place at the surface, and deals in detail with each of its components, with special emphasis on how the built environment affects them.

What is the surface energy balance?

The concept of an energy balance is derived from the First Law of Thermodynamics, which states that energy can neither be created nor destroyed, only converted from one form to another. When applied to a simple system, this means that energy input must equal the sum of energy output from it and the difference in energy stored within it:

Energy input = Energy output + change in stored energy

Note that energy input and output are not required to be equal at all times: in fact, although this is generally the case when the balance is calculated for relatively long time periods, energy input and output are most likely to be unequal at any given instant. Also, the input and output of energy from a system do not necessarily occur in the same form: typically several modes of energy transfer take place simultaneously, and it is the constantly changing balance among them that determines whether a system will be heating up or cooling down.

Before going on to introduce the elements of the energy balance, we must define the boundaries of the system we are dealing with. The previous chapter discussed the urban boundary-layer, which may be conceived as the entire volume that is affected by the presence of the built-up area (see Figure 1.1, Chapter 1). The upper limit of this volume is somewhat arbitrary, since the exchange of energy as well as water vapour and other gases occurs in an atmospheric continuum. The lower border of this system is likewise imprecise: the depth of soil that interacts with the air above, storing and releasing energy, may vary from a few centimetres to several metres, depending on the properties of the ground and the time scale of the process in question.

A further difficulty in drawing the limits of the system involves the definition of the urban surface itself. The diversity of size, shape, composition and arrangement of the elements within the urban canopy means that it is very difficult to assign an appropriate scale to each of the parameters that describe the urban surface. Highly detailed descriptions are necessarily limited to relatively small spatial tracts such as urban canyons, and describing the energy balance of a more extensive area requires further simplification or generalization.

Typically the urban surface energy balance is viewed as a local- or meso-scale phenomenon, with the built-up area represented as a textured surface that can be characterized by its average properties (such as aerodynamic roughness or albedo). The energy transfer between this surface and the atmosphere is quantified by measuring or modelling fluxes above the urban canopy, at a height which is sufficient to ensure that these fluxes are representative of the overall urban terrain.

Keeping in mind the above qualifications, the general form of the surface energy balance of an urban area can be expressed as follows:

$$Q^* + Q_F = Q_H + Q_E + \Delta Q_S + \Delta Q_A \qquad (2.1)$$

where Q^* is the net all-wave radiation, Q_F is the anthropogenic heat flux, Q_H is the convective (or turbulent) sensible heat flux, Q_E is the latent heat flux, ΔQ_S is the net storage heat flux and ΔQ_A is the net horizontal heat advection.

The energy balance equation given above, as it stands, tells us very little about the urban microclimate. It includes all possible modes of energy transfer

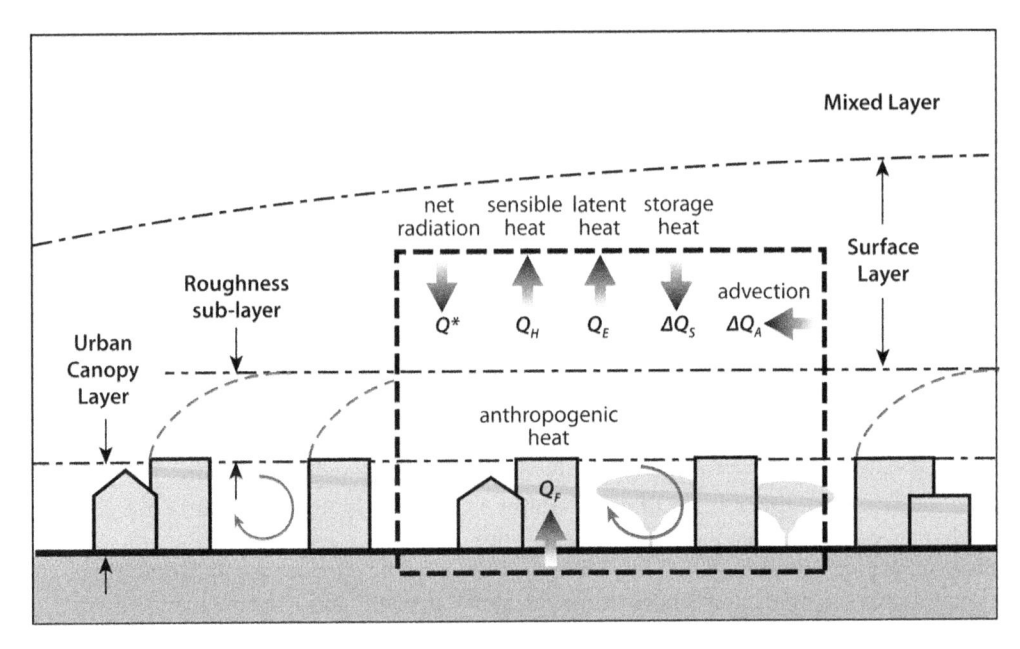

Figure 2.1 Schematic section showing urban surface energy balance (SEB) components

Note: Arrows pointing inward to the box marked by the dashed lines represent fluxes for which positive values represent energy gains to the system; positive values for arrows pointing outward (the turbulent fluxes Q_H and Q_E) represent energy losses from the system.

at the surface, although the magnitude of any component may equal zero at a particular point in time or space. A similar equation, containing the same terms, could be written for any other system. To understand what makes urban microclimate different, we must consider each of its component parts in detail, seeking in particular to identify those aspects that are affected by the presence of nearby buildings.

Radiation

In this section, we examine in detail the net exchange of radiation occurring in the urban canopy. The effect of urban form on the absorption of solar radiation and on long-wave radiation from the sky and from terrestrial surfaces is discussed, as are the overall effects of form and orientation on urban albedo.

The radiative exchanges occurring over any outdoor surface may be described by the following balance equation:

$$Q^* = (K_{dir} + K_{dif})(1-\alpha) + L\downarrow - L\uparrow \qquad (2.2)$$

where Q^* is the net radiative balance, K_{dir} is direct short-wave radiation (incident solar rays coming directly from the sun), K_{dif} is diffuse short-wave radiation (solar radiation that is reflected from clouds or aerosols in the atmosphere, and which makes the entire sky dome appear bright even if the sun itself is hidden), α is the albedo of the surface and $L\uparrow$ and $L\downarrow$ are the long-wave radiation emitted by the surface, and received by it from the sky, respectively.

Urbanization affects the absorption and reflection of incoming solar radiation as well as the absorption and emission of long-wave (far infra-red) radiation from the surface. This is due to the combined effects of urban geometry (which results in interference with the transmission of radiant energy), differences in the surface properties of man-made materials and air pollution.

Short-wave (solar) radiation

Solar radiation received at the surface of the Earth is the main source of energy in the urban canopy-layer (UCL). The geometry of the city affects the absorption of this radiation in complex ways. The mutual shading of tall buildings in a dense urban fabric may give rise to two seemingly contradictory phenomena. While multiple reflections of the sun's rays on building surfaces result in greater absorption overall compared to a flat horizontal surface, the amount of direct solar radiation penetrating to street level is lower. This description is particularly relevant to mid-latitude cities, and has a somewhat reduced effect in equatorial cities, where midday solar elevation is higher.

The proportion of energy that is reflected from the urban surface back to the atmosphere, rather than being absorbed and heating the surface, is determined at two levels:

1 *The properties of individual urban facets.* For a photon of light striking a terrestrial surface, the probability of being reflected is determined by the angle of incidence and by the wavelength-weighted and spatially averaged reflectivity of solar radiation (referred to as *albedo*). The albedo of typical

urban surfaces may vary from only 0.05 for dark asphalt to about 0.8 for whitewashed roofs (see Table 2.1).

2 *The three-dimensional arrangement of the individual facets that comprise the urban surface.* The albedo of a built-up area is affected not only by the reflectivity of individual elements, but also by the overall texture of the urban fabric. Certain configurations of buildings lead to an increased probability of multiple reflections and absorptions in the canopy-layer, resulting in a low urban albedo.

Table 2.1 The albedo and thermal emissivity of typical natural and man-made materials

Surface		Albedo (α)	Emissivity (ε)
man-made			
asphalt		0.05–0.20	0.95
concrete		0.10–0.35	0.71–0.90
brick		0.20–0.40	0.90–0.92
corrugated iron		0.10–0.16	0.13–0.28
fresh white paint		0.70–0.90	0.85–0.95
clear glass (normal incidence)		0.08	0.87–0.94
natural			
forest[1]		0.07–0.20	0.98
grass		0.15–0.30	0.96
soil[2]	wet	0.10–0.25	0.98
	dry	0.2–0.4	0.9–0.95

Notes:
1 The albedo of tropical rainforests lies in the lower part of this range, while that of coniferous or deciduous forests is in the upper part.
2 The albedo of soils depends, in addition to moisture content, on colour: it shows a high correlation with the Munsell colour value (Post et al, 2000).

Sources: Oke (1987); Garratt (1992).

Numerous studies have been carried out to assess the effect of urban geometry upon albedo, using a variety of methods – including analytical models, scale models and field observations – with somewhat varying results. However, sensitivity analysis carried out using models has resulted in a better understanding of the effect upon albedo of the following characteristics of urban form:

- *Plan area density* (the proportion of the city area covered by buildings): in dense areas, a large proportion of incoming solar radiation is reflected at roof level, and the effect of multiple reflections in the urban canyon is proportionately smaller. Urban albedo is also high in very low-density urban forms, because reflections from road surfaces are not intercepted by adjacent wall surfaces. Maximum absorption (or lowest albedo) occurs in medium-density configurations, for example when the street canyon width is approximately twice the width of the building blocks.

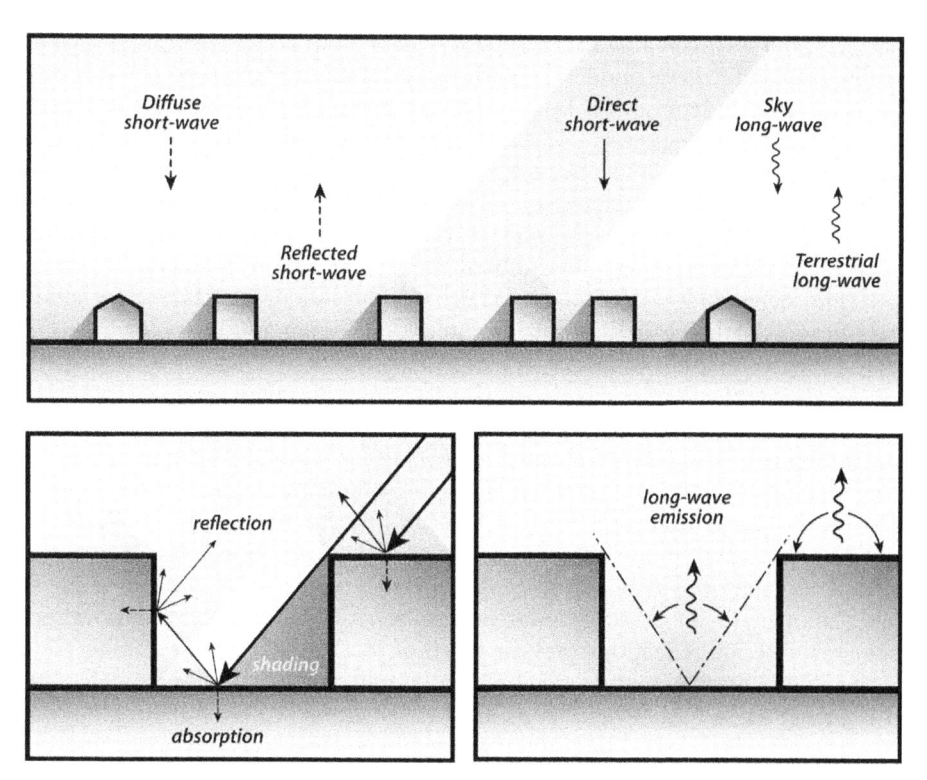

Figure 2.2 Generic effects of urban surface geometry on the penetration, absorption and reflection of solar radiation, and on the emission of long-wave radiation

- *Building height*: taller buildings create deeper urban canyons. For a given street width, this tends to increase the mutual reflection and absorption of radiation among building facets, and thus reduces albedo (see Figure 2.2). This is the main reason that the daytime peak values of *net radiation* (Q^*) tend to be higher for urban surfaces with deep canyons than for those with low buildings (refer to Figure 2.8).
- *Uniformity of building height*: when the roof surfaces of buildings in a city block are all at the same height, there is less likelihood that reflections off any roof surface will be intercepted at another building. Uniform building heights will therefore result in higher albedo, while buildings of varying heights will create a rougher (and less reflective) overall surface, absorbing more of the incoming solar radiation.
- *Orientation of roads*: although orientation affects penetration of direct sunlight to street level in patterns that vary with regular seasonal and diurnal patterns, the overall effect on urban albedo appears to be negligible.

While the reflectivity of most natural surfaces is almost independent of incidence angle (except for very acute solar zenith angles), the albedo of an urban area changes substantially with solar position. This is because the albedo of a city is not simply the area-weighted average of the albedo of individual surfaces, but is affected by the geometric relationship between surfaces such as walls, roofs and the ground. The *nadir view albedo* (NVA) used traditionally measures albedo from a fixed point directly above the city, regardless of solar angle, and has a single (i.e. constant) value. This measure fails to provide an accurate estimate of the proportion of solar radiation impinging upon the city that is absorbed over the course of a day, not only because the solar angle is not constant, but also because the intensity of sunlight varies during the diurnal cycle. The NVA may thus underestimate daily solar radiative loads by 11 to 22 per cent, depending on land use and urban morphology. An *energy weighted albedo* (EWA) that is a time-varying function of solar position and intensity may provide a better estimate.

As a general rule, the albedo of a surface increases with angle of incidence (note: incidence angle is measured from a line normal to the surface, so a 90 degree angle of incidence is parallel to the surface while zero degree incidence is perpendicular to it). Therefore, low sun angles result in higher reflection from flat roofs. This is true regardless of whether low elevation is the result of the time of day (early in the morning or late in the afternoon), season (winter, except in equatorial regions) or geographical latitude. Once the sun angle is large enough to allow substantial penetration of solar radiation into street canyons, internal reflections prevent much of this sunlight from escaping.

Sunlight entering a street canyon may be reflected from building walls, but if it encounters a glazed surface, it may be transmitted to the building interior. Modern office construction is characterized by extensive glazed areas, and the radiation thus absorbed may be a significant proportion of the incident sunlight. Numerical modelling has shown that although the albedo of relatively deep canyons (H/W>1) is less than about 0.2 for typical construction materials with diffuse reflection such as masonry, increasing the window-to-wall ratio results in a lower canyon albedo, for a wide range of sun angles. In very deep canyons (H/W>2) the predicted albedo for direct solar radiation from all sun angles, as well as for uniform diffuse solar radiation, is negligible – between 0.01 and 0.03.

Models, either physical or numerical, have generally tended to predict higher albedo than values produced by field studies. This is because models fail to reproduce the complexity of real urban environments. Real cities often have buildings with intricate facades, street furniture, vegetation, people and vehicles, while models typically resort to using simplified cubic arrays with uniform planar surfaces. The urban albedo simulated by such models has ranged from 0.23 to as much as 0.4 – much higher than the values reported by most field observations.

Characteristic urban surface albedo based on remote-sensing data reported in numerous studies is within a range of 0.09 to 0.27, with a mean value of approximately 0.14 for urban centres. Rural values are typically higher by about 0.05, probably because dark coloured roofing materials and the trapping role exerted by urban geometry result in less reflection compared with typical rural surfaces. Most US and European cities have an albedo in the range of 0.15 to 0.20, although there are large disparities among cities and between different neighbourhoods of the same city. Some North African towns have an albedo as high as 0.30 to 0.45 – possibly because they are uniformly low-rise, very dense and have flat whitewashed roofs.

Table 2.2 Sample of albedo values assigned to various land use classifications by several researchers

Study	Residential	Commercial	Industrial
Arnfield (1982)	0.18–0.20	0.08–0.10	0.13
Sailor (1995)	0.15–0.16	0.14	0.12–0.14
Seaman (1989)	0.12–0.18	0.20	0.20
Taha (1999)	0.16	0.18	0.18

Source: Sailor and Fan (2002).

Table 2.2 summarizes the results of several studies of the urban albedo, according to land use classifications.

Long-wave radiation

The relationship between the total hemispherical radiation emitted by a black body (i.e. a body that has an all-wave emissivity of 1.0) and its surface temperature is known as the Stefan-Boltzmann Law:

$$R^0 = \sigma T^4 \tag{2.3}$$

where R^0 is the total radiant energy in W m^{-2}, T is the absolute temperature in K and σ, known as the Stefan-Boltzmann constant, is 5.67×10^{-8} W m^{-2} K^{-4}.

The radiation given off by a real object may be calculated by introducing its total hemispherical emissivity, ε, which is, by definition, less than unity:

$$R = \varepsilon \sigma T^4 \tag{2.4}$$

(Representative values for the emissivity of various urban materials are given in Table 2.1).

The wavelength distribution of radiation emitted by a black body is given by Planck's Law:

$$R^0_\lambda(T) = \frac{C_1}{\lambda^5 [e^{(C_2/\lambda T)} - 1]} \tag{2.5}$$

where $R^0_\lambda(T)$ is the emittance at temperature T(K) for the wavelength λ(μm), and the constants are $C_1 = 3.741 \times 10^{-16}$ m^2 W and $C_2 = 0.014388$ m K.

This function approaches zero at very small and very large wavelengths. The wavelength at which a black body emits radiation with the highest intensity depends only on the temperature of the emitting surface, and may be calculated from Wien's Displacement Law, as follows:

$$\lambda_{max} \cdot T = 2897.8 \tag{2.6}$$

where λ_{max} is the wavelength of maximum emission, in μm, and T the absolute temperature of the radiating surface (K).

The radiation incident on a body may be absorbed, reflected or transmitted through it. The fractions of the absorbed, reflected and transmitted radiation are called *absorptivity* (α), *reflectivity* (ρ) and *transmissivity* (τ), respectively. The sum of these fractions is, by definition, unity:

$$\alpha + \rho + \tau = 1 \tag{2.7}$$

It should be noted that these values are total hemispherical values, and characterize the overall interaction between an object and the radiation impinging on it.

The relation between the emitting and absorbing properties of a body is given by Kirchoff's Law, which states that for every wavelength and for every direction of propagation, the directional spectral emissivity is equal to its directional spectral absorptivity:

$$\alpha_\lambda(T,\varphi,\theta) = \varepsilon_\lambda(T,\varphi,\theta) \tag{2.8}$$

In assessing the net radiative heat loss from a terrestrial surface (i.e. neglecting the effects of convection) the counter-radiation received from the sky, which is affected by atmospheric conditions, must also be taken into account.

The incoming atmospheric infra-red radiation can be expressed in two ways:

1. The sky may be assumed to behave like a black body. In this case, the radiation given off by the sky is given by the equation:

$$R_{sky} = \sigma T_{sky}^4 \tag{2.9}$$

   This equation requires a means of calculating the apparent temperature of the sky (the apparent sky temperature at a particular location and time is defined as the temperature a black body would have in order to radiate the same amount of energy as that received from the sky by a horizontal radiator);

   Or

2. The sky may be assumed to have a temperature equal to the ambient dry bulb temperature near the ground (T_a), in which case the differences in radiation emitted due to variations in atmospheric moisture content are accounted for by modifying the sky emissivity ε_{sky}:

$$R_{sky} = \sigma \varepsilon_{sky} T_a^4 \tag{2.10}$$

   where T_a is the dry bulb temperature of the air near the ground (K).

Both of these methods disregard the spectral distribution of the incoming sky radiation, and deal only with the total flux of radiant energy, assumed to have a continuous spectrum. These methods are applicable when the radiating surface approximates a black body, or is a grey body i.e. it absorbs all wavelengths indiscriminately. (Most natural materials are grey bodies, but several building materials, particularly polished metals, are spectrally selective, and have different emissivities in the long-wave part of the spectrum and in the solar spectrum.)

Table 2.3 Formulae to calculate the atmospheric emissivity of clear skies e_a

	Author	Equation	Remarks
1	Brunt (1932)	$\varepsilon_{a(0)} = 0.51 + 0.066 e_a^{1/2}$	Coefficients vary with geographic location
2	Swinbank (1963)	$\varepsilon_{a(0)} = 0.92 * 10^{-5} T_a^2$	For $T_a > 0°C$
3	Idso and Jackson (1969)	$\varepsilon_{a(0)} = 1 - 0.261 \exp\{-7.77 * 10^{-4}(273 - T_a)^2\}$	
4	Brutsaert (1975)	$\varepsilon_{a(0)} = 0.575 e_a^{1/7}$	Coefficient from Idso (1981)
5	Brutsaert (1982)	$\varepsilon_a = 1.24 (\frac{e_a}{T_a})^{1/7}$	
6	Idso (1981)	$\varepsilon_{a(0)} = 0.70 + 5.95 * 10^{-5} e_a \exp(1500/T_a)$	

Notes:
1 All equations use T_a in K and e_a in millibars.
2 The Swinbank and the Idso and Jackson relations require no calibration to local conditions, and they possess a high degree of spatial and temporal stability. The Brunt relation, on the other hand, requires an initial knowledge of local conditions for selection of appropriate regression coefficients. All expressions require correction for cloudy conditions.

Source: Oke (1987, p373)

Incoming long-wave radiation ($L\downarrow$) is not generally measured at meteorological stations. Various statistical correlations have therefore been proposed between $L\downarrow$ and meteorological parameters which are measured on a widespread basis and which may be used as surrogates for atmospheric emissivity. Some of these models of atmospheric emissivity are summarized in Table 2.3.

In the above models, the effect of altitude on long-wave radiation at the surface is incorporated indirectly through its effect on air temperature and atmospheric moisture content. The following model[1] proposes a parameterization scheme in which the effects of altitude are incorporated in two empirical coefficients:

$$L\downarrow = \sigma T_a^4 \{1 - x_s \exp(-Y_s e/T_a)\} \quad (2.11)$$

The empirical parameters X_s and Y_s have values of 0.35 and 10K hPa^{-1}, respectively, for lowland sites and values of 0.43 and 11.5K hPa^{-1} for mountain sites. Vapour pressure e is measured in hPa.

Clouds have a strong influence upon long-wave exchange in the atmosphere, because water has a very high absorptivity (and hence emissivity). The following modifications to the values for incoming sky radiation and for the net long-wave radiation may be used to compensate for cloud:

$$L\downarrow = L\downarrow_{(0)} (1 + an^2) \quad (2.12)$$

$$L^* = L^*_{(0)} (1 - bn^2) \quad (2.13)$$

Table 2.4 Values of the coefficients used in Equations 2.12 and 2.13 above to compensate for the effect of clouds on long-wave radiation in the atmosphere

Cloud type	Typical cloud height (km)	Coefficients a	b
Cirrus	12.20	0.04	0.16
Cirrostratus	8.39	0.08	0.32
Altocumulus	3.66	0.17	0.66
Altostratus	2.14	0.20	0.80
Cumulus		0.20	0.80
Stratocumulus	1.22	0.22	0.88
Stratus	0.46	0.24	0.96
Fog	0	0.25	1.00

Source: Oke (1987, p374)

where the constants 'a' and 'b' are a function of the cloud type (see Table 2.4), and 'n' is the fraction of the sky covered in cloud, expressed in tenths on a scale from zero to unity.

If cloud characteristics are not available, a simpler relationship may be applied:

$$L\downarrow = (1 + 0.0224n - 0.0035n^2 + 0.00028n^3)L\downarrow_{clear} \tag{2.14}$$

If the difference between the absolute temperatures of the surface and the sky is not large, the following linearized form of the Stefan-Boltzmann Law may be used to relate the environmental conditions to the net radiative heat transfer at the surface:

$$R_{net} = 4\varepsilon\sigma T_a^3 (T_r - T_s) \tag{2.15}$$

where R_{net} (W m^{-2}) is the net radiative heat loss, T_a (K) is the ambient air temperature, T_r (K) the radiator temperature and T_s (K) the equivalent sky temperature, and ε and σ are the emissivity and Stefan-Boltzmann constant, respectively.

Net radiative heat transfer may also be expressed by introducing a coefficient of radiant heat transfer at the surface. Setting this coefficient, h_r, to equal $4\varepsilon\sigma T_{air}^3$, Equation 2.15 above then becomes:

$$R_{net} = h_r(T_r - T_s) \tag{2.15}$$

The value of h_r has been determined experimentally for a range of temperatures, and was found to vary within a fairly narrow range – about 3.9 to 6.5 W m^{-2} K^{-1}. The typical diurnal range is about 0.5 W m^{-2} K^{-1}.

The effect of air pollution on radiant exchange in cities

Urban air pollution has a complex effect on radiation exchanges. The presence of aerosols in relatively high concentrations tends to reflect incoming solar radiation, and would thus be expected to lower daytime maximum temperatures. However, airborne particles also absorb outgoing long-wave radiation, diminishing the potential for nocturnal cooling of terrestrial surfaces, while the reduction in incoming solar radiation (K↓) is also offset to a great degree by increased downward long-wave radiation from the sky (L↓).

Urban–rural differences in levels of solar radiation attributed to air pollution in the form of aerosols vary widely from city to city (an aerosol is a suspension of fine solid particles or liquid droplets in a gas, e.g. smoke, oceanic haze, air pollution or smog). Some studies show an attenuation of up to 20 per cent, but most research suggests that this value is usually less than 10 per cent, since airborne particles tend to scatter direct radiation that is then received in the form of diffuse radiation. Evidence for both effects has been found in temperature and radiation records for Mexico City, one of the largest and most polluted cities in the world. As a result of this air pollution, global radiation in the city may be reduced by as much as 25 to 35 per cent relative to a rural site on clear days with low winds and high relative humidity. Temperature records show that although daytime maximum temperatures have declined slightly in the suburbs over the past 25 years, in downtown areas the urban heat island effect (see Chapter 3) dominates over the cooling effect of the aerosols. Increased absorption by airborne pollutants has also reduced long-wave radiative cooling, and the mean minimum temperatures have accordingly increased by nearly 2K over the same period.

Convective sensible heat flux

The exchange of sensible heat between the solid urban terrain and the atmosphere is discussed first at the scale of individual building facets, and then at the scale of the larger urbanized terrain.

Micro-scale convection

Sensible heat is transferred by convection between the air and the adjacent urban surface when there is a temperature difference between them. The size of the convective component of the surface energy balance (Q_H) depends on two factors: the magnitude of the temperature difference and the resistance to heat transfer between the surface and the adjacent air. The latter property is usually described in terms of its inverse, the convective heat transfer coefficient, so that the convective heat flux is given by the following expression:

$$Q_H = h_c (T_s - T_a) \qquad (2.17)$$

where Q_H is the rate of convective heat exchange (W m^{-2}), h_c is the convective heat transfer coefficient (W m^{-2} K^{-1}) and T_s and T_a are the temperature of the surface and ambient air (K), respectively.

The size of the heat transfer coefficient h_c cannot be obtained by analytical methods. It is affected not only by the properties of the air-flow, including its speed and the degree of turbulence, but also by the effect of the geometry of the solid body on the pattern of air-flow, by its surface characteristics and by the difference in temperature between the body and the surrounding fluid. Values for h_c have been obtained experimentally for use in various engineering applications (see Table 2.5). However, many of these correlations incorporate dimensionless numbers such as the Nusselt number and Sherwood number, which are in turn functions of the Prandtl number and Reynolds number. Setting a value for these numbers requires an appropriate representative length – which is difficult to define in complex and variable urban environments. For example, the non-dimensional heat transfer coefficient obtained from experiments in full-scale building surfaces is larger than that obtained in scale-model experiments with the same Reynolds number – probably because the representative length used to fix the Reynolds number, such as roof size, was inappropriate in the latter case.

There have also been several attempts to express h_c as a function of airspeed near outdoor surfaces. Figure 2.3 summarizes the findings of several such studies carried out near horizontal building surfaces, typically flat roofs. These are often similar, qualitatively, to correlations based on experiments carried out near vertical building surfaces (i.e. walls), illustrated in Figure 2.4.

All of the correlations involve specification of air speed, but the distance from the surface at which this speed is measured has varied among the studies from as little as 13cm to as much as 10m. In the context of a heterogeneous urban geometry, air speed changes substantially at this scale, so specifying an appropriate reference height is essential. A distance of about one metre is a suitable compromise between the desire to avoid the effect of inhomogeneity in the building surfaces – such as the effect of details of window sills or roof

Table 2.5 Empirical relationships for estimating the magnitude of the surface heat transfer coefficient for convection, h_c

	Author	Equation	Remarks
1	Clark and Berdahl (1980)	(a) $h_c = 0.8$	[a] The radiating surface is colder than ambient air, and wind speed is low enough ($u < 0.076$ m s^{-1}) to allow free convection, i.e. the flow is laminar
		(b) $h_c = 3.5$	[b] The radiating surface is warmer than ambient air and there is free convection ($u < 0.45$ m s^{-1})
		(c) $h_c = 1.8V + 3.8$	[c] Turbulent flow, $1.35 < u < 4.5$ m s^{-1}
		(d) $h_c = \dfrac{k(0.054 Re^{0.8} Pr^{0.33})}{L}$	[d] Turbulent flow, regardless of the surface temperature (u greater than the values noted above for the relevant surface temperatures)
2	Givoni (1982)	$h_c = 1 + 6 V^{0.75}$	
3	Hagishima and Tanimoto (2003)	$h_c = 3.96 + \sqrt{u^2 + v^2 + w^2} + 6.42$	Wind speed measured 13cm from surface
4	Clear et al (2003)	$h_x = \eta \dfrac{k}{L} 0.15 Ra_L^{1/3} + \dfrac{k}{x} R_f 0.0296 Re_x^{4/5} Pr^{1/3}$	Natural plus turbulent forced convection on a horizontal roof warmer than the air

Notes: V is wind speed in ms^{-1}, k is the thermal conductivity of the air (W m^{-2} K), Re the Reynolds number, Ra is the Rayleigh number and Pr the Prandtl number. L is the characteristic length of the radiating surface. η is a surface roughness coefficient. x is the distance from the edge of the surface.

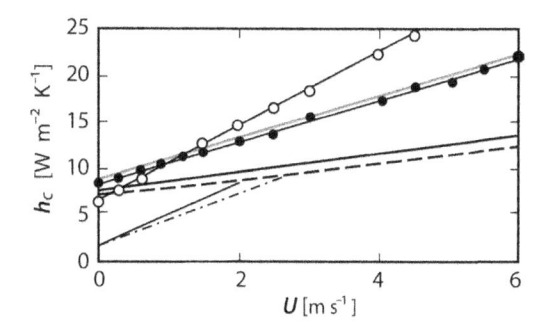

Figure 2.3 Measured convective heat transfer coefficient h_c for horizontal building roofs at various wind speeds U

Notes: The grey thick line marks results from Urano and Watanabe (1983). Thick solid and broken lines mark results of Kobayashi (1994) for measurements done under unstable conditions with S+1.5m and S+10m, respectively. Thin solid and broken lines are from Kobayashi and Morikawa (2000) for measurements done under stable conditions with S+1.5m and S+10m, respectively. The lines with white and black circles are from Hagishima and Tanimoto (2003) with S+0.13m and S+0.6m, respectively.

Source: Redrawn from Hagishima et al (2005).

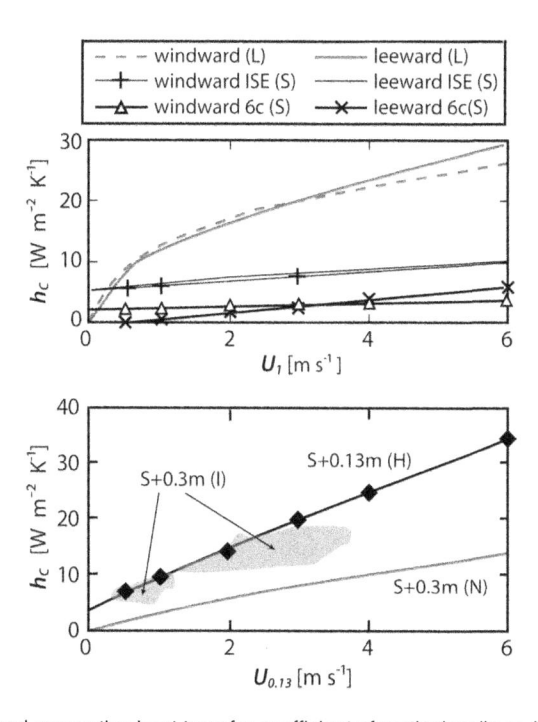

Figure 2.4 Measured convective heat transfer coefficient of vertical walls on buildings at various wind speeds

Note: '18E' indicates data observed at the edge of the wall of 18th floor and '6c' indicates the data observed at the central wall of the 6th floor. (H), (I), (L), (N) and (S) indicate the data of Hagishima and Tanimoto (2003), Ito et al (1972), Loveday and Taki (1996), Narita et al (1997) and Sharples (1984), respectively.

Source: Redrawn from Hagishima et al (2005).

parapets – and the need to obtain a sufficiently accurate estimate of the speed near a specific building element.

An additional complication arises from the fact that the heat transfer coefficient of a building surface is not spatially uniform. This is especially true for walls, which have a higher transfer coefficient near edges than at the centre, especially the top edge. Differences are less important in horizontal roof surfaces, which are typically exposed to a relatively homogeneous wind environment.

The effects of variations in surface temperature on the heat transfer coefficient are critical, especially when ambient wind speed is low. Warm surfaces (relative to the air) may induce noticeable convection in the absence of mechanical turbulence. Therefore, the heat transfer coefficient of the upper surface of a horizontal building element will be greater than that of its lower surface. Since adjacent building surfaces may exhibit large temperature differences due to unequal exposure to the sun, different thermal properties or even variations in moisture availability (in the case of porous materials or soil), the convective flux from a surface may be distinctly non-uniform.

In addition to the heat transfer coefficient and surface temperature, discussed in the preceding paragraphs, the exchange of sensible heat between a solid and the adjacent layer of air depends upon the temperature of air near the surface. Where terrain is flat and homogeneous, air temperature near the surface is generally uniform. However, the urban street canyon is a different case. Not only are surfaces not homogeneous in material, solar exposure and orientation, but also the effect of geometry on air-flow means that different surfaces may be exposed to different air velocities. Turbulent mixing tends to neutralize temperature gradients in the environment in general, so that the difference between air temperatures above and within a canyon is generally less than 1K. However, pockets of stagnant air (near the base of the walls) may remain undisturbed by the typical canyon vortex, and air temperature differences of up to 3K have been observed compared with the centre of the street. Air temperature within 0.5m of wall surfaces may also differ from that of the rest of the canyon volume.

The heterogeneous nature of the urban environment makes it difficult to characterize by means of a single representative temperature. However, many micrometeorological models of the urban environment are not detailed enough to obtain the temperature of individual facets comprising the urban surface as a whole, and require just such a temperature. Remote sensing by satellite or airborne infra-red sensors can provide a representative temperature of the area being surveyed. However, there are somewhat contradictory reports regarding the correlation between the surface temperature obtained by this means and the air temperature near the ground. The method is used fairly extensively in studies of global climate and has also been applied in several urban studies. However, although off-nadir observations from aerial sensors in the direction of the most shaded urban facet agreed most closely with a 'complete surface temperature' that takes into account the area-weighted temperature of all urban surfaces, estimates of surface temperature based on scans of the urban surface at different angles are probably not good enough to be useful for detailed modelling of urban microclimate.

Turbulent sensible heat flux

The discussion in this section has so far dealt only with sensible heat flux between ground (or building) surfaces and air immediately adjacent to them – that is, within the urban canopy-layer and the roughness sub-layer immediately above it. As described in Chapter 1, both of these layers tend to be extremely heterogeneous. In order to characterize the exchange of heat between the atmosphere and the larger urban surface, which is composed of various buildings, streets, trees and countless other elements, it is necessary to observe this patchwork from a sufficient height above the canopy so that the separate effects of these disparate elements will be spatially averaged. The range of heights which fits this description is denoted in Figure 1.1 (see Chapter 1) as the surface layer (also known as the inertial sub-layer), and it is characterized by a spatial homogeneity of vertical fluxes and by negligible advective fluxes.

As an urban surface is warmed through the absorption of solar radiation, cooler air flows over the rough surface, absorbs some of its heat and mixes with air higher up. This mixing is generated by *turbulence*, or the tendency of wind flow to exhibit random deviations in its characteristic properties, such as its

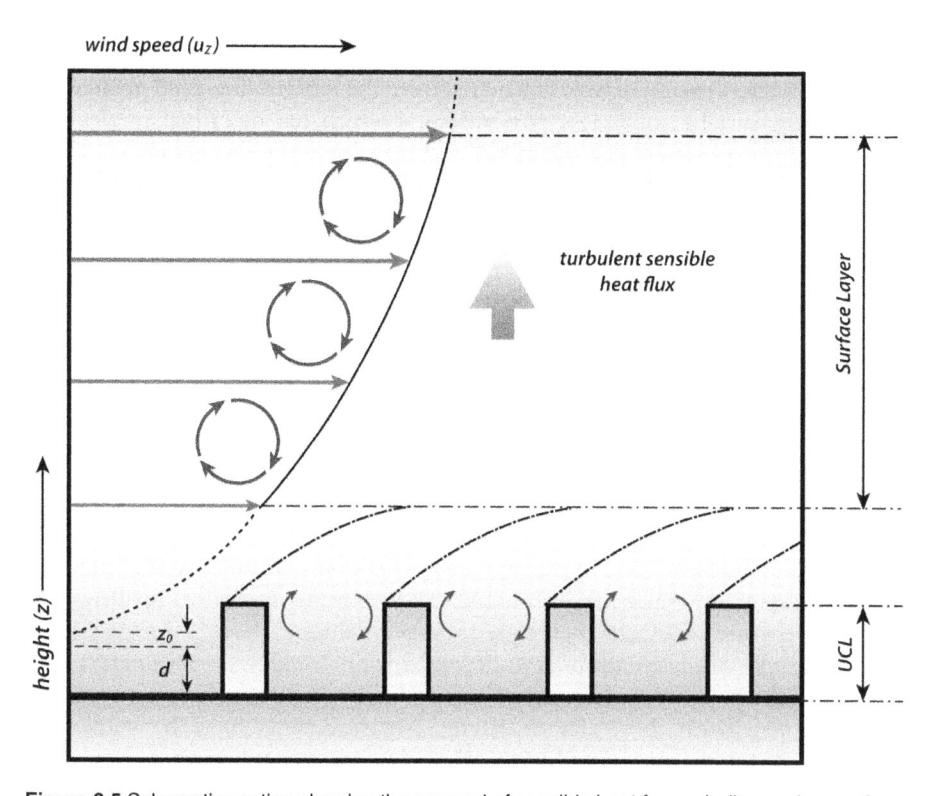

Figure 2.5 Schematic section showing the removal of sensible heat from a built-up urban surface by wind turbulence

speed and direction. The extent of the turbulence depends upon the properties of the fluid, the nature of the flow itself and the effect of physical obstacles the fluid may encounter (for an extended discussion of this subject, see Chapter 4). The rough urban texture exerts a drag on the wind flow, making it not only more turbulent but also decreasing its average velocity – so that wind speed is lowest near the surface and increases with height (see Figure 2.5). Within the surface layer, this increase with height is systematic but not linear; rather, the vertical wind speed profile takes the shape of a logarithmic curve.

Eddies are generated by shear stress between streamlines of air flowing at different speeds, and it is these eddies that carry warmer air up and cooler air down, through a process of mechanical mixing (as depicted in Figure 2.5). This process is known as the *turbulent flux of sensible heat*.

The turbulent sensible heat flux density Q_H (W m^{-2}) in a homogeneous surface layer may be calculated as:

$$Q_H = \rho c_p k u_* T_* \tag{2.18}$$

where ρ and c_p are the respective density (kg m^{-3}) and specific heat (J kg^{-1} K^{-1}) of air and k is von Karman's constant (taken as 0.4). Both the friction velocity u_* (m s^{-1}) and scaling temperature T_* (K) are considered constant with height within the surface layer over a given time interval, as determined by surface roughness and prevailing conditions.

The friction velocity may be calculated from the logarithmic wind profile with appropriate surface roughness parameters – which (as described in detail in Chapter 4) are closely dependent on the three-dimensional geometry of the buildings and other roughness elements that make up the urban surface. The scaling temperature T_*, which is an expression of the logarithmic vertical air temperature profile within the surface layer, can be calculated from temperature measurements at a series of heights and should be corrected for stability effects.

A commonly used approach for quantifying Q_H over actual urban surfaces is the *eddy covariance* (or eddy correlation) method, in which high-frequency readings are taken simultaneously of air temperature (T) and of the vertical component of the turbulent wind flow (w):

$$Q_H = \rho c_p \overline{w'T'} \tag{2.19}$$

where ρ and c_p are the density and specific heat of air, as in Equation 2.17. Sonic anemometers are typically used in combination with fine-wire thermocouples, to track the instantaneous deviations in vertical air-flow (w') and temperature (T') from their time-averaged values.

This type of calculation is independent of roughness parameters and stability effects, but requires a precise synchronization of measurements at a high frequency (on the order of 10Hz). Measurements must be made at a sufficient distance from any physical obstacle to capture the appropriate eddy circulation, depending on the path-length of the sonic anemometer and the time scale of the measurement.

Latent heat flux

One of the main differences between the urban environment and the rural one is the extent of exposed ground surfaces that absorb precipitation or lose moisture due to evaporation. The availability of moisture affects the magnitude of the latent heat flux, which in turn affects the extent to which available radiant energy causes the air temperature to rise. Transpiration from plants also has an effect on the balance of energy and moisture, and the relative lack of vegetation in built-up areas is often mentioned as being one of the main reasons for differences between urban and rural environments.

Evapotranspiration, the formation of dew and the urban water balance

Evaporation is the physical process by which a liquid is converted to its gaseous state. The evaporation of water into the atmosphere occurs from the surfaces of water bodies, from wet soils and from transpiring vegetation (*transpiration* is the process of evaporation of water that has passed through a plant). Soil evaporation and plant transpiration occur simultaneously in nature, and there is often no easy way to distinguish between the two processes. Therefore the term *evapotranspiration* (ET, or simply E) is used to describe the total process of water transfer into the atmosphere from vegetated land surfaces.

The urban water budget for a volume comprising the urban canopy layer and the underlying soil to a depth where no net exchange of water takes place during the time period relevant to the process under examination can be written as:

$$p + I + F = E + r + \Delta A + \Delta S \qquad (2.20)$$

where p is precipitation, I is the piped water supply of the city, F is the water vapour released due to anthropogenic activities such as combustion, E is evapotranspiration, r is run-off, ΔA is the net advection of moisture for the volume and ΔS is the change in water storage for the given period.

The water balance is linked to the energy balance through the term E, which is the mass equivalent of the latent heat flux Q_E:

$$Q_E = L_v E \qquad (2.21)$$

where L_v is the latent heat of vaporization, or the amount of energy required to evaporate a unit mass of a liquid. L_v is a physical property that varies with temperature and pressure, and at 30°C and 100kPa equals 2.43MJ (0.675kWh) per kilogram. Thus an evaporation rate of 1mm per hour of water is equivalent to a latent heat flux of 675W m^{-2}.

A microclimatic model of the urban water balance can be constructed from Equation 2.20 by setting net advection ΔA to zero (as it is defined in the surface layer) and assuming that anthropogenic moisture F is negligible. Such a model may be driven by standard climate data and a detailed description of the hydrological properties of the surface. This requires a partitioning of the urban area into three types of surfaces:

1. Impervious surfaces, such as roads, parking lots and buildings. These surfaces are considered to be either wet (saturated) during or immediately after rain, or dry.
2. Pervious un-irrigated, such as open untended park areas. These surfaces may have a moisture status ranging from totally wet (saturated) to totally dry.
3. Pervious irrigated, such as lawns and gardens, which are assumed to be always wet.

The availability of water is then calculated using conventional relations describing the hydrological properties of the surface and subsurface, including the retention capacity of the three types of surfaces and the soil storage capacity and field capacity of the pervious portion of the city.

Of special importance is the calculation of evapotranspiration, because of its effect on the urban energy balance. There are two possible conditions:

1. If the surface is wet or soil moisture is at field capacity, evaporation occurs at the potential rate, given by Priestley and Taylor:[2]

$$E = (\alpha/L_v)[s/(s+\gamma)](Q^* - \Delta Q_s) \qquad (2.22)$$

where E is evapotranspiration, L_v is the latent heat of vaporization, s is the slope of the saturation vapour pressure versus temperature relationship, γ is the psychrometric constant, Q^* is the net all-wave radiation flux density and ΔQ_s the subsurface (net storage) heat flux density. The (non-dimensional) coefficient α is the ratio of evaporation from a wet surface under conditions of minimal advection to the equilibrium evaporation, which is the lower limit to evaporation from moist surfaces. The value of α has been determined empirically, and is about 1.2 to 1.3 in suburban areas.

2. If the surface is moist or dry, evapotranspiration is restricted to a certain extent by water availability, and may be calculated by a modified version of Brutsaert and Stricker's[3] advection-aridity equation:

$$E = (1/L_v) \left\{ \begin{matrix} (2\alpha - 1)(s/s+\gamma))(Q^* - \Delta Q_s)\sum_{i=2}^{n} A_i \alpha_i' \\ -[AA(\gamma/(s+\gamma))E_a] \end{matrix} \right\} \qquad (2.23)$$

where A_i is the proportion of the catchment covered with the ith surface type, a'_i is an empirical coefficient of the ith surface type, defined as above and AA is the status of soil moisture related to area. E_a refers to the drying power of the air:

$$E_a = (C/\gamma)(\bar{e}^* - \bar{e}_a) \left\{ \begin{matrix} (\bar{u}/k^2)/[(\ln(z_v - d + z_{0v}/z_{0v})) \cdot \\ \ln(z_u - d + z_{0m})/z_{0m})] \end{matrix} \right\} \qquad (2.24)$$

where C is the heat capacity of dry air; $\bar{e}^*$ and $\bar{e}_a$ are the mean saturation and ambient vapour pressures at height z_v, respectively; u is the mean horizontal wind speed at height z_u; k is the von Karman constant (0.40);

d is the zero-plane displacement length and z_{0v} and z_{0m} are the water vapour and momentum roughness lengths, respectively (see Chapter 4 for explanation of the parameters k, d and z_0).

Evapotranspiration may account for 30 to 70 per cent of the annual external water balance (i.e. not including irrigation), even in temperate mid- and high-latitude cities. Irrigation during the dry season increases evapotranspiration rates and has a substantial effect on the energy balance near the surface.

The formation and deposition of dew on terrestrial surfaces is the converse of evaporation, and may have equally substantial effects on energy exchange. While small in magnitude – dew accumulation is on the order of several-tenths of a millimetre per night – dewfall is not a negligible term in the urban water balance. Furthermore, there are significant differences between dew formation on rural surfaces and on a variety of urban materials. Dewfall tends to be relatively abundant on grass or on low thermal mass surfaces in the city, such as exposed roof shingles, but tends to be absent from surfaces that stay warm throughout the night, such as pavements.

Partitioning energy between sensible and latent heat

In the absence of advection, surplus incoming energy not stored in the ground heats the air near the surface (increasing its sensible heat content) and also evaporates available surface water, thus increasing the latent heat content of the air. If there is no moisture available, all of the surplus energy is converted to sensible heat, often resulting in a substantial rise in air temperature. The availability of water, and the potential for evaporative cooling which it embodies, thus has a major effect on air temperature near the surface.

Many dry urban surfaces, such as paved asphalt roads, channel their entire net radiant surplus during the daytime into stored or convected sensible heat, warming the substrate or the adjacent air. Natural terrain is rarely totally impervious, and absorbed moisture may cause some of the surplus radiant energy to be converted into latent heat. However, much of the water received from precipitation or irrigation may percolate into the depths of the soil, so that it is not available at the surface. On the other hand, impervious urban materials may hold rainwater at the surface for some time (depending on drainage), during which considerable evaporation may occur, increasing the latent heat content of the air at the expense of its sensible heat. In terms of climatic response, therefore, impervious surfaces can cover the full moisture range from 'wet' (after rain) to 'dry' in a very short period, while pervious natural surfaces can cover a similar range over more extended periods and with a much slower response.

Urban environments may vary widely in their permeability and moisture availability, from city centres consisting almost entirely of masonry, concrete, asphalt and glass, to suburban developments with dense vegetation and well-irrigated lawns. The former may contribute to a very dry system with very little latent heat, while the latter create more humid microclimates that are dominated by the effects of evapotranspiration. In the extreme case of a large body of water, such as a sea or lake, mixing of the water reduces diurnal temperature fluctuations near the surface while high atmospheric humidity restricts evaporation – so both sensible and latent heat fluxes may be small.

The *Bowen ratio* (β), which is the ratio between sensible heat flux and latent heat flux in a given location ($\beta = Q_H / Q_E$), provides a simple method of describing the relative importance of latent heat in the surface energy balance. When there is a shortage of water and evapotranspiration is limited, $\beta>1$, reaching values of 10 or more in desert conditions. The Bowen ratio for temperate areas is typically 0.4–0.8.

Cities differ substantially in the extent of vegetation, in the availability of water and in the size of the incoming radiant flux during the daytime. Accordingly, the Bowen ratio of several North American cities has been estimated at about 1.5 where precipitation is limited and irrigation is practised, compared with a value of about 0.8–1.0 for cities with frequent summertime precipitation. The daytime Bowen ratio is affected strongly by the extent of the irrigated area in the cities, there being a clear inverse relationship between β and the irrigated area. Considerable variability in the size of the fluxes is typically found on a day-to-day basis, but on average peak daily values for Q_E are in the range of 150–200W m^{-2}, while the magnitude of peak Q_H (sensible heat flux) typically varies from about 200–300W m^{-2}.

While the Bowen ratio gives an indication of the relative importance of latent heat flux compared to sensible heat, the magnitude of both these components of the surface energy balance may vary substantially on a seasonal basis. In some cases the total turbulent flux (the sum of sensible and latent heat) may be quite small, accounting for less than 20 per cent of net radiation, or even exhibit negative values. In this case, net storage may account for most of the mean daily net radiation. This condition is most likely to occur in cool humid conditions with high levels of soil moisture and relatively weak sunshine: most of the (weak) incoming solar flux is absorbed in the soil, which due to its high moisture content has a large thermal capacity and exhibits little change in temperature. High atmospheric humidity limits evaporation, so both the sensible and latent heat fluxes remain small both in absolute terms and in comparison with the net radiant flux.

The following expressions may be used to estimate the sensible and latent heat fluxes near the surface:

$$Q_H = \frac{(1-\alpha)+(\gamma/s)}{1+(\gamma/s)}(Q^* - \Delta Q_s) - \beta \qquad (2.25)$$

$$Q_E = \frac{\alpha}{1+(\gamma/s)}(Q^* - \Delta Q_s) + \beta \qquad (2.26)$$

where s is the slope of the saturation vapour pressure versus temperature curve; γ is the psychrometric constant; and α and β are empirical parameters. The dimensionless parameter α depends on the soil moisture status, and accounts for the strong correlation of Q_H and Q_E with $Q^*-\Delta Q_S$, whereas β (in W m^{-2}) accounts for the uncorrelated portion.

Equation 2.22 is essentially the same as the Priestley-Taylor equation (2.22) which was originally proposed to calculate evaporation in the presence of unlimited moisture (over large bodies of water or saturated soil). Extension to non-saturated areas is enabled by the addition of the empirical factor β and by selecting appropriate values for α. It is relatively simple, and its accuracy depends on whether the values of α and β are appropriate for the conditions.

Table 2.6 shows typical values of α and β for a variety of landscapes. α increases from nearly zero in hyper-arid conditions to a maximum of about 1.2 to 1.4, but the size of β appears to be independent of local conditions. The heterogeneity within cities and variations among them means that in practice, it is unlikely that α will have a single representative value for all or even most cities. In fact, when values of α and β were fitted to data from well-documented observations in several North American cities, substantial variations were found. As Table 2.7 shows, the value of α ranged from 0.19 in dry Mexico City to 0.65 in cool and humid Chicago, with an average value of 0.45, while β ranged from –0.3 in Mexico City to 8.4 in Tucson, averaging only 2.8 W m^{-2}.

Table 2.6 Values of the α and β parameters in different landscapes

	α	β (W m^{-2})
Dry desert with no rain for months	0.0–0.2	20
Arid rural area	0.2–0.4	20
Crops and field, midsummer during periods when rain has not fallen for several days	0.4–0.6	20
Urban environments, some parks	0.5–1.0	20
Crops, fields or forests with sufficient soil moisture	0.8–1.2	20
Large lakes or ocean with land more than 10km distant	1.2–1.4	20

Source: Hanna and Chang (1992).

Table 2.7 Average β (W m^{-2}) and α for several urban areas

City	α	β (W m^{-2})
Tucson	0.28	8.4
Chicago[a]	0.65	6.1
Sacramento	0.56	2.9
Vancouver[b]	0.33	1.4
Miami	0.51	2.3
Los Angeles[c]	0.50	1.2
Mexico City	0.19	–0.3
Mean	0.45	2.8

Notes: [a] average of two separate sites; [b] average of three separate sites; and [c] average of three separate sites.

Source: Grimmond and Oke (2002).

Urban evapotranspiration rates

Evapotranspiration (ET) may be an important flux in urban areas, typically accounting for 20 to 40 per cent of the daytime net all-wave radiation in residential neighbourhoods and an even higher portion of the daily (24-hour) radiation. The evapotranspiration rates in downtown and light industrial sites tend to be much lower, due to the relative absence of vegetation. As Figure 2.6 shows, evapotranspiration rates in residential neighbourhoods in developed countries are often almost independent of regional climate, since irrigation sustains evaporation in the absence of rainfall, even in desert cities such as Tucson. The limit on evapotranspiration in urban areas is therefore closely related to the extent of green space within the built-up area, which often is dominated by dry paving and other impermeable surfaces.

It has been shown that the proportional latent heat flux can be closely predicted by the vegetated fraction of the city (i.e. the ratio of landscaped to total urban area), and that this connection is even closer when the total is taken not only in terms of the city's horizontal area, but also in terms of its complete three-dimensional surface area – which includes the vertical walls of buildings as well as roof and ground surfaces (see Figure 2.7). This implies that buildings, which in the vast majority of cases are composed of dry, non-transpiring materials, also have a limiting effect on the city's ability to moderate heat gain through evaporative cooling.

Thermal storage

The continual change in the amount of heat stored in the urban fabric, or the *net storage heat flux* (ΔQ_S), is clearly an important component of the surface energy balance – it may commonly account for up to half of daytime net radiation. Radiant energy – whether from the sun, from the atmosphere or from other terrestrial surfaces – is absorbed in all of the surfaces that define the urban canopy. The thermal and optical properties of these surfaces, whether

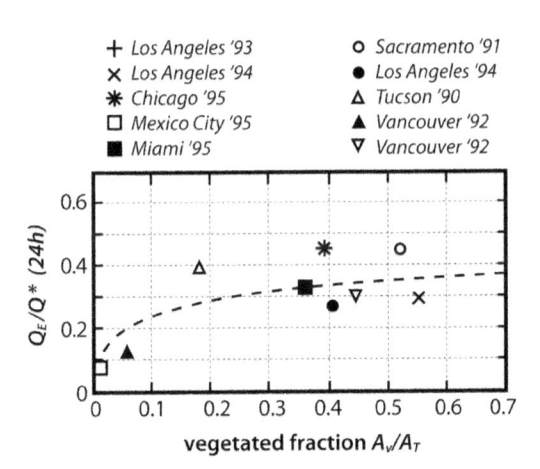

Figure 2.6 Relationship between average ET at a site and fraction of the surface cover vegetated

Source: Redrawn from Grimmond and Oke (1999b).

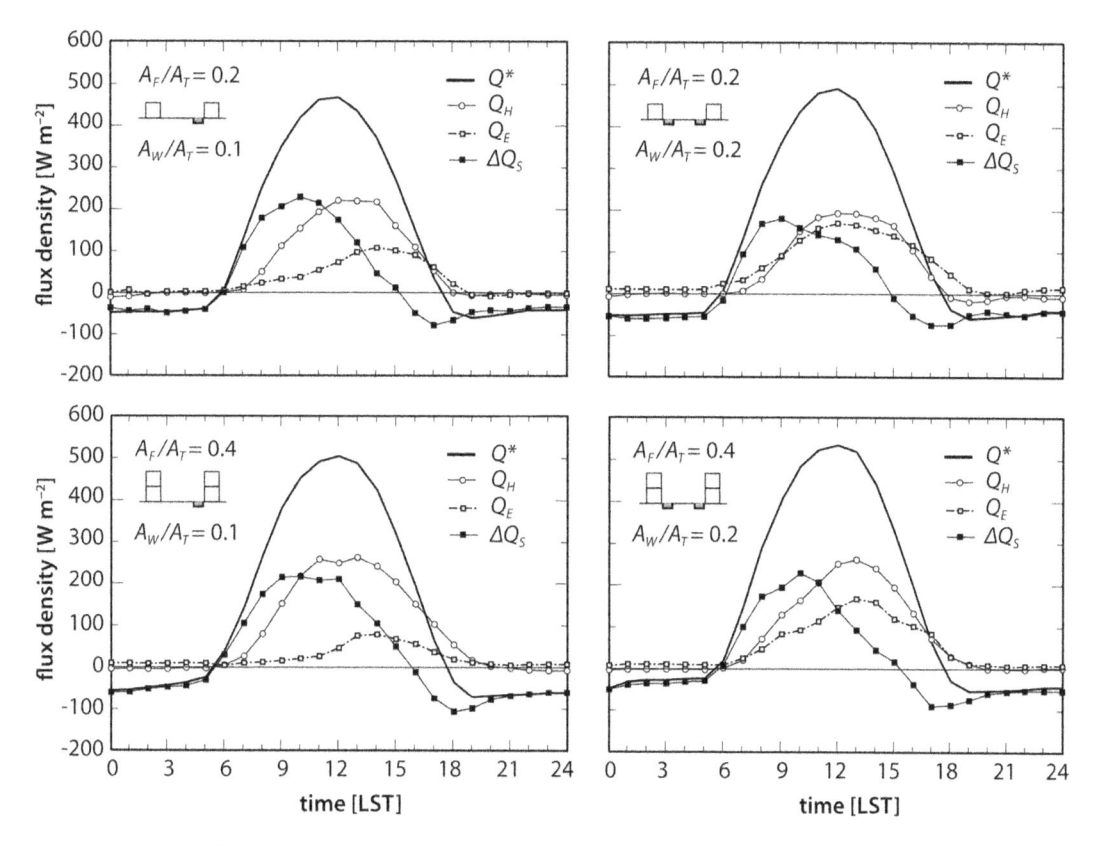

Figure 2.7 Energy fluxes over an open-air scaled urban array, for different configurations of 3D geometry and water availability

Note: It can be seen that the latent heat flux Q_E is highest when the fraction of evaporating area (A_W/A_T) is maximized with respect to total urban surface area, as represented by the frontal density (A_F/A_T).

Source: Based on Pearlmutter et al (2009).

they are paved streets or the walls of buildings, are often different from those of natural surfaces. Their ability to absorb, store and emit radiant energy has a substantial effect on urban microclimate. Furthermore, it is not only the properties of the materials but also the size and spatial arrangement of the surface areas that affects the storage of energy in the city. Since the process of storage also affects the temperature of urban surfaces, it is significant for the thermal comfort of people exposed to this environment.

The storage heat flux is driven by energy exchange at the surface: it is considered positive if the net effect of all heat transfer mechanisms results in an increase in the energy content of the ground, the structures and, to a much smaller extent, the air within the volume of interest (see Figure 2.7). Over a daily 24-hour cycle the net storage flux is typically small, as the surface gradually accumulates heat in summer and dissipates heat in winter, and over a yearly cycle it is assumed to be negligible. In the long term it is assumed to equal zero, unless there is a significant net input of external energy, such as anthropogenic heat from the combustion of fossil fuels.

The rate at which energy is absorbed or released from the ground is determined not only by the external forcing (i.e. the incoming energy which drives the surface energy balance), but also by the thermal properties of the material itself – namely its *thermal conductivity* (k) and *heat capacity* ($C = \rho c_p$, where ρ is density and c_p specific heat). The heat capacity is a measure of the amount of energy required to raise the temperature of a given volume of material by a given number of degrees – and massive materials with a large heat capacity are said to have a high *thermal inertia*, because they register a relatively small diurnal temperature change even when exposed to intense incoming and outgoing energy fluxes. Table 2.8 gives the thermal properties of several common soil types and urban paving materials.

A parameter that combines the properties of both thermal conduction and heat capacity is the *thermal admittance* ($\mu = kC^{-1/2}$): materials with a high admittance absorb heat readily and transmit it to the substrate, only to release it easily when the ambient air becomes cooler. Typical values of thermal admittance for both rural and urban surfaces vary over a wide range – from about 300 J m^{-2} s$^{1/2}$ K^{-1} for dry peat soil and foamed concrete to approximately 2500 J m^{-2} s$^{1/2}$ K^{-1} for wet sandy loam or dense concrete. Massive materials such as the latter are responsible large storage fluxes, while materials with a very small mass – such as the air between buildings – store very little heat.

Table 2.8 The thermal properties of typical natural soils and man-made materials

Material	Remarks	ρ Density and (kg m^{-3})	c Specific heat and (J kg^{-1} K^{-1})	C Heat capacity and (kJ m^{-3} K^{-1})	k Thermal conductivity and (W m^{-1} K^{-1})	κ Thermal diffusivity and (m^2 s^{-1} × 10^{-6})	μ Thermal admittance and (J m^{-2} s$^{-1/2}$ K^{-1})
Natural soils:							
Sandy soil (40% pore space)	dry	1600	800	1280	0.30	0.24	620
	saturated	2000	1480	2960	2.20	0.74	2550
Clay soil (40% pore space)	dry	1600	890	1420	0.25	0.18	600
	saturated	2000	1550	3100	1.58	0.51	2210
Peat soil (80% pore space)	dry	300	1920	580	0.06	0.10	190
	saturated	1100	3650	4020	0.50	0.12	1420
Water	pure, at 4°C	1000	4180	4180	0.57	0.14	1545
Man-made construction materials:							
Asphalt		580	800	1940	0.75	0.38	1205
Building brick		1970	800	1370	0.83	0.61	1065
Concrete	dense	2300	650	2110	1.51	0.72	1785
Polystyrene	expanded	30	0.88	0.02	0.03	1.50	25
Steel	mild	7830	500	3930	53.3	13.6	14,475

Source: Oke (1987, Tables 2.1 and 7.4).

While the thermal admittance undoubtedly has an effect on the surface temperature, and thus on the ambient air temperature, the complexity of the urban environment makes it very difficult to assess the overall effect of the differences between urban and rural materials. This difference depends to a great extent on the properties of the soil in the rural area, in particular its moisture content – which is susceptible to frequent change in many climates. Whereas the surface properties of urban areas are generally constant over time (with the exception of parks and gardens), changes in the rural environment, particularly soil moisture content, may be substantial, and thus could have a dominant effect on the magnitude of the urban heat island (see Chapter 3). Thus differences in thermal admittance (or in *thermal diffusivity*, which is the simple ratio between k and C) may generate an urban–rural temperature difference of as much as 6K if rural diffusivity is very low. (This effect is comparable in magnitude to the effect of radiative geometry, as discussed below). If rural diffusivity is very high, the net effect on air temperature difference may be negligible.

Storage flux may be measured quite easily at any given point using heat flux plates, but it is difficult to obtain a representative value for storage in a typically heterogeneous urban area by direct measurement. The large variety of materials present in a typical city, and the fact that each surface may be exposed to a unique combination of radiant, convective and latent heat fluxes, limit the utility of such point measurements. Most studies of the urban microclimate have therefore determined the storage heat flux (ΔQ_S) as the residual in the energy balance equation, based on direct observations of the net all-wave radiation, sensible heat and latent heat flux. This indirect approach assumes, rather than demonstrates, the closure of the overall energy balance (i.e. that all fluxes sum to zero), and as such is susceptible to the accumulation of errors in measuring the other fluxes. Anthropogenic heat is quite often ignored in this balance of fluxes, because data are difficult to obtain or because it is assumed that its magnitude is relatively small. Likewise, advection between dissimilar urban patches is neglected because most models lack the detailed spatial description of the surrounding area required to deal with this component of the energy balance, and because on an urban scale the contributions of very small patches are described within an average value for larger grid elements.

The net storage flux may fluctuate substantially over short periods of time, even under steady radiative forcing, as the result of variability in the convective fluxes. However, the process of energy storage is driven primarily by changes in the net radiant load, and early attempts to evaluate its magnitude assumed that it had a linear relationship to net radiation (Q^*). The process of energy storage, the proposition of a linear relationship between storage and net radiation does not explain the typical diurnal pattern of changes in the storage flux on sunny days (see Figure 2.8). During the first third of the night urban surfaces release large amounts of heat stored during the daytime. This results in positive values of sensible heat (Q_H) even after net radiant exchange becomes negative around sunset. Where radiant losses to the sky are restricted by small sky view factors (as in dense urban canyons) the heat released from street surfaces is a major source of the urban heat island that typically forms at this time. In most urban locations, unlike rural

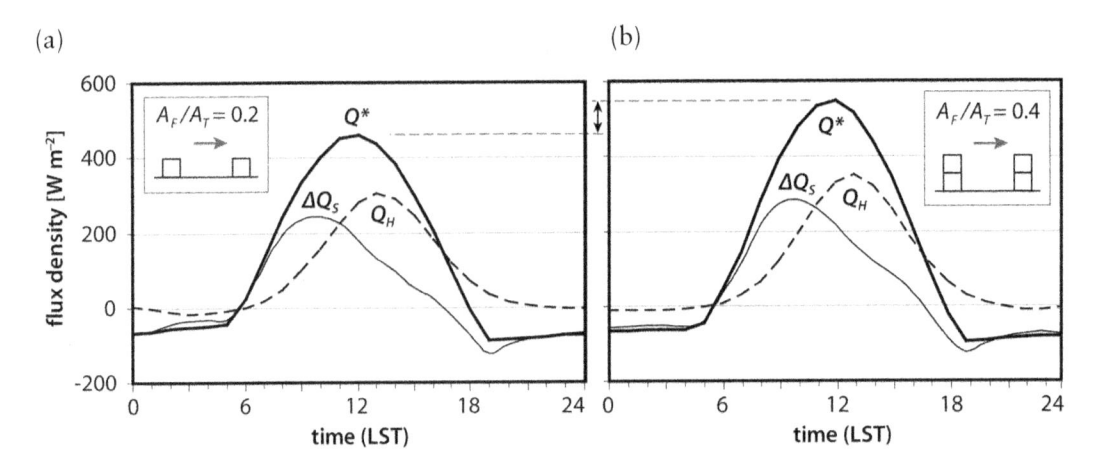

Figure 2.8 Daily progression of energy flux components over two dry open-air scaled urban surfaces, showing the signature pattern common to urban environments: the peak in net storage heat flux ΔQ_S precedes that of net radiation Q^*, which in turn precedes Q_H. In the late afternoon ΔQ_S becomes negative, with heat dissipating throughout the night.

Note: Peak net radiation, and in turn peak storage, are lower in (a) the shallow array than in (b) the deep array.

Source: Based on Pearlmutter et al (2005).

areas, Q_H remains directed away from the surface throughout the night. Several hours after sunset, the radiative drain and the storage loss reach a balance. In the morning hours, when the net radiant load becomes positive again, the store is recharged ($\Delta Q_S > 0$). The atmosphere is usually relatively stable at this time, and sensible heat flux is small. In the afternoon, when the atmosphere is generally less stable, the coupling of the surface and atmosphere is better and turbulent heat flux into the air is more efficient.

The typical daily pattern of heat storage described above confirms a distinct phase lag between Q^* and ΔQ_S: peak storage generally precedes maximum radiation levels by between one and two hours. Where ground surfaces are homogeneous, this typical diurnal pattern may be described by means of a hysteresis loop function (Figure 2.9):

$$\Delta Q_s = a_1 Q^* + a_2 \frac{\partial Q^*}{\partial t} + a_3 \qquad (2.27)$$

where t is time; the parameter a_1 indicates the overall strength of the dependence of the storage heat flux on net radiation; a_2 determines whether the curves ΔQ_S and Q^* are exactly in phase ($a_2 = 0$) or ΔQ_S precedes Q^* ($a_2 > 0$); and a_3 is the size of ΔQ_S when Q^* becomes negative: a large value of a_3 indicates that ΔQ_S becomes negative much earlier than Q^*.

The objective hysteresis model (OHM) embodies an implicit assumption that the energy stored in the soil and in building envelopes is derived only from radiant sources, such as the sun (short-wave) and the atmosphere (long-wave). This assumption is not always justified: it is most likely to be valid in daytime, and if the anthropogenic contribution Q_F is relatively small compared to the net radiative

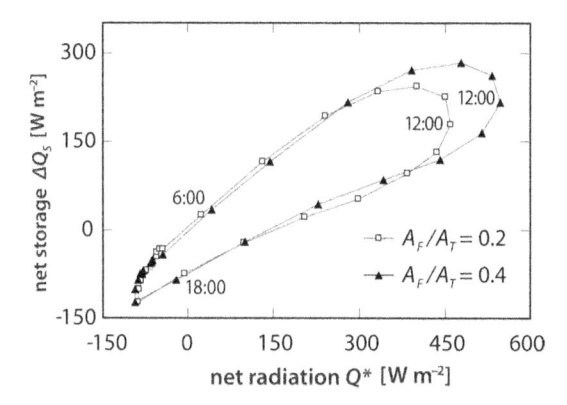

Figure 2.9 Correlation between the net storage heat flux ΔQ_s and net radiation Q^* for the two open-air scaled urban surface arrays depicted in Figure 2.8

Note the hysteresis loop formed by consecutive hourly measurements over the daily cycle.

Source: Based on Pearlmutter et al (2005).

flux. At night, the net radiant flux is smaller in absolute terms and the anthropogenic flux may become relatively larger, so it may not always be neglected.

To be useful, the objective hysteresis model requires appropriate values of the coefficients a_1, a_2 and a_3 for each surface category. Mean values for the coefficients of the OHM on the basis of empirical data from a number of sites are shown in Table 2.9 for several classes of surface types.

The formulation of the objective hysteresis model presented above describes heat storage in individual surfaces. A similar method may be applied to describe the pattern of heat storage in a complex array of surfaces, characteristic of the three-dimensional urban surface. Each of the component surface types of a particular urban neighbourhood is weighted by its relative area, and the resulting values are summed for the area as a whole:

$$\Delta Q_s = \sum_{i=1}^{n} \{a_{1i} Q^* + a_{2i} \frac{\partial Q^*}{\partial t} + a_{3i}\} \tag{2.28}$$

The effect of geometric properties such as aspect ratio of an urban street canyon or the orientation of its main axis on net storage flux may be analysed by means of

Table 2.9 Values of the coefficients used in the objective hysteresis model (OHM) to describe storage heat flux in several classes of surface types

Surface type	a_1	a_2 (h)	a_3 (W m^{-2})
Green space/open	0.34	0.31	−31
Paved/impervious	0.70	0.33	−38
Rooftop*	0.12	0.39	−7

Note: * denotes average of six values for different materials and locations.

Source: Grimmond and Oke (2002).

a parametric study in which the summation procedure described by Equation 2.28 is applied to various street configurations. For typical street canyons in mid-latitude locations, the following conclusions may be drawn:

- Canyon orientation has only a minor effect on overall energy stored, although the partitioning between different surfaces is affected.
- Increasing the aspect ratio (giving a deeper canyon) results in a larger net radiation and a larger proportion of the solar flux being stored.
- Deep canyons may display a greater time lag between peak radiation and maximum storage rate than shallower ones.

Anthropogenic heat

Human activity requires energy – whether for transport, heating (or cooling) buildings or various industrial activities. The amount of energy used depends not only on the climate but also on the layout of the city, the type of transport used and the efficiency with which heat and light are provided in buildings.

The magnitude of the anthropogenic heat flux may be assessed by separate analyses of its three principal components:

$$Q_F = Q_V + Q_B + Q_M \tag{2.29}$$

whereby the total input Q_F is the sum of inputs from vehicles Q_V, buildings Q_B and metabolism Q_M.

Heat from vehicular traffic may be estimated on the basis of detailed hourly traffic counts on major and minor roadways throughout a metropolitan area (these are available to transport engineers in many cities). Traffic patterns in most cities display a pronounced diurnal and weekly pattern, with well-defined rush-hour peaks on weekdays and much lower levels at night and on weekends.

Heat from buildings comprises electricity consumption, which powers lighting, air-conditioning and equipment, and heating fuels (such as natural gas) which may be used to provide space heating in cold climates. Data on electricity consumption are easier to obtain on a detailed scale than information on the use of heating fuels. Modelling the latter is often done on the assumption that overall consumption for a period can be distributed over all buildings in a given area on the basis of floor area, while the rate of use is proportional to the difference between ambient air temperature and some arbitrary fixed interior air temperature.

There are several methods for estimating anthropogenic heat from buildings in a city, starting with an inventory approach based on the mapping of building energy consumption due to thermal loads. This approach is considered practical when the availability of detailed data is limited, but it may underestimate the sensible heat actually removed by HVAC (Heating, Ventilation and Air-Conditioning) systems, and even more so the latent heat removed by evaporative cooling. A micrometeorological approach, in which anthropogenic heat is estimated as the residual in the surface energy budget, overcomes this problem but may be limited in accuracy because closure of the energy balance

Table 2.10 Average annual anthropogenic heat flux densities

Urban area	Latitude	Year	Pop. density (persons km^{-2})	Per capita energy use (GJ yr^{-1})	Q_F (W m^{-2})	Q^* (W m^{-2})	Q_F/Q^*
Manhattan	40°N	1965	28,800	169	159	93	1.71
Moscow	56°N	1970	7,300	530	127	42	3.02
Montreal	45°N	1961	14,100	221	99	52	1.90
Budapest	47°N	1970	11,500	118	43	46	0.93
Hong Kong	22°N	1971	37,200	28	33	~110	0.30
Osaka	35°N	1970–74	14,600	55	26	n/a	n/a
Los Angeles	34°N	1965–70	2,000	331	21	108	0.19
West Berlin	52°N	1967	9,800	67	21	57	0.37
Vancouver	49°N	1970	5,400	112	19	57	0.33
Sheffield	53°N	1952	10,400	58	19	56	0.34
Fairbanks	64°N	1967–75	550	314	6	18	0.33

Note: All data relate to areas within the urbanized limits of the cities, not their surrounding territories.

Source: Adapted from Oke (1988), whose sources were Bowling and Benson (1978); Kalma and Newcombe (1976); Ojima and Moriyama (1982); Oke (1987); SMIC (1971).

incorporates accumulated errors in the measurement of radiation, storage and turbulent fluxes. An alternative approach is based on building energy modelling, in which detailed building energy simulation results are integrated with an urban canopy meteorological model or with a GIS database that reflects the characteristics of different building prototypes. In this way, the city's anthropogenic heating may be more realistically disaggregated into local-source heat islands that have different diurnal and seasonal characteristics.

Industrial heat releases tend to be more concentrated point sources, from individual factories or industrial areas. The strength of these sources, emanating essentially from industrial buildings, may be estimated using the different methods described above for Q_B.

In addition to these three major sources (vehicles, buildings and industry), heat is also released from human metabolism. Large-scale movements of people commuting to and from work, mostly in downtown locations, affect the spatial distribution of the output of metabolic heat. However, except in extreme cases, this component contributes only 2–3 per cent of the total anthropogenic heat flux.

In the absence of a detailed database of heat sources in a city, the local anthropogenic flux in a given location may be related to the mean flux for the urban area as a whole through the vegetation ratio at the site:

$$Q_F = (1 - R_g)Q_{F(0)} \tag{2.30}$$

where $Q_{F(0)}$ is the density of anthropogenic heat released when the vegetation ratio R_g is equal to zero. (The vegetation ratio is the ratio between the vegetated area and the overall area of the site.)

Magnitude

The magnitude of anthropogenic heat varies greatly between cities. It is affected by per capita energy use and by population density, and depends on the climate (due to the demand for space heating or cooling), the degree and type of industrial activity and the type of urban transport system.

An estimate of the average anthropogenic heat flux in a given urban area may be obtained by dividing the total amount of energy consumed by its plan area. From a modelling point of view, this methodology raises several problems:

- Scale of grid cell: in the absence of net advection, the anthropogenic heat flux into a given urban canyon originates from adjacent buildings only. The model should therefore accommodate input of data at an appropriate scale (if available) and not necessarily city-wide averages. A very fine spatial mesh – for example 100 metres between adjacent points – may be needed to account for intra-urban variation, but will require an extremely detailed database.
- Location of heat source: anthropogenic heat may be allocated uniformly to the whole grid cell at ground level, as is commonly done in meso-scale models. This is a gross simplification, however, because in high-rise buildings energy flow through the building envelope is distributed along the entire surface area of the building, and much of it will not affect conditions in the urban canyon directly. This is especially true in hot climates, where heat exchangers for air-conditioning equipment of multi-storey buildings are often located on the roof. Whereas wall or window-mounted air-conditioners dump the excess heat directly onto the street where it contributes to the urban canopy-layer heat island, central air-conditioning systems in high-rise buildings in effect transport energy from the canopy-layer near street level to the roughness sub-layer above the roof, where it is quickly dissipated.
- Mode of heat transfer: energy may be emitted (or absorbed) in the form of sensible heat, e.g. in heat exchangers of air-conditioners, contributing directly to the urban canopy-layer heat island. However, it is also exchanged by radiation, for example from warm building surfaces, and may be in the form of latent heat through vaporization. Each of these processes must be accounted for in models of the urban environment, according to the level of spatial detail and time step being simulated.
- Correlation between energy consumption and heat flux to the environment: ultimately all consumed energy is transformed into heat, but energy consumption may not necessarily affect the surface energy balance. In many buildings (such as hotels), as much as 50 per cent of the energy consumed is required to heat water – much of which is later released into the sewage system, and thus has only a minor effect on local air temperature.

An alternative approach is to assess anthropogenic heat by considering heat conduction through building envelopes. If the interior temperature of the building and the thermal properties of its external envelope are known, there is no need to assemble overall energy consumption data, other than inputs due to vehicles and other external sources. This is the approach employed in many urban canyon models, especially if they are not designed to provide feedback to meso-scale models. To simplify the calculation, a basic equation of steady-state heat transfer is used, similar to the following:

$$Q_F = U A \Delta T_{b-\infty} \qquad (2.31)$$

where U is the thermal conductance of the building envelope [W m^{-2} K], A is the surface area [m^2] and $\Delta T_{b-\infty}$ is the difference in temperature between the internal and external surfaces of the building.

However, this method, too, has several potential pitfalls:

- The internal temperature of most buildings is not necessarily constant. In many buildings all around the world heating or cooling systems are operated intermittently, only when they are occupied, to conserve energy. If weather is not extreme, temperature may be allowed to float within a fairly broad range.
- The temperature of the external surface of the building is often difficult to estimate accurately: although it is frequently fairly close to the ambient air temperature, especially at night or in windy conditions, it may diverge substantially during daytime in response to large radiant (mostly solar) loads.
- Since neither the internal nor, especially, the outdoor temperature is constant, heat transfer is not governed by steady-state conditions, so the thermal capacity of the building elements affects the rate and timing of the heat flux through the building envelope.

These effects are well-known to researchers and engineers working in the field of building energy simulation, and are accounted for in even the most basic software used by them. However, the detailed description of each and every building element that is required to run building energy simulation is typically not incorporated into models of the urban microclimate, so the error in assessing the time-varying anthropogenic heat flux by this method might be substantial.

Spatial variability

Average values for the heat flux of entire cities mask great spatial variability within the metropolitan area. For example, anthropogenic heat density in urban cores of US cities may be five to ten times greater (and upwards) than the magnitudes of city-wide averages, reflecting the great disparity in building height and the concomitant concentration of human activity in central business districts (CBDs). In downtown office blocks anthropogenic heat flux in cold climates can be 1500W m^{-2} or more in winter. At the other extreme, in mild climates where heating and air-conditioning represent a relatively small proportion of total energy consumption, the anthropogenic heat flux of a typical low-density suburb may be as small as 1–5 W m^{-2}, compared to 25W m^{-2} or more in the CBD of the same city.

Temporal variability

Mean annual values of energy consumption mask great temporal as well as spatial variability. Anthropogenic heat emissions parallel levels of human activity, and therefore have daily, weekly and seasonal cycles. Most cities have the same typical diurnal pattern, irrespective of season, location or weather: anthropogenic heat is at a minimum at night, with consumption more than doubling during the daytime between about 7.00am and 4.00pm.

Seasonal variations in energy demand reflect changing demand for space conditioning, artificial lighting, etc. However, the effect of these absolute changes in the magnitude of the fluxes may be less important than the change in the relative magnitude of the fluxes due to changes in meteorological conditions, such as solar insolation and ambient air temperature. Artificial heat generation may therefore be the equivalent of as little as one-fifth of the net radiant flux to over three times as much (see Table 2.11).

Each of the three primary components of anthropogenic heat has a different temporal pattern:

- Heat from vehicles varies on two main time scales: diurnal and weekly. Rush-hour traffic is reflected in two distinct daily peaks that are observed in nearly all cities, at about 8.00am and 4.00pm. Traffic emissions – of energy as well as of air pollution – are also substantially lower on weekends than on working days. However, apart from reduction observed in some cities during major holidays, the contribution to anthropogenic heat from vehicles does not vary significantly on seasonal basis.
- Heat from buildings varies on a seasonal basis in addition to displaying a regular diurnal and weekly pattern. The latter variations reflect occupancy: offices, for example, are occupied during daytime on weekdays, and are nearly empty on weekends and at night. Office demand typically peaks at the beginning of the working day, as space conditioning equipment comes online in response to near simultaneous occupation of facilities, and then declines slowly throughout the day. Hotels, on the other hand, typically have lower demand throughout the day and a large surge in the evening. Residential demand has twin peaks, both in the morning before people leave for work or school, and in the evening. However, it is the seasonal variations, which are related to weather, that have the greatest impact on building energy consumption in most regions other than the tropics. Buildings may require heating, cooling – or neither. Artificial lighting, which may comprise as little as 10 per cent or as much as one-third of the total energy consumption of buildings, is affected by the availability of daylight, which may exhibit very substantial seasonal variations. Industrial heat production is more continuous than that of residential or commercial buildings, but naturally depends on the plant schedule and the nature of the process.
- Human metabolic heat represents a relatively small proportion of total anthropogenic heat. However, large concentrations of people, e.g. at sporting events, may nevertheless generate non-negligible localized heat sources.

Mapping anthropogenic heat from buildings and vehicles poses different practical problems. Energy emitted from vehicles, whether through exhaust tail pipes or from cooling systems, contributes almost immediately to the surface energy balance in its immediate vicinity. However, although the time lag from consumption of energy to its emission to the environment is negligible, the location of a vehicle changes almost continuously. To assess the contribution of vehicle emissions, their location must be mapped, at least in aggregated form representing typical traffic distribution over the road network.

Table 2.11 Diurnal and seasonal variations in anthropogenic heat flux of several cities

Urban area	Year	Pop. density (persons/km²)	Season	Q_F (W m⁻²) min	mid-day	max	Notes
Sydney (Kalma and Newcombe, 1976)	1970		summer	6	15	16	CBD only
			winter	7	18	19	CBD only
Brisbane (Khan and Simpson, 2001)	1996			17	33	66	Major urban areas only. Vehicles comprise 72% of Q_F
Atlanta (Sailor and Lu, 2004)	2000	1221	summer	4	10	13	Max occurs at 1600 hours
			winter	4	10	13	Max occurs at 0800 hours
Chicago (Sailor and Lu, 2004)	2000	4924	summer	10	35	42	
			winter	32	62	75	
Los Angeles (Sailor and Lu, 2004)	2000	3041	summer	9	28	32	
			winter	11	26	33	
Philadelphia (Sailor and Lu, 2004)	2000	4337	summer	10	40	46	
			winter	22	62	65	
Salt Lake City (Sailor and Lu, 2004)	2000	643	summer	2	7	8	
			winter	4	10	12	
San Francisco (Sailor and Lu, 2004)	2000	6419	summer	17	53	58	
			winter	22	58	67	

Notes: (a) data from Sailor and Lu (2004) obtained graphically from Figure 6; (b) data from Kalma and Newcombe (1976) obtained graphically from Figure 4.

Advection

Most cities are highly heterogeneous, exhibiting a broad range of land use patterns. Factors such as building density and the extent of planted areas affect the surface energy balance, creating hot spots and relatively cooler areas, often in close proximity. This leads to transport of heat and moisture from one location to another. While many studies of urban climate neglect this process in order to simplify modelling, the diversity of conditions in the city contributes to quality of life. Advection must therefore be examined in order to allow designers to understand its magnitude and the spatial extent of the influence of local features such as city parks.

Field studies have shown that energy fluxes over a supposedly homogeneous suburban residential area may vary by up to 40 per cent within horizontal scales of only 100 to 1000 metres.[4] These variations are comparable in magnitude to urban–rural differences. Such horizontal variations of vertical turbulent energy fluxes in the presence of a mean flow must induce advection. This implies that 'micro-advection' may have an important effect on the energy balance of urban locations. The studies showed that spatial variation of net radiant flux is relatively small, while anthropogenic heat may vary more substantially, on both spatial and temporal scales. However, the most important differences may be found in the partition of sensible and latent heat flux, and in storage heat, resulting from differences between paved and vegetated surfaces, especially if the soil is moist.

The extent and distance of the source area for a given quantity may be modelled using a reverse plume scheme. Changing wind directions imply that the source area for heat advected to a given location may be time-dependent. Furthermore, the typical diurnal pattern of stability may also affect the distance from which energy or moisture may be transported. During the daytime, under unstable atmospheric conditions, the source areas affecting fluxes at a given urban location are most likely contained within an area with a radius of about 500 metres upwind. At night, as the atmosphere becomes neutral or stable, the source areas become narrower and more elongated and may extend as much as 2000 metres upwind (though distant sources have a much smaller effect than near ones).

Notes

1   Iziomon et al (2003).
2   Priestley and Taylor (1972).
3   Brutsaert and Strickler (1979).
4   Schmid and Oke (1990); Schmid et al (1991).

References

Arnfield, J. (1982) 'An approach to the estimation of the surface radiative properties and radiation budgets of cities', *Physical Geography*, vol 3, pp97–122

Bowling, S. and Benson, C. (1978) 'Study of the subarctic heat island at Fairbanks, Alaska', Environmental Monitor Report No. EPA-600/4-78-027, US EPA Research, Triangle Park, NC

Brunt, D. (1932) 'Notes on radiation in the atmosphere', *Quarterly Journal of the Royal Meteorological Society*, vol 58, pp389–420

Brutsaert, W. (1975) 'On a derivable formula for long wave radiation from clear skies', *Water Resources Research*, vol 11, no 5, pp742–744

Brutsaert, W. (1982) *Evaporation into the Atmosphere*, Kluwer Academic Publishers, Dordrecht

Brutsaert, W. and Stricker, H. (1979) 'An advection-aridity approach to estimate actual regional evapotranspiration', *Water Resources Research*, vol 15, no 2, pp443–450

Clark, G. and Berdahl, P. (1980) 'Radiative cooling: Resource and applications', *Proceedings of the Fifth National Solar Conference*, Amherst, MA, 20–22 October 1980

Clear, R. D., Gartland, L. and Winkelmann, F. C. (2003) 'An empirical correlation for the outside convective air-film coefficient for horizontal roofs', *Energy and Buildings*, vol 35, no 8, pp797–811

Garratt, J. R. (1992) *The Atmospheric Boundary Layer*, Cambridge University Press, Cambridge, UK

Givoni, B. (1982) 'Cooling by long wave radiation', *Passive Solar Journal*, vol 1, no 3, pp131–150

Grimmond, C. S. B. and Oke, T. R. (2002) 'Turbulent heat fluxes in urban areas: Observations and a local-scale urban meteorological parameterization scheme (LUMPS)', *Journal of Applied Meteorology*, vol 41, pp792–810

Hagishima, A. and Tanimoto, J. (2003) 'Field measurements for estimating the convective heat transfer coefficient at building surfaces', *Building and Environment*, vol 38, no 3, pp873–881

Hagishima, A., Tanimoto, J. and Narita, K. (2005) 'Intercomparisons of experimental convective heat transfer coefficients and mass transfer coefficients of urban surfaces', *Boundary-Layer Meteorology*, vol 117, no 3, pp551–576

Hanna, S. and Chang, J. (1992) 'Boundary-layer parameterizations for applied dispersion modeling over urban areas', *Boundary-Layer Meteorology*, vol 58, no 3, pp229–259

Idso, S. (1981) 'A set of equations for full spectrum and 8–14μm and 10.5–12.5μm thermal radiation from cloudless skies', *Water Resources Research*, vol 17, pp295–304

Idso, S. and Jackson, R. (1969) 'Thermal radiation from the atmosphere', *Journal of Geophysical Research*, vol 74, pp5397–5403

Ito, N., Kimura, K. and Oka, J. (1972) 'A field experiment on the convective heat transfer coefficient on exterior surface of a building', *ASHRAE Transactions*, vol 78, pp184–191

Iziomon, M. G., Mayer, H. and Matzarakis, A. (2003) 'Downward atmospheric longwave irradiance under clear and cloudy skies: Measurement and parameterization', *Journal of Atmospheric and Solar-Terrestrial Physics*, vol 65, no 10, pp1107–1116

Kalma, J. D. and Newcombe, K. J. (1976) 'Energy use in two large cities: A comparison of Hong Kong and Sydney, Australia', *Environmental Studies*, vol 9, no 1, pp53–64

Khan, S. and Simpson, R. (2001) 'Effect of heat island on the meteorology of a complex urban airshed', *Boundary-Layer Meteorology*, vol 100, no 3, pp487–506

Kobayashi, S. (1994) 'Convective heat transfer characteristics of rooftop surface in summer', *Journal of Architecture, Planning and Environmental Engineering*, vol 465, pp11–17 (in Japanese)

Kobayashi, S. and Morikawa, K. (2000) 'Convective heat transfer coefficient of rooftop surface in downward heat flow', *Journal of Architecture, Planning and Environmental Engineering*, vol 536, pp21–27 (in Japanese)

Loveday, D. and Taki, A. (1996) 'Convective heat transfer coefficients at a plane surface on a full-scale building façade', *International Journal of Heat and Mass Transfer*, vol 39, pp1729–1742

Narita, K., Nonomura, Y. and Ogasa, A. (1997) 'Real scale measurement of convective mass transfer coefficient at window in natural wind', *Journal of Architecture, Planning and Environmental Engineering*, vol 491, pp49–56 (in Japanese)

Ojima, T. and Moriyama, M. (1982) 'Earth surface heat balance changes caused by urbanization', *Energy and Buildings*, vol 4, no 2, pp99–114

Oke, T. (1987) *Boundary Layer Climates*, Methuen, London and New York

Oke, T. (1988) 'The urban energy balance', *Progress in Physical Geography*, vol 12, no 4, pp471–508

Pearlmutter, D., Berliner, P. and Shaviv, E. (2005), 'Evaluation of urban surface energy fluxes using an open-air scale model', *Journal of Applied Meteorology*, vol 44, pp532–545

Pearlmutter, D., Krüger, E. L. and Berliner, P. (2009) 'The role of evaporation in the energy balance of an open-air scaled urban surface', *International Journal of Climatology*, vol 29, pp911–920

Post, D. F., Fimbres, A., Matthias, A. D., Sano, E. E., Accioly, L., Batchily, A. K. and Ferreira, L. G. (2000) 'Predicting soil albedo from soil color and spectral reflectance data', *Soil Science Society of America Journal*, vol 64, pp1027–1034

Priestley, C. and Taylor, R. (1972) 'On the assessment of surface heat flux and evaporation using large-scale parameters', *Monthly Weather Review*, vol 100, pp81–92

Sailor, D. (1995) 'Simulated urban climate response to modifications in surface albedo and vegetative cover', *Journal of Applied Meteorology*, vol 34, no 7, pp1694–1704

Sailor, D. and Fan, H. (2002) 'Modeling the diurnal variability of effective albedo for cities', *Atmospheric Environment*, vol 36, no 4, pp713–725

Sailor, D. and Lu, L. (2004) 'A top-down methodology for developing diurnal and seasonal anthropogenic heating profiles for urban areas', *Atmospheric Environment*, vol 38, no 17, pp2737–2748

Schmid, H. P. and Oke, T. R. (1990) 'A model to estimate the source area contributing to turbulent exchange in the surface layer over patchy terrain', *Quarterly Journal of the Royal Meteorological Society*, vol 116, pp965–988

Schmid, H. P., Cleugh, H. A., Grimmond, S. B. and Oke, T. R. (1991) 'Spatial variability of energy fluxes in suburban terrain', *Boundary-Layer Meteorolgy*, vol 54, no 3, pp249–276

Seaman, N. (1989) 'Numerical studies of urban planetary boundary-layer structure under realistic synoptic conditions', *Journal of Applied Meteorology*, vol 28, no 8, pp760–781

Sharples, S. (1984) 'Full-scale measurements of convective energy losses from exterior building surfaces', *Building and Environment*, vol 19, pp31–39

SMIC (1971) *Inadvertent Climate Modification*, MIT Press, Cambridge, MA

Swinbank, W. C. (1963) 'Long-wave radiation from clear skies', *Quarterly Journal of the Royal Meteorological Society*, vol 89, pp339–348

Taha, H. (1999) 'Modifying a mesoscale meteorological model to better incorporate urban heat storage: A bulk parameterization approach', *Journal of Applied Meteorology*, vol 38, no 4, pp466–473

Urano, Y. and Watanabe T. (1983) 'Heat balance at a roof surface and time-varying effect of the film coefficient on its thermal response', *Journal of Architecture, Planning and Environmental Engineering*, vol 325, pp93–103 (in Japanese)

Additional reading

Aida, M. (1982) 'Urban albedo as a function of the urban structure – a model experiment', *Boundary-Layer Meteorology*, vol 23, no 4, pp405–413

Aida, M. and Gotoh, K. (1982) 'Urban albedo as a function of the urban structure – a two-dimensional numerical simulation', *Boundary-Layer Meteorology*, vol 23, no 4, pp415–424

Akagawa, H., Oka, T. and Komiya, H. (1995) 'Research on heat fluxes to the atmosphere in urban areas – observation of heat fluxes in the center of urban area and the Bay of Tokyo', *Pan Pacific Symposium on Building and Urban Environmental Conditioning in Asia*

Arnfield, J. A. and Grimmond, C. S. B. (1998) 'An urban canyon energy budget model and its application to urban storage heat flux modeling', *Energy and Buildings*, vol 27, no 1, pp61–68

Arnfield, J. and Mills, G. (1994a) 'An analysis of the circulation characteristics and energy budget of a dry, asymmetric east-west urban canyon. I. Circulation characteristics', *International Journal of Climatology*, vol 14, no 2, pp119–134

Arnfield, J. and Mills, G. (1994b) 'An analysis of the circulation characteristics and energy budget of a dry, asymmetric east-west urban canyon. II. Energy budget', *International Journal of Climatology*, vol 14, no 3, pp239–261

Bozonnet, E., Belarbi, R. and Allard, F. (2005) 'Modelling solar effects on the heat and mass transfer in a street canyon, a simplified approach', *Solar Energy*, vol 79, no 1, pp10–24

Camuffo, D. and Bernardi, A. (1982) 'An observational study of heat fluxes and their relationships with net radiation', *Boundary-Layer Meteorology*, vol 23, no 3, pp359–368

Chimklai, P., Hagishima, A. and Tanimoto, J. (2004) 'A computer system to support albedo calculation in urban areas', *Building and Environment*, vol 39, no 10, pp1213–1221

Elnahas, M. M. and Williamson, T. J. (1997) 'An improvement of the CTTC model for predicting urban air temperatures', *Energy and Buildings*, vol 25, no 1, pp41–49

Fuggle, R. F. and Oke, T. R. (1970) 'Infra-red flux divergence and the urban heat island', in *Urban Climates, WMO Technical Note No. 108*, pp70–78

Fuggle, R. F. and Oke, T. R. (1976) 'Long-wave radiative flux divergence and nocturnal cooling of the urban atmosphere I: Above roof level', *Boundary-Layer Meteorology*, vol 10, no 2, pp113–120

Grimmond, C. S. B. and Oke, T. R. (1986) 'Urban water balance 2. Results from a suburb of Vancouver, British Columbia', *Water Resources Research*, vol 22, no 10, pp1404–1412

Grimmond, C. S. B. and Oke, T. R. (1991) 'An evapotranspiration-interception model for urban areas', *Water Resources Research*, vol 27, no 7, pp1739–1755

Grimmond, C. S. B. and Oke, T. R. (1995) 'Comparison of heat fluxes from summertime observations in the suburbs of four North American cities', *Journal of Applied Meteorology*, vol 34, no 4, pp873–889

Grimmond, C. S. B. and Oke, T. R. (1999) 'Evapotranspiration rates in urban areas', *Impacts of Urban Growth on Surface Water and Groundwater Quality*, IAHS

Grimmond, C. S. B. and Oke, T. R. (1999b) 'Heat storage in urban areas: Local-scale observations and evaluation of a simple model', *Journal of Applied Meteorology*, vol 38, pp922–940

Grimmond, C. S. B. and Oke, T. R. (2002) 'Turbulent heat fluxes in urban areas: Observations and a Local-scale Urban Meteorological Parameterization Scheme (LUMPS)', *Journal of Applied Meteorology*, vol 41, pp792–810

Grimmond, C. S., Cleugh, H. A. and Oke, T. R. (1991) 'An objective heat storage model and its comparison with other schemes', *Atmospheric Environment, Part B: Urban Atmosphere*, vol 25, no 3, pp311–326

Grimmond, C. S. B., Oke, T. R. and Steyn, D. G. (1986) 'Urban water balance 1. A model for daily totals', *Water Resources Research*, vol 22, no 10, pp1397–1403

Harman, I. N., Best, M. J. and Belcher, S. E. (2004a) 'Radiative exchange in an urban street canyon', *Boundary-Layer Meteorology*, vol 110, pp301–316

Harman, I. N., Barlow, J. F. and Belcher, S. E. (2004b) 'Scalar fluxes from urban street canyons, Part II: Model', *Boundary-Layer Meteorology*, vol 113, no 3, pp387–410

Ichinose, T., Shimodozono, K. and Hanaki, K. (1999) 'Impact of anthropogenic heat on urban climate in Tokyo', *Atmospheric Environment*, vol 33, pp3897–3909

Jauregui, E. and Luyando, E. (1999) 'Global radiation attenuation by air pollution and its effects on the thermal climate in Mexico City', *International Journal of Climatology*, vol 19, no 6, pp683–694

Kalma, J. D. (1974) 'An advective boundary-layer model applied to Sydney, Australia', *Boundary-Layer Meteorology*, vol 6, pp351–361

Kalma, J. D. and Newcombe, K. J. (1976) 'Energy use in two large cities: A comparison of Hong Kong and Sydney, Australia', *Environmental Studies*, vol 9, no 1, pp53–64

Kalma, J. D., Aston, A. R. and Millington, R. J. (1972) 'Energy use in the Sydney area', in H. A. Nix (ed) *City as a Life System?* Ecological Society of Australia

Kondo, A., Ueno, M., Kaga, A. and Yamaguchi, K. (2001) 'The influence of urban canopy configuration on urban albedo', *Boundary-Layer Meteorology*, vol 100, no 2, pp225–242

Lowry, W. (1967) 'The climate of cities', *Scientific American*, vol 217, pp15–23

Martin, M. (1989) 'Radiative cooling', in J. Cook (ed) *Passive Cooling*, MIT Press, Cambridge, MA

Montávez, J. P., Jiménez, J. I. and Sarsa, A. (2000) 'A Monte Carlo model of the nocturnal surface temperatures in urban canyons', *Boundary-Layer Meteorology*, vol 96, no 3, pp433–452

Monteith, J. L. (1981) 'Evaporation and surface temperature', *Quarterly Journal of the Royal Meteorological Society*, vol 107, pp1–27

Moriyama, M. and Matsumoto, M. (1988) 'Control of urban night temperature in semi-tropical regions during summer', *Energy and Buildings*, vol 11, pp213–220

Nakamura, Y. and Oke, T. R. (1988) 'Wind, temperature and stability conditions in an east–west oriented urban canyon', *Atmospheric Environment*, vol 22, no 12, pp2691–2700

Niemelä, S., Räisänen, P. and Savijärvi, H. (2001) 'Comparison of surface radiative flux parameterizations. Part I: Longwave radiation', *Atmospheric Research*, vol 58, no 1, pp1–18

Nunez, M. and Oke, T. R. (1976) 'Long-wave radiative flux divergence and nocturnal cooling of the urban atmosphere II: Within an urban canyon', *Boundary-Layer Meteorology*, vol 10, no 2, pp121–135

Nunez, M. and Oke, T. R. (1977) 'The energy balance of an urban canyon', *Journal of Applied Meteorology*, vol 16, no 1, pp11–19

Nunez, M., Eliasson, I. and Lindgren, J. (1998) 'Spatial variability of longwave radiation in Goteborg, Sweden', in S. Grimmond (ed) *Second Urban Climate Symposium*, American Meteorological Society, Boston, MA

Offerle, B., Grimmond, C. S. B. and Oke, T. R. (2003) 'Parameterization of net all-wave radiation for urban areas', *Journal of Applied Meteorology*, vol 42, no 8, pp1157–1173

Oke, T. R. (1981) 'Canyon geometry and the nocturnal urban heat island: Comparison of scale model and field observations', *International Journal of Climatology*, vol 1, no 3, pp237–254

Oke, T. R. (1998) 'On the confounding role of rural wetness in assessing urban effects on climate', in S. Grimmond (ed) *Second Urban Environment Symposium*, American Meteorological Society, Boston, MA

Oke, T. R. and Fuggle, R. F. (1972) 'Comparison of urban/rural counter and net radiation at night', *Boundary-Layer Meteorology*, vol 2, no 3, pp290–308

Oke, T. R., Johnson, G. T., Steyn, D. G. and Watson, I. D. (1991) 'Simulation of surface urban heat islands under "ideal" conditions at night. Part 2: Diagnosis of causation', *Boundary-Layer Meteorology*, vol 56, no 4, pp339–358

Oliveti, G., Arcuri, N. and Ruffolo, S. (2003) 'Experimental investigation on thermal radiation exchange of horizontal outdoor surfaces', *Building and Environment*, vol 38, no 1, pp83–89

Raupach, M. R. (1994) 'Simplified expressions for vegetation roughness length and zero-plane displacement', *Boundary-Layer Meteorology*, vol 71, pp211–216

Richards, K. and Oke, T. (1998) 'Dew in urban environments', in S. Grimmond (ed) *Second Urban Environment Symposium*, American Meteorological Society, Boston, MA

Rosenberg, N. (1974) *Microclimate: The Biological Environment*, John Wiley and Sons, New York

Roth, M. (2000) 'Review of atmospheric turbulence over cities', *Quarterly Journal of the Royal Meteorological Society*, vol 126, pp941–990

Soler, M. R. and Ruiz, C. (1994) 'Urban albedo derived from direct measurements and LANDSAT 4 TM satellite data', *International Journal of Climatology*, vol 14, no 8, pp 925–931

Spronken-Smith, R. (1998) 'Comparison of summer and winter-time energy fluxes over a suburban neighborhood, Christchurch, New Zealand', in S. Grimmond (ed) *Second Urban Climate Symposium*, American Meteorological Society, Boston, MA

Spronken-Smith, R. and Oke, T. R. (1998) 'The thermal regime of urban parks in two cities with different summer climates', *International Journal of Remote Sensing*, vol 19, no 11, pp2085–2104

Spronken-Smith, R., Oke, T. and Lowry, W. (1998) 'Advection and the surface energy balance across an irrigated urban park', in S. Grimmond (ed) *Second Urban Climate Symposium*, American Meteorological Society, Boston, MA

Taha, H., Douglas, S. and Haney, J. (1997) 'Mesoscale meteorological and air quality impacts of increased urban albedo and vegetation', *Energy and Buildings*, vol 25, no 2, pp169–177

Terjung, W. H. and Louie, S. (1973) 'Solar radiation and urban heat islands', *Annals of the Association of American Geographers*, vol 63, no 2, pp181–207

Tsangrassoulis, A. and Santamouris, M. (2003) 'Numerical estimation of street canyon albedo consisting of vertical coated glazed facades', *Energy and Buildings*, vol 35, no 5, pp527–531

Voogt, J. A. and Oke, T. R. (1991) 'Validation of an urban canyon radiation model for nocturnal long-wave fluxes', *Boundary-Layer Meteorology*, vol 54, no 4, pp347–361

Voogt, J. A. and Oke, T. R. (1997) 'Complete urban surface temperatures', *Journal of Applied Meteorology*, vol 36, pp1117–1132

Yap, D. and Oke, T. R. (1974) 'Sensible heat fluxes over an urban area – Vancouver, B.C.', *Journal of Applied Meteorology*, vol 13, no 8, pp880–890

Yoshida, A., Tominaga, K. and Watatani, S. (1991) 'Field measurements on energy balance of an urban canyon in the summer season', *Energy and Buildings*, vol 15, pp417–423

3
The Urban Heat Island

The urban heat island is one of the most important manifestations of the urban climate, and has been the subject of much research since it was first described for the city of London by Luke Howard in 1818. Its intensity varies significantly on a diurnal and seasonal basis, and the phenomenon is known to be a complex one. This chapter reviews the wealth of field studies on the urban heat island, seeking to illuminate the relationship between the intensity of the urban heat island and the various factors that contribute to its formation. Starting with the basic relationship between city size and the maximum urban–rural temperature difference, a series of progressively detailed models will be introduced to examine the causative factors of the urban heat island.

Definition

Under certain weather conditions a substantial difference in temperature may be observed between a city and its surrounding rural areas. When isotherms are drawn for the area in question, the city is apparent as a series of concentric, closed lines of higher temperature, with maximum values recorded at or near the densest part of the urban area (Figure 3.1). This condition is known as the 'urban heat island'.[1]

The conventional measure of the intensity of the urban heat island, ΔT_{u-r}, expresses the temperature difference between two measurement locations – one representing an 'urban' condition, the other a 'rural' one. However it is difficult, in reality, to select appropriate pairs of urban–rural measuring stations that would be subject to the same meso-scale weather conditions. In climatology as in other aspects of urban studies, the urban–rural dichotomy describes extreme cases of what is often in reality a continuum. As discussed in the Introduction, the characterization of a site as being either urban or rural is a coarse distinction, and does not allow for an accurate description to be made of the complexity of land use types found in and around urbanized areas. There are very few cities where undisturbed landscapes can be found close to the urban core. Often the area around cities is devoted to agriculture, or has been so in the past. Truly rural climate measuring stations are thus often located at a substantial distance from the city centre. This creates the risk that meso-scale climate effects may come into play, at least during isolated episodes (such as the passage of a cold front), making co-temporal comparisons between them difficult. An alternate definition of ΔT_{u-r} may be based upon the difference between temperatures actually measured in the urban location in question and the temperature that would have been recorded at the same place in the hypothetical event that urban development in the region had not occurred.

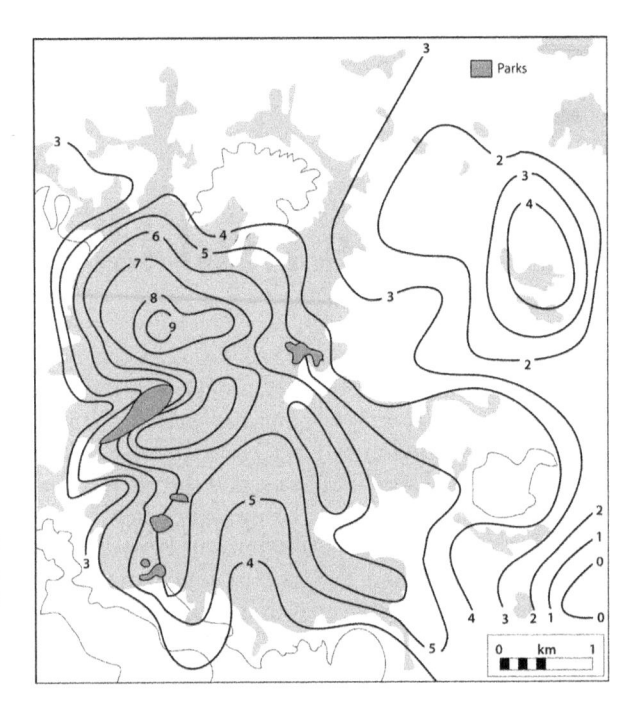

Figure 3.1 Isotherms showing the mean minimum temperature for November 1981 in Mexico City, demonstrating the existence of a nocturnal urban heat island (UHI) in the city

Source: Jauregui (1986).

Although this definition is conceptually sound it is, however, of little value in the selection of appropriate urban–rural station pairs for estimating the urban heat island.

As a general phenomenon, the idea of the urban heat island has generated great interest not only in the scientific community but also among the non-professional public. Some link the UHI to the issue of global warming and various authors have suggested mechanisms that attempt to explain how changes in local temperature measurements, as seen in the classical urban heat island, may in fact contribute to observed global surface warming at regional and larger scales.[2]

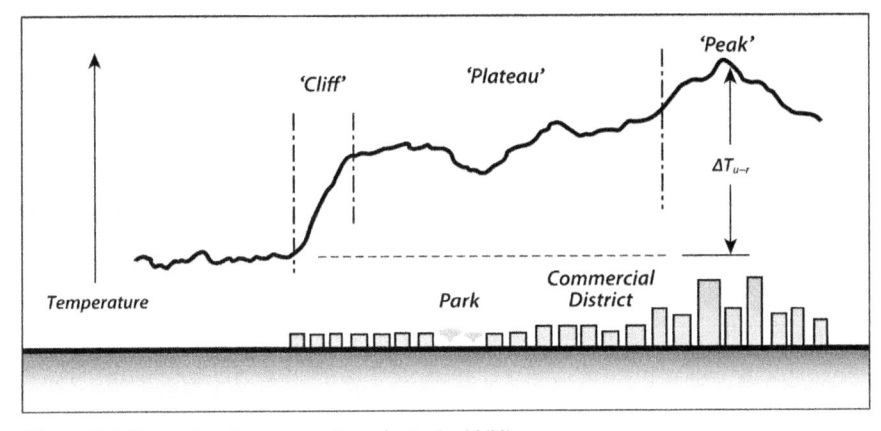

Figure 3.2 Generalized cross-section of a typical UHI

Source: Redrawn from Oke (1976).

The popular image of the urban heat island structure, as shown in Figure 3.2, is a fairly schematic pattern by which temperature rises from the urban periphery to the downtown core.

However, it should be noted that many studies assume the existence of this pattern somewhat too freely. Indeed, as the following quote (from Oke, 1998) suggests, the concept of a city-wide heat island may be misleading:

> The well known change in air temperature at screen-level ... has a steep gradient at the edge of the city, but the distribution is much flatter over most of the rest of the urban area except for relatively 'hot' and 'cool' spots in particularly densely built-up (high rise, narrow canyons) or open and/or vegetated (parks, vacant land) areas, respectively. Again, one must remember that the nature of the urban canopy-layer climates is dominated by the immediate surroundings, not distance from the edge or the centre.

Types of urban heat island

Urban heat islands may be observed both at the surface (*surface heat islands*) and in the atmosphere in and above the city (*atmospheric heat islands*). The latter type may be sub-divided into canopy-layer heat islands and boundary-layer heat islands. These categories differ in their intensity, temporal behaviour, spatial form and degree of homogeneity. Although their formation is the result of the interaction of several physical processes, they are not necessarily observed concurrently (in time or space), and their properties are different.

- A *surface heat island* (SHI) forms when the temperature of urban surfaces is greater than that of the surrounding rural (natural) surfaces. This type of heat island is common where the city is surrounded by moist soil or by vegetated areas, which tend to be cooler than dry impervious urban surfaces. However, in desert surroundings, the dry rocky or sandy soil may actually be warmer than many urban surfaces (see Figure 3.3). Urban SHIs are largest during the daytime, especially in sunny conditions with little wind, and are generally weaker at night.
- The *canopy-layer heat island* (CLHI) is observed in the layer of air closest to the surface in cities, extending upwards to approximately the mean building height. It is typically observed at night in stable atmospheric conditions with little cloud or wind, and is weaker or non-existent during the daytime.
- The *boundary-layer heat island* (BLHI) forms a dome of warmer air that extends downwind of the city. It may be one kilometre or more in thickness by day, shrinking to hundreds of metres or less at night. Wind often changes the dome to a plume shape.

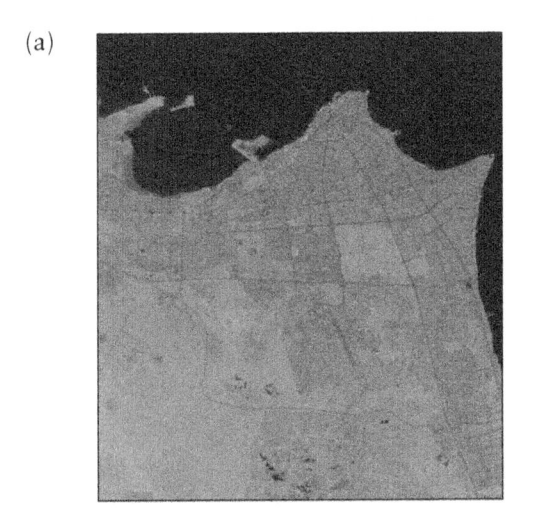

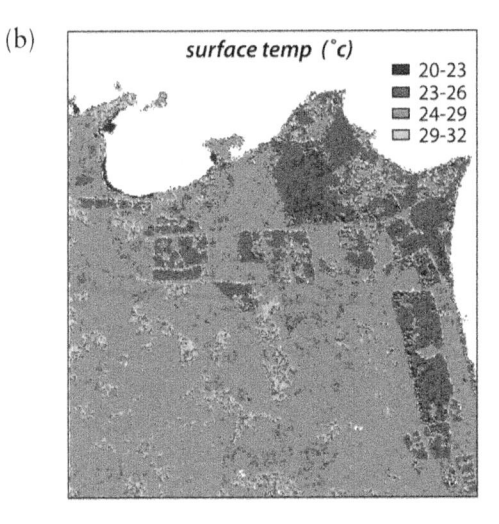

Figure 3.3 The surface heat island of Kuwait city. (a) Composite image created from Landsat images showing the urban area of Kuwait and the adjacent desert; (b) Surface temperature distribution for the same area, in which the temperature difference between the cooler urban surfaces (dark grey) and the warmer desert soils (light grey) is clearly discernible.

Images were taken on the morning of 6 March 2001.

Source: Redrawn from Kwarteng and Small (2007).

The formation of urban heat islands and factors affecting their intensity

The formation of urban heat islands reflects the sum effect of the multitude of man-made alterations to the natural environment that continually take place in the city. Even a single building may create a measurable disturbance to the land in its natural state, but to understand how urban heat islands are formed, the vast complexity of the city must be reduced to relatively simple physical processes. In particular, the formation of the urban heat island can be understood by examining the differences in the surface energy balance between the warm urban area and the relatively cooler rural surroundings. It is the energy balance at any given moment that determines whether cooling or heating takes place at a surface, and the rate at which these processes occur.

Although urban heat islands have been reported during the daytime, the phenomenon is more typically observed at night – particularly in dense low-latitude cities with a large anthropogenic heat flux. As temperatures begin to decline in the late afternoon and early evening, the cooling rate in the city is often lower than in the rural area. As a result, a temperature difference is formed, typically reaching a maximum several hours after sunset (see Figure 3.4). The trend is reversed shortly after sunrise, when urban warming occurs at a slower rate than in the rural surroundings. This process has been observed in numerous studies all over the world, in cities of all sizes and shapes, albeit with different intensity and variations in specific timing. Thus the general urban heat island phenomenon is often referred to as the 'nocturnal heat island'.

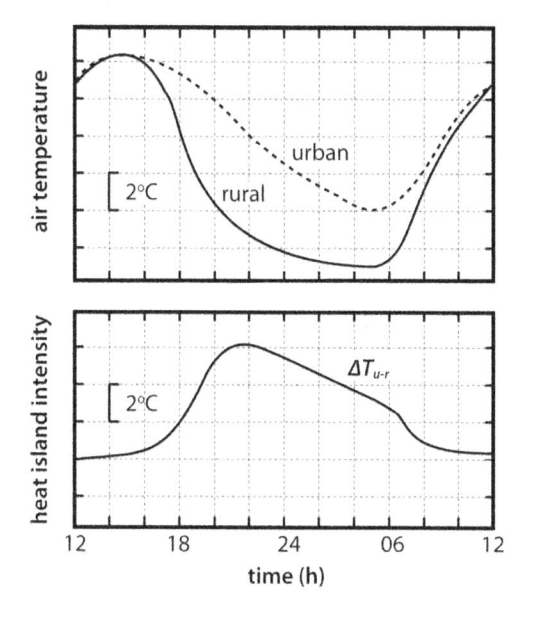

Figure 3.4 Typical diurnal variation of urban and rural air temperature (top) and the resulting nocturnal UHI intensity (bottom)

Note: The nocturnal UHI is formed as the result of relatively rapid cooling in rural areas in the late afternoon and early evening, compared with slower cooling in the city. The maximum intensity of the UHI occurs several hours after sunset, and it is completely eroded as rural areas heat up more quickly after sunrise.

Source: Redrawn from Oke (1987).

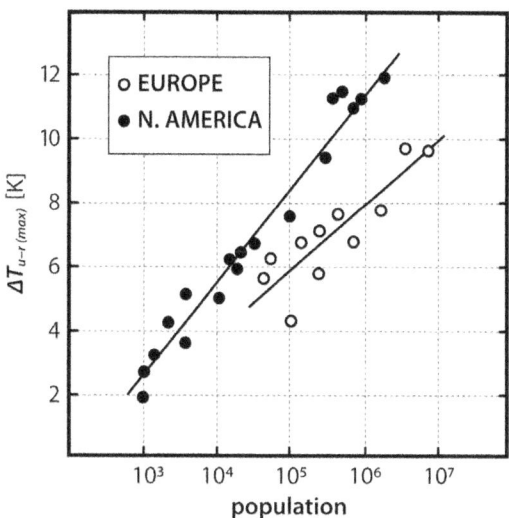

Figure 3.5 Relation between maximum observed heat island intensity and the population of North American and European cities

Source: Redrawn from Oke (1973).

Early empirical findings indicated that in mid-latitude locations, the maximum intensity of the urban–rural temperature difference was correlated with the size of the city, as measured by its population (see Figure 3.5). However, subsequent studies have made it clear that population size is merely a proxy for the physical structure of the city, and for the confluence of energy-exchange processes that operate within it to form heat islands. How the physical form of a city affects each of the elements of the surface energy balance is of primary importance, but weather, geographical location and even the season and time of day affect the intensity of urban heat islands, as does the amount of heat released by human activity.

Urban form

An implicit but often ignored aspect of the development of the nocturnal urban heat island is that the magnitude of the urban–rural difference is more sensitive to the rate of rural cooling than that of cooling in the city. The urban heat island is relatively small when rural cooling rates are low, for instance in humid and overcast conditions. It is when rural cooling rates are high that the urban heat island is fully developed. Notwithstanding, the actual heating of the city is clearly dependent on the properties of the city and of the urban open spaces within it.

Cities differ from their rural surroundings in a multitude of ways, many of which have a direct bearing on the surface energy balance and hence on the formation of heat islands. Urban form is affected first and foremost by building dimensions and spacing, but also by the characteristics of artificial surfaces (most of which are impervious) and by the amount of green space.

Building density

The most obvious characteristic of cities is the concentration of buildings in a fairly dense pattern in a given space. Buildings are where most human activity occurs, and the impetus of urban clustering has led to ever-denser construction in and around city centres. As large, tall buildings have risen along city streets, the spaces between them have come to resemble artificial canyons (as described in Chapter 1). In many cases these urban canyons are deeper than they are wide, and are defined on both sides by nearly continuous building facades.

The presence of a dense matrix of buildings promotes the creation of urban heat islands through a variety of processes. First among these is the trapping of solar energy due to multiple reflection and absorption within canyons, which reduces the urban albedo and increases the amount of heat stored in the urban fabric. Secondly, the restricted sky view factor of deep and/or narrow canyons

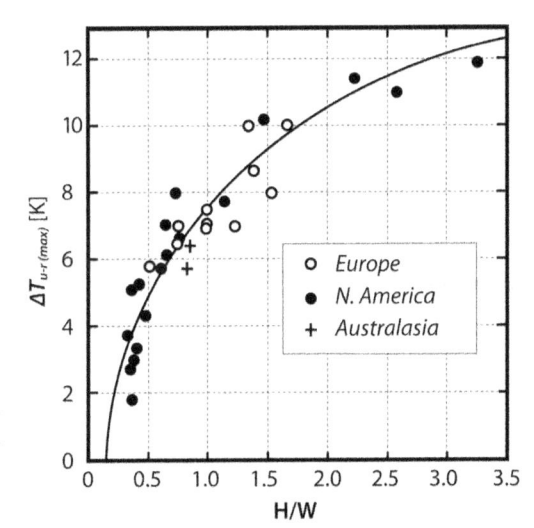

Figure 3.6 Relation between maximum observed heat island intensity and the H/W ratio of a sample of street canyons at the centre of 31 cities

Source: Redrawn from Oke (1987).

inhibits the net emission of long-wave radiation to the sky, and in turn the rate of cooling which occurs after sunset. Figure 3.6 shows the relationship between the sky view factor (and the related H/W, or aspect ratio) at the centre of a large sample of cities and the maximum urban heat island intensity recorded in them. Finally, the dense urban structure reduces wind speeds near the ground and limits the rate of air-flow through the canopy spaces, significantly impairing ventilation cooling.

While canyon geometry, as represented by the sky view factor, has a great effect on radiant exchange in the city, its contribution to the urban heat island remains a complex issue. For example, high correlations are usually obtained between the sky view factor and *surface* temperatures in the street – but correlations with *air* temperature in the same street may be substantially lower. Furthermore, while the maximum urban heat island measured in any given city may be predicted by Figure 3.6, it is much harder to predict intra-urban differences in temperature based upon geometry alone. A possible explanation for this inconsistency is that micro-scale diversity in air temperature is reduced by advection, so that the temperature measured at a particular canyon reflects the spatially averaged energy balance in a larger urban area.

Impervious surfaces

A large proportion of the ground surface of the city is covered by impervious surfaces – pavement consisting of materials such as concrete, asphalt or interlocking masonry bricks. These surfaces become fully wet during precipitation, and the available water may contribute to a rapid evaporative cooling of the air as sensible heat is converted to latent heat. If drainage is efficient, however, such surfaces may dry within a short period after the rain stops, due to evaporation. In the absence of available moisture, a positive net radiant balance contributes to a rapid increase in sensible heat near the surface, which is registered as an increase in air temperature. In rural areas, where most of the ground surface is pervious, the reduction in air temperature during precipitation is less pronounced: at least some of the available water will percolate into the pervious soil, leaving less to be evaporated. However, after rain has stopped falling the water thus stored may be released slowly over a period of time, often several days. During this time, the evaporation of soil moisture leads to a reduced sensible heat flux and hence to lower air temperatures, especially during daytime when there is a positive net radiant balance.

Vegetation

The complex and varied effects of vegetation on the urban microclimate are discussed at length in Chapter 9, but a brief mention will also be made here. The presence of vegetation affects the surface energy balance in several ways: it intercepts solar radiation (thus shading the surface), it blocks incoming long-wave radiation (from the sky) and outgoing radiation emitted by the ground, it reduces air speed when wind is blowing and it provides moisture through evapotranspiration.

There is little doubt that the presence of vegetation can produce daytime surface temperatures which are lower than those of exposed paved surfaces or even bare soil. The extent of the reduction can vary widely depending on the type of planting and upon water availability. In the presence of unrestricted water supply, plant surfaces may be cooled by evapotranspiration to a temperature approaching that of the ambient air, whereas exposed pavement may be between 5 and 20K warmer. A city with little plant cover surrounded by cropland or forest may display a substantial surface heat island during the daytime. At night, the temperature of urban surfaces may remain warmer than the air, and many studies show a small net positive sensible heat flux throughout the night.

The effect of vegetation on the atmospheric heat island is manifested not only indirectly, in the form of a reduction of sensible heat flux from the cooler surface, but also directly in the form of evaporative cooling. Most field studies support the argument that a lack of vegetation in the city would tend to result in elevated daytime air temperature, and concomitantly, that a large-scale planting campaign may lead to a reduction of the daytime urban heat island.

Properties of urban materials

Man-made features of the city, such as buildings and paved surfaces, might be expected to differ in their thermal and optical properties from natural surfaces. Of special significance in this context is the fact that while a given urban surface (like a plastered wall or pathway) tends to be relatively homogeneous over its area and has properties that change little with time, this is rarely the case with rural surfaces. Two features of rural surfaces in particular lead to substantial variation in their thermal and optical behaviour:

1. The soil increases in moisture content as it absorbs precipitation, and subsequently exhibits a drying phase. Variations in soil moisture change the thermal conductivity, volumetric heat capacity, thermal diffusivity and thermal admittance of the ground surface – all of which affect its role as a thermal store and its interaction with the atmosphere (for thermal properties of typical natural and man-made materials see Table 2.8). The albedo of a soil also changes with moisture content: solar radiation is trapped by internal reflection at air–water interfaces between soil particles and the inter-particle pores, so as moisture content increases, albedo decreases.
2. Seasonal changes in vegetation may result in variations in the albedo of the area in question, because the albedo of a vegetated plot of land in full foliage is typically lower than that of many soils (see Table 2.1).

The precise effect of urban material properties on heat island intensity may be difficult to quantify because of the large variability in the properties of the reference rural environment (as well as the inhomogeneity of urban surfaces). As a general rule, however, the intensity of SHIs in particular stands to be reduced if highly absorptive materials such as asphalt or dark-coloured roof tiles are replaced in sufficient quantity with lighter, more reflective materials for paving and roofing.

Weather

Weather, and in particular winds and cloud cover, affects the intensity of heat islands. Heat island magnitudes are largest under calm and clear weather conditions, since strong winds mix the air and erode the heat island, both during the daytime and at night.

Increasing cloud cover reduces radiative cooling at night, and the difference between urban and rural nocturnal cooling is a major contributor to heat island formation. Thus it is only to be expected that under overcast conditions, when radiant cooling is weak in both the city and its surroundings, heat island development tends to be minimal.

Geographic location

Geographic location dictates the regional climate and topography of the area in which the city is situated. Regional or local weather influences, such as local wind systems, may impact heat islands. For example, coastal cities may experience cooling in the summer when sea surface temperatures are lower than the land and winds blow onshore. Where cities are surrounded by wet rural surfaces, slower cooling by these surfaces can reduce heat island magnitudes, especially in warm humid climates.

Heat released by human activity

Human activity modifies the urban atmosphere in various ways, including the emission of industrial pollutants and exhaust fumes from vehicles. It also affects the intensity of the urban heat island, both directly and indirectly.

The direct effect consists of anthropogenic heat, which contributes to an elevation in air temperature the extent of which depends not only on the density of the heat flux but also upon interaction among the other environmental processes. Anthropogenic heating usually has the largest impact under cold winter conditions in the downtown core of the city, where thermal energy escaping from heated buildings can raise outdoor air temperatures significantly. However, densely developed cities may also have significant summertime anthropogenic heating, primarily as a result of waste heat from refrigerative air-conditioning systems. Evaporative cooling of buildings, on the other hand, generates latent rather than sensible heat and can contribute to higher humidity and heat stress in the city.

Indirect effects include the emission of carbon dioxide (CO_2) into the urban atmosphere from fossil fuel combustion in vehicles, power plants and industry. CO_2 concentrations above cities can be measurably higher than the global atmospheric average, contributing to the formation of an urban-scale greenhouse effect (i.e. by transmitting solar radiation and absorbing long-wave radiation emitted from the urban terrain). The emission of black carbon (or soot) also promotes urban heating, since unlike other aerosols which tend to reflect solar radiation, it is highly absorptive and effectively acts as a greenhouse gas.

Urban cool islands

The existence of a weak daytime cool island was reported by Luke Howard in his study *The Climate of London* (1818), which is better known for the first known record of the urban heat island:

> The excess of the Temperature of the city varies through the year, being least in spring, and greatest in winter; and it belongs, in strictness, to the nights; which average three degrees and seven-tenths warmer than in the country; while the heat of the day, owing without doubt to the interception of a portion of the solar rays by a veil of smoke, falls, on a mean of years, about a third of a degree short of that in the open plain.

Likewise, Oke (1982) noted that:

> The absence of a peak in warming, such as that experienced in the countryside, probably is due to the combined effects of canyon shading at low sun angles, higher thermal admittance and the lack of a capping inversion within the lowest few hundred metres of the urban atmosphere. The existence of a 'cool island' in the middle of the day usually is attributed to canyon shading in the city centre.

Although there is some empirical evidence indicating that daytime urban cool islands do in fact form on a regular basis – see for example Figure 3.7 – the phenomenon has received much less attention than the nocturnal heat island. This may be because daytime cool islands, where they occur, are typically weaker than nocturnal heat islands or may be masked by anthropogenic heat released, for example, by air-conditioning systems. Also, it is more difficult to obtain sufficiently accurate temperature readings during the daytime: dissimilar exposure to sunlight among different locations may create measurement error of the same order of magnitude as the temperature differences being recorded. The mechanisms responsible for the evolution of daytime cool islands are thus less well understood, and deserve some discussion.

In a densely built-up area, much of the incoming solar radiation is intercepted by building walls and other solid elements. The ground surface, and even the lower portions of adjacent walls, may remain in shade for much of the

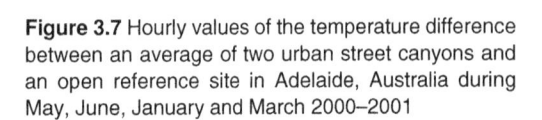

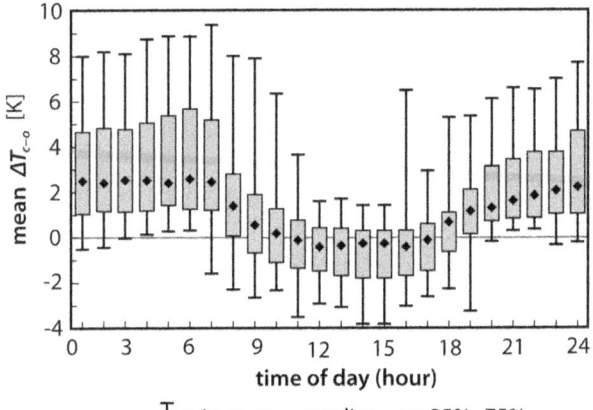

Figure 3.7 Hourly values of the temperature difference between an average of two urban street canyons and an open reference site in Adelaide, Australia during May, June, January and March 2000–2001

Note: Negative values indicate the existence of a canyon cool island.

Source: Erell and Williamson (2007).

day, so that their solar exposure is limited to diffuse radiation from the relatively constricted sky vault, and to reflected radiation from other wall surfaces – which may also be minimal if those surfaces have a low albedo. Air at ground level may be expected to absorb little heat from the shaded ground, and if mixing is weak then this air may indeed remain cooler than it would be in spaces with higher solar exposure.

It should be remembered, however, that the radiation incident on the walls of buildings, even at a considerable height above the ground, is not removed from the system. That portion which is reflected outward is largely redistributed among the other urban facets, so that the average rise in surface temperature may be small but the absorbing area is large. Much of the radiation is absorbed in the walls and transmitted through windows, heating the building and potentially amplifying the waste heat generated by air-conditioning. Depending on the heat capacity of the building materials and the associated time lag, as well as the actual circulation of air, much of the absorbed energy may be re-radiated or convected into the urban space at night, amplifying the nocturnal heat island.

Thus the daytime cool island, as it occurs in this scenario, is actually a redistribution of heat in space and time. Such redistribution may be beneficial in a hot-dry climate with wide temperature fluctuations, to the extent that outdoor heat stress is intense in the daytime and becomes a non-issue at night. In more humid regions, though, this is often not the case.

Factors affecting the intensity of urban cool islands

Geographic latitude

Because the interception of direct solar radiation by buildings depends both on the canyon aspect ratio and orientation and on the relative solar position, even fairly shallow canyons may be shaded by adjacent buildings if solar altitude is low. Therefore, daytime urban cool islands may be more likely to occur in high-latitude locations than in the tropics.

Canyon geometry and surface characteristics

Urban geometry has an effect on both radiant exchange and on energy storage, as well as on the complex interaction between them. Incoming solar radiation is absorbed over a much larger surface area in street canyons compared to open sites. A flat, unobstructed rural surface that is exposed to direct solar radiation continuously throughout the day may experience a substantial rise in temperature, unless much of the radiant flux is converted to latent heat in the presence of moisture. In a street canyon, by contrast, individual facets are exposed to direct sunlight in sequence, each for only several hours of the day. This results in reduced insolation per unit area of each canyon surface, especially if the canyon is deep in relation to its width. Although a street canyon may absorb more solar radiation overall than an unobstructed flat rural site due to multiple reflections among canyon surfaces, absorption over a larger surface area allows the thermal mass to moderate extremes of surface temperature, and hence reduces peaks of sensible heat flux. The higher overall absorption of solar radiation may, however, be reflected in a higher average air temperature in the canyon over the diurnal cycle. The release of this excess heat is typically in evidence at night: long-wave radiant loss is inhibited by a small sky view factor, so – unlike exposed rural soil – canyon surfaces may remain warmer than the air, resulting in a small positive sensible heat flux all night.

Thermal storage

The effect of urban thermal mass on air temperature may be seen as being analogous to the effect of thermal mass on interior temperatures of buildings: irrespective of other factors, one would expect the daily amplitude of urban air temperature to be reduced compared with the surrounding environment, and the minimum and maximum temperatures to be time-lagged to a certain extent. The damping effect of urban thermal mass on air temperatures is seen clearly in Figure 3.8, which shows that the diurnal range in an urban street canyon may be a constant fraction of the range in a reference non-urban station, irrespective of weather conditions. This damping effect may be attributed to the effects of urban morphology on radiant exchange as well as to the effects of thermal mass. The fact that the relationship is strongly linear and shows no seasonal dependence, as one would expect with solar radiation effects, favours the latter explanation. The dominant role of thermal mass is also consistent with the time lag observed between the peak of the net radiant load on the surface (about noon) and the maximum intensity of the urban cool island which typically occurred two to three hours later. In this view, the daytime cool island and the nocturnal heat island are, to a certain extent, related phenomena.

Anthropogenic heat

The size of the anthropogenic flux depends on the density of the city, as well as on climate and on building construction. In most cities it is quite small – most major US cities have anthropogenic fluxes of 15 to 75W m^{-2}. Nevertheless, even a moderate mean anthropogenic flux of 50W m^{-2} may be larger than Q^* in

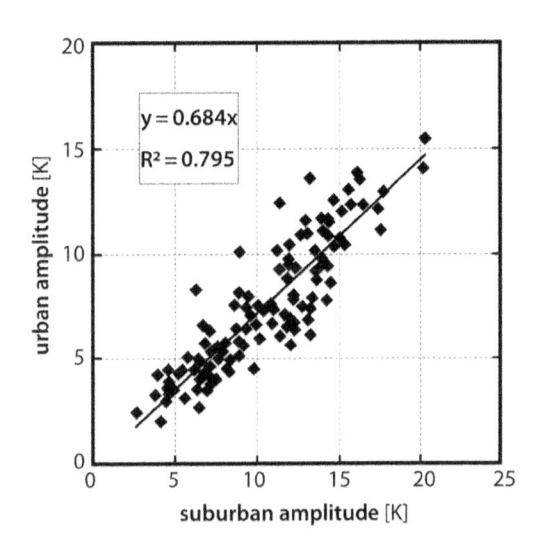

Figure 3.8 Correlation between the diurnal temperature range recorded at a street canyon site and concurrent records from a standard station in a nearby suburb of Adelaide, Australia

Source: Erell and Williamson (2007).

some cities during winter. In such conditions, a daytime urban cool island is unlikely to occur. However, where climate is warmer (so there is less heat loss from buildings) and insolation greater, anthropogenic heat is unlikely to dominate the urban energy balance. In such cases, the combination of factors listed above suggests a possible strategy for reduction of daytime air temperature in dense urban cores.

To summarize, although daytime cool islands may be more common than the relative paucity of published data on this subject suggests, the conditions in which they are likely to occur may not necessarily be found in all cities. A daytime canopy level cool island is more likely to occur if (a) the urban structure is dense, (b) the anthropogenic heat flux (Q_F) is small in proportion to the net radiant flux (Q^*) and (c) if a substantial proportion of the incoming solar radiation is absorbed by building surfaces that are not in contact with air at street level.

UHI mitigation

The urban heat island is not necessarily detrimental, especially in cold climates. However, in warm-climate cities, there are compound benefits from a reduction in surface and screen level air temperatures. The potential benefits include, in addition to a decreased demand for cooling energy, a decrease in some photochemical reaction rates and thus lower ozone levels, a decrease in temperature-dependent biogenic hydrocarbon emissions from vegetation and a decrease in evaporative losses. All of these factors may also contribute to an improvement in the overall quality of the outdoor areas enjoyed by pedestrians, and may lead to more intensive use of urban space. However, any strategy to mitigate heat islands should be evaluated in the context of complex interrelated effects of the varied controls on the urban microclimate.

Controlling solar gain is probably the first step in planned modification of the urban microclimate. Solar reflective (high-albedo) alternatives to traditionally absorptive surfaces such as rooftops and roadways can reduce cooling energy use at almost no cost (see also Chapter 8). All else being equal, the application of high-albedo materials reduces the temperature of surfaces exposed to direct sunlight by reducing absorption of solar radiation. The main effect may be observed during the daytime, when high surface temperatures result in greater sensible heat flux and thus elevated air temperature, but residual effects may be felt throughout the diurnal cycle as energy stored in the substrate is gradually released. The scale of modification possible depends on the area of solid surfaces such as rooftops, streets and other paved areas as a proportion of the total urban area. The use of high-albedo paving can also have a number of indirect effects, such as visual glare and increased reflected radiation on pedestrians and building facades (including on glazed openings).

Landscaping, specifically the incorporation of planted areas in the urban fabric, seeks to minimize differences between natural terrain and the urban surface. However, an irrigated lawn requires the introduction of additional water from outside the immediate system; it is the evaporation of this water that converts sensible into latent heat and lowers the temperature above the lawn. This has implications not only for resource usage in water-scarce regions, but for the extent of cooling itself: planted areas in a city tend to reduce daytime maximum temperatures, but have little or no effect on night-time minima. In fact, the main effect of trees is often to reduce radiant exchange at the ground surface: this may reduce daytime maximum temperature, but may also restrict nocturnal cooling, leading to higher minima.

UHIs and global warming

Urban heat islands play a role in the much broader phenomenon of global warming, in at least two ways. Firstly, urban heating contributes in some measure to large-scale temperature trends, and secondly, urban areas are large producers of greenhouse gases.

The effect of urbanization on long-term meteorological records

Much scientific inquiry has focused in recent years on the contribution of urban heat islands to observed rises in global near-surface temperature. The models which provide evidence of a warming trend are typically based on temperature records from large meteorological networks, whose stations are often in the proximity of cities and therefore are influenced by local urban conditions.

The effects of urbanization on these stations over time can in fact lead to contamination of the temperature record (in the context of global climate research), which must be considered in evaluating the long-term change in background temperature which is applicable to the atmosphere on a global scale. Using a variety of methods, researchers have thoroughly homogenized the time series of temperature for a large sample of weather stations, employing statistical methods to adjust for differences between urban and rural stations that are not related to the urban effect as such (e.g. effects of differences in elevation or distance from the sea or differences in instrumentation). These studies indicate that the direct impact of urbanization and other land use changes on the long-term trend of global temperature is noticeable, but of a relatively small magnitude (of the order of 10 per cent of the overall anthropogenic warming trend, with the remainder attributed to the effects of greenhouse gas emissions).

The contribution of cities to global CO_2 levels

Cities cover only a tiny fraction of the Earth's surface. However, over half of humanity now lives in urban areas – with the proportion projected to increase as predominantly rural societies in Asia and Africa become more urbanized – and these metropolitan areas are also the main centres of fuel-intensive industry, commercial activity and daily commuting. Consequently, most greenhouse gas emissions (related to human activity) come from urban areas, and contribute to both local and global-scale weather and climate modification.

The design and operation of cities are essential to the success of any initiative designed to promote carbon-free economic growth. To have a measurable effect on global production of atmospheric CO_2, substantial changes will need to occur not only in lifestyle, but also in urban form. Cities will mostly become denser, to allow public transport to operate efficiently. An unintended and often overlooked consequence of such a trend is that although dense cities consume far less energy per capita than cities that sprawl over larger areas, they are characterized by the very features that might promote the development of larger or more intense urban heat islands: high aspect-ratio streets, reduced vegetation, lower wind speeds and higher anthropogenic heat flux per unit surface area. (See Chapter 11 for a modelling study of the interaction of microclimate and building-scale effects in cities with different climates.)

Notes

1   The term probably appeared for the first time in the English language in 1958 in a paper by Gordon Manley in the *Quarterly Journal of the Royal Meteorological Society*, although it may have been coined earlier elsewhere.
2   See, for example, De Laat and Maurellis (2006).

References

De Laat, A. T. J. and Maurellis, A. N. (2006) 'Evidence for influence of anthropogenic surface processes on lower tropospheric and surface temperature trends', *International Journal of Climatology*, vol 26, pp897–913

Erell, E. and Williamson, T. (2007) 'Intra-urban differences in canopy layer air temperature at a mid-latitude city', *International Journal of Climatology*, vol 27, no 9, pp1243–1255

Howard, L. (1818) *The Climate of London Deduced from Meteorological Observations*, W. Phillips, London

Jauregui, E. (1986) *The Urban Climate of Mexico City in Urban Climatology and its Applications with Special Regard to Tropical Areas*, WMO 652, World Meteorological Organization, Geneva

Kwarteng, A. and Small, C. (2007) 'Remote sensing analysis of Kuwait City's thermal environment', *Proceedings of the Urban Remote Sensing Joint Event*, 11–13 April 2007, Paris

Manley, G. (1958) 'On the frequency of snowfall in metropolitan England', *Quarterly Journal of the Royal Meteorological Society*, vol 84, pp70–72

Oke, T. (1973) 'City size and the urban heat island', *Atmospheric Environment*, vol 7, no 8, pp769–779

Oke, T. (1982) 'The energetic basis of the urban heat island', *Quarterly Journal of the Royal Meteorological Society*, vol 108, pp1–24

Oke, T. (1987) *Boundary Layer Climates*, 2nd edition, Methuen, London

Oke, T. (1998) 'Observing urban weather and climate', *Proc. WMO Tech. Conf. on Meteorology and Environmental Instruments and Methods of Observation*, World Meteorological Organization, Geneva, WMO/TD-No. 877, pp1–8

Oke, T. R. (1976) 'The distinction between canopy and boundary-layer urban heat islands', *Atmosphere*, vol 14, pp268–277

Additional reading

Arnfield, J. (2003) 'Two decades of urban climate research: A review of turbulence, exchanges of energy and water, and the urban heat island', *International Journal of Climatology*, vol 23, no 1, pp1–26

Bärring, L., Mattsson, J. O. and Lindqvist, S. (1985) 'Canyon geometry, street temperatures and urban heat island in Malmö, Sweden', *Journal of Climatology*, vol 5, no 4, pp433–444

Chandler, T. J. (1965) *The Climate of London*, Hutchinson, London

Changnon, S. A. (1992) 'Inadvertent weather modification in urban areas: Lessons for global climate change', *Bulletin of the American Meteorological Society*, vol 73, no 5, pp619–627

Choi, Y., Jung, H., Nam, Y. and Kwon, W. (2003) 'Adjusting urban bias in the regional mean surface temperature series of South Korea, 1968–99', *International Journal of Climatology*, vol 23, pp577–591

Chow, W. and Roth, M. (2006) 'Temporal dynamics of the urban heat island of Singapore', *International Journal of Climatology*, vol 26, no 15, pp2243–2260

Eliasson, I. (1990–1991) 'Urban geometry, surface temperature and air temperature', *Energy and Buildings*, vol 15, nos 1–2, pp141–145

Eliasson, I. (1996) 'Intra-urban nocturnal temperature differences: A multivariate approach', *Climate Research*, vol 7, pp21–30

Emmanuel, R. (1997) 'Summertime urban heat island mitigation: Propositions based on an investigation of intra-urban air temperature variations', *Architectural Science Review*, vol 40, no 4, pp155–164

Gedzelman, S., Austin, S., Cermak, R., Stefano, N., Partridge, S., Quesenberry, S. and Robinson, D. (2003) 'Mesoscale aspects of the urban heat island around New York City', *Theoretical and Applied Climatology*, vol 75, pp29–42

Goward, S. N. (1981) 'Thermal behavior of urban landscapes and the urban heat island', *Physical Geography*, vol 2, pp19–33

Jauregui, E. (1990–1991) 'Influence of a large urban park on temperature and convective precipitation in a tropical city', *Energy and Buildings*, vol 15, nos 3–4, pp457–463

Kim, Y. and Baik, J. (2002) 'Maximum urban heat island intensity in Seoul', *Journal of Applied Meteorology*, vol 41, no 6, pp651–659

Landsberg, H. E. and Maisel, T. N. (1972) 'Micrometeorological observations in an area of urban growth', *Boundary-Layer Meteorology*, vol 2, no 3, pp365–370

Livada, I., Santamouris, M., Niachou, K., Papanikolaou, N. and Mihalakakou, G. (2002) 'Determination of places in the great Athens area where the heat island effect is observed', *Theoretical and Applied Climatology*, vol 71, nos 3–4, pp219–230

Lowry, W. P. (1977) 'Empirical estimation of urban effects on climate: A problem analysis', *Journal of Applied Meteorology*, vol 16, no 2, pp129–135

Lu, J., Arya, J. P., Snyder, W. H. and Lawson, R. (1997) 'A laboratory study of the urban heat island in a calm and stably stratified environment. Part I: Temperature field', *Journal of Applied Meteorology*, vol 36, pp1377–1391

Magee, N., Curtis, J. and Wendler, G. (1999) 'The urban heat island effect at Fairbanks, Alaska', *Theoretical and Applied Climatology*, vol 64, pp39–47

Morris, C. J. G., Plummer, N. and Simmonds, I. (2001) 'Quantification of the influences of wind and cloud on the nocturnal urban heat island of a large city', *Journal of Applied Meteorology*, vol 40, pp169–182

Myrup, L. O. (1969) 'A numerical model of the urban heat island', *Journal of Applied Meteorology*, vol 8, no 6, pp908–918

Nunez, M. and Oke, T. R. (1977) 'The energy balance of an urban canyon', *Journal of Applied Meteorology*, vol 16, pp11–19

Oke, T. R. (1981) 'Canyon geometry and the nocturnal urban heat island: Comparison of scale model and field observations', *International Journal of Climatology*, vol 1, no 3, pp237–254

Oke, T. R. (1982) 'The energetic basis of the urban heat island', *Quarterly Journal of the Royal Meteorological Society*, vol 108, pp1–24

Oke, T. R., Johnson, G. T., Steyn, D. G. and Watson, I. D. (1991) 'Simulation of surface urban heat islands under "ideal" conditions at night. Part 2: Diagnosis of causation', *Boundary-Layer Meteorology*, vol 56, no 4, pp339–358

Post, D., Fimbres, A., Matthias, A., Sano, E., Accioly, L., Batchily, A. and Ferreira, L. G. (2000) 'Predicting soil albedo from soil color and spectral reflectance data', *Soil Science Society of America Journal*, vol 64, pp1027–1034

Rosenfeld, A. H., Akbari, H., Bretz, S., Fishman, B. L., Kurn, D. M., Sailor, D. and Taha, H. (1995) 'Mitigation of urban heat islands: Materials, utility programs, updates', *Energy and Buildings*, vol 22, no 3, pp255–265

Runnalls, K. and Oke, T. R. (2000) 'Dynamics and controls of the near-surface heat island of Vancouver, British Columbia', *Physical Geography*, vol 21, no 4, pp283–304

Saaroni, H., Ben-Dor, E., Bitan, A. and Potchter, O. (2000) 'Spatial distribution and microscale characteristics of the urban heat island in Tel-Aviv, Israel', *Landscape and Urban Planning*, vol 48, pp1–18

Steinecke, K. (1999) 'Urban climatological studies in the Reykjavik subarctic environment, Iceland', *Atmospheric Environment*, vol 33, pp4157–4162

Sundborg, Å. (1950) 'Local climatological studies of the temperature conditions in an urban area', *Tellus*, vol 2, no 3, pp221–231

Terjung, W. H. and Louie, S. (1973) 'Solar radiation and urban heat islands', *Annals of the Association of American Geographers*, vol 63, no 2, pp181–207

Watkins, R., Palmer, J., Kolokotroni, M. and Littlefair, P. (2002a) 'The London Heat Island: Results from summertime monitoring', *Building Service Engineering*, vol 23, no 2, pp97–106

Watkins, R., Palmer, J., Kolokotroni, M. and Littlefair, P. (2002b) 'The balance of the annual heating and cooling demand within the London urban heat island', *Building Service Engineering*, vol 23, no 4, pp207–213

4
Urban Air-Flow

The nature of air movement in urban spaces holds key importance for pedestrian comfort as well as for building ventilation, air quality and energy use. The irregularity of urban terrain, however, makes patterns of air-flow in built-up areas notoriously complex.

At each level of scale, physical man-made and natural features have distinct modifying effects on wind speed, direction and intensity of turbulence. In the following discussion, these overlapping effects will be examined sequentially, starting with the isolated impact of a single building on the ground and progressing toward the larger-scale impacts of urbanized terrain.

Wind near the ground: air-flow and disturbance

On average, over level ground, wind flows horizontally – although always with some measure of *turbulence*, or deviation in its speed and its horizontal and vertical direction relative to the average of these flow properties over a given period of time. The source of the horizontal flow may be regional winds generated by pressure differences (e.g. due to differences between land and sea surface temperatures), and if the terrain is smooth and flat, then the frictional drag imposed by the ground on this free flow of air near the surface may be minor. Any change from level ground – due to the topography, vegetation or the built structures that are typical of urban areas – will obstruct the flow and modify the pattern. The portion of air in which the effects of the solid surface are felt is known as the *boundary-layer*.

Obstruction by an isolated obstacle

A fundamental distinction can be made between disturbances to air-flow by obstacles which cause separation of the flow (sharper-edged obstacles such as rectilinear buildings) and those which allow the flow to adhere to their surface (rounder obstacles such as moderate hills and valleys). This discussion will focus on the former type of obstacle, known as a *bluff body*, which is characteristic of most urban construction.

It may be useful to first consider a simplified two-dimensional object. When a stream of air flowing parallel to the ground encounters this type of built obstacle, at least three zones are created in which the movement of air is distinctly different from the undisturbed flow. These zones are located, respectively, at the approach to a building (on its upwind side), above its roof, and for some distance downwind, in what is known as its *wake* (see Figure 4.1).

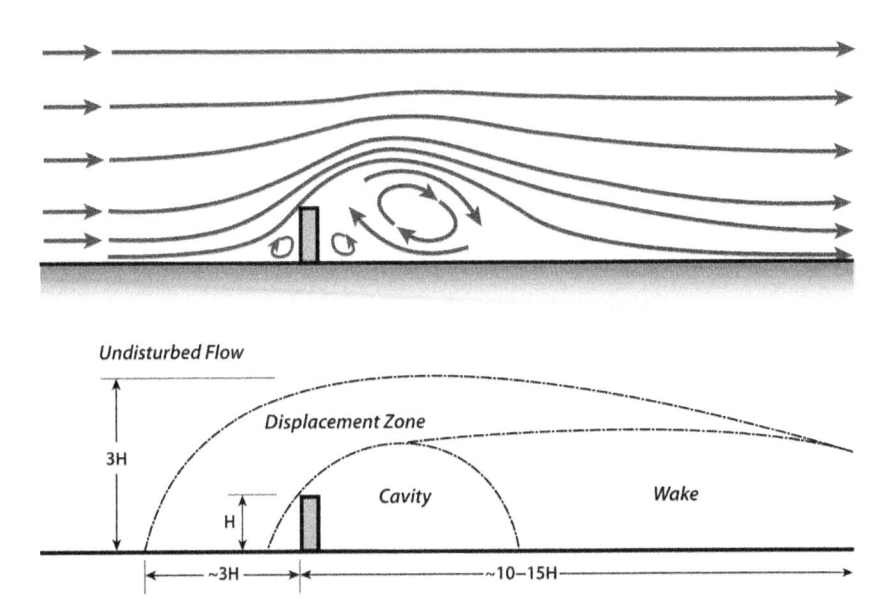

Figure 4.1 Schematic section showing typical pattern of air-flow over an isolated building, depicted as streamlines (top) and general flow zones (bottom)

Note: The extent of disturbance upwind, above and downwind of the building are shown as approximate multiples of the building's height.

A built-up area with isolated, widely spaced bluff-body structures will be characterized by this type of flow pattern.

Flow around buildings

Unlike the simplified object discussed in the preceding section, buildings are three-dimensional, permitting air-flow around their ends as well as above them. The disturbance that this creates can induce high wind speeds at ground level, due to two quite separate mechanisms (or pressure fields). The first type of flow is caused by the pressure distribution on the windward face of a building, which increases with height and which is related to the local dynamic wind pressure. The second type of flow is caused by the pressure difference between the low-pressure wake regions (leeward and side faces) and the relatively high-pressure regions at the base on the windward face. Flow directly between these two regions through arcades or around corners can cause very high local wind speeds. The low wake pressure is dependent on the velocity along the top free boundary, i.e. the free stream velocity at the top of the building. Hence the taller the building, the lower the wake pressure and the higher the velocities that are induced through arcades and around corners (see Figure 4.2).

It is clear from Figure 4.2 that upon encountering the impermeable building, the air is either deflected over the top, down the front or around the sides. The air pushing against the building creates relatively high pressures near the upper middle part of the wall where the wind is actually brought to a standstill, and pressure decreases outwards from this *stagnation point*. If the building has

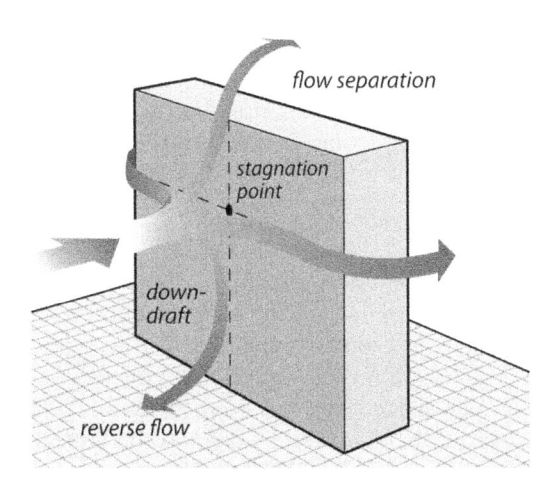

Figure 4.2 Air-flow pattern around a tall slab building

sharp corners the flow accelerating over the top and around the sides becomes separated from the surface. Therefore the sides, roof and leeward wall experience suction. Since air moves from high to low pressure, these areas are characterized by reverse flows. This is responsible for the lee eddy circulation, which extends up into the strong suction zone above the roof. In plan view a double eddy circulation at ground level characterizes the cavity zone.

Modelling studies with smoke streams have shown the strong effect that high-rise buildings can have on both the intensity and the direction of the air-flow. Upon encountering an especially tall building within a low-rise built-up area, the main stream flowing above the uniform-height buildings tends to divide into two streams. Part of the stream passes upwards, while the greater part is deflected downwards, reaching the space in between rows and then separating into a bilateral stream flowing sideways from the

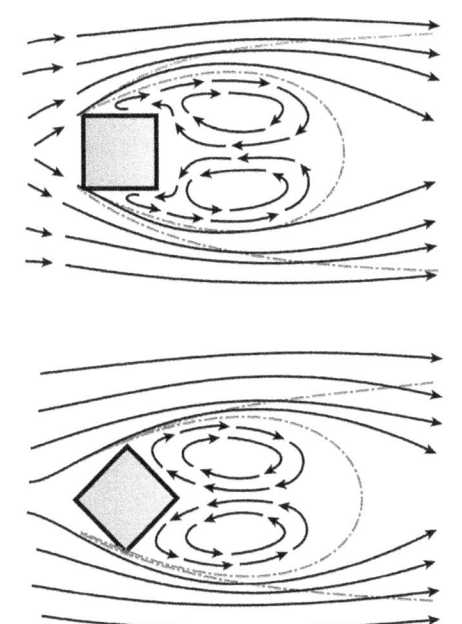

Figure 4.3 Flow pattern around a sharp-edged building

Source: Based on Oke (1987).

building. A high-pressure zone is typically observed on the windward side of the tall building and a low-pressure zone (suction) on the leeward side. When high-rise buildings form a street, the combination of pressure and suction zones can result in a stronger stream flowing from one zone to the other.

Wind in the urban canopy

Within the urban canopy-layer, wind speed and direction are extremely variable. In general, observations show a sharp drop in the average wind speed below roof level, but micro-scale changes in geometry may result in localized areas with very high wind speed. Wind direction is also affected by the form of buildings, the pattern of streets and open spaces, and the local topography. In terms of velocity, canopy air-flow may be characterized by calm at the bottom of deep spaces, strong winds along streets oriented in the direction of the wind and eddies across streets perpendicular to winds.

Canyon wind flow regimes

Wind tunnel studies have shown that for a simple street canyon within an urban array which is oriented with its axis perpendicular to the wind direction three distinct wind regimes may be identified, depending on the canyon's aspect ratio (see Figure 4.4). Each regime describes the pattern of disturbance to the free flow due to the built obstacles which enclose the canyon.

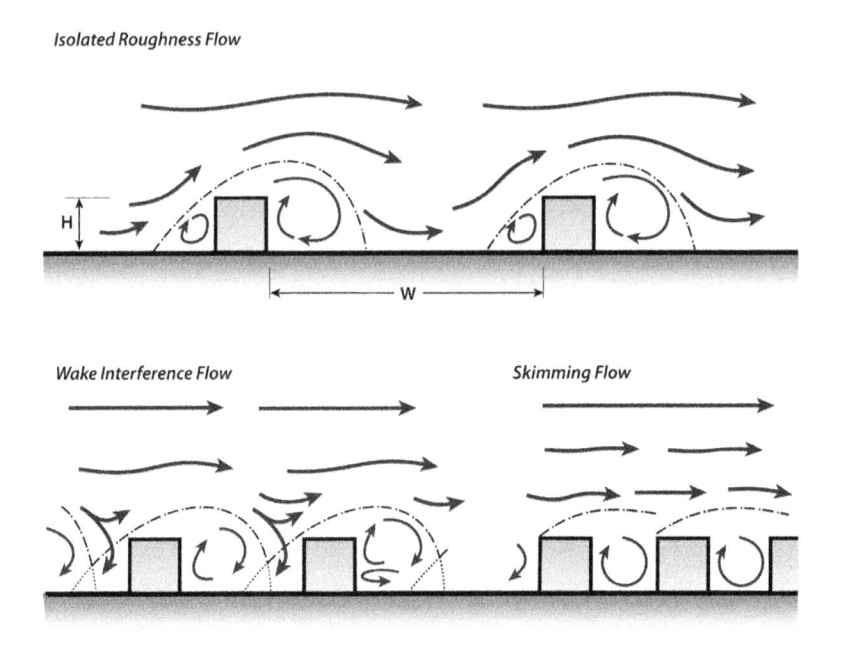

Figure 4.4 Flow regimes associated with different urban geometries, drawn by Oke (1987) on the basis of wind tunnel experiments carried out by Hussain and Lee, 1980.

Source: Based on Oke (1987).

Isolated roughness flow regime

A single obstacle such as a building, placed in the path of the near ground level wind flow, will produce the following disturbance patterns:

- In the *displacement zone*, located at the approach to the building, a bolster eddy vortex is formed. This pattern is characterized by flow down the windward face of the building, with relatively high pressures over most of the wall. Maximum pressure occurs near the upper middle part of the wall, where the wind is essentially brought to a standstill, and pressure decreases outward from this stagnation point.
- If the building has sharp corners, the flow of air over the top and around the sides will become separated from the surface, creating zones of suction. If the two-dimensional section of a continuous urban canyon is considered, this 'cavity zone' of negative pressure is experienced over the roof and leeward wall of the building, where air is drawn into a 'lee eddy' in a reverse circulation from that of the main air stream.
- Downwind from the obstacle is the *wake*, or low-pressure zone, in which the flow separation creates a more turbulent condition than that of the free flow. As a result of this separation, the wind force is lessened near the ground and lower velocities are experienced.

When the spacing between building obstacles is relatively large, i.e. the H/W ratio is less than 0.3–0.5, the flow fields of consecutive buildings do not interact. Thus their patterns of disturbance are similar to that of an isolated building.

Wake interference regime

At greater aspect ratios (0.5<H/W<0.65), secondary flows are generated within the canyon space, where the downward flow of the cavity eddy is reinforced by deflection down the windward face of the next building downstream. Thus the bolster and lee eddies work together to increase turbulence, due to interference in the initial building's wake zone flow. Despite the more turbulent circulation, however, average wind speeds are generally lower in this regime than in the previous pattern of isolated obstacles.

Skimming flow regime

When successive building blocks are tightly spaced, such that the H/W ratio is greater than 0.65, the canyon may be considered sheltered from the direct impact of winds perpendicular to its axis. In this case, a stable circulatory vortex is established within the canyon space by momentum transfer, but the bulk of the air-flow does not enter. Instead, the main flow 'skims' over the buildings and winds at street level are weak. Naturally, this condition provides greatest shelter to pedestrians from undesirable winds, but at other times may impede necessary ventilation of the urban space.

In practice, urban canyons are not bounded by continuous buildings of infinite length. The actual transitions between air-flow regimes are governed not only by H/W ratio, but also by the proportion between the canyon's length

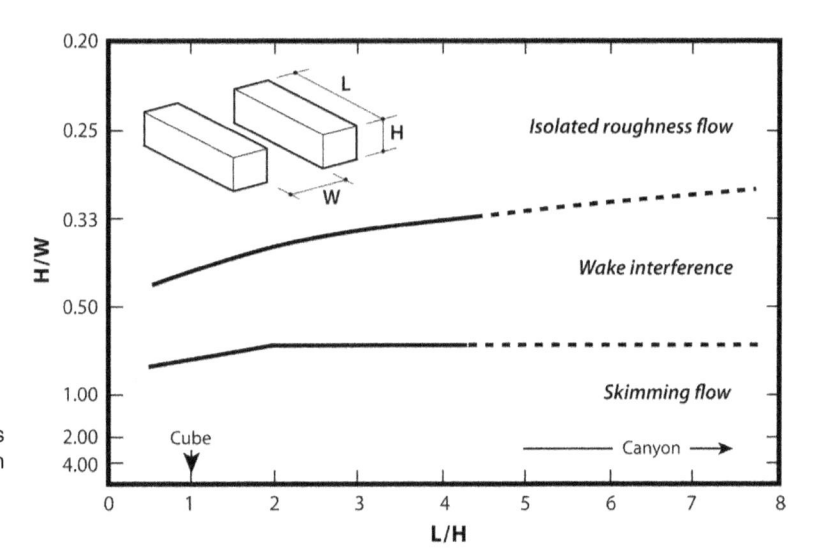

Figure 4.5 Threshold lines dividing flow regimes as a function of building and canyon geometry

Source: Based on Oke (1988).

and width (L/W), as determined by the length of the building normal to the air-flow. Figure 4.5 shows the critical combinations of H/W and L/W which divide between regimes, as observed in wind tunnel tests. It may be seen that while the transition from wake interference to skimming flow is relatively constant, the H/W at which isolated roughness flow is disturbed by wake interference decreases slightly with building length.

Subsequent mathematical modelling has refined the transition points between regimes, which were previously identified using wind tunnel observations. While the transition point from skimming to wake interference was confirmed, the transition from wake interference to isolated roughness flow was found to occur at aspect ratios as low as 0.2 for longer street canyons.

Canyon wind speed attenuation

Although the pattern of air-flow in a street canyon is quite complex, it is sometimes useful to obtain a simple estimate of wind speed near the middle of the street, as a function of the free wind speed above:

$$u_c = u_r P \tag{4.1}$$

In this approximation, horizontal wind speed in the centre of the canyon (u_c) is linearly related to the speed of perpendicular winds above roof level (u_r), as corrected by a diminution factor (P) which depends on the H/W ratio and height of measurement. First-order estimates have shown that for wind speeds of up to 5m/s, with an H/W ratio of one, and canyon/roof measurements at heights of $0.06H$ and $1.2H$ respectively, the diminution factor (P) is approximately 0.66. In other words, the shelter of the urban canyon under these conditions reduces the prevailing wind speed by about one-third.

Beyond such a rough estimate, wind attenuation varies widely depending on the actual canyon aspect ratio and orientation. Scale-model measurements in the open air have shown that for a given canyon H/W ratio, a clear relation exists

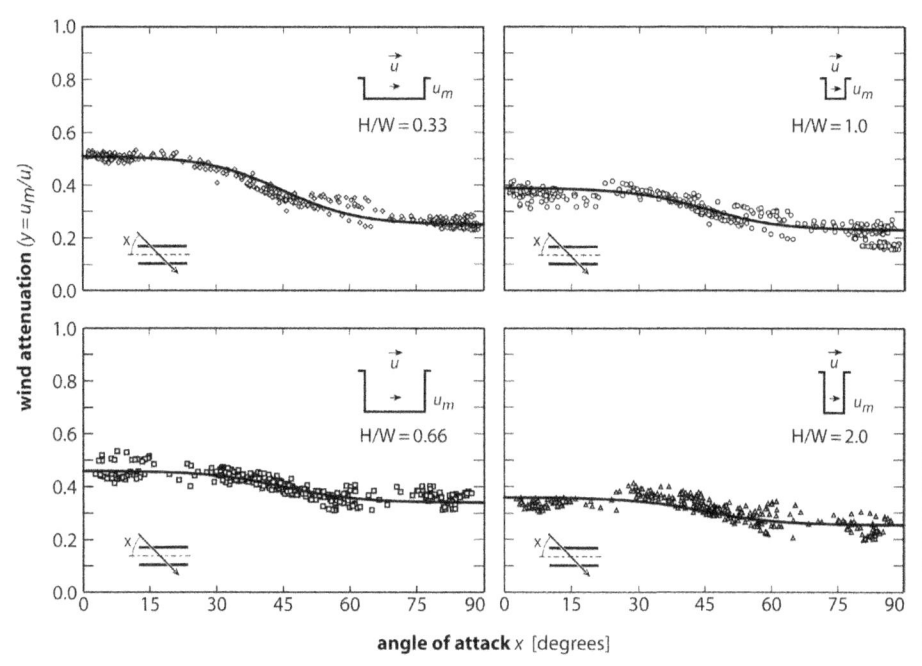

Figure 4.6 Correlation between wind speed attenuation and angle of attack for street canyons of varying aspect ratio

Source: Based on Pearlmutter et al (2005).

between wind speed attenuation and the 'angle of attack' between the street axis and prevailing wind direction (see Figure 4.6). As might be expected, wind speed is most severely attenuated at the maximum angle of attack (cross-canyon flow) and less so at lower attack angles (along-canyon flow). However this relationship is not linear, taking instead the form of an 'S' curve, with a greater slope at intermediate oblique angles than at near-parallel or near-perpendicular ones.

Figure 4.6 shows that when flow is near-parallel (attack angles of zero to 20 degrees), the attenuation factor decreases incrementally from about $P = 0.5$ for a wide street cross-section (H/W = 0.33) to about $P = 0.35$ for a very narrow one (H/W = 2.0). When flow is near-perpendicular, however, the attenuation approaches $P = 0.25$ in all cases (though cross-canyon flow is somewhat higher for the H/W = 0.66 street, presumably due to the complex wake-interference flow pattern in the canyon relative to the point of measurement). This severe attenuation reflects the fact that air-flow in the urban canopy is affected by the overall roughness of the urban surface and not just the proportions of the individual space.

Detailed air-flow patterns in an urban canyon

When air flows across a two-dimensional rectangular notch of depth H and width W (i.e. the cross-section of an urban canyon), a vortex is formed (see Figure 4.7). The transverse (horizontal) component of the flow (u) and the vertical component (w) may be described by the following equations:

$$u = u_0(1-\beta)^{-1}[\gamma(1+ky) - \beta(1-ky)/\gamma]\sin(kx) \quad (4.2)$$

$$w = -u_0 ky(1-\beta)^{-1}[\gamma - \beta/\gamma]\cos(kx) \quad (4.3)$$

92 URBAN MICROCLIMATE

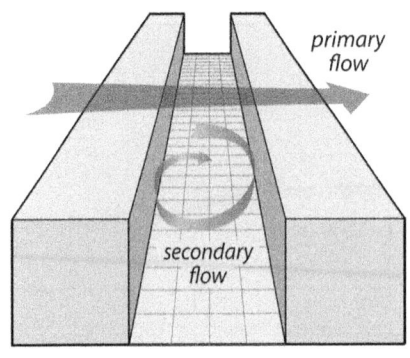

Figure 4.7 An idealized representation of the lee vortex formed in an urban street canyon by above-roof wind blowing at normal incidence to the canyon axis

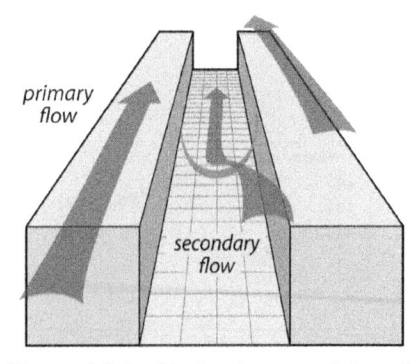

Figure 4.8 An idealized representation of the flow in an urban street canyon generated by above-roof wind blowing parallel to the canyon axis

Source: Based on Hotchkiss and Harlow (1973) and Yamartino and Wiegand (1986).

where $k = \pi/B$; $\beta = \exp(-2kH)$; $\gamma = \exp(ky)$; $y = z-H$; and u_0 is the transverse wind speed above the canyon (and at the point $x = B/2$, $z = H$).

When the wind is directed parallel to the canyon axis (as in Figure 4.8), the longitudinal (along-canyon) flow has a logarithmic vertical profile and the wind speed at a given height (z) can be estimated by:

$$v(z) = v_r \frac{\log\left[\dfrac{z + z_0}{z_0}\right]}{\log\left[\dfrac{z_r + z_0}{z_0}\right]} \qquad (4.4)$$

where v_r is the along-canyon component of the wind speed at reference height r above the canyon and z_0 is the *roughness length*.

The general case, in which the above-roof wind that drives the vortex is neither perpendicular to the canyon axis nor exactly parallel to it, may be characterized by a corkscrew-like flow which is the result of a superposition of the transverse flow and the longitudinal flow components (see Figure 4.9).

Note that this formulation assumes the following:

- neutral atmospheric stability and height-independent shearing stress;
- z_0 has different values according to different angles of the approach flow with respect to the longitudinal axis of the street;
- canyon parallel and transverse flows are often largely decoupled from one another.

Numerical models as well as scale-model simulations show that when skimming flow is present, the aspect ratio of the canyon determines the number and strength of the vortices formed in the street. For H/W equalling approximately unity, a single vortex forms, with its centre a little downwind relative to the

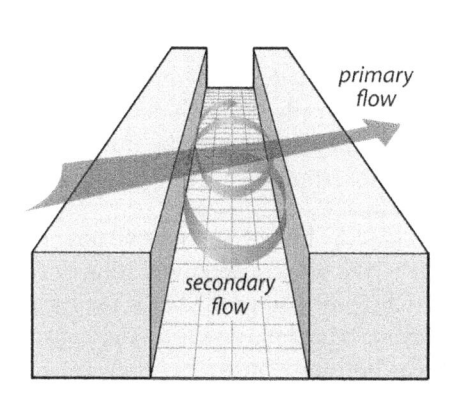

Figure 4.9 An idealized representation of the lee vortex formed in an urban street canyon by above-roof wind blowing at an angle to the canyon axis

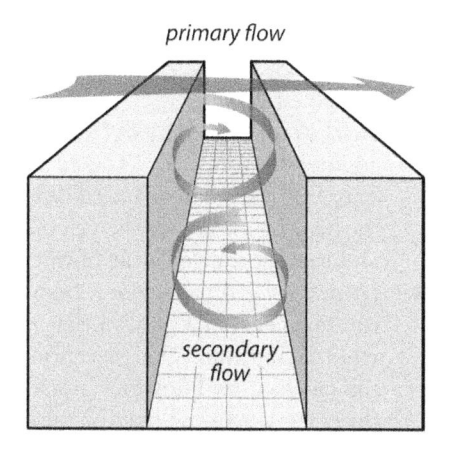

Figure 4.10 An idealized representation of two counter-rotating vortices formed in a deep street canyon by above-roof wind blowing perpendicular to the canyon axis

canyon centre. Theory suggests that deeper canyons may exhibit two counter-rotating vortices (see Figure 4.10): the vertical velocity vector of the primary vortex is independent of the canyon aspect ratio. The downward flow near the downwind wall of the canyon is stronger than the upward flow in the lee of the windward wall.

The conventional view of persistent recirculation within the street, in the form of vortices with small-scale turbulent fluctuations about the mean flow, is consistent with some field studies, but much of the evidence now shows that although a lee vortex is often formed, it may be much weaker than the unsteady turbulent fluctuations. The position of a shear layer formed by the upstream roof of the street canyon is responsible for the unsteady circulation within the street and also for the main mechanism of transporting air (and pollutants) from street level into the roughness layer above the roofs.

Effect of stability and thermal differentials on canyon air-flow

A possible explanation for the failure of some field studies to detect clear evidence for a vortex in urban canyon flow is that most models fail to account for thermal effects of differential solar heating of some canyon surfaces. The effects of solar heating on individual surfaces may create substantial thermal flows affecting the mechanical, wind-induced patterns. If the downwind wall is exposed to direct solar radiation and is substantially warmer than other canyon surfaces, an upwards thermal flow may form near the wall surface. This flow tends to counteract the downwards advective flow, and may lead to the creation of two counter-rotating vortices normally associated with deeper canyons. The formation of a multi-vortex pattern reduces vertical exchanges, primarily of pollutants but also of heat.

When wind is weak and radiant loads are strong, buoyancy effects are strong and disrupt the symmetrical lee vortex. The disruption depends on the orientation of the heated surface relative to the approaching wind (Figure 4.11):

- *Heating of lee wall*: the lee vortex remains symmetrical but is reinforced in magnitude. More ejection of canyon air occurs as a result of buoyant flow near the lee wall.
- *Heating of wind-facing wall*: buoyancy divides the lee vortex into two counter-rotating cells. The advection cell is typically larger than the thermal one, but the relative magnitude of the two depends upon the intensity of the heating and upon the velocity of the above-roof flow. Air flows upwards and may be ejected near both canyon walls.
- *Heating of ground surface*: buoyancy divides the lee vortex into two counter-rotating cells, in a pattern that is similar to the one created by heating of the wind-facing wall. The advection cell may become compressed near the top of the canyon, as buoyancy prevents it from extending down to the canyon floor. Upward flow may be observed near both canyon walls.

When winds are stronger, advection dominates even in the presence of strong radiant loads, and the overall structure of the canyon flow is affected by thermal buoyancy only to a minor extent.

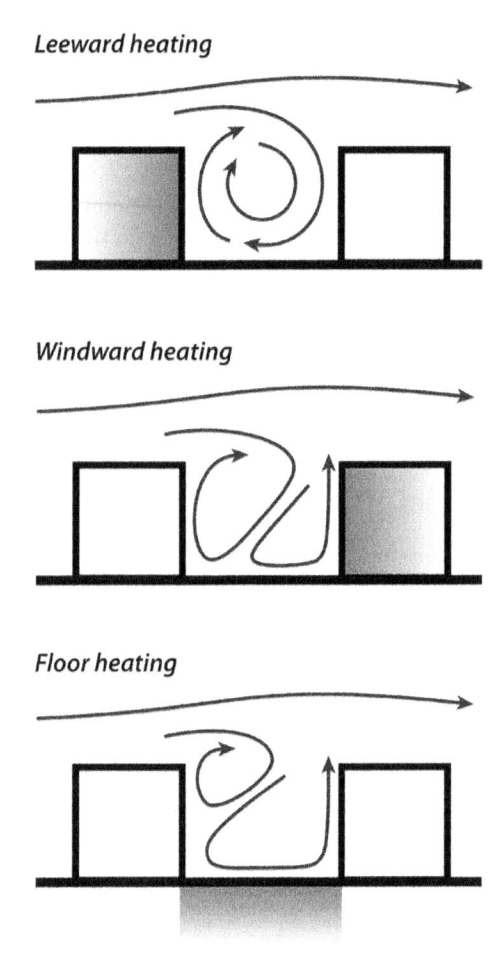

Figure 4.11 Effect of differential heating of canyon surfaces on the lee vortex generated by relatively weak above-roof wind

Source: Based on Xie et al (2005).

Wind modification in the urban boundary-layer (UBL)

When regional winds blow over a city, the air-flow is modified due to its contact with the urban surface, which is rougher than most natural surfaces. This roughness derives from its patchy and heterogeneous mixture of three-dimensional elements, many of which are sharp-edged buildings. Because the texture of the urban surface tends to be so different from the surroundings, the nature of turbulence – and in turn, the turbulent transfer of heat – that are observed in the urban boundary-layer above the city tend to be quite different from what is measured at the same height upwind of the city. As described in Chapter 1, however, these flow characteristics become adapted to the underlying surface only within a relatively shallow surface layer, whose thickness gradually grows as air flows over the modified surface. In the upper part of the urban boundary-layer, these flow characteristics may not be in equilibrium with the surface below, but may instead reflect the characteristics of the surface upwind.

Depending on the height and location of measurement, therefore, the air-flow (as well as the exchange of heat and pollutants) above the urban surface will be conditioned by a certain area of upwind terrain. The extent of this terrain is known as the source area, and its size and location depend on the wind speed and direction, surface roughness and atmospheric stability.

Frictional drag due to roughness

Wind speed in the Earth's atmospheric boundary-layer (also known as the planetary boundary-layer, or PBL) increases with height above the surface. Early models proposed that the mean wind speed $\bar{u}$ at any height z above the surface could be calculated by a simple power law:

$$\bar{u}_z = V_G \left(\frac{z}{z_G}\right)^\alpha \tag{4.5}$$

where V_G is gradient velocity or geostrophic wind, z_G. It is the same for all wind profiles and represents the wind at a height z 'at which the influence of the ground friction transmitted upwards through the eddy viscosity has a negligible effect on the velocity of the wind as it responds to the pressure gradient'.[1] The value of α depends both on the surface roughness and atmospheric stability, and may range from about 0.1 for smooth water to about 0.4 for well-developed urban surfaces. Empirical evidence showed that the rough urban surface not only changed the shape of the velocity profile, but also increased the height of the boundary-layer (Table 4.1).

While the power law relationship fits empirical measurements of the wind profile fairly well, physical analysis leads to the conclusion that in a neutrally stable atmosphere, the wind speed $\bar{u}$ at height z above the surface depends not only on height but also on the surface drag and on the density of the fluid.

These last two factors are embodied in a quantity known as the *friction velocity* (u_*), which is proportional to the product of the shear stress imposed

Table 4.1 Vertical wind profile parameters for different terrain types

Terrain type	α	z_G (m)
Open country, flat	0.16	274
Suburban settlement	0.28	396
Urban centres	0.40	518

Note: The height of the geostrophic wind was originally given by Davenport in feet (900ft, 1300ft and 1700ft).

Source: Based on Davenport (1965).

by the surface and the density of the air. Using u_*, the wind speed at height z may be described by a logarithmic decay function whose slope increases with surface roughness (see Figure 4.12):

$$\bar{u}_z = \frac{u_*}{k} \ln\left(\frac{z-d}{z_0}\right) \quad (4.6)$$

The ratio between friction velocity (u_*) and von Karman's constant (k – approximately 0.40) is an expression of the *shear stress* which, through a vertical flux of horizontal momentum, causes the textured surface to exert a *drag* on the free air stream. Drag may be defined as the total shear stress on the rough surface, or the downward flux density of streamwise momentum. The *roughness length* (z_0) is defined as the height at which the vertical wind profile extrapolates to a zero wind speed. It is related to the average height of roughness elements such as buildings and trees and may be estimated from their average density in plan and in the windward direction. This length may be more accurately represented in relation to an elevated plane whose height is defined by the *zero-plane displacement* (d), which in many cases is approximately equal to two-thirds of the average height (h) of roughness elements.[2]

Figure 4.12 An idealized representation of the vertical profile of the mean wind speed above an urban area

Note: The logarithmic curve in the surface layer (i.e. inertial sub-layer) extrapolates to a zero wind speed at a height equal to the sum of the zero-plane displacement (*d*) and roughness length (z_0).

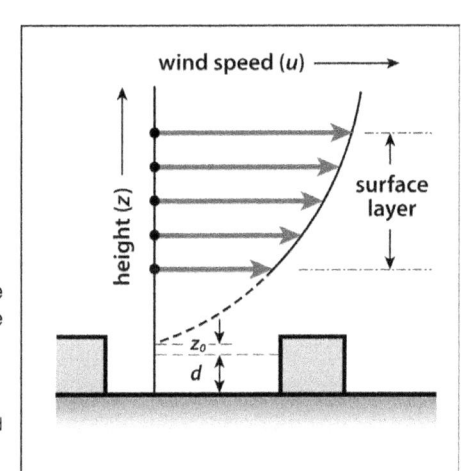

Friction velocity (u_*)

According to Equation 4.6 above, estimation of the wind speed at a given height above the city requires a knowledge of the friction velocity u_*, which is a relatively constant property of flow within a given adapted surface layer over a defined homogeneous roughness. The friction velocity is defined according to the relation:

$$u_* = \left(\frac{\tau}{\rho}\right)^{1/2} \tag{4.7}$$

where ρ is the air density and τ is the shear stress, which is a measure of flow retardation per unit horizontal area and is dependent on a drag coefficient (C_D). Since neither the drag coefficient nor the total shear stress are easily determined empirically, the friction velocity is more commonly determined from the above logarithmic profile formula, which requires measurement of wind speed and the determination of roughness length and zero-plane displacement.

Roughness length (z_0)

It has been demonstrated that the aerodynamic resistance of a rough surface such as a city may be described by universal laws involving the geometry of the surface and the nature of the boundary-layer associated with it. This resistance, or drag, is caused in various measures by the roughness of individual ground or building surfaces, and of the larger urban surface according to the composition of its roughness elements, such as buildings. Such roughness may be characterized by particular quantitative parameters, and the estimation of these parameters for typical urban surfaces is an ongoing topic of research in micrometeorology. While such studies often assume neutral stratification, conditions in an unstable surface layer have been considered as well.

There are two different methods to describe the roughness of the surface: the roughness length z_0 and the drag coefficient $C_D(z)$. The size of the drag coefficient depends on the choice of reference height, so z_0, which is independent of reference height (over a homogeneous terrain), is often preferred as a basic descriptive parameter of the surface roughness.

The roughness length is a parameter which directly expresses the geometrical roughness of the surface. The statement that 'z_0 is the height at which wind speed becomes zero' is true in an algebraic sense only, because it implies extrapolation of the logarithmic profile below its limit of validity (see Figure 4.12).

Zero-plane displacement (d)

For a dense canopy of surface-covering objects like buildings, only a small fraction of total shear stress is taken up by the bottom surface, with the remaining stress carried by the canopy elements, with a vertical drag distribution depending on their shape. The use of an appropriate value of d adjusts the reference level of the logarithmic profile to the effective level of mean drag on the surface canopy elements (see Figure 4.12).

Estimating the roughness parameters of a given urban surface

When possible, the most reliable way to estimate the roughness length and zero-plane displacement of an existing urban area is through micrometeorological (or anemometric) field observations, calculating their values directly from wind profile measurements. The displacement height is determined from the semi-logarithmic wind profile (using Equation 4.6) as the value of d which yields the highest possible coefficient in the linear correlation between the height function $ln(z-d)$ and mean wind speed $\bar{u}_z$. Using this optimal value of d, the roughness length z_0 is then calculated as the y-intercept of the linear relation between $ln(z-d)$ and $\bar{u}_z$.

Table 4.2 gives typical values of the roughness length for a variety of surface types, derived from on-site anemometer measurements. It should be noted that since the values shown in the table were measured over homogeneous surfaces, the roughness length of heterogeneous terrain characterized by wake-interference flow would be significantly higher.

Effect of urban geometry on roughness parameters

In practice, anemometric measurements in actual urban areas tend to be expensive and complex, and the accuracy of roughness parameter estimates may be compromised by the fact that they fail to consider critical aspects of this inherent complexity. Difficulties in estimating z_0 and d arise in many urban settings due to the heterogeneous nature of the surface, and because the properties of the source area affect the results – that is, the values are highly dependent on wind direction and changes in the upwind terrain.

Because it can be so difficult to directly determine the roughness parameters in a particular case, *morphometric models* have been developed which use algorithms to relate z_0 and d to generic measures of surface geometry. These models may be based on empirical observations of wind profiles in actual urban areas or in controlled settings, such as scale-modelled urban surfaces. In Table 4.3, first-order estimates of the roughness parameters of urban areas are shown for general categories of urban form, with the sole geometric measure being the average building height H. Using a convenient rule of thumb, z_0 may be approximated as one-tenth the canopy height, and d as approximately two-thirds of H.

Table 4.2 Typical roughness length (z_0) of homogeneous surfaces

Surface type	Roughness length (m)
Concrete, flat desert	0.0002–0.0005
Fallow ground	0.001–0.004
Short grass	0.008–0.03
Continuous bushland	0.35–0.45
Mature pine forest	0.8–1.6
Tropical forest	1.7–2.3
Dense low buildings (suburb)	0.4–0.7
Regularly built large town	0.7–1.5

Source: Based on Wieringa (1993).

A more versatile geometric measure used to express the form of buildings in a city is the *frontal area density*, or the ratio between the 'silhouette area' of the average obstacle A_F (i.e. the average vertical area 'seen' by the wind) and the average plan area per obstacle A_T (i.e. the total horizontal surface divided by the number of obstacles). A_T is defined so that if n is the number of obstacles in a given lot and A is the area of this lot, then $A_T = A/n$. As seen in Figure 4.13, the frontal area density may also be calculated as $A_F/A_T = \overline{L_y}H/\overline{D_x}\overline{D_y}$, where $\overline{L_y}$ is the mean breadth of the roughness elements perpendicular to the wind direction, H is their mean height, and $\overline{D_x}$ and $\overline{D_y}$ the average spacing between element centroids in the along-wind and crosswind directions, respectively. Another measure is the *plan area index*, or the ratio A_P/A_T, where A_P is the plan area covered by the roughness elements and A_T is the total area.

Early experiments showed that in simple geometric arrays, roughness length increases with the frontal area density (A_F/A_T) according to the linear function:[3]

$$z_0 = 0.5H\, A_F/A_T \qquad (4.8)$$

Table 4.3 Typical roughness properties of homogeneous zones in urban areas

Urban surface form	*H* (m)	*d* (m)	*z₀* (m)
Low height and density	5–8	2–5	0.3–0.7
Medium height and density	7–11	4–7	0.4–1.4
Tall and high density	11–18	7–13	1.0–2.2
High-rise	>18	>10	>2.0

Source: Grimmond and Oke (1998).

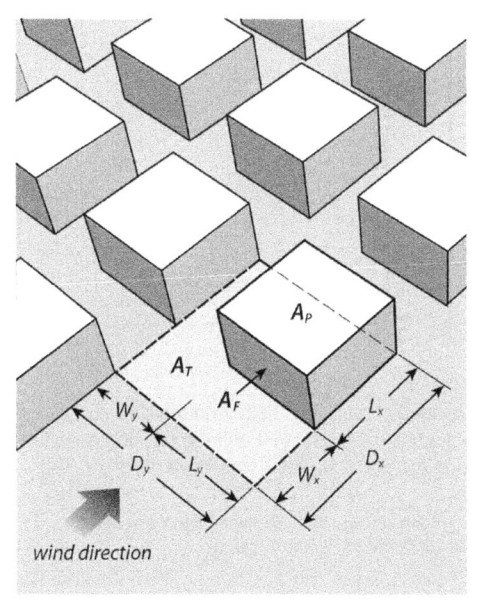

Figure 4.13 Definition of surface dimensions used in morphometric analysis, for describing the frontal area density (A_F/A_T) and plan area density (A_P/A_T)

More recent models[4] have shown that such an increase in roughness length is only applicable up to a frontal area density of approximately 0.1–0.2, or a plan area density of about 0.3–0.4, after which roughness levels off or even decreases with density due to smothering by consecutive roughness elements as skimming flow is reached, as depicted in Figure 4.14.

However this type of relationship between surface roughness and density has mainly been identified under controlled conditions, using for instance scale-model studies in wind tunnels – which often are not capable of reproducing a sufficiently long fetch or boundary-layer height to achieve similarity with realistic urban surfaces (and obviously not accounting for radiative and other thermal effects). Nonetheless, wind tunnel models have been used to provide general indications of the relationship between urban geometry and roughness parameters. For example, such experiments have found that building spacing may have less effect on roughness than does roof shape (at least in relatively dense configurations, characterized by skimming flow),[5] and that staggered building blocks increase roughness when compared to a regular grid.[6]

Using an open-air scaled urban surface,[7] roughness parameters have also been systematically defined under actual atmospheric conditions, relative to the height of regular block arrays. For a scaled building array with a frontal area density (A_F/A_T) of 0.2, the height-normalized roughness length (z_0/H) ranged from 0.13 to 0.19, and the normalized displacement (d/H) was in the range of 0.6–0.7. When the array density was doubled ($A_F/A_T = 0.4$), z_0/H decreased to 0.09–0.11 and d/H increased slightly to 0.7–0.8. As seen in Table 4.4, these values closely correspond to the ranges given in a wide-ranging survey of morphometric models.

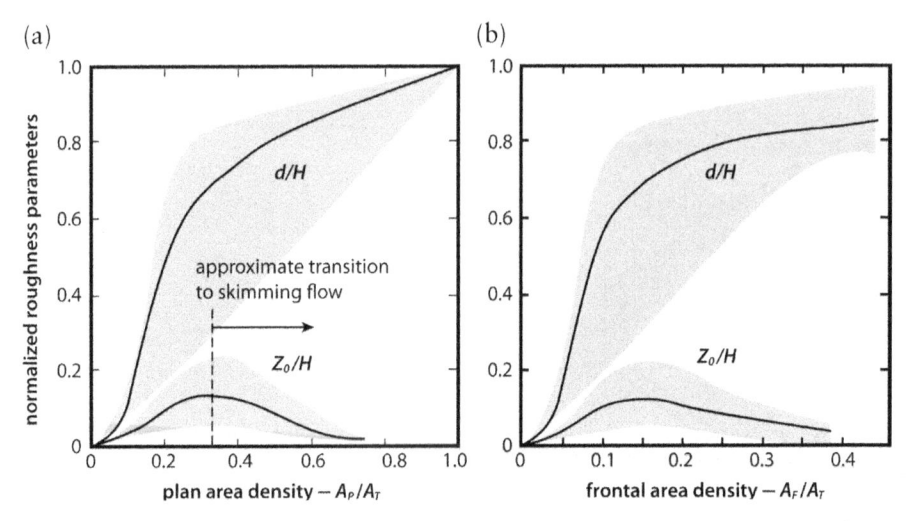

Figure 4.14 Conceptual representation of the relation between height-normalized roughness parameters (zero-plane displacement d/H and roughness length z_0/H) and the packing density of roughness elements, using (a) the plan area index A_P/A_T and (b) the frontal area density A_F/A_T

Note: The surface roughness rises to a peak at medium density, and then declines as the flow is 'smothered'. Shaded areas represent reasonable zones of variation.

Source: Redrawn from Grimmond and Oke (1999).

Table 4.4 Roughness parameters as a proportion of the urban canopy height, determined through (a) measurements above scale-modelled urban arrays (Pearlmutter et al, 2005) and (b) morphometric models surveyed by Grimmond and Oke (1999)

Frontal area density		Normalized roughness length (z_0/H)	Normalized zero-plane displacement (d/H)
$A^*/A' = 0.2$	(a)	0.13–0.19	0.60–0.70
	(b)	0.11–0.18	0.40–0.80
$A^*/A' = 0.4$	(a)	0.09–0.11	0.68–0.80
	(b)	0.07–0.12	0.65–0.95

It can be seen from Table 4.4 that in general terms, displacement height follows the rule by which d is close to $0.6H$–$0.7H$ and increases with density, while values of z_0/H do indeed decrease with the transition from medium to high density. It has been estimated that spreads of +/–25 per cent or more are to be expected from experimentally derived roughness parameters.[8]

Transforming a wind speed measured at a given height and terrain to another height or terrain

Unless wind speed is measured at an actual site we will need to rely upon data taken from a nearby meteorological station. Typically these measurements will be from an airport and recorded at a standard height of 10m. Applying such data in a different terrain type and/or at a different height requires the data to be transformed. Two methods of transformation can be used depending on whether we assume a power law or logarithmic wind profile:

A power law wind profile

It follows from the fundamental statement of the power law (Equation 4.5), and because the magnitude of the gradient wind V_G is assumed the same in all terrains in a given location, that the wind speed $\overline{U}(z_A)$ in one terrain measured at height z_A can be related to the wind speed $\overline{U}(z_B)$ in another terrain at height z_B by:

$$\overline{U}(z_B) = \overline{U}(z_A) \frac{(z_B)^\alpha (z'g)^{\alpha'}}{(z_A)^{\alpha'} (zg)^\alpha} \tag{4.9}$$

Here the primed values denote the values in terrain A, i.e. the terrain in which the wind speed is measured.

If now we define two terms β and β' such that:

$$\beta = \frac{(zg)^\alpha}{(zg)^\alpha} \text{ and } \beta' = \frac{(z'g)^{\alpha'}}{(zg)^\alpha} \tag{4.10}$$

then Equation 4.9 can be re-written as:

$$\overline{U}(z_B) = \overline{U}(z_A) \frac{\beta(z_B)^\alpha}{\beta'(z_A)^{\alpha'}} \qquad (4.11)$$

If it is assumed that the standard wind measurements $\overline{U}(z_A)$ are always taken in terrain class 2 as described in Table 4.5, for example at an airport in a flat open terrain, then the term $\dfrac{(z'_g)^{\alpha'}}{(z_g)^\alpha}$ can be normalized and determined for each terrain category.

Values of α and β for various terrain classes as shown in Table 4.5.

Table 4.5 Terrain factors

Terrain Class	Description	α	β
1	Ocean or other body of water with at least 5km of unrestricted expanse	0.10	1.37
2	Flat terrain with some isolated obstacles, e.g. buildings or tress well separated from each other	0.15	1.00
3	Rural areas with low buildings, trees, etc.	0.20	0.73
4	Urban, industrial or forest areas	0.25	0.53
5	Centre of large city	0.35	0.27

Source: Terrain descriptions and α values from Sherman (1980).

A logarithmic wind profile

If the wind speed is measured in terrain A and the log law (Equation 4.6) is applied then:

$$\overline{U}(z_A) = \frac{u_{*A}}{k} \ln\left(\frac{z_A - d_A}{z_{0A}}\right) \qquad (4.12)$$

where k is von Karman's constant (0.4).

Hence:

$$u_{*A} = \frac{k\overline{U}(z_A)}{\ln\left(\dfrac{z_A - d_A}{z_{0A}}\right)} \qquad (4.13)$$

For large scale atmospheric boundary-layers in synoptic winds a geostrophic drag coefficient may be defined such that $C_g = u_*/U_g$ where u_* is the friction velocity and U_g is the geostrophic wind speed.[9]

The Rossby number, R_0, is given by:

$$R_0 = \frac{U_g}{fz_0} \tag{4.14}$$

where f is the Coriolis parameter ($2\Omega\sin\lambda$, where Ω is the angular velocity at latitude λ).

The geostrophic drag coefficient may be obtained from either of the following relationships:[10, 11]

$$C_g = \frac{u_*}{U_g} \approx 0.16 R_0^{-0.09} \tag{4.15}$$

$$C_g \approx 0.111 R_0^{-0.07} \tag{4.16}$$

If we take the geostrophic wind to be the same in different terrains then a transformation of wind speeds from one terrain to another may be derived. In terrain A therefore:

$$U_g^{0.91} = \frac{u_{*A}}{0.16(fz_{0A})^{0.09}} \tag{4.17}$$

As U_g is the same in both terrains, in terrain B:

$$U_g^{0.91} = \frac{u_{*B}}{0.16(fz_{0B})^{0.09}} \tag{4.18}$$

Hence:

$$u_{*B} = \left(\frac{z_{0B}}{z_{0A}}\right)^{0.09} u_{*A} \tag{4.19}$$

Now calculate the wind speed at height z_B in terrain B using the log law:

$$\bar{U}(z_B) = \frac{u_{*B}}{k} \ln\left(\frac{z_B - d_B}{z_{0B}}\right) \tag{4.20}$$

Therefore to calculate the wind speed $\bar{u}(Z_B)$ at height Z_B in terrain B from a wind speed measurement $\bar{u}(Z_A)$ taken at height z_A in terrain A:

$$\bar{U}(z_B) = \left(\frac{z_{0B}}{z_{0A}}\right)^{0.09} \frac{\ln\left(\frac{z_B - d_B}{z_{0B}}\right)}{\ln\left(\frac{z_A - d_A}{z_{0A}}\right)} \bar{U}(z_A) \tag{4.21}$$

Effect of atmospheric stability on air-flow

The logarithmic wind profile described above (see Figure 4.12 and Equation 4.6) is valid in the absence of thermal buoyancy – that is, when a packet of air will have a tendency to neither rise nor subside. However, such a condition, described as *neutral* atmospheric stability, does not always exist: often the atmosphere is either *stable* (causing a parcel of air to subside) or *unstable* (causing it to rise).

Atmospheric stability is generally described by one of the following parameters:

1 The *Richardson number* (*Ri*) is the ratio of buoyancy forces (caused by vertical temperature differences) to inertial forces (caused by horizontal wind pressure) in the atmosphere, and may be calculated from gradients of temperature and wind speed:

$$Ri = \frac{g}{\overline{T}} \cdot \frac{(\Delta \overline{T}/\Delta z)}{(\Delta \overline{u}/\Delta z)^2} \qquad (4.22)$$

where g is the acceleration due to gravity, $\overline{T}$ is the mean temperature in a layer of air whose thickness is described by the height difference Δz and $\overline{u}$ is the mean horizontal wind speed in the layer. It can be seen that the absolute value of R_i increases as the vertical temperature difference ($\Delta \overline{T}$) becomes large in comparison to the vertical difference in wind speed ($\Delta \overline{u}$), signifying unstable conditions when Ri is negative, or stable conditions when it is positive. Conversely, when the thermal gradient is relatively small ($-0.01 < Ri < +0.01$), convection is considered to be 'fully forced' and stability is described as neutral.

2 The *Obukhov length*[12] is a function of fluxes of heat and momentum. It corresponds to the height at which the shear and buoyant production of turbulent kinetic energy are equal. It is negative under unstable conditions, infinite at neutral stability and positive in a stable atmosphere.

$$L = -\frac{\rho c_p T u_*^3}{kg Q_H} \qquad (4.23)$$

where ρ, c_p and T are the density of air, its specific heat and its absolute temperature, u_* is the friction velocity, k is the von Karman constant, g is the acceleration due to gravity and Q_H the turbulent sensible heat flux.

If atmospheric stability is not neutral, then the log-profile relationship (Equation 4.6) must be modified to account for buoyancy effects, as follows:

$$u_z = \frac{u_*}{\kappa}\left[\ln\left(\frac{z-z_d}{z_0}\right) - \Psi_m\left(\frac{z}{L}\right)\right] \qquad (4.24)$$

where ψm is a stability function and L is the Obukhov length.

Urban-scale wind

In near-calm conditions with relatively weak winds and clear skies, urban-scale thermal flows might become more dominant than regional winds. A thermally induced circulation may be generated due to the rising of heated air over the relatively warm urban terrain, and the subsequent convergence of air drawn in from the surroundings. Such a flow is directed radially inward towards the city centre at lower levels, and outward from the city centre at higher levels.

Urban-scale thermal winds have been predicted by several urbanized versions of meso-scale meteorological models, but empirical evidence remains mixed. Some studies suggest that while an *intra-urban thermal breeze* (IUTB) is possible, it occurs only at night (not in the daytime) and only in very specific meteorological conditions:

- if the urban heat island is strong,
- if there is a strong ground-based inversion and
- if the meso-scale wind is very weak.

Under such conditions, a decoupling of the lower layer of the atmosphere has been observed, with a weak surface flow (of about 0.3m s^{-1}) towards the city centre and a return flow of about the same magnitude found at rooftop level.

When the urban heat island generates a thermal breeze, the resulting advection may act as a self-regulating mechanism that reduces the urban–rural temperature difference: relatively cooler rural air is drawn into the city near the surface while warmer air is ejected upward and outward, thus eroding the temperature differential generating the flow.

A variant of the IUTB may occur in the presence of a fairly large park (~1km^2 in area) surrounded by built-up areas. In stable weather conditions with weak regional winds, a park cool island ($\Delta T_{u-p}>0$) is likely to occur, which may induce a local-scale thermal flow sometimes referred to as a park breeze. Air tends to subside over the relatively cool park, and a local air-flow of up to 0.5m s^{-1} is created outwards toward the built-up surroundings in all directions. Such flows are necessarily limited in extent, and may be felt less than 250m from the park border. They are best developed between two and six hours after sunset.

Notes

1. Davenport (1960).
2. Experimental work based on scintillometer measurements of atmospheric fluxes over a large source area suggests that the magnitude of the zero-plane displacement may vary with changes in atmospheric stability. Unstable conditions result in larger fluxes and hence stronger vertical flows, leading to greater mixing of the air in the canopy-layer and to smaller values of d.
3. Originally proposed by Lettau (1969), based on experiments using arrays of bushel baskets on a frozen lake.
4. See for example Raupach (1994), Bottema (1997) and MacDonald et al (1998)
5. Rafailidis (1997)
6. Bottema (1999)

7   Pearlmutter et al (2005)
8   MacDonald et al (1998)
9   Holmes (2007)
10 Lettau (1959)
11 Swinbank (1974)
12 The Monin-Obukhov similarity theory (MOST) provides the conceptual framework for describing the mean and turbulence structure of the stratified surface layer (the part of the atmosphere which is fully adapted to the surface but is above the height affected by individual roughness elements). This theory proposes that in a horizontally homogeneous layer the mean flow and turbulence characteristics depend only on four independent variables: the height above the surface (z); the friction velocity (u_*), the surface kinematic heat flux ($H_0/\rho c_p$); and the buoyancy variable (g/T_0). The theory requires several simplifying assumptions, as follows: the flow is horizontally homogeneous and quasi-stationary; the turbulent fluxes of momentum and heat are constant with height; molecular exchanges are insignificant in comparison with turbulent exchanges; Coriolis effects may be ignored; and the influence of surface roughness, boundary-layer height and geostrophic winds is fully accounted for through u_*. Because independent variables in the MOST involve three fundamental dimensions (length, time and temperature), according to Buckingham's theorem one can formulate only one independent dimensionless combination of them. The combination used in MOST is the buoyancy parameter ξ, so that $\xi = z/L$, where L is the Obukhov length. It is worth noting that experimental evidence suggests that in very stable conditions, the assumption of height-independent momentum flux may not be always be justified (Pahlow et al, 2001). Furthermore, Feigenwinter et al (1999) note that the assumption that turbulent fluxes are constant with height is not justified over rough urban terrain, except at very small spatial scale.

References

Aynsley, R., Melbourne, W. and Vickery B. (1977) *Architectural Aerodynamics*, Applied Science Publishers, London

Bottema, M. (1997) 'Urban roughness modelling in relation to pollutant dispersion', *Atmospheric Environment*, vol 31, no 18, pp3059–3075

Bottema, M. (1999) 'Towards rules of thumb for wind comfort and air quality', *Atmospheric Environment*, vol 33, pp4009–4017

Davenport, A. G. (1960) 'Rationale for determining design wind velocities', *Proceedings of the American Society of Civil Engineers: Structural Division*, vol 86, pp39–63

Davenport, A. G. (1965) 'The relationship of wind structure to wind loading', in *National Physical Laboratory, Symposium No. 16, Wind Effects on Buildings and Structures*, Her Majesty's Stationery Office, London, pp54–102

Feigenwinter, C., Vogt, R. and Parlow, E. (1999) 'Vertical structure of selected turbulence characteristics above an urban canopy', *Theoretical and Applied Climatology*, vol 62, pp51–63

Grimmond, C. S. B. and Oke, T. R. (1999) 'Aerodynamic properties of urban areas derived from analysis of surface form', *Journal of Applied Meteorology*, vol 38, pp1262–1292

Holmes, J. (2007) *Wind Loading of Structures*, Taylor & Francis, London

Hotchkiss, R. and Harlow, F. (1973) *Air Pollution Transport in Street Canyons*, EPA-R4-73-029, U. S. Environmental Protection Agency, Washington, DC

Hussain, M. and Lee, B. E. (1980) 'A wind tunnel study of the mean pressure forces acting on large groups of low rise buildings', *Journal of Wind Engineering and Industrial Aerodynamics*, vol 6, pp207–225

Lettau, H. H. (1959) 'Wind profile, surface stress and geostrophic drag coefficients in the atmospheric surface layer', *Symposium on Atmospheric Diffusion and Air Pollution*, New York, Academic Press

Lettau, H. (1969) 'Note on aerodynamic roughness-parameter estimation on the basis of roughness-element description', *Journal of Applied Meteorology*, vol 8, no 5, pp828–832

MacDonald, R. W., Griffiths, R. F. and Hall, D. J. (1998) 'An improved method for the estimation of surface roughness of obstacle arrays', *Atmospheric Environment*, vol 32, no 11, pp1857–1864

Oke, T. R. (1987) *Boundary Layer Climates*, Methuen, London and New York

Oke, T. (1988) 'Street design and urban canopy layer climate', *Energy and Buildings*, vol 11, pp103–113

Pahlow, M., Parlange, M. B. and Porté-Agel, F. (2001) 'On Monin-Obukhov similarity in the stable atmospheric boundary layer', *Boundary-Layer Meteorology*, vol 99, no 2, pp225–248

Pearlmutter, D., Berliner, P. and Shaviv, E. (2005) 'Evaluation of urban surface energy fluxes using an open-air scale model', *Journal of Applied Meteorology*, vol 44, no 4, pp532–545

Rafailidis, S. (1997) 'Influence of building areal density and roof shape on the wind characteristics above a town', *Boundary-Layer Meteorology*, vol 85, no 2, pp255–271

Raupach, M. R. (1994) 'Simplified expressions for vegetation roughness length and zero-plane displacement as functions of canopy height and area index', *Boundary-Layer Meteorology*, vol 71, pp211–216

Sherman, M. H. (1980) 'Air Infiltration in Buildings', PhD thesis, Lawrence Berkeley Laboratory, University of California, Berkeley

Swinbank, W. C. (1974) 'The geostrophic drag coefficient', *Boundary-Layer Meteorology*, vol 7, no 1, pp125–127

Wieringa, J. (1993) 'Representative roughness parameters for homogeneous terrain', *Boundary-Layer Meteorology*, vol 63, no 4, pp323–363

Xie, X., Huang, Z., Wang, J. and Xie, Z. (2005) 'The impact of solar radiation and street layout on pollutant dispersion in street canyons', *Building & Environment*, vol 40, no 2, pp201–212

Yamartino, R. J. and Wiegand, G. (1986) 'Development and evaluation of simple models for the flow, turbulence and pollutant concentration fields within an urban street canyon', *Atmospheric Environment*, vol 20, no 11, pp2137–2156

Additional reading

Alberts, W. (1982) 'Modeling the wind in the town planning process', *Energy and Buildings*, vol 4, no 1, pp71–76

Al-Sallal, K. A., AboulNaga, M. M. and Alteraifi, A. M. (2001) 'Impact of urban spaces and building height on airflow distribution: Wind tunnel testing of an urban setting prototype in Abu-Dhabi City', *Architectural Science Review*, vol 44, no 3, pp227–232

Baik, J., Park, R., Chun, H. and Kim, J. (2000) 'A laboratory model of urban street-canyon flows', *Journal of Applied Meteorology*, vol 39, no 9, pp1592–1600

Cermak, J. E. (1995) 'Physical modelling of flow and dispersion over urban areas', in J. E. Cermak, A. G. Davenport, E. J. Plate and D. X. Viegas (eds) *Wind Climate in Cities*, Kluwer Academic Publishers, Dordrecht, The Netherlands

DePaul, F. T. and Sheih, C. M. (1986) 'Measurements of wind velocities in a street canyon', *Atmospheric Environment*, vol 20, no 3, pp455–459

Eliasson, I. and Upmanis, H. (2000) 'Nocturnal airflow from urban parks – implications for city ventilation', *Theoretical and Applied Climatology*, vol 66, pp95–107

Garratt, J. R. (1992) *The Atmospheric Boundary Layer*, Cambridge University Press, Cambridge

Givoni, B. and Paciuk, M. (1972) *Effect of High-Rise Buildings on Airflow Around Them*, Building Research Station, Technion, Haifa, Israel

Goliger, A. M. and Milford, R. V. (1991) 'The influence of upwind topography on the development of the boundary layer profile over a city centre', *Journal of Wind Engineering and Industrial Aerodynamics*, vol 38, nos 2–3, pp123–130

Grimmond, C. S. B., King, T. S., Roth, M. and Oke, T. R. (1998) 'Aerodynamic roughness of urban areas derived from wind observations', *Boundary-Layer Meteorology*, vol 89, pp1–24

Haeger-Eugensson, M. and Holmer, B. (1999) 'Advection caused by the urban heat island circulation as a regulating factor on the nocturnal urban heat island', *International Journal of Climatology*, vol 19, no 9, pp975–988

Hunter, L. J., Watson, I. D. and Johnson, G. T. (1990–1991) 'Modeling air flow regimes in urban canyons', *Energy and Buildings*, vols 15–16, nos 3–4, pp315–324

Hunter, L. J., Watson, I. D. and Johnson, G. T. (1991) 'Modeling air flow regimes in urban canyons', *Energy and Buildings*, vol 15, pp315–324

Johnson, G. T. and Hunter, L. J. (1999) 'Some insights into typical urban canyon airflows', *Atmospheric Environment*, vol 33, no 24, pp3991–3999

Johnson, G. T., Hunter, L. J. and Arnfield A. J. (1990) 'Preliminary field test of an urban canyon wind flow model', *Energy and Buildings*, vol 15, nos 3–4, pp325–332

Louka, P., Belcher, S. E. and Harrison, R. G. (2000) 'Coupling between air flow in streets and the well-developed boundary layer aloft', *Atmospheric Environment*, vol 34, no 16, pp2613–2621

MacDonald, R. W. (2000) 'Modelling the mean velocity profile in the urban canopy layer', *Boundary-Layer Meteorology*, vol 97, no 1, pp25–45

Plate, E. J. (1999) 'Methods of investigating urban wind fields – physical models', *Atmospheric Environment*, vol 33, pp3981–3989

Rooney, G. G. (2001) 'Comparison of upwind land use and roughness length measured in the urban boundary layer', *Boundary-Layer Meteorology*, vol 100, no 3, pp469–486

Uehara, K., Murakami, S., Oikawa, S. and Wakamatsu, S. (2000) 'Wind tunnel experiments on how thermal stratification affects flow in and above urban street canyons', *Atmospheric Environment*, vol 34, no 10, pp1553–1562

Yersel, M. and Goble, R. (1986) 'Roughness effects on urban turbulence parameters', *Boundary-Layer Meteorology*, vol 37, no 3, pp271–284

5
The Energy Balance of a Human Being in an Urban Space

Human thermal comfort is both physiological and perceptual. Each person may experience differently the thermal qualities of a particular place at a given point in time, but the underlying basis for this thermal sensation is the manner in which that person's body is physically heated, and in turn dissipates heat to the surrounding environment.

Recent studies have uncovered a wide range of variability in the limits of temperature, humidity and other climatic descriptors that together define the comfort zone, since different populations tend to become acclimatized to different sets of conditions – and even within a given population, the sense of discomfort may arise due to a person's physical activity or even frame of mind. Nevertheless, it is well understood that thermal discomfort is essentially caused by heating or cooling of the body that is too rapid. Our physiology includes mechanisms for maintaining thermal equilibrium with the environment, and our preferences tend to lead us, both instinctually and consciously, to avoid the extreme loss or gain of thermal energy. Therefore, any understanding of how the design of the urban environment may promote thermal comfort (or discomfort) will necessarily include a description of the mechanisms through which the body exchanges energy with its surroundings.

In an outdoor urban setting, which typically provides less shelter from sun and wind than the interior of a building, there are two important mechanisms of this sort that are closely dependent on the architectural attributes of the space, and which will be discussed in this chapter:

- the absorption and emission of energy in the form of radiation;
- the absorption – or, most commonly, dissipation – of heat by convection.

Under warm conditions the body also dissipates heat by evaporation (through sweating and respiration, as discussed below within the context of overall thermal stress). To the extent that the body comes in direct contact with other surfaces, it will also gain or lose heat by conduction (this mechanism will be discussed largely with respect to clothing effects).

Radiation

Radiation is a highly variable, and often dominant, component of the energy balance in urban open spaces.[1] Within the confines of a building a person is likely to be shielded from intense solar radiation, and the temperature of room surfaces often remains close to that of the interior air – to the extent that the indoor thermal environment may in many cases be described by a simple temperature, without regard for the 'radiant field' surrounding an occupant.

Outdoor spaces that make up the urban environment differ fundamentally from the enclosed room; pedestrians experience wide fluctuations in thermal stimuli due to radiation in two forms. The first of these is short-wave radiation, emitted from the extremely hot surface of the sun and commonly referred to as sunlight, although about half of this radiation in fact lies in the non-visible, near infra-red range of the spectrum. The second is long-wave (or thermal) radiation, which is emitted by the atmosphere and by lower-temperature terrestrial surfaces that surround us in the built environment. Both forms of radiation may be expressed in terms of the rate at which energy is absorbed (or emitted) by a unit area of the surface of our body (W m^{-2}), and combined as a total net exchange of radiation R_n between the body and the urban environment (see Figure 5.1):

$$R_n = (K_{dir} + K_{dif} + K_h + K_v)(1-\alpha_s) + L_d + L_h + L_v - L_s \qquad (5.1)$$

In this equation, the short-wave portion of the pedestrian radiation balance R_n is further sub-divided into the following components:

- K_{dir} – direct short-wave radiation incident on the body
- K_{dif} – diffuse short-wave radiation incident on the body
- K_h – indirect radiation incident on the body, reflected from horizontal surfaces
- K_v – indirect radiation incident on the body, reflected from vertical surfaces.

with α_s representing the albedo of the skin and/or clothing, such that $(1-\alpha_s)$ is the proportion of all incident short-wave radiation that is absorbed by the body.

In the same equation, the long-wave radiation is sub-divided as:

- L_d – long-wave radiation incident on the body, emitted downwards by the sky
- L_h – long-wave radiation incident on the body, emitted by horizontal surfaces
- L_v – long-wave radiation incident on the body, emitted by vertical surfaces
- L_s – long-wave radiation emitted by the body to the environment.

All the above radiation components represent energy sources which cumulatively heat the body, except for the last – outgoing long-wave emission from the body itself – which represents cooling, and is therefore a negative term in the equation. The following discussion illustrates how the magnitude of each term is influenced by the design of the urban environment.

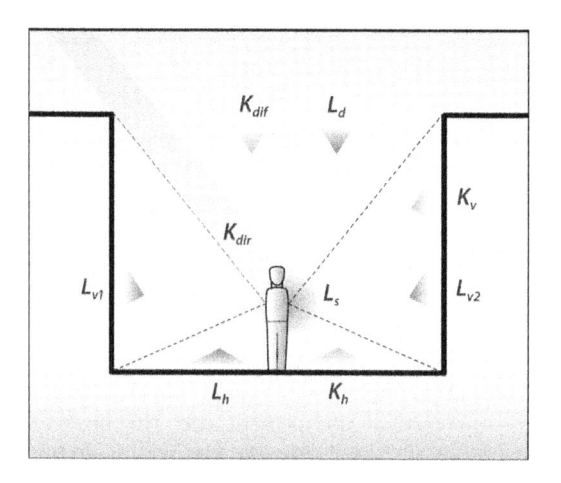

Figure 5.1 Schematic depiction of radiation exchanges between a pedestrian and the surrounding urban environment (see text for definition of components)

Source: Based on Monteith and Unsworth (1990); Pearlmutter et al (1999; 2006).

Short-wave radiation

In mid-latitude regions, pedestrians are liable to suffer most severely from thermal stress due to overheating during the midday hours of the summer season. It is during this period that solar (i.e. short-wave) radiation is most intense, and the extent to which people and surfaces are exposed to this radiation is likely to be the over-riding determinant of thermal comfort within city spaces. A pedestrian's body may be unshaded, and thus exposed to solar rays arriving directly from the direction of the sun (i.e. *direct radiation*). It may also absorb solar energy indirectly, by way of *diffuse radiation* which is scattered by the atmosphere and thus arrives from the entire vault of the sky, or due to the reflection of sunlight from adjacent building and ground surfaces (*reflected radiation*). The sun's short-wave radiation also heats the body in an even more indirect way, by raising the temperature of adjacent surfaces and increasing the emission of long-wave radiation (see more detailed discussion later in this chapter).

Direct radiation, because of its directionality, is decisively influenced by geometry – that is, by the three-dimensional geometry of the urban space and by the solar geometry (the relative position of the sun in the sky at a particular time and location). Exposure to direct radiation is further influenced by a person's particular body shape, as well as his or her posture (e.g. sitting, standing, facing toward or away from the sun, etc.).

The body's exposure may also be differentiated by its different parts, distinguishing for example between the varied effects of direct sun on the face or limbs or between the absorption on clothed or bare areas. For a useful description of solar exposure in a given urban space, however, the shape of the human body may be approximated by a simple geometric form. A common model used to represent a standing or walking pedestrian is an upright cylinder with defined proportions of vertical (outward-facing) and horizontal (upward-facing) surface area, as seen in Figure 5.1.

Using this cylindrical approximation of a standing body, the exposure of a pedestrian to direct short-wave radiation is given by:

$$K_{dir} = I_{dir}(\frac{\tan\theta_z}{\pi}SC_{sv} + SC_{sh}) \quad (5.2)$$

in which I_{dir} is the intensity of direct radiation on a horizontal plane (i.e. the difference between measured global and diffuse radiation) in W m^{-2}, and θ_z is the zenith angle of the sun (or the complement of its altitude, which is measured as the angle of elevation above the horizon). The terms SC_{sv} and SC_{sh} are the respective shading coefficients for the vertical side surface and horizontal top surface of the cylinder, which define the proportions of total body surface that are actually exposed to direct sun (a shading coefficient of one means that the entire surface of the body is exposed to direct sunlight, and a value of zero is complete shade).

It should be noted that I_{dir} is the vertical component (i.e. the intensity measured normal to the horizontal plane) of the solar beam, and is thus distinct from direct beam intensity, which is measured normal to a plane tilted to face the sun at the given time and location (see Figure 5.2).

The sun's zenith angle θ_z, which is the complement of the solar altitude angle ($ALT = 90 - \theta_z$), is a function of geographic location (primarily latitude) and time (hour of the day and day of the year):

$$\cos\theta_z = \sin ALT = \sin L \sin d + \cos L \cos d \cos h \quad (5.3a)$$

where L is latitude (in degrees north or south), d is the solar declination angle (between the sun's rays and the equatorial plane, as a function of the day of the year):

$$d = -23.4\cos[360(day + 10)/365] \quad (5.3b)$$

and h is the hour angle, a function of the local apparent solar time t:[2]

$$h = 15(12 - t) \quad (5.3c)$$

Using a symmetrical model of the human body (such as the vertical cylinder described above), the shading coefficients SC_v and SC_h may be determined from

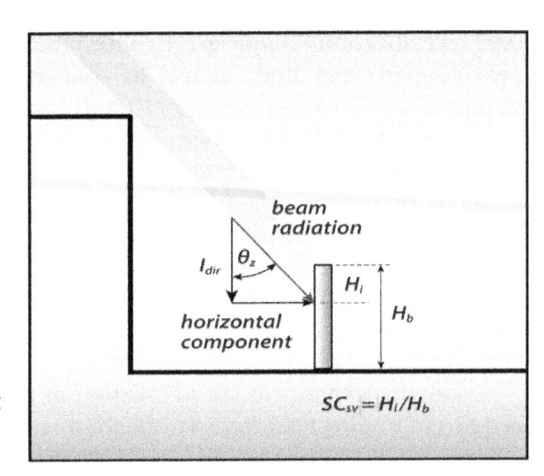

Figure 5.2 Schematic section showing components in the calculation of direct radiation on a pedestrian body, looking perpendicular to the solar rays

the geometry of the walls, trees and other obstacles which cast shadows on the body by blocking direct solar rays at a given point in time. In order to account for the location and/or direction of obstructions which cast a shadow on the body at a given point in time, the solar azimuth angle AZ (in degrees, clockwise from north) is also required:

$$\cos AZ = (\cos L \sin d + \sin L \cos d \cos h) / \sin \theta_z \quad (5.4)$$

(when t > 12, the angle value is subtracted from 360°).

Methods for quantifying the shading coefficient vary depending on the complexity of the space, and are discussed in Chapter 10 for the special case of an urban street canyon. For irregular arrangements, 3D solid modelling software can be used to provide visual (and in some cases quantitative) expressions of shadows on a defined object at a particular location. Regardless of the type of space, the relative exposure of vertical and horizontal body surfaces depends on the specific cylinder proportions (i.e. height and diameter) used, though typically the upward-facing top surface accounts for less than 10 per cent of the total area.

Diffuse radiation is assumed to come from a source which is evenly distributed across the sky, i.e. it is isotropic, which is a useful approximation in most cases. The exposure of a pedestrian's body to the diffuse component K_{dif} is limited, therefore, by its angle of view towards the sky, and given by:

$$K_{dif} = I_{dif} \overline{SVF} \quad (5.5)$$

I_{dif} is the intensity of diffuse radiation on an open horizontal plane (as measured, for example, by a pyranometer with an opaque band obstructing the direct solar rays). The diffuse component is typically equal to between 15 and 20 per cent of the global radiation under clear skies, but this ratio rises with cloudiness (see Figure 5.3). $\overline{SVF}$ is the average SVF as 'seen' by a pedestrian.

The SVF is presented in Chapter 1 as a descriptor of the urban space geometry, in which case it is normally measured from a point on the horizontal upward-facing ground. A point on the vertical cylinder surface representing a standing person can be exposed, at most, to half the sky vault, so its maximum average SVF is 0.5. As seen in Figure 5.1, the body is exposed to walls and ground as well, and the total of all these view factors will add up to one. An average view factor may be obtained by integrating over the height of the body, or it may simply be calculated at a representative height such as the mid-point or the head-height.

As with the shading coefficient, the pedestrian SVF may be estimated by a number of methods, each of which is appropriate for a different set of urban space types. For a regular urban canyon the calculation is relatively straightforward (as described in Chapter 10). For complex and irregular spaces fish-eye lens imaging or numerical modelling may be required (see Chapter 1).

Reflected radiation is also treated as a diffuse input, emanating from each surface – walls, paving, soil, vegetation, etc. – that is 'seen' by the pedestrian's body. While a person in an urban space of interest is likely to be surrounded by a multitude of different elements made of various materials, some simplifying

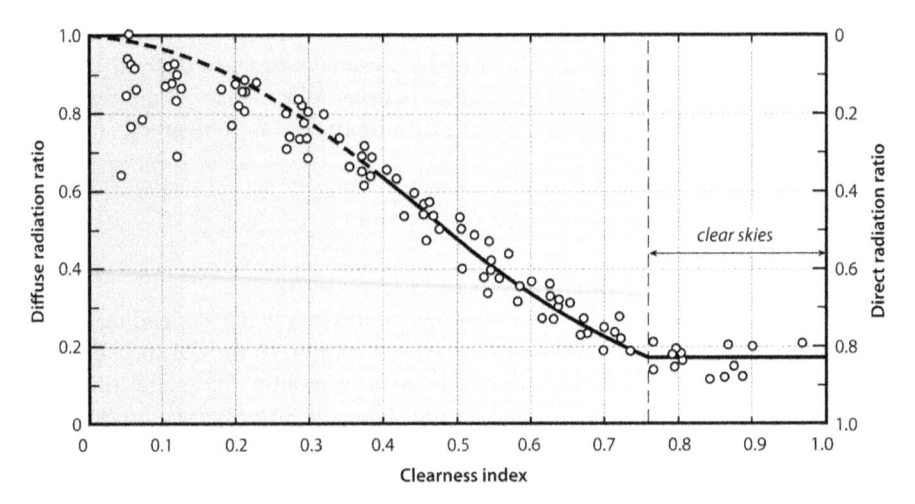

Figure 5.3 The relation between the diffuse component of global radiation and the cloudiness index

Source: Based on Liu and Jordan (1960).

assumptions may be made to characterize these surfaces. The first distinction that may be made is between horizontal surfaces, mainly at ground level, and vertical facets of buildings and other objects of significant height. The exposure of a pedestrian to reflected radiation from the horizontal ground plane K_h is given by:

$$K_h = I_{dir} SC_h \alpha_h \overline{FVF} \tag{5.6}$$

where I_{dir} is, as above, the incoming direct radiation incident on a fully exposed horizontal plane; SC_h is the shading coefficient (the proportion of the actual ground plane which is exposed to direct sun), α_h is the albedo, or solar reflectivity, of this plane, and $\overline{FVF}$ is the average floor view factor (FVF) which expresses the angle of exposure between the pedestrian body and the ground surface.

The shading coefficient of the ground surface may be a simple function of the urban space and solar geometry, as in the case of a regular street canyon (see Chapter 10) or it may involve complex patterns of shade cast by trees, structures and other objects. In the latter case, 3D solid modelling or site photography may aid in its estimation. The albedo of paving and landscape materials varies with the brightness of their colour as well as with their texture, and can be estimated by referring to data such as the sample values in Table 2.1 (Chapter 2). The floor view factor, as with the previously described SVF, may be averaged over the body height or calculated at a representative point. In the case of a regular street canyon its value may be calculated directly (see Chapter 10), and for other types of spaces, methods such as 3D modelling or fish-eye lens photography are once again useful.

If the ground surface surrounding a pedestrian comprises a variety of materials and cannot be reasonably characterized by a single reflectivity value, then K_h may be estimated cumulatively for each upward-facing part of the landscape by summing the separate products of shading coefficient, albedo and view factor.

Vertical surfaces are likely to be a smaller source of reflected radiation than horizontal surfaces facing upward, because they often receive less direct sunlight themselves – either when midday sun angles are high, or when they are 'self-shaded' (i.e. facing away from the sun). In other cases, however, reflection from walls is a significant component of the radiation balance. The exposure of a pedestrian to reflected radiation from a vertical surface (K_v) is given by:

$$K_v = I_{dir}(\frac{\tan\theta_z \cos\phi}{2})SC_v\alpha_v \overline{WVF} \qquad (5.7)$$

where I_{dir} is direct radiation (as above), θ_z is once again the zenith angle, ϕ is the azimuth angle of the sun relative to the wall (i.e. the angle of incidence as seen in plan view), SCv is the wall's shading coefficient and α_v its albedo, and $\overline{WVF}$ is the average wall view factor between the pedestrian and the upright wall surface (refer to Figure 5.1).[3]

Quantification of individual wall view factors may be far from straightforward in a variegated urban setting, though the calculation is simplified in a regular street canyon (Chapter 10). Even for irregular spaces, it is possible to quantify the total WVF (i.e. of all surrounding vertical surfaces) as the 'residual' in the overall field of view, once SVF and FVF are known:

$$WVF = 1 - (SVF + FVF) \qquad (5.8)$$

Note that in order to use this overall view factor in estimating the body's exposure to reflection from multiple walls, it is necessary to take a weighted average of the reflected radiation intensity emanating from each surface (as given by the other terms in Equation 5.7).

It bears mentioning that the exposure of building facades to direct solar radiation is crucial to the internal energy balance of the buildings, as well as that of the outdoor space. This is most pertinent for those wall areas containing glazed openings, which may transmit excessive radiation under hot conditions or be utilized for solar gain in winter. An accurate accounting of the solar exposure of window openings will usually include indirect (i.e. diffuse and reflected) radiation as well as direct radiation, and it is important to note that Equation 5.7 above – which is useful for outdoor spaces – expresses the reflection from walls based only on the direct radiation that is incident on the walls themselves.

While the body is exposed to direct, diffuse and reflected radiation as detailed thus far, it will only absorb a portion of this energy. The actual short-wave absorption is influenced firstly by the person's clothing (including any sun hat, parasol or other implements used), and secondly by the actual absorptivity ($1-\alpha_s$) of the body itself. When characterizing the radiant load within a given urban space, it is necessary to define these attributes and hold them constant in any direct comparison of design alternatives. For typical summer conditions, it is common to simplify the calculation by assuming light clothing and applying to the whole body a skin albedo in the range of $\alpha_s = 0.3–0.4$.

Long-wave radiation

A person standing between buildings and other elements in an urban space is exposed to the long-wave radiation that is emitted from each of these upright surfaces, as well as from the ground and the sky. The extent of the pedestrian's exposure to emission from each of these sources will depend upon the temperature and upon the emissivity of the respective part of the surrounding environment and upon its corresponding view factor.

Downward long-wave radiation emitted by the atmosphere (L_d) is given by:

$$L_d = L\downarrow \overline{SVF} \qquad (5.9)$$

in which $L\downarrow$ is the intensity of long-wave radiation emitted by the sky, which may be estimated by a variety of methods, as described in Chapter 2. One such method uses the air temperature at screen height, assigning an appropriate emissivity to obtain a close approximation of measured atmospheric radiation in most conditions. The value of the *sky emissivity* thus defined is typically in the range of 0.75–0.85, increasing with the concentration of water vapour in the air. As seen in Figure 5.4, this means that emissivity rises with both temperature and relative humidity, and it is still higher when skies are not clear, with the proportional increase a function of the fraction of sky covered by clouds or fog.

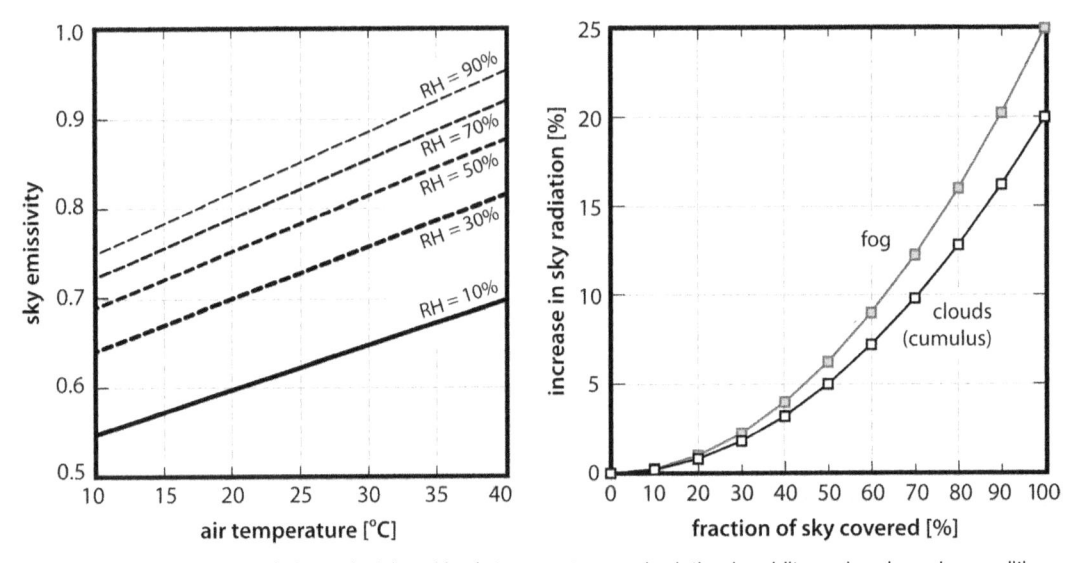

Figure 5.4 The variation of sky emissivity with air temperature and relative humidity under clear-sky conditions (left), and the percentage increase in long-wave radiation as a function of cloud or fog cover (right)

Note: Based on Equation 2.12 and Table 2.4 (see Chapter 2).

Outgoing long-wave radiation emitted respectively by horizontal (L_h) and vertical (L_v) surfaces is computed as:

$$L_h = \varepsilon_h \sigma T_h^4 \overline{FVF} \tag{5.10}$$

and:

$$L_v = \varepsilon_v \sigma T_v^4 \overline{WVF} \tag{5.11}$$

with the subscripts h and v referring to horizontal and vertical surfaces, and the view factors $\overline{FVF}$ and $\overline{WVF}$ defined as previously. The surface emissivity of most materials commonly found in urban settings, as seen in Table 3.2, is in the range of 0.90–0.95. The prominent exceptions are metals such as polished aluminium and galvanized steel – materials whose low emissivity (and, by definition, low absorptivity) in the far infra-red range of the spectrum essentially makes them 'heat mirrors'.[4]

The radiant temperatures of horizontal and vertical surfaces (T_h and T_v respectively) are in many cases similar to the adjacent outdoor air temperature, especially when shaded. However, when these paving and wall materials are exposed to direct sun their surface temperature may be elevated by as much as tens of degrees. This surface temperature, which is influenced by solar absorption as well as contact with the air, may be approximated by the *sol-air temperature* (see Box 5.1).

The radiant field within an urban space may also be described by the mean radiant temperature (MRT), which provides an integrated expression of the incoming radiation at a particular point[5] (see Box 5.2). The MRT is a central element in thermal comfort indices such as the physiological equivalent temperature (PET), which is discussed in Chapter 6.

Finally, in addition to incoming radiation absorbed by the body due to all of the sources mentioned thus far, long-wave radiation is emitted from the body to the environment, with this flux (L_s) calculated simply as:

$$L_s = \varepsilon_s \sigma T_s^4 \tag{5.15}$$

where the emissivity ε_s of skin and/or clothing may be estimated as 0.9 and its surface temperature T_s may be usefully approximated as 34–35°C (about 308K). The actual temperature of the body will depend on the entire energy balance and will change with time upon exposure to a given set of outdoor conditions. As detailed below, however, the body regulates its temperature through mechanisms such as metabolic activity and sweat secretion, and therefore T_s normally varies only within a small range of several degrees.

Box 5.1 Sol-air temperature

The sol-air temperature ($T_{sol-air}$) is defined as the outdoor temperature which will cause the same rate of heat flow at the surface and the same temperature distribution throughout the material as results from the actual outdoor air temperature and net radiation exchange between the surface and its environment. It may be estimated as follows:

$$T_{sol-air} = T_a + \frac{(K_{abs} - \varepsilon L^*)}{h_o} \tag{5.12}$$

where T_a is the temperature of air in the immediate vicinity, K_{abs} is the intensity of short-wave radiation absorbed by the surface, L^* is the net long-wave radiation at the surface, ε is the surface's long-wave emissivity and h_o is a heat transfer coefficient. K_{abs} is given in terms similar to those in Equations 5.6 and 5.7:

$$K_{abs} = (1 - \alpha_h) I_{dir} SC_h \quad \text{(for horizontal surfaces)} \tag{5.13}$$

$$K_{abs} = (1 - \alpha_v)(\tan\theta_z \cos\phi) I_{dir} SC_v \quad \text{(for vertical surfaces)} \tag{5.14}$$

The long-wave balance L^* is difficult to estimate if the temperature of the surface is unknown. When estimating $T_{sol-air}$ in a dense urban setting with a narrow SVF, this term may be neglected since the temperature differences and thermal exchanges between adjacent surfaces are likely to be small. However, if the surface is exposed to direct sunlight, it may be necessary to obtain it by iterative calculation of the expression above until $T_{sol-air}$ is obtained to any desired accuracy. The coefficient h_o depends on several factors, such as the shape of the surface and its orientation, and, most importantly, on airspeed. (For a more detailed discussion see Chapter 2; examples of empirical correlations between air speed and the transfer coefficient are given in Table 2.4.)

Given the uncertainties involved in calculating sol-air temperatures accurately from solar radiation and air temperature, a useful estimation of long-wave radiation may require measuring radiant surface temperatures directly. Obviously this approach is more feasible in existing urban spaces than in those being planned, although physical scale models (with appropriate thermodynamic scaling, as discussed in Chapter 11) have recently been used for the latter purpose as well. The measurement of radiant wall and ground surface temperatures may be done remotely with infra-red sensors and thermal imagery (requiring a close estimate of the surface emissivity) or with shielded sensors in contact with the relevant surface. Pyrgeometers can also be used to obtain long-wave intensity directly from each direction (sky, ground and various wall orientations) if such an instrumental set-up is feasible.

Box 5.2 Mean radiant temperature

The mean radiant temperature (MRT) is defined as the uniform temperature of an imaginary enclosure in which radiant energy exchange with the body equals the radiant exchange in the actual non-uniform enclosure. While the concept of MRT is fairly straightforward in the confined setting of an enclosed room, its estimation outdoors is subject to considerable complexities and uncertainties.

One way of estimating the MRT in a complex urban space is by using globe thermometers, which were originally developed for measuring MRT indoors. A number of researchers have refined the use of this tool for outdoor application, replacing the standard 150mm blackened hollow copper sphere with smaller, lighter variations. Calculation of the MRT from globe temperature is based on an assumed equilibrium between the radiation balance and convective heat exchange of the globe. However, the thermal response time of the metal ball (20–30 minutes) is often too slow for this equilibrium to be maintained in practice when exposed to rapidly changing outdoor conditions.

To overcome this problem, a version of the globe thermometer has been adopted in recent years that comprises a 38mm diameter acrylic grey-globe, made by painting a ping-pong ball with a flat grey coating (RAL 7001) to approximate the typical absorptivity of skin and clothing. The globe temperature, which is taken to represent the average temperature of the sphere's outer surface, is measured by placing a temperature sensor at the centre of the ball. However, calculation of the MRT based on this temperature requires an accurate estimate of the air temperature and velocity in the immediate vicinity, and is quite sensitive to radiation asymmetry and other variables. The equation given by ASHRAE (2001) with empirical coefficients recently refined by Thorsson et al (2007) is:

$$MRT = \left[(T_g + 273.15)^4 + \frac{1.335 \times 10^8 v_a^{0.71}}{\varepsilon_g \times D^{0.4}} \times (T_g - T_a)\right]^{1/4} - 273.15$$

where T_g is the globe temperature (°C), V_a is air velocity (m s⁻¹), T_a is air temperature (°C), D is the globe diameter (mm) and ε_g is the globe emissivity.

Convection

A body exchanges heat with the surrounding air through thermal convection due to local air temperature differences and through forced convection due to wind. In typical outdoor situations where the latter is dominant, the rate of convective heat transfer C per unit area of the body may be given (in W m⁻²) as:

$$C = h_c \Delta T \tag{5.16}$$

where h_c is a heat transfer coefficient (W m⁻²K⁻¹) dependent on wind speed, and ΔT (K) is the mean difference between body surface temperature T_s (which may be taken for general purposes as a constant 35°C) and the surrounding air temperature T_a.

For a rotationally symmetric standing or walking person, represented by a vertical cylinder of diameter 0.17m (see Figure 5.5), the transfer coefficient h_c may be estimated by the empirical relation:[6]

$$h_c = 8.3v^{0.6} \qquad (5.17)$$

where v is the horizontal wind speed (in ms^{-1}) averaged over the height of the body.

Note that the heat transfer by convection is expressed in the same units of energy flux density (W m^{-2}) as all of the radiation components described above. Under most conditions (unless air temperature is above 35°C), the convective exchange represents heat removed from the body, i.e. cooling.

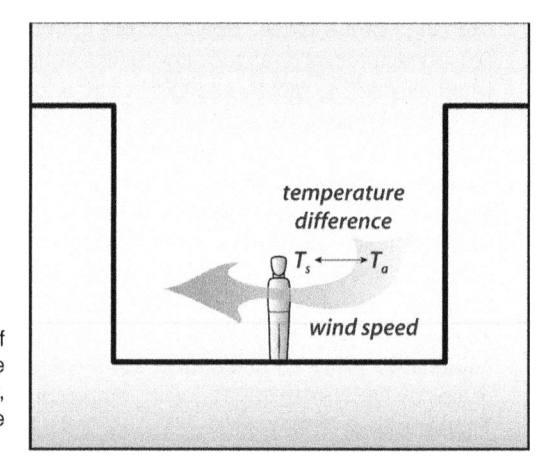

Figure 5.5 Schematic depiction of convective heat exchange between the standing body and urban environment, as a function of the skin–air temperature difference and horizontal wind speed

Metabolism, work, perspiration and thermal stress

The discussion in this chapter so far has dealt with the energy exchange between a human being and the urban environment by radiation and by convection. However, in warm conditions heat loss due to evaporation from the body must also be accounted for. One way to deal with this evaporative cooling is by means of a model for physiological heat exchange, such as the Index of Thermal Stress (ITS)[7]. The ITS expresses the overall thermal exchange between the body and its surroundings under warm conditions, with evaporation accounted for in a detailed manner. An additional feature of the ITS is that it allows physiological heat exchange under warm conditions to be expressed in terms of perceived thermal sensation, based on empirical observations of subjective comfort response that have been made under measured conditions, as discussed below. It has been characterized as the most comprehensive index for the general evaluation of environmental heat stress.[8]

The ITS is a measure of the rate at which the human body must give up moisture to the environment in order to maintain thermal equilibrium. Under warm conditions, the human body attempts to maintain thermal equilibrium through several mechanisms of evaporative cooling, particularly through the production of sweat. The index is based on the assumption that the weight loss of the body, through sweating and evaporation, may serve as an indication of the overall thermal stress to which the body is subjected. According to this assumption, the body regulates sweat secretion at such a rate as to achieve the actual evaporative cooling required by (a) metabolic heat production and (b) heat exchange with the environment.

While metabolism is a function of body characteristics and activity, and is therefore not in itself an environmental parameter, heat exchange with the environment is composed of radiation and convection components as described previously. The one environmentally based variable, which is as yet unaccounted for, is the level of efficiency at which evaporative cooling is generated through sweat secretion. This efficiency is a function not only of the previously mentioned environmental parameters that govern radiative and convective exchanges, but also of the moisture content, or humidity, of the surrounding air.

The value of the ITS is computed as the sweat rate required for thermal equilibrium, given in terms of its equivalent latent heat (in total watts) by:

$$ITS = E \times \frac{1}{f} \qquad (5.18)$$

in which E is the cooling rate (W) produced by sweat which is required for equilibrium, and f is the (dimensionless) cooling efficiency of sweating. The required cooling rate E is equivalent to the total load, consisting of metabolic heat production and heat exchange with the environment, given as:

$$E = (M - W) \pm R_n \pm C \qquad (5.19)$$

where M is the body's metabolic rate, W is the metabolic energy transformed into mechanical work, and R_n and C are the respective environmental exchanges due to radiation and convection, as calculated previously (all component flux densities in W m^{-2} may be multiplied by the DuBois body surface area to yield fluxes in watts).

It may be seen from Equation 5.18 that the cooling efficiency f is in fact the ratio between the required cooling load E and the total latent heat of the sweat secreted (ITS). Its value is given by the empirical equation:

$$\frac{1}{f} = \exp[0.6(\frac{E}{E_{max}} - 0.12)] \qquad (5.20)$$

in which E_{max} is an expression of the evaporative capacity of the air, calculated (in kcal h^{-1}, and converted to W) as:

$$E_{max} = pV^{0.3}(42 - Pv_a) \qquad (5.21)$$

where p is a clothing coefficient (equal to 20.5 for light summer clothing, which does not appreciably alter radiative or convective exchanges), V is wind speed (m s^{-1}) and Pv_a is the vapour pressure of the air (mm Hg). This latter value, which expresses the moisture content of the air and in turn determines the efficiency of evaporative cooling from sweat, is taken relative to the vapour pressure of the skin, which at 35°C is equal to 42 mm Hg. The vapour pressure of air may be computed from measured relative humidity RH (per cent) as:

$$Pv_a = 7.52 \times (RH/100) \times Pv_s \qquad (5.22)$$

where Pv_s is saturation vapour pressure (kPa), which is in turn derived from air temperature T (°C) as:

$$Pv_s = \exp[16.6536 - (\frac{4030.183}{T+235})] \qquad (5.23)$$

In a series of empirical experiments,[9] values of ITS were correlated with subjective thermal sensation, as perceived by test groups subjected to carefully monitored conditions. In these studies, subjects were exposed to varying thermal stimuli and their responses – characterized by evaluations ranging from 'comfortable' (number four on a cold-to-hot scale of zero to seven) to 'very hot' – were compared with simultaneous physiological and climatic observations. The resulting correlation between thermal sensation and thermal stress indicated that a limit to comfort may be found at an ITS value of approximately 160W, with the upper thresholds for 'warm' and 'hot' conditions occurring at successive increments of about 120W each.

The validity of this correlation between ITS and actual thermal sensation has recently been re-examined under outdoor conditions, since the original experiments were conducted in controlled indoor climate chambers. Preliminary results of a field study[10] combining pedestrian comfort surveys with detailed outdoor measurements indicate that the ITS provides a fairly robust correlation with reported thermal sensation, and that the threshold between comfortable and overheated conditions does indeed occur in the vicinity of 140–160W. However, the transitions from 'warm' to 'hot' and 'very hot', appear to be at considerably higher increments than the original indoor results suggested. It is possible that this divergence reflects the a fundamental difference in people's perceptual response to outdoor – as opposed to indoor – conditions, or it could be a consequence of any number of methodological issues.

What appears evident is that the sense of thermal comfort in any given individual at any given moment will depend on many more variables than physiological heat balance alone. Comfort in the urban environment undoubtedly involves behavioural, psychological and cultural aspects as well, and these will be touched upon in the next chapter.

Notes

1. See Chapter 2 for an introduction to radiation and the urban energy balance.
2. Local apparent solar time may vary from local standard time (LST) by up to about 17 minutes depending on the time of year, and may be obtained using a correction based on the Equation of Time.
3. The specific form of Equation 5.7 refers to a straight wall which is considered semi-infinite, as in a street canyon (see further discussion in Chapter 10).
4. Invisible metallic coatings with low emissivity are increasingly applied to the glass windows and glazed facades of buildings. It is important to note that while these 'low-e' coatings may influence the temperature T_v of the vertical glass surface facing the urban space, they do not change its emissivity. This is because the coating is typically applied to one of the inner surfaces of a window with multiple layers of glass, leaving the outermost surface with the radiative properties of regular glass.

5   ASHRAE (2001); Thorsson et al (2007); Lindberg et al (2008).
6   Mitchell (1974).
7   Developed by Givoni (1963) and applied for outdoor spaces by Pearlmutter et al (2007).
8   Vogt et al (1981).
9   Originally reported by Givoni (1963).
10 The study was conducted at the campus of the Institutes for Desert Research in Israel, during the summer of 2009. Further details available from the authors.

References

ASHRAE (2001) *ASHRAE Fundamentals Handbook 2001* (SI Edition), American Society of Heating, Refrigerating, and Air-Conditioning Engineers, Atlanta, GA

Givoni, B. (1963) 'Estimation of the effect of climate on man-development of a new thermal index', PhD Thesis, Technion, Israel Institute of Technology

Lindberg, F., Holmer, B. and Thorsson S. (2008) 'SOLWEIG 1.0 – Modelling spatial variations of 3D radiant fluxes and mean radiant temperature in complex urban settings', *International Journal of Biometeorology*, vol 52, no 7, pp697–713

Liu, B. Y. H. and Jordan, R. C. (1960) 'The interrelationship and characteristic distribution of direct, diffuse and total solar radiation', *Solar Energy*, vol 4, no 3, pp1–19

Mitchell, D. (1974) 'Convective heat transfer from man and other animals', in J. L. Monteith and L. E. Mount (eds) *Heat Loss from Animals and Man: Assessment and Control*, Butterworths, London

Monteith, J. L. and Unsworth, M. (1990) *Principles of Environmental Physics*, Edward Arnold, London

Pearlmutter, D., Bitan, A. and Berliner, P. (1999) 'Microclimatic analysis of "compact" urban canyons in an arid zone', *Atmospheric Environment*, vol 33, pp4143–4150

Pearlmutter, D., Berliner, P. and Shaviv, E. (2006) 'Physical modeling of pedestrian energy exchange within the urban canopy', *Building and Environment*, vol 41, no 6, pp783–795

Pearlmutter, D., Berliner, P. and Shaviv, E. (2007) 'Integrated modeling of pedestrian energy exchange and thermal comfort in urban street canyons', *Building and Environment*, vol 42, no 6, pp2396–2409

Thorsson, S., Lindberg, F., Eliasson, I. and Holmer, B. (2007) 'Different methods for estimating the mean radiant temperature in an outdoor urban setting', *International Journal of Climatology*, vol 27, no 14, pp1983–1993

Vogt, J. J., Candas, V., Libert, J. P. and Daull, F. (1981) 'Required sweat rate as an index of thermal strain in industry', in K. Cena and J. A. Clark (eds) *Bioengineering, Thermal Physiology and Comfort*, Elsevier, Amsterdam

Additional reading

Ali-Toudert, F., Djenane, M., Bensalem, R. and Mayer, H. (2005) 'Outdoor thermal comfort in the old desert city of Beni-Isguen, Algeria', *Climate Research*, vol 28, no 3, pp243–256

Auliciems, A. and Szokolay, S. V. (1997) *Thermal comfort*, International PLEA Organisation and University of Queensland, Brisbane

Brown, R. D. and Gillespie, T. J. (1995) *Microclimatic Landscape Design: Creating Thermal Comfort and Energy Efficiency*, Wiley, New York

Burt, J. E., O'Rourke, P. A. and Terjung, W. H. (1982) 'The relative influence of urban climates on outdoor human energy budgets and skin temperature. I. Modeling considerations', *International Journal of Biometeorology*, vol 26, no 1, pp3–23

Fanger, P. O. (1972) *Thermal Comfort*, McGraw-Hill, New York

Givoni, B. (1976) *Man, Climate and Architecture*, Van Nostrand Reinhold, New York

Höppe, P. (1992) 'A new procedure to determine the mean radiant temperature outdoors', *Wetter unt Leben*, vol 44, pp147–151

Höppe, P. (1999) 'The physiological equivalent temperature – a universal index for the biometeorological assessment of the thermal environment', *International Journal of Biometeorology*, vol 43, no 2, pp71–75

Höppe, P. (2002) 'Different aspects of assessing indoor and outdoor thermal comfort', *Energy and Buildings*, vol 34, no 6, pp661–665

Johansson, E. (2006a) 'Urban Design and Outdoor Thermal Comfort in Warm Climates', PhD Thesis, Lund Institute of Technology, Lund, Sweden

Johansson, E. (2006b) 'Influence of urban geometry on outdoor thermal comfort in a hot dry climate: A study in Fez, Morocco', *Building and Environment*, vol 41, no 10, pp1326–1338

Johansson, E. and Emmanuel, R. (2006) 'The influence of urban design on outdoor thermal comfort in the hot, humid city of Colombo, Sri Lanka', *International Journal of Biometeorology*, vol 51, no 2, pp119–133

Matzarakis, A. and Mayer, H. (1991) 'The extreme heat wave in Athens in July 1987 from the point of view of human biometeorology', *Atmospheric Environment*, vol 25B, pp203–211

Matzarakis, A., Mayer, H. and Iziomon, M. G. (1999) 'Applications of a universal thermal index: physiological equivalent temperature', *International Journal of Biometeorology*, vol 43, no 2, pp76–84

Mayer, H. and Höppe, P. (1987) 'Thermal comfort of a man in different urban environments', *Theoretical and Applied Climatology*, vol 38, no 1, pp43–49

Nikolopoulou, M. and Steemers, K. (2003) 'Thermal comfort and psychological adaptation as a guide for designing urban spaces', *Energy and Buildings*, vol 35, no 1, pp95–101

Nikolopoulou, M., Baker, N. and Steemers, K. (2001) 'Thermal comfort in outdoor urban spaces: Understanding the human parameter', *Solar Energy*, vol 70, no 3, pp227–235

Nishi, Y. (1981) 'Measurement of thermal balance of man', in K. Cena and J. A. Clark (eds) *Bioengineering, Thermal Physiology and Comfort*, Elsevier, Amsterdam

6
Thermal Preferences

Introduction

Thermal comfort and associated notions of increased health and efficiency were the main reason for introducing the new technology of air-conditioning into buildings from the beginning of the 20th century. The introduction of the concept of thermal comfort and the specification of desirable environmental conditions for air-conditioned buildings provided a level playing field for companies competing in the burgeoning industry. By adopting an accepted standard condition that all would deliver they could vie for contracts on the basis of cost, quality of their equipment and the service they provided. However, along with technological changes, people's expectations of comfort also changed; these expectations have moved from conditions inside the buildings to outdoor spaces. A growing theme in the academic literature on urban design is the issue of what specification 'should obtain between people and the environments they occupy' in order to make the conditions comfortable.[1] These proposed conditions usually represent a direct translation of the assumptions and judgments regarding the indoor environment to outdoor spaces. As with indoor thermal comfort literature, the thinking concerning outdoor thermal comfort 'reflects and embodies a cocktail of contrasting and often competing concepts'.[2] On one hand comfort is seen as a universally definable state of affairs and on the other hand a socio-cultural achievement. We can see that if the former is accepted then the standardized concepts and conventions of comfort will lead inevitably to certain design outcomes that in a sense are pre-determined. If the latter is true then decision-making does not have a single trajectory but will require a detailed consideration of a multitude of issues including environmental, social and economic factors.

In either case the implications for urban design theory and practice are significant.

Assessment of human thermal environments and comfort indices

Environmental comfort indices

The thermal energy balance of the human body in an urban space was discussed in Chapter 5. Using this or similar mathematical models, as well as mathematical models based on field studies, researchers have attempted to derive the conditions people find acceptable. Generally these models have been designed to predict acceptability when people are indoors, but they are sometimes applied with little modification for conditions outside buildings.

The systematic study of thermal comfort can be traced back to the early 1900s and is therefore one of the oldest areas of building science. Early studies on thermal comfort were undertaken by heating and ventilating engineers.[3,4] These initial studies were generally laboratory-based, often with only a small number of subjects, involving experiments based on measuring the energy exchanges between the human body and 'his' (usually male) environment and obtaining a simultaneous subjective verbal reaction to the physical conditions, such as 'hot', 'slightly warm', 'comfortable', 'uncomfortable' or 'cold'. Although Houghton and Yagloglou[5] proposed the notion of a thermal comfort zone (a range of air conditions plotted on a psychrometric chart) in which a majority of people expressed a sensation of neutrality, the emphasis was usually on discovering a preferred temperature which could be used as the basis for air-conditioning design and thermostat set points. The Effective Temperature scale developed by Houghton and Yagloglou used the concept of a standard environment to derive a thermal index. They defined Effective Temperature as 'an index of the degree of warmth which a person will experience for all combinations of temperature and humidity'[6]. Using the idea of a standard environment an extension of the Effective Temperature scale is the New Effective Temperature which is the temperature of a (hypothetical) standard environment in which a subject would experience the same total heat loss from the skin, ie the same skin wettedness and mean skin temperature, as in the actual environment.

Bedford, who studied the thermal sensation assessments of factory workers in the UK and related their impressions on a seven-point scale of warmth to simultaneous environmental measurements, demonstrated a method for numerical treatment of subject responses to verbal prompts.[7] His work was unusual for its time, since most early researchers based their research on laboratory-based experiments rather than upon field studies.

A different approach to assessing a satisfactory thermal environment, in particular for addressing requirements related to free-running buildings, was developed by Victor and Aladar Olgyay. Their idea, constructed specifically as a tool for designers, was termed a 'bioclimatic approach'. It followed from the concept that a designer was interested in knowing, subject to climate effects and human needs, the widest possible range of conditions in which thermal comfort would be possible. The Olgyay Bioclimatic Chart is shown in Figure 6.1.

The Olgyay Bioclimatic Chart has two axes that define a basic comfort zone: dry bulb temperature and relative humidity. The chart shows how this relatively narrow comfort range may be extended by taking into account the effects of various design options on mean radiant temperature (e.g. admitting solar radiation and raising the temperature of surfaces), air movement and evaporative cooling. The authors warn that the use of their chart is directly applicable only to inhabitants of the temperate climates of the United States, below around 300m in elevation, wearing normal indoor clothing and undertaking only sedentary or light activity.[8]

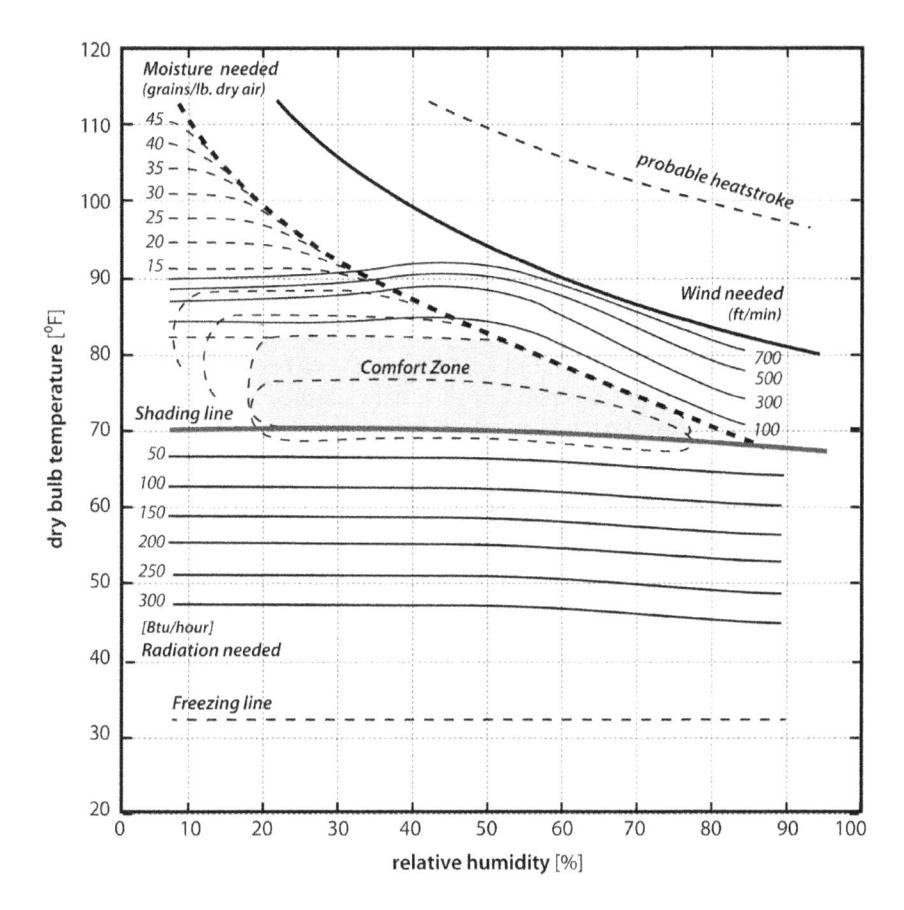

Figure 6.1 An example of the Olgyay Bioclimatic Chart

Source: Olgyay and Olgyay (1963).

Into the 1960s and 1970s many scientists, engineers and others continued to maintain that the state of thermal comfort was a universal condition that could be determined by scientific experimentation. During this period experimenters[9,10,11] refined and extended the laboratory-based experimental techniques to larger numbers of subjects. The notions of a stimulus/response mechanism were applied to this type of experiment during the 1960s.[12] These investigations purported to demonstrate that the thermal sensation responses concerning the environment showed consistent relationships to a number of measurable physiological mechanisms, to the exclusion of other influences such as social customs. A number of indices of thermal comfort assessment were developed: the New Effective Temperature scale and the Standard Effective Temperature, which, together with indices based on models that predict thermal sensation using skin temperature and skin wettedness (TSENS, a prediction of a vote on the seven-point thermal sensation scale and DISC, a prediction of a vote on a scale of thermal discomfort) are all based on the outcomes of laboratory investigations.

The New Effective Temperature is based on a two-node thermal heat balance model,[9] and is the temperature of a (hypothetical) standard environment (here defined as an environment in which air temperature is equal to the mean radiant temperature, relative humidity is 50 per cent and airspeed is less than

0.15ms^{-1}) in which a subject would experience the same skin wettedness and mean skin temperature as in the actual environment. Its applicability is generally limited to conditions of low metabolic rate and light clothing.

The Standard Effective Temperature extended the applicability of Effective Temperature to include a range of activities and clothing levels. It is defined as 'the equivalent air temperature of an isothermal environment at 50 per cent RH in which a subject, while wearing clothing standardized for the activity concerned, has the same heat stress and thermoregulatory strain as in the actual environment'.[13] Similar to the Effective Temperature scale, it requires that in this standard environment, the same physiological strain, i.e. the same skin temperature and skin wettedness and heat loss to the environment, would exist as in the real environment. A version of this scale adapted for outdoor use has also been developed (OUT-SET*), with promising results in field studies.[14]

The work of Fanger[10] and his equation for the 'predicted mean vote' (PMV) and 'predicted percentage dissatisfied' (PPD) is perhaps the best-known outcome of laboratory-based comfort research. Fanger showed that given a set of environmental variables (dry bulb temperature, mean radiant temperature, vapour pressure and relative wind speed) the predicted mean vote of a population expressed on a seven-point thermal sensation scale (–3 to +3) may be calculated, compatible with an assumed metabolic rate and clothing level. The PMV technique was generally perceived as a significant breakthrough in assessing the thermal environment and formed the basis of the international standard *ISO 7730 Moderate Thermal Environments – Determination of the PMV and PPD indices and the specification of the conditions for thermal comfort* (first published in 1984, revised in 1994 and updated most recently in 2005 with an amended title *ISO 7730:2005 Ergonomics of the thermal environment – Analytical determination and interpretation of thermal comfort using calculation of the PMV and PPD indices and local thermal comfort criteria*). Computer code for programming the PMV/PPD calculations is given in the standard.[15]

The PMV equation rests on steady-state heat transfer, a state that hardly ever occurs in everyday life, particularly in an outdoor environment. A state of dynamic thermal equilibrium would best describe the situation of most people. Therefore, when calculating PMV at a particular time, there may be an error arising from the body's ever-changing thermal state. This error for a sample of individuals is likely to behave in a quasi-random manner, and suggests that the PMV may be of limited value as an index for assessing outdoor environments.

In recent years, a new index, the Physiological Equivalent Temperature (PET), first proposed by Höppe,[16] has been used extensively. Like ET*, it is a temperature index, so it gives designers a better feel of the thermal environment than an artificial scale such as the PMV. The Physiological Equivalent Temperature at any given place (outdoors or indoors) is equivalent to the air temperature at which, in a typical indoor setting, the heat balance of the human body is maintained with core and skin temperatures equal to those under the conditions being assessed. It assumes that the metabolic rate is fairly low (80W of light activity are added to basic metabolism) and that the heat resistance of clothing is 0.9clo (see Table 6.1 for indicative metabolic rates of adults engaged in various activities and Table 6.2 for the typical insulation value of clothing). PET has been used for the evaluation of different thermal environments within

Table 6.1 Indicative metabolic rates of adults engaged in various activities

Activity	Metabolic rate (W m^{-2})	(met)
Sleeping	46	0.8
Seated relaxed	58	1.0
Sedentary activity	70	1.2
Teaching	95	1.6
Walking on the level (2kmh)	110	1.9
Digging with a spade	380	6.5
Running (15kmh)	500	9.5

Table 6.2 Typical insulation value of clothing

Garment description	Insulation value (m^2 K W^{-1})	(clo)
Shorts	0.009	0.06
T-shirt	0.014	0.09
Long-sleeved shirt	0.039	0.25
Trousers	0.039	0.25
Sweater	0.054	0.35
Jacket	0.054	0.35
Parka	0.109	0.70

cities, including the consequences of a changed thermal environment caused by different planning variations and the effect of different kinds of greenery or increasing green areas planted with trees.[17]

The adaptive approach

A major criticism of models for predicting thermal comfort based solely on laboratory investigations is that field surveys consistently show that people adapt to their surroundings and accept conditions that would appear to lie outside the established comfort range. Researchers undertaking field studies assert the importance of environmental factors and claim that in practice, people are comfortable in a wide range of environments as they respond to the complex situations encountered in their daily lives. This does not mean that, given the opportunity, they would not vote for a comfort temperature in accordance with that predicted by the laboratory models. It only means that in complex real-life situations, behaviour patterns are modified so that comfort may be perceived at temperatures close to those to which people are actually exposed. This line of thinking about thermal comfort, which became known as the *adaptive approach*, was pioneered by Michael Humphreys when he presented an analysis of 36 field surveys, totalling over 200,000 observations performed by other researchers who had studied the issue of human thermal comfort.[18] He found a strong relationship between the 'neutral temperature'[19] indicated by respondents in free-running buildings and the outdoor mean temperature. The work of Auliciems in Australia also supports this type of relationship.[20]

Much of the recent thermal comfort literature is concerned with the contentious theoretical issues that arise from different conclusions derived from the laboratory-based models and the field-based adaptive models. A common criticism levelled at field studies is that they are generally not able to measure the variables with the same accuracy as the laboratory methods, thus throwing some doubt on their findings. Many claim that within the bounds of experimental error the results are the same. However, the differences carry significant implications for the types of possible building designs, the means by which their thermal environments are controlled and the amounts of energy they consume in the quest to achieve acceptable indoor conditions. A project commissioned by the American Society of Heating, Refrigerating and Air-Conditioning Engineers (ASHRAE) analysed a large amount of data in an attempt to reconcile the differences. The project concluded that two standards were the most appropriate for use in practice: one standard for use in the design and operation of air-conditioned buildings where occupants had little or no adaptive opportunity, and one for use in naturally ventilated buildings where occupants had access to operable windows and other adaptive opportunities. Subsequent updates of both ASHRAE standard 55:2004 *Thermal Environmental Conditions for Human Occupancy, Thermal Environmental Conditions for Human Occupancy* and the European Standard EN 15251:2007 *Indoor environmental input parameters for design and assessment of energy performance of buildings addressing indoor air quality, thermal environment, lighting and acoustics* recognized the adaptive model as an optional method applicable to naturally conditioned, free-running buildings.

By assuming that occupants will take measures such as altering clothing, posture and schedules or activity levels, the adaptive model of comfort allows for a wider range of temperatures to be considered as compatible with comfort. However, it should be emphasized that although some of the field studies cited in support of the adaptive approach were carried out in outdoor conditions, the majority of studies were carried out indoors. The main concern of its authors has been to allow more flexible definitions of acceptable standards for indoor thermal comfort, and hence to allow substantial energy savings; less attention has been devoted to an assessment of the environmental conditions that affect human behaviour outdoors.

Measuring compound environmental indicators

As described in Chapter 5, an alternative to mathematical modelling of thermal conditions in urban spaces based on individual energy fluxes is to derive the mean radiant temperature from the globe temperature, measured with a globe thermometer.

The *wet bulb globe temperature* (WBGT) is an extension of the globe temperature. The WBGT gives a composite index (a weighted temperature) that can be applied to estimate the effect of temperature, humidity, wind speed and solar radiation on humans. In practice this may be used to avoid thermal stress by determining appropriate exposure levels to high temperatures. It is derived from three separate measurements using the following formula:

$$WBGT = 0.7T_w + 0.2T_g + 0.1T_d \tag{6.1}$$

where humidity is described by T_w, the wet bulb temperature (°C); solar radiation is accounted for by means of the globe temperature, T_g (°C), and air temperature is described by the dry bulb temperature, T_d (°C).

Indoors, or when solar radiation is negligible, the following formula is used:

$$WBGT = 0.7T_w + 0.3T_g \qquad (6.2)$$

The process for determining the WBGT is described in ISO 7243:1989, *Hot Environments – Estimation of the Heat Stress on Working Man, based on the WBGT Index*. This standard sets threshold limit values of WBGT, which can be used for evaluating the heat stresses on an individual. It applies to the evaluation of the mean effect of heat during a period representative of activity, but it does not apply to very short periods, nor does it specify zones of comfort. The inconvenience of measuring with three different instruments may be overcome by using a wet globe thermometer consisting of a dial thermometer with the heat sensing portion enclosed by a blackened copper sphere approximately 60mm in diameter that is completely covered with two layers of a wetted black cloth supplied with distilled water from a reservoir. Temperature readings from this instrument correlate so well with the more complicated WBGT index that this single easy measurement may be used to assess outdoor thermal environments.[19]

Fieldwork-based assessments of urban spaces

While direct measurement of environmental conditions can be applied only to existing spaces, the information gathered from such work is invaluable in providing an understanding of environmental conditions to inform design decision-making. The largest field assessment of urban spaces was probably the RUROS project (Rediscovering the Urban Realm of Open Spaces) which was conducted under the auspices of the European Union Fifth Framework Programme (1998–2002) and included an extensive survey of urban spaces in seven cities throughout Europe representing a range of climates from Copenhagen, Denmark to Athens, Greece. Assessments included the thermal, visual and acoustic aspects of the spaces. Ambient environmental conditions were measured and users of the spaces were interviewed. Overall 81 per cent of respondents expressed a perception of comfort in the outdoor urban environment in which they were being interviewed, whereas the calculated thermal index of PMV suggested that only around 60 per cent would be satisfied (i.e. in the range –1 to +1). The difference was attributed to adaptation, which is described as 'the processes which people go through to improve the fit between the environment and their requirements, both at a physical and psychological level'.[21]

Because of these differences the researchers concluded that 'a purely physiological approach is inadequate to characterize the thermal comfort conditions outdoors' and they stated that 'the consistent discrepancy between actual and theoretical comfort conditions outdoors gave us ground to investigate and develop models for thermal comfort conditions, based on the empirical data gathered from field surveys with nearly 10,000 interviews across

Europe'.[22] For each city studied, a regression relationship was developed between the actual sensation vote (ASV) of the users and the ambient meteorological conditions of air temperature, incident solar radiation, wind speed and relative humidity. The resulting design assessment guides are assumed to have applicability in cities with similar climates. However the complicated form of these relationships and doubt over their relevance in different situations means they are probably of little practical use for the urban designer.

Defining the design problem

So how should we proceed? If our main concern is to give useful advice regarding the thermal environment for urban design, then we need a framework for tackling this challenge. However, deriving a theoretical approach to thermal design problems that has general applicability poses several problems:

> Discussion of and research into human thermal comfort has a long history. The results are illuminating but far from unambiguous. In all cases, at least of the more thorough work, the authors have had to limit and qualify their conclusions. Sometimes they hold only for a limited range of environments, or a special group of people (in terms of age, ethnic group, acclimatization or work conditions), and usually they involve acceptance of a theoretical standpoint with regard to the definition, and hence the measurement, or even the measurability, of 'comfort' itself. (Markus and Morris, 1980)

Although researchers are probably fully aware of these issues, there appears to be a widespread, if possibly unfounded, belief among urban and building designers that reliable mathematical models can be produced to predict the conditions, both external and internal to buildings, which designers should aim to achieve in the full range of circumstances. This confusion is due at least in part to the lack of emphasis given by thermal sensation researchers to important questions that address the actual applicability of instrumental approaches proposed to specify the thermal climate which designers should aim to achieve in urban spaces. In addition, the continuing emphasis on theoretical models leads to 'a ratcheting of thermal environment expectations that converge on design solutions that escalate resource use and largely involve outcomes that can be seen as not sustainable'.[23]

Since we are interested in providing practical information for designers, it is useful to discuss something of the nature of the problems of designing urban spaces, and to then discuss the important design-related concepts of thermal preferences and acceptability.

Design requirements, means and contexts

The purposeful nature in the design of urban spaces can be considered in terms of the ends of all the various people involved and the means by which these requirements can and should be addressed. Ends may be considered as states or processes experienced by humans. Few, other than those related to issues of safety and security, can meaningfully be described as states or processes which the spaces must provide for humans. Required states or processes, which can be designated as design requirements, must therefore be understood in a relative and contextual sense. Design requirements may include the broad goals of the various stakeholders involved in the overall process of creating the urban environment, down to the individual requirements of a user of the space. Requirements can also be expressed as a composite description of a desired outcome, e.g. 'providing opportunities for social interactions'. A contextual approach becomes even more necessary when the requirements are expressed in such a manner.

Design means are concerned with the way by which the design requirements are realized in the material world. They may include, but are not limited to, *mechanism means* (which cause or allow an action to achieve some requirement, e.g. air movement and sun penetration in a space); *object means* (materials, components, etc.); and *assessment means* (which anticipate the outcomes of design decisions, e.g. manual design aids, computer simulation). In conceptualizing the problem it must be recognized that the design requirements and design means can only be understood in relation to each other. Requirements cannot be understood as pure abstraction, since they gain their meaning by interpretation of the consequences in relation to a completed and functioning design: for example, a requirement such as thermal satisfaction can be understood only in the context of particular subjects and the design means by which it might be achieved, or fail to be achieved (such as a wind barrier or shade mesh protecting a children's play area, see Figure 6.2). Assessment methods and techniques to evaluate design proposals can be misleading and even dangerous unless they relate to the particular physical and societal context of the problem: imagine calculating the effects of a shading device for a location different to the proposed project, or suggesting hard paving for an area destined to be a children's playground.

A lack of awareness of the essential inter-relatedness of design requirements and the design means in issues such as thermal comfort allows misleading

Figure 6.2 Object means: shade covering a children's playground in (a) Yeroham, Israel and in (b) Darling Harbour, Sydney, Australia

Photographs: Evyatar Erell and Terry Williamson.

concepts to flourish, for example, the idea that acceptable conditions can be determined without consideration of the social and economic context. To look at human thermal requirements from the perspective of a particular design problem, the concept of thermal preferences is useful.

Thermal preferences

Thermal preferences can be defined as the combination of physical factors influencing thermal sensation (air temperature, humidity, air movement, radiation, clothing and activity) which a person in a particular physical environment would choose when constrained by climate and existing physical, social, cultural and economic influences, including general social expectations of the urban space.

This definition not only includes the same six variables used in thermal sensation models, but it is also more relevant than thermal sensation to many built environments, because it points to the need to account for real-world influences such as customs or costs.

To analyse design problems, it is useful to conceptualize three sets of potential preferences which relate to thermal attributes of environments:

1. Preferences regarding attributes of the climatic environment: the air temperature, radiation, humidity and air movement of the internal or external climate of buildings.
2. Preferences regarding attributes of the built environment: the buildings, technology, equipment and other physical means by which the climate set of preferences can be addressed.
3. Preferences regarding attributes of the human environment: this very broad set includes all the aspects of people's beliefs and behaviour which affect their other thermal preferences; for example, on the everyday level, customs and preferences regarding clothing and activity levels, and on the wider level, the ways in which societies make decisions about satisfaction of thermal preferences (surveys and user consultations are two ways this is accomplished).

To be applicable in design, these preferences need to be conceptualized as real-world preferences, rather than as what people might want in some vaguely defined ideal world. In analysing design problems, thermal preferences will usually need to be considered in relation to many non-thermal preferences. For example, thermal preferences regarding attributes of the built environment will be influenced commonly by the costs of various alternatives (perhaps seen as construction costs or as the rates or taxes levied by a local council), and the costs of satisfying thermal preferences will need to be weighed against the costs of satisfying other, non-thermal, preferences.

The design problem of providing some relief from near-zero temperatures in a Paris train station is illustrative here. In theory a solution would be to heat the entire volume of the station, and in a new design this might be considered as a possibility. However for an existing station, in effect a semi-outside space, such a resource-intensive solution would be impractical. The solution of small

Figure 6.3 Passengers waiting for a train stand around radiant heaters when the temperature is close to zero (Gare du Nord, Paris)

Photograph: Terry Williamson.

radiant heaters, as seen in Figure 6.3, addresses the many competing requirements. It is highly unlikely that a decision would have been taken to employ such devices based on modelling their thermal effect, yet user testing quickly showed that they met relevant thermal preferences.

Acceptability

In considering people's preferences for climatic attributes – air temperature, radiation, air movement and humidity – an essential issue is the question whether, for particular design problems, information is needed on thermal neutrality, or some sort of optimal value (e.g. the ideal air movement), or on some kind of upper and lower limits to the range of 'acceptable' conditions (e.g. ranges of air speeds that are acceptable for outdoor eating). The concept of acceptability is particularly important in urban design, as it establishes the boundaries of the climatic conditions which should be achieved. These may include, for example, lower and upper temperature limits, maximum wind speed or a limit of exposure to levels of solar radiation. Acceptability used this way must always be context-dependent. Computer simulation of complex spaces, including computational fluid dynamics (CFD) analysis of air-flows, while perhaps not accurate in an absolute sense, may be sufficient to understand environmental limits and thus test acceptability of proposed designs.

It is evident from casual observation of the world that the climatic conditions which people accept vary widely: people in Sweden may accept skiing in the snow in freezing weather, while Australians may accept sitting on a beach in the heat and sun. The acceptance of these conditions, and of less extreme climatic conditions, can best be understood by reference to the cultural, social, economic, temporal and physical contexts in which they occur. Everyday experience in Western cultures such as those dominant in Europe or North America suggests that expectation and perceived control play a major influence on acceptability: the climatic conditions which people accept when required to be in an outdoor space may differ markedly from those they accept when *choosing* to read a paper on a park bench, and both may differ from what they accept when walking through the space. Figure 6.4, which shows a family picnic on a hot day (around 34°C) in Adelaide, Australia, illustrates this point: the older people and the youngest congregate under the shade of the tree, while the teenagers and healthy adults (out of photo) play football nearby. All found the conditions a 'bit warm' but acceptable because they were doing what they wanted, and all had a great party.

It is important to distinguish this use of the term 'acceptable' from its use in much thermal comfort literature. For example, the widely used International Standard ISO 7730 (2005) defines 'acceptable' in a way that is independent of context. Clearly, the standard concept of 'acceptable' is different from the acceptance shown by Swedes in the snow or Australians in the sun. The standard recognizes that there are circumstances in which people accept conditions which are 'not acceptable', but it provides no means of identifying these paradoxical situations. For application in design, it would also be important to know how much it mattered if conditions were not always acceptable.

Design problem / research problem

When designers use research for prediction of acceptable thermal limits, it seems that they may have the unenviable choice between an approach such as the PMV, which is relatively precise but possibly irrelevant, or an intensive contextual field study which is relevant to the particular field in which the study took place, but perhaps not to the field of the design problem. The alternative of an approach based on field studies (such as the RUROS study) is even less promising: it is likely to be both ambiguous and of doubtful relevance.

Figure 6.4 A family party under a tree in a park, Adelaide, Australia (ambient temperature 34°C)

Photograph: Terry Williamson.

One of the implications of this dilemma is that the choice of a research method should be appropriate to the particular design problem at hand. Here we avoid the need to pass overall judgements on the merits and failings of mathematical models, field studies or physical models, as the appropriate approach (if any) will follow from the nature of the problem to be addressed: it is a question of finding the best tools for the particular job. If the problem is the relative effect on comfort of different air speeds that may result from different building forms, then a PMV or a PET index may have much to offer in conjunction with an urban thermal simulation model. If the problem is whether sun shading should be provided for a children's playground then a context-specific field study seems an appropriate source of information on relevant preferences.

Another research approach that ultimately has value for design is parametric analysis, which looks at the way a phenomenon (such as thermal comfort) is influenced by variations in basic descriptors (like the height–width ratio of streets). In this case, the goal is not to precisely diagnose a specific real-world site, with its many details and idiosyncrasies, but to reveal relationships that can inform the fundamental decisions of urban designers.

How does outdoor comfort affect indoor energy consumption?

Architects and urban designers understand that the spaces outside a building can often influence the perceptions and use of a building on the inside:

> Artistically, the essence of the builder's art is always to create a whole. When a building succeeds, it is because we perceive it, feel it, to be a magnificent whole, whole through and through, one thing ... We cannot make something whole unless we unite it with its surroundings. So, to be whole, it has to be 'lost', that is, not separate from its surroundings, part and parcel of them. (Alexander, 2002)

While designers intuit this requisite for good design, there is little empirical evidence through case studies and the like to support the idea; this is especially true of the way the use of a building may translate to measurable factors such as energy consumption.

Studies have shown that the design of a house, and in particular the connection between inside and outside spaces, may affect the behaviour and attitude of its occupants and thus influence heating and cooling energy consumption. The connection between the inside and outside living spaces of houses may affect (to varying degrees) the way the occupants use the spaces and perceive the environment. Importantly, one such study found a strong inverse correlation between energy consumption and the use and satisfaction with an outdoor living area.[24] Put simply, if people were outside they were not inside, consuming energy for heating or cooling. Anecdotal evidence suggests such a finding would equally apply at an urban scale, linking improvement in the usability of outdoor spaces directly to a reduced level of reliance on conditioned interiors, thus encouraging more, rather than less sustainable outcomes.

Notes

1. Cooper (1982).
2. Chappells and Shove (2005).
3. Houghton and Yagloglou (1923a).
4. Winslow et al (1937; 1938).
5. Houghton and Yagloglou (1923b)
6. Houghton and Yagloglou (1923c)
7. Bedford (1936).
8. Olgyay and Olgyay (1963).
9. Gagge et al (1971).
10. Rohles and Nevins (1971).
11. Fanger (1972).
12. Stevens et al (1969).
13. ASHRAE (2001).
14. Spagnolo and de Dear (2003).
15. Marc Fountain and Charlie Huizenga at the Center for the Built Environment, University of California, Berkeley, have written a software package WinComf© that will calculate a number of thermal comfort indices.
16. Höppe (1999).
17. Matzarakis et al (1999).
18. Humphreys (1975).
19. The neutral temperature is that temperature which 50 per cent of a sample population will indicate on a seven-point thermal sensation scale as in the range one to four and 50 per cent in the range four to seven. It is usually considered synonymous with comfort temperature.
20. Auliciems (1983).
21. Botsford (1971).
22. Nikolopoulou (2004).
23. Shove (2003).
24. Thomas (2006).

References

Alexander, C. (2002) *The Nature of Order – Book Two: The Process of Creating Life*, The Center for Environmental Studies, Berkeley, CA

ASHRAE (2001) *Handbook of Fundamentals*, American Society of Heating, Refrigerating and Air-Conditioning Engineers, New York,

Auliciems, A. (1983) 'Psycho-physiological criteria for global thermal zones of building design', *International Journal of Biometeorology*, vol 26, pp69–86

Bedford, T. (1936) *The Warmth Factor in Comfort at Work*, HMSO, London

Botsford, J. H. (1971) 'A wet globe thermometer for environmental heat measurement', *American Industrial Hygiene Association Journal*, vol 32, pp1–10

Chappells, H. and Shove, E. (2005) 'Debating the future of comfort: Environmental sustainability, energy consumption and the indoor environment', *Building Research & Information*, vol 33, pp32–40

Cooper, I. (1982) 'Comfort theory and practice – barriers to the conservation of energy by building occupants', *Applied Energy*, vol 11, pp243–288

Fanger, P. O. (1972) *Thermal Comfort: Analysis and Applications in Environmental Engineering*, McGraw-Hill, New York

Gagge, A. P., Stolwijk, J. A. J. and Nishi, Y. (1971) 'An effective temperature scale based on a simple model of human physiological regulatory response', *ASHRAE Transactions*, vol 9, pp247–262

Höppe, P. (1999) 'The physiological equivalent temperature – a universal index for the biometeorological assessment of the thermal environment', *International Journal of Biometeorology*, vol 43, pp71–75

Humphreys, M. A. (1975) *Field Studies in Thermal Comfort Compared and Applied*, Building Research Establishment, Garston, UK

Markus, T. A. and Morris, E. N. (1980) *Buildings, Climate and Energy*, Pitman, London

Matzarakis, A., Mayer, H. and Iziomon, M. G. (1999) 'Applications of a universal thermal index: Physiological equivalent temperature', *International Journal of Biometeorology*, vol 43, pp76–84

Nikolopoulou, M. (ed) (2004) *Designing Open Spaces in the Urban Environment: A Bioclimatic Approach*, Centre for Renewable Energy Sources (CRES), Greece

Olgyay, V. and Olgyay, A. (1963) *Design With Climate*, Princeton University Press, Princeton, NJ

Rohles, F. H. and Nevins, R. G. (1971) 'The nature of thermal comfort for sedentary man', *ASHRAE Transactions*, vol 77, pp239–246

Shove, E. (2003) *Comfort, Cleanliness and Convenience*, Berg, Oxford

Spagnolo, J. and de Dear, R. (2003) 'A field study of thermal comfort in outdoor and semi-outdoor environments in subtropical Sydney, Australia', *Building and Environment*, vol 38, pp721–738

Stevens, J. C., Marks, L. E. and Gagge, A. P. (1969) 'The quantitative assessment of thermal discomfort', *Environmental Research*, vol 2, pp149–165

Thomas, M. (2006) 'Inside outside: A relationship that moves me!', in S. Shannon, V. Soebarto and T. J. Williamson (eds) *Proceedings of 40th Annual ANZAScA Conference*, The University of Adelaide, Adelaide (published on CD)

Winslow, C. E. A., Herrington, L. P. and Gagge, A. P. (1937) 'Physiological reactions of the human body to varying environmental temperatures', *American Journal of Physiology*, vol 120, pp1–22

Winslow, C. E. A., Herrington, L. P. and Gagge, A. P. (1938) 'Physiological reactions and sensations of pleasantness under varying atmospheric conditions', *Transactions of the American Society of Heating and Ventilating Engineers*, vol 44, pp179–196

Additional reading

Dear, R. de, Brager, G. and Cooper, D. (1997) 'Developing an adaptive model of thermal comfort and preference', Final Report on ASHRAE RP-884, Macquarie Research Ltd, Sydney

Gagge, A. P., Fobelets, A. P. and Berglund, L. G. (1986) 'A standard predictive index for human response to the thermal environment', *ASHRAE Transactions*, vol 92, pp709–731

Humphreys, M. A. (1977) 'The optimum diameter for a globe thermometer for use indoors', *Annals of Occupational Hygiene*, vol 20, pp135–140

Humphreys, M. A. and Fergus Nicol, J. (2002) 'The validity of ISO-PMV for predicting comfort votes in every-day thermal environments', *Energy and Buildings*, vol 34, pp667–684

Olgyay, V. and Olgyay, A. (1954) 'Appendix Report No. 1 – Man as a physiological measure in architecture', in A. M. Cole and J. H. Orendroff (eds) *Application of Climatic Data to House Design*, US Government Printing Office, Washington, DC

Parsons, K. C. (1993) *Human Thermal Environments*, Taylor and Francis, London

Yaglou, C. P. and Minard, D. (1957) 'Control of heat casualties at military training centres', *American Medical Association Archives of Industrial Health*, vol 16, pp302–305

7
Application of Climatology in Urban Planning and Design

This chapter serves as an introduction to the third section of the book, which is dedicated to microclimatic considerations in urban planning and design. It is devoted to a discussion of how our understanding of the urban microclimate may be applied in practice.[1] The question is not as simple as it seems, because an architect designing urban space must resolve numerous, often conflicting, demands that relate to diverse aspects of planning. These may include, for example, space requirements for traffic infrastructure or pressure by developers to maximize the economic return on expensive urban land. Furthermore, the architect should bear in mind that a sound design response may need to deal simultaneously with climatic stress on pedestrians and on buildings – and that responding to both might sometimes lead to contradictory requirements.

Subsequent chapters in this section deal in a general way with issues such as solar access, control of air-flow, the effects of vegetation and the use of different landscaping materials. The principles discussed here may be applied in most types of urban space, including open space such as parks and plazas, linear spaces such as streets and small, semi-enclosed spaces such as courtyards and patios. A more detailed discussion of specific issues that characterize linear space – urban street canyons – will be dealt with in a subsequent chapter.

Applications of microclimatology in urban planning

Microclimate has an effect on a very broad range of issues encompassed in the field of urban planning and design. These include:[2]

- optimization of land use patterns in relation to different activities to be carried out in towns;
- identification and development of suitable microclimates for various activities, such as parks or recreation;
- identification of adverse microclimatic factors likely to affect the detailed design of urban systems, such as high local winds;
- optimization of building form in relation to external climatic inputs, such as solar radiation and wind;
- optimization of building form in relation to microclimatic modification of the immediate exterior domain of the building, such as the high winds induced near ground level by tall buildings;

- structural safety, especially with respect to high winds;
- selection of appropriate building materials;
- planning of the construction process in view of climatic constraints;
- control of water run-off;
- assessment of building running costs (HVAC, lighting, etc.) in advance of construction;
- optimization of the operating environment of transport systems, e.g. avoidance of ice hazards;
- control of the environmental impact of a transport system on its adjacent urban systems, for example with respect to air pollution by vehicles.

To summarize this diverse list, it is useful to organize these effects into two main categories:

1. *The effect of microclimate on human activity, especially pedestrian, in the spaces between buildings.* The urban fabric consists of both buildings and open space, which may in turn be classified according to intended patterns of use. In locations where pedestrian access is considered desirable the design of outdoor spaces should provide optimal conditions, as appropriate to the local climate. To the extent that the use of urban space by pedestrians is encouraged, the enhancement of outdoor comfort may in turn reduce the reliance on mechanically conditioned buildings and vehicles.
2. *The effect of microclimate on the performance of buildings, especially with respect to energy conservation.* The magnitude of modifications to the microclimate resulting from the effects of the urban fabric has drawn the attention of researchers to the need for tools for predicting them and for devising design strategies to respond to them. The impetus for some of the research has been the proliferation of computer software for building thermal analysis, which relies on meteorological data to predict interior conditions. While many building simulation codes are now considered to be quite accurate, significant errors may be introduced to the simulations as a result of weather data which is based on regional averages but which may not be representative of site-specific conditions.

Useful consideration of urban microclimate issues in the design process may be achieved if the following guidelines are adhered to:

Clear and measurable benefits

For a particular recommendation based on urban climate considerations to be adopted by planners, the proposed strategy should have clear and measurable benefits. In the absence of quantitative studies on the effect of proposed designs upon climate, decision-makers will tend to downgrade the importance of climatic considerations. There is therefore a need for sufficiently accurate and reliable predictive tools, capable of testing different scenarios. For example, the effect of urban climate modification on building energy consumption could be estimated, taking into account the urban heat island – as has been demonstrated by using measured temperature data for a number of cities, as well as by using computer modelling to predict the magnitude of urban effects on temperature or wind speed.

Economic viability

The recommendations of urban climatologists with respect to city planning may often have significant economic implications. Urban development is driven to a great degree by economic considerations, and zoning regulations often reflect the desire of city planners to attract investment by real estate developers. Street width, for instance, is generally determined by the requirements of vehicular access, while building height reflects the desire to maximize the value of land. Thus, any recommendation concerning the height to width ratio of streets, which has a major influence on the canopy-layer climate of cities, may also have considerable economic implications. Any explanation for the relative lack of success in implementing climate-related strategies in urban planning must therefore also consider the lack of a practical framework to assess their economic effects.

Sustainability

Evaluating economic viability is a necessary but insufficient metric to assess a planning project and its climate consequences. Increasingly, climate considerations must incorporate other aspects of sustainable planning which account for social and environmental concerns.

Subsidiarity

As mentioned above, architects and planners must deal with a multitude of factors. Often the demands of different aspects of the plan introduce conflicting requirements, so the design of urban space quite frequently involves a process of optimization (although this is usually done intuitively rather than by a clearly defined formal method). It is thus of great value to be able to establish the motivation for a particular approach in terms of the benefits, without resorting to a unique policy required to achieve the desired goal. Climate considerations may have a profound effect on urban form, and must often be dealt with as early as possible in the design process because appropriate climatic strategies can rarely be applied retroactively to rectify errors made in the initial stages of the design. However, if more than one approach can yield the required result, the preferred solution is that which may be applied as late as possible in the planning process, and which thus allows maximum flexibility in other aspects of the design. This approach, of seeking the solution for a particular issue at the lowest possible level of the planning process, may be termed 'subsidiarity'.

Complexity

A common shortcoming of some attempts to apply scientific methods to urban planning is that in order to analyse a particular question, researchers often simplify the issue, studying its effects in isolation from the other factors which may be involved. This has clear advantages as far as analysis of the physical processes is concerned, yet great care must be used in the synthesis of research results into an overall planning strategy that may be applied to a specific urban location. For example, deriving an optimal urban form on the basis of exposure to solar radiation risks overlooking the effects of other factors, such as the effect of density on energy consumption in transport. The formulation of design recommendations on the basis of such research must be done with great care.

Comprehensive approach to problem solving

In order to apply urban climatology effectively in the process of town planning, a comprehensive approach must be adopted. Recommendations must be based on analysis of all factors influencing the urban microclimate. Conclusions based upon the study of one or even several factors in conjunction may be misleading if they fail to take into account the effect of other, significant processes. With the increase in computing power, computerized modelling may be capable of providing accurate and comprehensive analysis of the urban microclimate. Once such models become reliable and accurate enough, they should be applied wherever possible to inform the decision-makers of the microclimatic implications of urban planning strategies under consideration. For the models to be useful, they must allow the study of the particular issues that are foremost in the architect's mind. In other words, they must be formulated so that the inputs include parameters related directly to the architect's decision-making process.

The rest of this section will explore the tools available to the architect and urban planner seeking to respond to the challenge of generating effective climatic responses in the design of spaces between buildings.

Notes

1 This chapter draws extensively on material published in Erell (2008), see below. Some of this material was also included in the paper 'Climate information for improved planning and management of mega cities', by H. Cleugh, R. Emmanuel, W. Endlicher, E. Erell, G. McGranahan, G. Mills, E. Ng, A. Nickson, J. Rosenthal and K. Steemer at the World Climate Conference 3 – Better Information for a Better Future, World Meterological Organization, Geneva, Switzerland, 31 August–4 September 2009.
2 Page (1972).

References

Erell, E. (2008) 'The application of urban climate research in the design of cities', *Advances in Building Energy Research*, vol 2, pp95–121

Page, J. K. (1972) 'The problem of forecasting the properties of the built environment from the climatological properties of the green-field site', in J. A. Taylor (ed) *Weather Forecasting for Agriculture and Industry*, David and Charles, London

Additional Reading

Page, J. K. (1968) 'The fundamental problems of building climatology considered from the point of view of decision-making by the architect and urban designer', *Symposium on Urban Climates and Building Climatology*, World Meteorological Organization, Geneva

8
Microclimate Design Strategies in Urban Space

This chapter will discuss the application of strategies to control solar access and air-flow in urban areas, and will examine the effect that building and paving materials have on the microclimate of adjacent urban spaces. Although vegetation may be used to modify both solar access and air-flow, the complex nature of its interaction with the microclimate of urban spaces warrants separate and detailed analysis. This will be provided in Chapter 9. Finally, although some of the discussion in this chapter applies primarily to urban street canyons, a more detailed discussion of the design of these prototypical urban spaces will be presented in Chapter 10.

Controlling solar access

The degree of exposure to solar radiation is one of the main controls on microclimatic conditions. In comparison with streets and semi-enclosed spaces, open spaces such as parks are usually more exposed, and shading may be restricted to small, localized patches. This section will introduce the concept of solar access in general terms. A more detailed discussion will be included in Chapter 10, which discusses linear spaces.

Solar rights for buildings

Solar access is an essential requirement for passive solar heating of buildings, so much so that the concept has sometimes been referred to as 'solar rights'. These may be defined as a guarantee of exposure to direct sunlight in a predetermined period, typically several hours each day during winter. The building surfaces that must receive the benefits of sunlight are usually vertical (i.e. walls) and equator-facing (south in the northern hemisphere, north in the southern one). However, the proliferation of photovoltaic cells and of solar collectors for hot water, which are usually mounted on roofs, requires consideration of the overshadowing of these surfaces by adjacent structures as well (see example in Figure 8.1).

Mandating solar access involves establishing limits on the height or volume of buildings that are determined from the apparent position of the sun, which may be plotted on a variety of charts or calculated by computer, based on the geographic location (latitude and longitude) of the site in question. The

Figure 8.1 The flat-plate solar collectors installed on the roof of the terrace building are shaded by the taller building on higher ground to the south

Photograph: Oded Potchter.

equations for calculating apparent solar position for any given location and time, in terms of azimuth and elevation above the horizon, are given in Chapter 5. Such limits are referred to as *solar envelopes*, a concept pioneered by Knowles.[1]

There are several ways to define appropriate criteria for solar access rights. The following discussion is, however, limited to simple angular criteria, since these are sufficient to illustrate the main issues involved. Such criteria are based on defining an obstruction angle, which may be based on the sun's altitude at a given time on a specified date.

This raises three questions:

1. What are the critical time and date? Requiring full exposure for several hours (say 9.00am to 3.00pm) on the winter solstice guarantees full access for the rest of the year – but implies very low angles of elevation, which in turn require very large unobstructed spaces between adjacent buildings, especially in high-latitude locations. Selecting a different time (e.g. noon) means that the sun might be obstructed at all other times on the day in question.
2. Where should the obstruction angle be measured from? If ground level at the base of the solar facade is taken, the effect of low, nearby obstructions such

as fences or even single-storey buildings will be exaggerated and result in unnecessarily stringent limits with respect to the actual collector surfaces.
3   Which facade orientations warrant guaranteed solar exposure? Obviously an equator-facing surface will theoretically enjoy the most insolation. However, some deviation from this ideal is inevitable in practice, and the loss of potential solar gains is not substantial for orientations of about 25 to 30 degrees away from due south (or north). Furthermore, unique features of the local climate, such as frequent early-morning cloud or fog, may mean that the optimal orientation deviates somewhat from the theoretical requirement for an equator-facing surface.

An example of the application of solar envelopes in practice to support passive heating of buildings by direct gain is shown in Figure 8.2, redrawn from the planning bylaws of the Neve Zin neighbourhood at Sde Boqer, Israel. No part of the building to the south may project above the limiting plane, drawn from ground level at the setback line of the northern plot. The angle of the restricting plane defining the solar envelope in this case was designed to permit unobstructed solar access between 9.00am and 3.00pm on the winter solstice, thus ensuring maximum exposure to the sun year round. Further details on the climatic aspects of the design of this neighbourhood are given in Case Study 1 (Chapter 12).

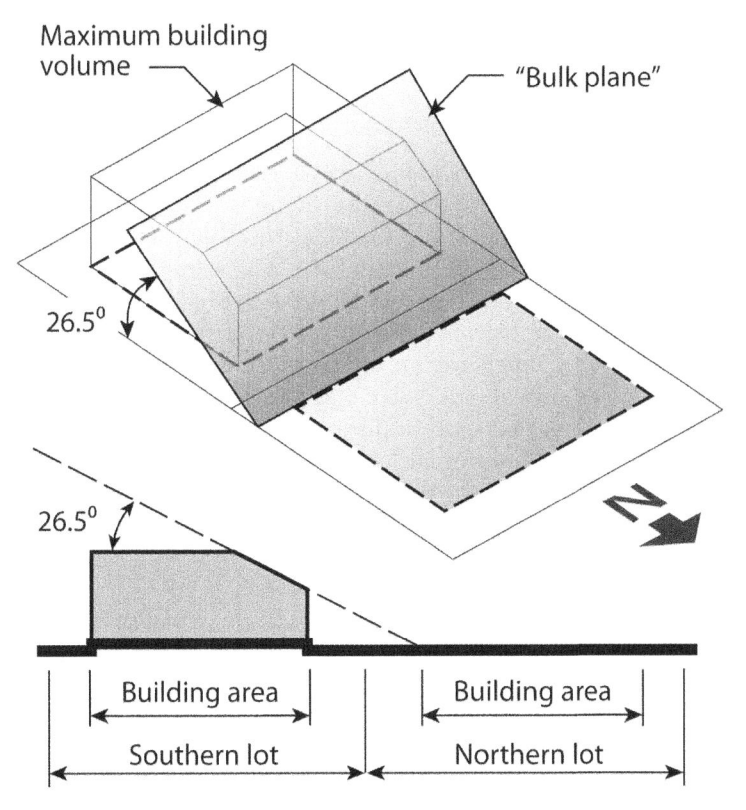

Figure 8.2 A simple 'solar envelope' guaranteeing solar access to a building, defined by an imaginary inclined plane, above which no part of the adjacent building may project

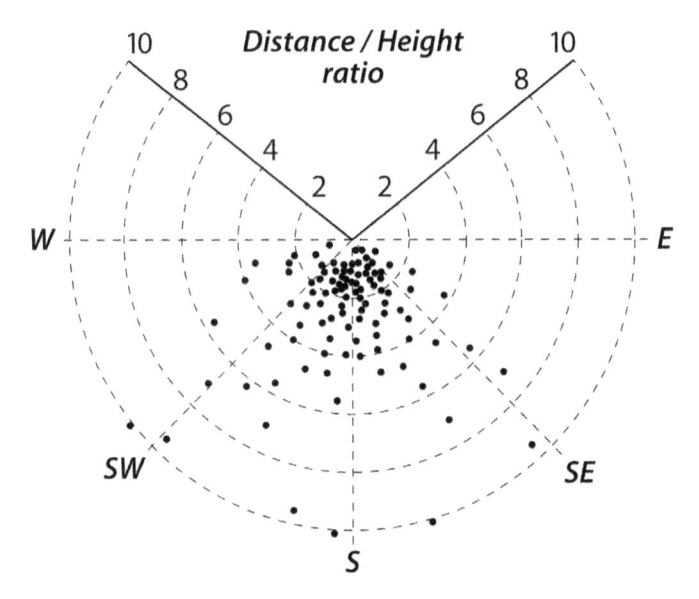

Figure 8.3 Solar gain indicator for a vertical, south-facing window in Manchester, UK

Note: Each dot represents 1 per cent of the total solar gain during the heating season, based on actual insolation for the locality. The distance from the centre of the diagram represents the ratio of the distance of a potential obstruction from the reference point to its height above it. The majority of the solar potential is found within a fairly narrow sector from southeast to southwest, at medium to high solar elevations. Very little additional energy is available from lower parts of the horizon or at solar azimuths outside this sector.

Source: Redrawn from Littlefair (1998).

Applying a stringent geometric limit to guarantee solar access throughout the winter is unrealistic in dense urban development at high-latitude locations. A preferable approach is based on mapping the solar resource for a given building surface, calibrated in terms of solar heat gain through the heating season. Such a procedure, illustrated in Figure 8.3, highlights the fact that for the entire heating season, the relative heat gain from portions of the sky close to the horizon is very small for an equator-facing surface. Conversely, the penalty for failing to provide full solar access to this part of the sky dome is negligible. This suggests that more realistic restrictions, in terms of the critical angle of elevation for the limiting surface, would nevertheless allow substantial solar gains even in fairly dense urban areas.

Controlling solar access for pedestrians

As has been demonstrated in Chapter 5, human thermal comfort in outdoor spaces may depend as much on the radiant load to which a pedestrian is exposed as on the temperature of the air. Furthermore, while our ability to control air temperature in outdoor spaces is very limited, it is fairly simple to control exposure to the sun, at least conceptually. The apparent position of the sun may be computed using any of several computer programmes in the public domain for any date and time, given the geographic coordinates of the location. Most computer-aided design (CAD) software also facilitates studies of shading cast by building elements or dedicated shading devices, once their geometry has been fixed. The problem lies in making the appropriate decisions concerning solar exposure at each of several levels in the design process. The effects of street orientation, canyon geometry and building form on this issue are discussed in Chapter 10. However, it should be noted that strategies such as providing shade by restricting the width of a street are fairly crude tools: shade may also be provided by means of trees along the pavements or by means of pedestrian arcades integrated at the street level of the adjacent buildings. In fact, bearing in mind the principle of subsidiarity, it may sometimes be preferable to do so. However, there are several drawbacks to this approach:

- It is more expensive. Whereas a very narrow street might be self-shading, a broader one will require additional outlays to provide shade.
- It requires the addition of specialized elements that are not essential to the core of the design, and might therefore not be implemented, especially if budgetary constraints become evident during the course of construction.
- It allows adoption of designs that are sub-optimal in the first instance, on the assumption that the situation may be rectified at a later stage.

Once the decision has been made regarding the period in which solar exposure is desirable, geometric restrictions must be established to prevent adjacent structures from casting a shadow on pedestrian areas where sun is required.

Figure 8.4 Pedestrian arcades protecting the pavement from the sun (or rain) may be constructed as an integral part of the building (left) or a light-weight add-on to it (right)

Photographs: Evyatar Erell.

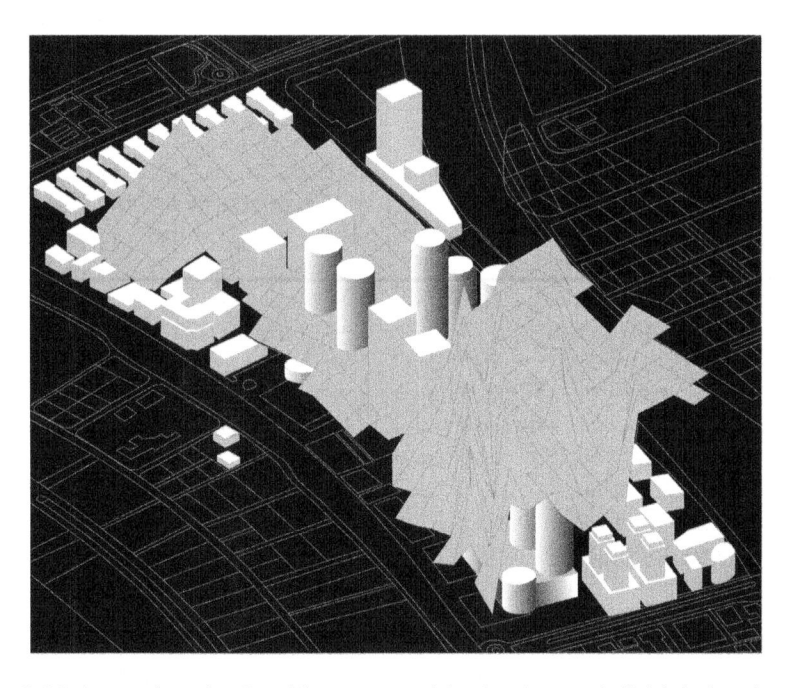

Figure 8.5 Solar envelope developed for a commercial redevelopment in Tel Aviv, Israel

Note: Buildings projecting above the mesh will cast a shadow beyond the limits of the solar envelope, which was generated in response to complex requirements for solar access to the adjacent neighbourhood and to main streets within the development.

Source: Redrawn from Capeluto et al (2003).

In the case of a simple rectilinear space the restriction may take the form of a plane inclined at an appropriate angle to the horizon, above which no construction is allowed. However, urban open space is often irregular in form. It is comprised of streets and plazas with different proportions and different orientations. This means that an appropriate solar envelope established in response to predetermined exposure criteria can only be calculated by computer.

Figure 8.5 shows the solar envelope for a commercial redevelopment in Tel Aviv, Israel, which was generated in response to a complex set of criteria. The proposed construction of a dense matrix of tall office blocks was modified in response to the requirements that solar access to an adjacent residential neighbourhood to the east would not be reduced; that pedestrian areas on the main east–west avenues within the development have winter sun all day; and that pedestrian areas in the main north–south road remain sunny during lunchtime in winter.

Controlling air-flow

Wind affects pedestrian use of open space at two levels. Firstly, air-flow results in turbulent mixing of energy and moisture, thus eroding any micro-scale differences in climate between adjacent patches. Secondly, it promotes the exchange of energy at the human skin, enhancing evaporation of sweat in warm conditions and introducing a wind-chill effect in cold ones.

Design of windbreaks in open spaces requires familiarity with the specific conditions at the site: wind speed and direction should be analysed on a seasonal and diurnal basis to provide a guide to what is both desirable and possible to achieve at a given location. The following discussion is based on the assumption that such analysis has in fact been carried out, and seeks to provide some guidance regarding the effects of several control strategies on air-flow in the city. The discussion is limited to understanding how to control air-flow in general: specific measures that apply to well-defined linear spaces are described in Chapter 10.

Shelterbelt trees

The purpose of a shelterbelt is to reduce wind velocity in an area on its lee side. While a solid barrier would appear to be best suited to achieve this aim, theoretical and experimental studies show that a porous barrier is in fact more effective. While a solid barrier prevents air-flow through it, turbulence is generated behind it, typically in the form of a lee vortex. Allowing some of the air to flow through the barrier – in effect making it porous to a certain extent – may prevent the formation of the vortex and result in a lower peak air speed behind the barrier.

The value of a shelterbelt of trees depends on its ability to reduce wind speed and to do so over a substantial distance. The effectiveness of this method depends upon orientation of the row of trees with respect to the angle of incidence of the wind, the porosity of the shelterbelt, the height of the trees and their distance from the area to be protected. The porosity of the shelterbelt in turn depends on the type of tree, the distance between adjacent trees and the overlap, if any, between rows.

When air blows towards a porous shelterbelt, wind speed decreases on the windward side of the barrier, and continues decreasing within a few multiples of the height of the barrier (H) on its lee side, before gradually recovering to the undisturbed background level. The decrease in wind speed starts to become noticeable at about 5H in front of the belt, and the recovery distance on the lee side may be as great as 30H.

The *incidence angle* (IA) of the wind with respect to the shelter (normal incidence is defined as IA = 0, and parallel as IA = 90°) has a substantial effect on air-flow. With increasing IA, the minimum wind speed decreases for lower density shelterbelts, but increases for higher density barriers. Three factors may contribute to these apparently contradictory effects of oblique flows: firstly, an increase of effective density of the shelterbelt due to the longer path through the shelter; secondly, a less effective reduction of the parallel component of the flow, compared to the perpendicular one; a third effect concerns the rotation of the wind vector as the flow returns to its original direction. In low-density shelterbelts, the first factor is more important, while in dense shelters or solid barriers, the second factor dominates.

The *porosity of the barrier* also affects the location of the area: a solid barrier has the greatest impact on the area adjacent to it, with a maximum reduction being felt at a distance that is equal to about twice the height of the barrier. As porosity increases, the maximum reduction in wind speed in the lee of the barrier is less substantial, and it occurs at a greater distance (see Figure 8.6). The region affected by a porous barrier is also greater than that of a solid one. An optimum porosity may be identified, in terms of the reduction of wind speed and the size of the area affected: in the case of unobstructed flow over a flat terrain upwind of the barrier, this is approximately 0.35.

An urban location does not typically include sizeable unobstructed areas. Rather, a city may be seen as a matrix of obstructions, such as buildings of different dimensions, arranged at varying angles to one another and at different distances. A wind shelter, such as a hedge or a belt of trees, must therefore be

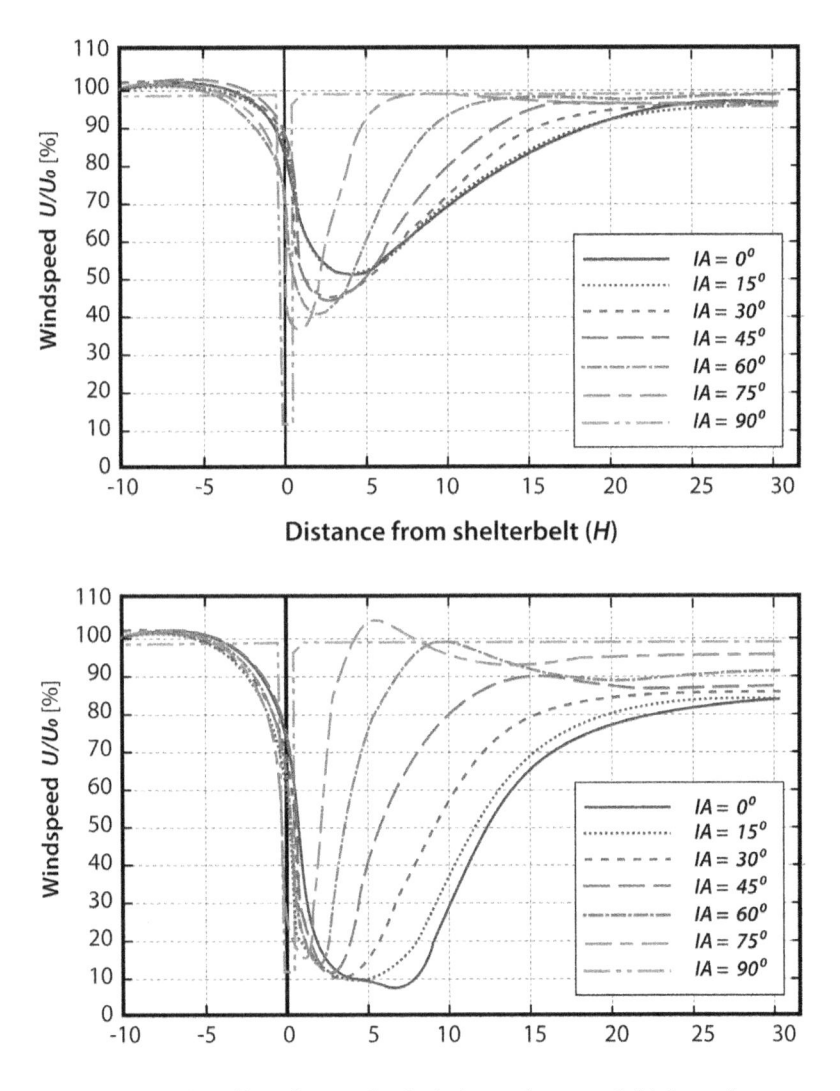

Figure 8.6 Horizontal profiles of normalized wind speed at z = 0.1H for various approach wind incidence angles for a shelterbelt with W = 0.5H and a porosity of 75 per cent (top) and 43 per cent (bottom)

Source: Redrawn from Wang and Takle (1996) Figures 3b and 3c.

designed with an understanding of its inter-relationship with adjacent buildings. In general, an adjacent building may be considered as being either windward of a barrier or leeward of it. If an adjacent building is located fairly close to the barrier, at a distance of approximately four times its height, the standing vortex in front of the building dominates air-flow in the region between the two bodies, and a porous barrier behaves similarly to a solid one. The effect of porosity becomes noticeable once the distance downwind from the barrier exceeds this ratio.

Urban air quality

Airborne particles in the urban atmosphere may originate either within the city or outside of it. However, with the exception of desert cities, where natural dust may be the main component of airborne particles, most urban aerosols are anthropogenic in origin. A large proportion of these result from combustion processes – in buildings but also in automobiles, which are typically the main source of ultra-fine particles in urban streets. Several studies show that particle number concentrations at street level are linearly correlated with traffic volume (as well as being inversely correlated with wind speed). In time, motor vehicles and other machines at the disposal of humans may have far reduced emissions but in the interim, cities should be designed so as to promote the dispersal of undesirable airborne material. Urban form affects the diffusion of pollutants – in gaseous or particle form – so urban air quality may be improved by appropriate planning.

Measuring urban air quality

Air quality for human activity is affected by the presence and concentration of several pollutants, which may be found in gaseous form or as small airborne particles – aerosols. The size of aerosols may vary by two orders of magnitude, from as little as several nanometres to a millimetre or more. Furthermore, the size distribution of aerosols varies with location and time, so there is an important difference between particle number concentrations (PNC) and the mass of airborne particulate matter (PM), e.g. PM_{10} ($D_p \leq 10\mu m$) or $PM_{2.5}$ ($D_p \leq 2.5\mu m$). This distinction has important ramifications: although toxicological studies show that ultra-fine particles ($D_p < 0.1\mu m$), which make up the main component of ambient particles by number, are more toxic than coarser particles per unit mass, air quality regulations in many countries limit mass concentrations, not particle number concentrations. Furthermore, fine particles ($D_p < 1.0\mu m$) are either not included in the regulatory limits, or have little effect on them, because such fine particles contribute very little to the total PM. PNC may be a better indicator of air quality with respect to human health, but the lack of standard methods and instrumentation to measure it has proven to be a barrier to its adoption.

Effect of urban geometry on diffusion of vehicle emissions

The dispersion of aerosols in general, and of airborne pollutants (which may be present in gaseous form too), depends on wind, and in particular on turbulence.

To understand how flushing of pollutants from street level takes place, it is useful to recall the basic characteristics of canyon flows and pollutant dispersion (for a more extended discussion see Chapter 4).

A typical street canyon and its associated flow patterns are shown in Figure 8.7. Two vortex types can be identified:

1. A *lee vortex* is formed in the middle of the canyon (with respect to its longitudinal axis). It is driven by the atmospheric cross-flow above roof level, and may develop if wind speeds above roof level are greater than 1.5ms^{-1}, and the angle between the approaching flow and the longitudinal axis of the street is more 30°. Depending on atmospheric stability and roof geometry, clean air may be entrained at roof height and directed downwards and into the canyon near the windward wall. At ground level, flow is directed opposite to the above-roof wind. Automobile emissions from the middle of the street are carried to the base of the leeward wall and then sucked upwards by the vortex flow. They are partially entrained into the atmospheric flow above the roof.

2. *Corner eddies* form at street intersections as a result of the shear force created by the interaction between air flowing along one street and the more protected air in the street perpendicular to it. They may provide additional ventilation if they transport clean air from above the roof directly into the street near ground level and their contribution to air quality in a dense urban matrix is extremely important. The effect of corner eddies is felt up to a distance of about three to four street widths, so limiting the length of individual city blocks and avoiding long street canyons with continuous building fronts are key elements in a planning strategy designed to assist in the removal of pollutants (such as automobile exhaust fumes) from street level.

The air-flow patterns in an unobstructed street canyon, characterized by vertical flows of varying strength and direction (either upward or downward)

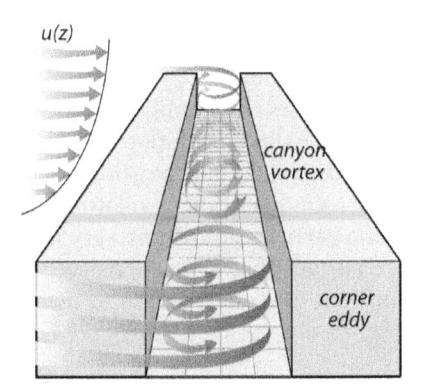

Figure 8.7 Simplified flow field and fundamental vortex structures in a street canyon with aspect ratios of H/W = 1 and L/W = 10 for flow perpendicular to the canyon axis

Source: Redrawn from Gromke and Ruck (2009, Figure 3).

result in a non-uniform concentration of pollutants in the volume defined by the buildings. The location of regions of high concentration of pollutants is affected by the geometry of the street canyon, specifically its aspect ratio and the difference in height (if any) between buildings on opposite sides of the street.

It is useful to first examine the case of a semi-infinite symmetrical street canyon with an aspect ratio of one. As Figure 8.8 shows, the air-flow in such a canyon is characterized by a fairly symmetrical lee vortex whose centre (indicated by *) coincides with the geometric centre of the canyon. Measured at street level, pollutant concentration is relatively lower near the downwind wall, because the downward flow induced by the lee vortex introduces fresh air from outside, and is highest at the bottom of the upwind wall. The upward velocity near this wall is smaller, on average, than the downward velocity near the windward wall, so there is only partial entrainment of canyon air in the free flow at the top of this wall.

Deep symmetric canyons are characterized by a skimming flow pattern, so the coupling between canyon flow and the above-roof flow is weak. As might be expected, this results in less effective removal of pollutants from the street level in deep canyons than in shallower ones. However, it is not only the concentration levels that change, but the location of the highly polluted regions as well (see Figure 8.9). The downward flow along the downwind wall may be unable to reach the canyon floor, creating a region of stagnant air which is highly polluted – more so even than the comparable area at the base of the upwind wall. This region, which may also be highly polluted, at least enjoys partial flushing due to the upward flow of air along the wall.

In the case of asymmetrical street canyons, the relative height of buildings on opposite sides of the street also affects air-flow patterns, and thus the concentration of pollutants at different points in the canyon. It is useful to distinguish between two conditions with respect to the approaching (above-canyon) air-flow: the downwind building may be either taller than the upwind building (and the canyon is thus a 'step-up notch') or it may be lower (and the canyon is thus a 'step-down notch').

In the case of a step-up notch, the primary lee-vortex is shifted upwards, relative to a symmetrical canyon. This effect is more pronounced in the case of a narrow street canyon (see Figure 8.10) than in a shallower street.

In the case of a step-down notch, the lee vortex is also shifted upwards. However, it may also be moved further downwind. If the street canyon is narrow, this vortex may occur above the roof of the downwind building (see Figure 8.11).

In both cases, although the centre of the lee vortex is found at a higher level above the street, the increased turbulence that is created by the asymmetric buildings results in better coupling between the air at street level and the above-roof flow, and therefore leads to better flushing of pollutants. This is especially true in the case of deep canyons: although in absolute terms they still suffer from higher concentrations of pollutants than shallower ones, the improvement obtained by the asymmetry in building heights is relatively greater.

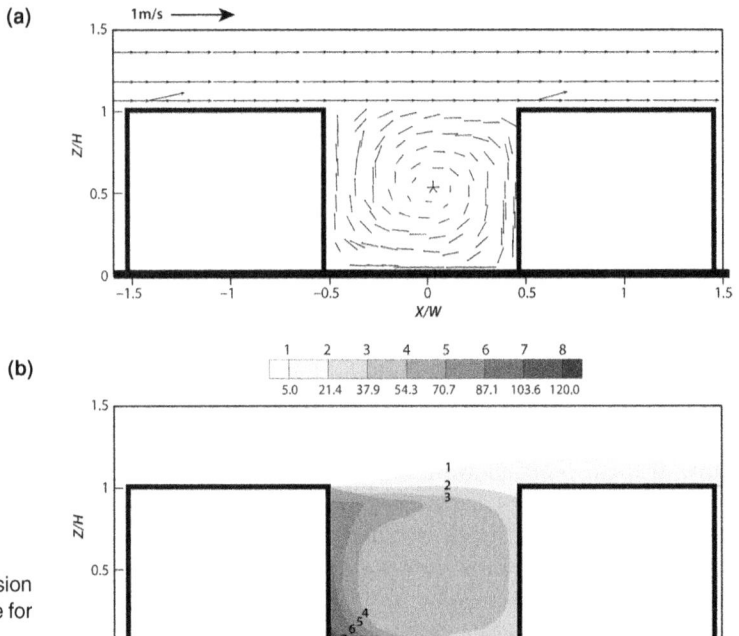

Figure 8.8 Wind field (a) and pollutant dispersion (b) as computed by the MIMO computer code for a square canyon (symmetric case)

Source: Redrawn from Assimakopoulos et al (2003).

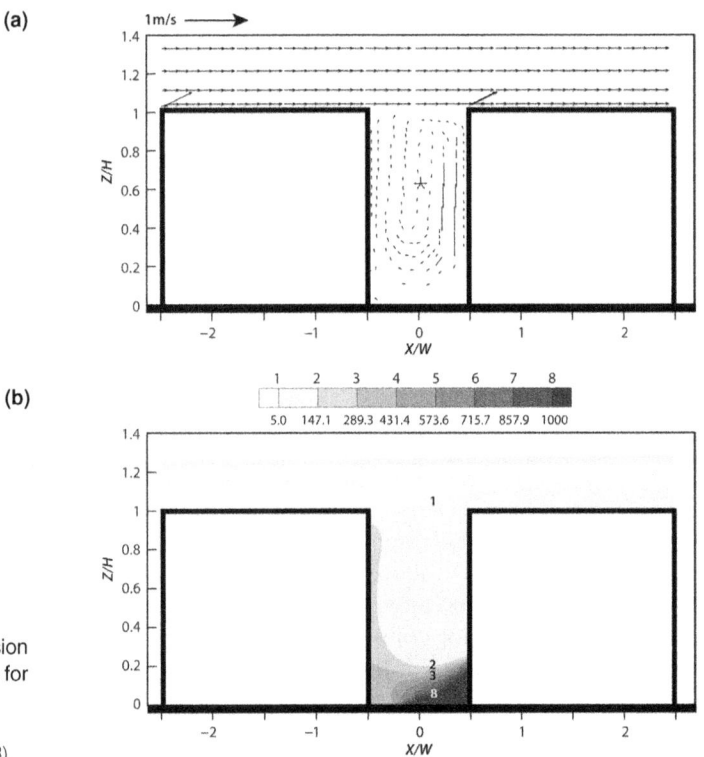

Figure 8.9 Wind field (a) and pollutant dispersion (b) as computed by the MIMO computer code for a deep symmetrical street canyon

Source: Redrawn from Assimakopoulos et al (2003).

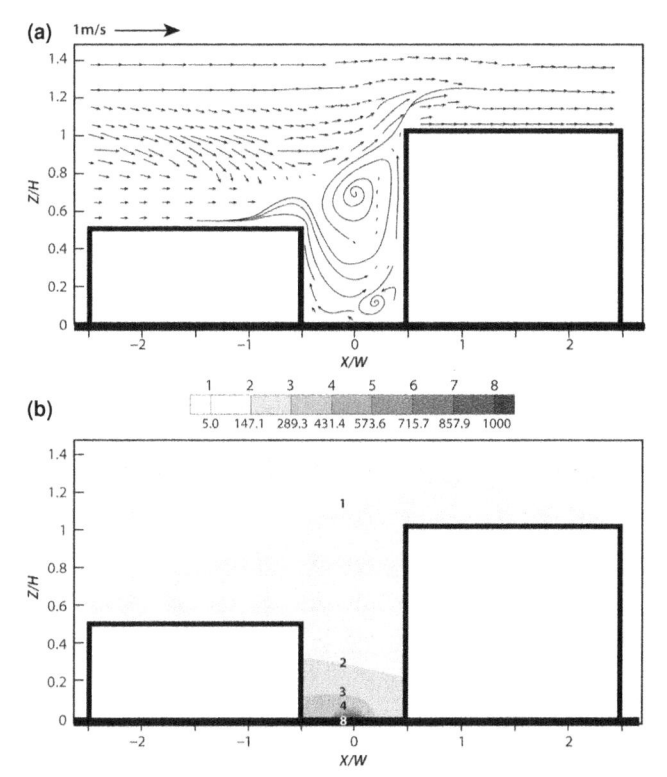

MICROCLIMATE DESIGN STRATEGIES IN URBAN SPACE 157

Figure 8.10 Wind field (a) and pollutant dispersion (b) as computed by the MIMO computer code for a deep asymmetric street canyon (step-up notch)

Source: Redrawn from Assimakopoulos et al (2003).

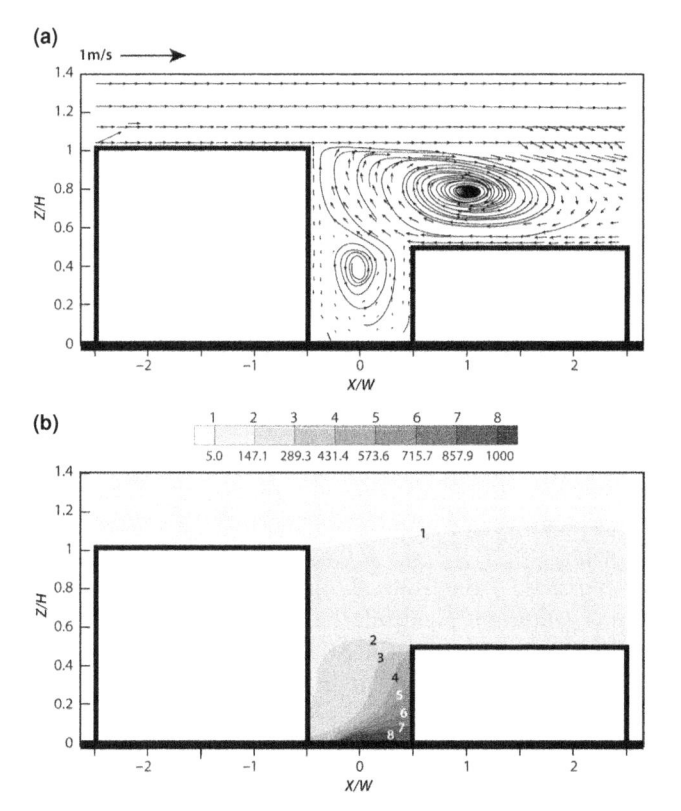

Figure 8.11 Wind field (a) and pollutant dispersion (b) as computed by the MIMO computer code for a deep asymmetrical street canyon (step-down notch)

Source: Redrawn from Assimakopoulos et al (2003).

Effect of street obstructions on air-flow and pollutant dispersion

The discussion has so far considered air-flow in unobstructed streets. Our understanding of the behaviour of air in such spaces is based mostly upon wind tunnel investigation with reduced scale models and upon computer modelling. Models – whether virtual or hardware – are necessarily simplifications of reality. It is clear, for example, that the general flow patterns that may be observed in unobstructed streets will be affected by the presence of obstructions such as kiosks, road signs or bus shelters.

The improvement in modelling techniques has allowed more complex environments to be investigated, and some generalizations regarding the effect of obstructions may be made based upon such studies. The following comments concerning the effect of solid (as opposed to porous) objects are based on the work of Gayev and Savory[2]. The effect of the latter category of objects, specifically trees, will be discussed in Chapter 9.

- Solid objects reduce average along-canyon wind speed, thus reducing the potential for ventilation of buildings. Pedestrian comfort may be enhanced if wind protection is desired (as in cold windy climates) or compromised if air-flow promotes thermal comfort (as in warm, humid locations).
- Solid objects may interfere with the characteristic lee vortex, impairing the flushing of pollutants from street level.
- Solid objects tend to make flow more turbulent, with greater variation in time and space within the street canyon. This may result in localized jets where air velocity is increased as a result of being compressed into narrow spaces, or in sharp changes in the direction of flow – vertically or horizontally. The increased mixing may thus assist in the removal of pollutants from street level, especially if the obstruction is not great enough to interfere with the general circulation in the street.

Planning for better urban air quality

Good air quality may be obtained in cities by applying a comprehensive strategy with several components, only some of which affect the fabric of the city itself. In general terms, such a strategy may be considered to be threefold:

1 *Reduce emissions from sources within the city or in its immediate surroundings.* The success of many cities in developed countries once known for poor air quality – such as London, Pittsburgh or Essen – in reducing airborne pollution is founded primarily on closing down fixed emission sources such as factories and in enforcing more stringent standards on automobile emissions.
2 *Reduce exposure to emissions from sources outside the city.* In humid climates where natural vegetation is plentiful, the concentration of aerosols in rural areas is typically lower than that in cities. However, in some arid regions, natural dust may contribute a substantial proportion of the total airborne particulate mass. Controlling the emission of dust particles from rural surfaces may seem to be beyond the capacity of man, but human

activity is in fact responsible for the state of much of the land surface in most countries. Over-grazing is responsible for decimating natural vegetation in many dryland regions, and together with poor agricultural practices is the cause of desertification. The Dust Bowl created in parts of the southern United States in the 1930s as a result of poor soil management resulted not only in massive dislocation of farming communities, but also in severe degradation of air quality in the communities affected.

3 *Provide an effective ventilation strategy to flush away pollutants in the urban canopy layer.* Once the overall quantity of airborne pollutants is reduced, strategies are required to flush the remaining particles and gases from the urban canopy layer where people carry out their activity. Effective ventilation of urban streets in order to reduce concentrations of pollutants may be promoted by applying the following general guidelines:

- Uniformity in building height, canyon width and canyon length should be avoided. Non-uniformly constructed roof heights provide better ventilation.
- Pitched roofs increase turbulence and create stronger vertical mixing in street canyons than flat roofs, thus assisting in the provision of fresh air and the removal of pollutants from street level.
- Wider canyons promote better pollutant diffusion. The canyon geometry should be restricted to the threshold value for skimming flow.
- The length of street canyons should be kept as short as is practical, to promote flushing at street intersections by corner eddies.
- Where the distance between adjacent intersections is large, ventilation may be improved by avoiding long, continuous facades at street level: flushing of pollutants may take place in the gaps between buildings, if they are large enough.

Building and paving materials

Roofing materials, wall finishes and paving blocks are typically specified by architects for a variety of reasons such as cost, durability and appearance. Their thermal properties, especially insulation, are usually assessed in the context of the energy budget of the building. However, the properties of the materials that form the surfaces that make up the urban canopy also have an effect on urban microclimate, which may be modified through the selection of suitable finishes.

The materials that make up the urban surface have a great influence on its thermal and hydrological balance. The absorptivity and thermal admittance of a surface affect its temperature in changing conditions, and in turn influence air temperature. However, surface temperature also determines radiant exchange with pedestrians, a major factor in their thermal comfort. Wavelength-selective coatings, recently developed, may be used on paving or roofing materials to alter the balance between their visual and thermal properties, and may also have an effect on the overall energy balance of a city if used extensively.

The role of materials in the formation of the urban heat island has been the subject of some conjecture. Experiments with reduced scale models have demonstrated that the nocturnal urban heat island could be explained not only by the effects of street canyon geometry on long-wave radiant exchange but also by differences in the thermal properties of urban and rural surfaces. However, in reality, differences in thermal admittance between urban and rural materials are too small, and are in any case affected to a great degree by rural soil moisture. Furthermore, differences in thermal inertia between rural and urban sites may be accounted for by considering the role of increased surface area in the city, as well as differences in moisture availability. The difficulty of measuring the storage flux on a neighbourhood scale directly in situ has so far limited efforts to explain this mechanism satisfactorily.

The thermal properties of the substrate have a significant effect on temperature and hence on the magnitude of the energy fluxes at the surface. For example, asphalt has a lower thermal conductivity than concrete. Even allowing for the difference in colour, asphalt becomes warmer than concrete in the presence of strong sunshine. Higher daytime temperature results both in greater emission of long-wave radiation and a higher sensible heat loss: a pedestrian walking on an asphalt surface is exposed to both higher air temperature and to a larger long-wave radiant load than if they were walking on a comparable surface made of concrete paving blocks. Conversely, an asphalt surface also cools down more quickly than concrete at night.

Buildings in the warmer parts of the Mediterranean are often whitewashed to reduce the absorption of radiant energy by the envelope during the daytime, and thus to moderate their surface temperature. The same strategy has been proposed to reduce convective heat transfer from pavements and buildings to the air, although the temperature of air near the surface is also affected by several additional factors. Paving materials with a variety of colours and textures have been investigated by several researchers to evaluate the effect of exposure to intense sunlight on surface temperature. The studies found that during the daytime all paving materials had a mean temperature higher than that of the ambient air, while at night all surfaces were cooler, in some cases by almost 6 degrees. However, differences among the samples are illuminating: compared to an exposed concrete tile serving as the reference, some of the coatings tested resulted in mean daytime temperatures lower by about 4 to 5 degrees, with a maximum difference in excess of 7 degrees. The difference between white marble, which is one of the coolest paving materials, and fresh asphalt, which is one of the warmest, may be as much as 22 degrees.

The benefit (in warm climates) of reducing absorption of solar radiation by paving materials, resulting in lower surface temperatures, is offset to some extent by the effects of increased reflection. Highly reflective surfaces, such as freshly whitewashed masonry, may create an uncomfortable visual environment because of excessive glare. Furthermore, the solar radiation reflected from the pavement and walls adds substantially to the radiant load on pedestrians in the space. Thus, the contribution to thermal comfort from slightly lower air temperature and from reduced infra-red emission from the surface needs to be assessed in the context of the overall energy balance of a pedestrian, as discussed in Chapter 5.

The albedo of roof surfaces may have less effect on air temperature in the canopy-layer than the properties of the pavement or the ground, because it affects heat transfer above roof level. However, since it affects the energy performance of a house directly, it has been the subject of much research. The obvious strategy with respect to roofing materials in hot climates is to employ light-coloured materials. However, progress in the production of wavelength-selective paints now allows other colours to be specified, which are fairly dark in appearance but which nevertheless have relatively high albedo. The so-called 'cool coatings' can reduce the temperature of roof tiles having the same appearance (i.e. colour) by between 1.5 and 10 degrees (for green and black tiles, respectively). Some of the coatings have been tested to evaluate the long-term effects of exposure to ultraviolet (UV) radiation and mechanical damage, and show relatively little deterioration over extended periods. Some of the reduction in reflectance is attributed to soiling and can therefore be reversed by rinsing.

High surface temperatures contribute directly to pedestrian discomfort by imposing a long-wave radiant load, and may also affect air temperature nearby. However, the thermal properties of urban surfaces may also have an effect on the climate of a city as a whole: if roof albedo is modified on a large proportion of city roofs, the cumulative effect on the climate of a city may be significant. A computer model of Sacramento, California, predicted that maximum air temperature (in the early afternoon in summer) could be reduced by about 4 degrees if urban albedo was increased from 0.25 to 0.4, while reducing urban albedo to only 0.1 would result in an increase of more than 4 degrees relative to the base case.[3] Similar modelling has shown that feasible albedo changes could lower daytime maximum temperatures in central Los Angeles by up to 2 degrees, although reductions predicted for the suburbs are less substantial. The actual albedo of most urban areas varies from about 0.1 to about 0.2 with a mean value of about 0.14 for urban centres, so there appears to be substantial potential for cooling, if the large-scale application of high-albedo surfaces can in fact be attained. The scale of modification possible depends on the area of solid surfaces such as rooftops, streets and other paved areas as a proportion of the total urban area. However, the micro-scale intra-urban variation of air temperature in the urban canopy, observed in several field studies, means that the benefits of such a strategy may not be felt uniformly over the entire city.

Notes

1 For an extended discussion of this concept, see Knowles (1981).
2 Gayev and Savory (1999).
3 Taha et al (1997).

References

Assimakopoulos, V. D., ApSimon, H. and Moussiopoulos, N. (2003) 'A numerical study of atmospheric pollutant dispersion in different two-dimensional street canyon configurations', *Atmospheric Environment*, vol 37, no 29, pp4037–4049

Capeluto, I. G., Yezioro, A. and Shaviv, E. (2003) 'Climatic aspects in urban design – a case study', *Building and Environment*, vol 38, no 6, pp827–835

Gayev, Y. and Savory, E. (1999) 'Influence of street obstructions on flow processes within urban canyons', *Journal of Wind Engineering and Industrial Aerodynamics*, vol 82, nos 1–3, pp89–103

Gromke, C. and Ruck, B. (2009) 'On the impact of trees on dispersion processes of traffic emissions in street canyons', *Boundary-Layer Meteorology*, vol 131, no 1, pp19–34

Knowles, R. (1981) *Sun, Rhythm, Form*, MIT Press, Cambridge, MA

Littlefair, P. (1998) 'Passive solar urban design: Ensuring the penetration of solar energy into the city', *Renewable and Sustainable Energy Reviews*, vol 2, no 3, pp303–326

Taha, H., Douglas, S. and Haney, J. (1997) 'Mesoscale meteorological and air quality impacts of increased urban albedo and vegetation', *Energy and Buildings*, vol 25, no 2, pp169–177

Wang, H. and Takle, E. (1996) 'On shelter efficiency of shelter belts in oblique wind', *Agricultural and Forest Meteorology*, vol 81, nos 1–2, pp95–117

Additional reading

Asaeda, T., Ca, V. T. and Wake, A. (1996) 'Heat storage of pavement and its effect on the lower atmosphere', *Atmospheric Environment*, vol 30, no 3, pp413–427

Bourbia, F. and Awbi, H. B. (2004a) 'Building cluster and shading in urban canyon for hot dry climate. Part 1: Air and surface temperature measurements', *Renewable Energy*, vol 29, no 2, pp249–262

Bourbia, F. and Awbi, H. B. (2004b) 'Building cluster and shading in urban canyon for hot dry climate. Part 2: Shading simulations', *Renewable Energy*, vol 29, no 2, pp291–301

Bretz, S. and Akbari, H. (1997) 'Long-term performance of high-albedo roof coatings', *Energy and Building*, vol 25, no 2, pp159–167

Bretz, S., Akbari, H. and Rosenfeld, A. (1998) 'Practical issues for using solar-reflective materials to mitigate urban heat islands', *Atmospheric Environment*, vol 32, no 1, pp95–101

Doulos, L., Santamouris, M. and Livada, I. (2004) 'Passive cooling of outdoor spaces: The role of materials', *Solar Energy*, vol 77, no 2, pp231–249

Emmanuel, R. (1997) 'Summertime urban heat island mitigation: Propositions based on an investigation of intra-urban air temperature variations', *Architectural Science Review*, vol 40, no 4, pp155–164

Givoni, B. (1989) *Urban Design in Different Climates*, World Meteorological Organization, Geneva

Gupta, V. K. (1984) 'Solar radiation and urban design for hot climates', *Environment and Planning B: Planning and Design*, vol 11, no 4, pp435–454

Kolokotroni, M., Giannitsaris, I. and Watkins, R. (2006) 'The effect of the London urban heat island on building summer cooling demand and night ventilation strategies', *Solar Energy*, vol 80, no 4, pp383–392

Levinson, R., Akbari, H. and Reilly, J. (2007) 'Cooler tile-roofed buildings with near-infrared-reflective non-white coatings', *Building and Environment*, vol 42, no 7, pp2591–2605

Li, W., Wang, F. and Bell, S. (2007) 'Simulating the sheltering effects of windbreaks in urban outdoor open space', *Journal of Wind Engineering and Industrial Aerodynamics*, vol 95, no 7, pp533–549

Robinson, D. and Stone, A. (2004) 'Solar radiation modelling in the urban context', *Solar Energy*, vol 77, no 3, pp295–309

Santamouris, M. (2001) *Energy and Climate in the Urban Built Environment*, Earthscan, London

Santamouris, M., Papanikolaou, N., Livada, I., Koronakis, I., Georgakis, C., Argiriou, A. and Assimakopoulos, D. N. (2001) 'On the impact of urban climate on the energy consumption of buildings', *Solar Energy*, vol 70, no 3, pp201–216

Santiago, J. L., Martín, F., Cuerva, A., Bezdenejnykh, N. and Sanz-Andrés, A. (2007) 'Experimental and numerical study of wind flow behind windbreaks', *Atmospheric Environment*, vol 41, no 30, pp6406–6420

Synnefa, A., Santamouris, M. and Livada, I. (2006) 'A study of the thermal performance of reflective coatings for the urban environment', *Solar Energy*, vol 80, no 8, pp968–981

Synnefa, A., Santamouris, M. and Apostolakis, K. (2007) 'On the development, optical properties and thermal performance of cool colored coatings for the urban environment', *Solar Energy*, vol 81, no 4, pp488–497

Taha, H. G. (1978) 'An Urban Micro-Climate Model for Site-Specific Building Energy Simulation: Boundary Layers, Urban Canyon and Building Conditions', PhD thesis, University of California, Berkeley, CA

Taha, H. (1997) 'Urban climates and heat islands: Albedo, evapotranspiration and anthropogenic heat', *Energy and Buildings*, vol 25, no 2, pp99–103

Taha, H., Akbari, H., Rosenfeld, A. and Huang, J. (1988) 'Residential cooling loads and the urban heat island – the effects of albedo', *Building and Environment*, vol 23, no 4, pp271–283

Taha, H., Konopacki, S. and Gabersek, S. (1999) 'Impacts of large-scale surface modifications on meteorological conditions and energy use: A 10-region modeling study', *Theoretical and Applied Climatology*, vol 62, pp175–185

Williamson, T. and Erell, E. (2008) 'The implications for building ventilation of the spatial and temporal variability of air temperature in the urban canopy layer', *International Journal of Ventilation*, vol 7, no 1, pp23–35

9
Vegetation

Urban vegetation is credited with providing numerous benefits, such as mitigating the urban heat island, reducing air-conditioning costs in buildings, improving air quality and providing a psychologically superior setting for human activity. To what extent is this in fact the case?

Landscaping, specifically the incorporation of planted areas in the urban fabric, may modify the microclimate of the areas in question, as well as the surrounding area. Typically, the availability of water and the resulting increase in evaporation result in lower surface temperatures. A recently irrigated lawn will therefore be cooler (during the daytime) than an otherwise similar lawn suffering a shortage of water. However, the effect of vegetation is quite complex, and varies with the type of plant, meteorological conditions and time of day. Under certain conditions, an urban park may even be slightly warmer than the surrounding built-up area.

The effects of vegetation on the energy balance are compound. In a thickly vegetated area, the ground surface is no longer the most appropriate datum for the surface energy balance: radiative, sensible and latent heat fluxes are spatially variable within the vegetative canopy, and must be dealt with taking into account the following factors:

- Reduced penetration of short-wave solar radiation to the ground surface.
- Interception of long-wave (infra-red) radiation from the ground surface to the atmosphere.
- Lower wind speed and reduced advection.
- Reduced surface run-off of water (after rain events) compared with paved surfaces or bare ground.

Energy storage in plants, unlike that in inanimate surfaces, consists of two separate components:

1 Physical heat storage.
2 Biochemical energy storage (the result of photosynthesis and CO_2 exchange).

Latent heat exchange occurs not only as a result of condensation or evaporation at the ground surface, but to a large extent due to transpiration from plant leaves.

The study of these effects has for many years been the subject of crop and forest meteorology. However, it is also of great importance in cities because although planted areas may comprise only a small percentage of the overall urban surface, they are very different in character from built-up or paved areas. The interactions between the two types of areas may often be significant.

The effects of vegetation in non-homogeneous areas

In a hypothetical homogeneous surface of unlimited horizontal extent all the fluxes would be perpendicular to the surface, i.e. vertical. However, the Earth's surface, particularly in urban areas, is like a patchwork quilt made from different materials. The horizontal non-homogeneity results in unequal fluxes of energy, and hence in advection. Urban areas are characterized by a variety of surfaces, and air passing over them is continually adjusting to the changing properties. The adjustment that occurs when air passes from a dry, bare surface to a vegetated one (or vice versa), as illustrated in Figure 9.1, is of particular importance.

As air passes from one surface type to another, climatically different surface, it must adjust to a new set of boundary conditions. The line of discontinuity is called the leading edge (see Figure 9.2). The adjustment is not immediate throughout the depth of the air layer: rather, it is generated at the surfaces and diffuses upward. The layer of air affected by the new surface is referred to as the internal boundary-layer (IBL) and its depth grows with fetch downwind from the leading edge. Conditions are fully adjusted to the properties of the new surface only in the lower 10 per cent of the internal boundary-layer. The remainder of the layer is a transition zone where the air is modified by the new surface but not fully adjusted to it. The properties of the air above the internal boundary-layer are determined by upwind influences and not by the surface immediately below.

At the leading edge, assuming a two-dimensional flow perpendicular to the border between the two surfaces, the dry warm air induces a sharply increased

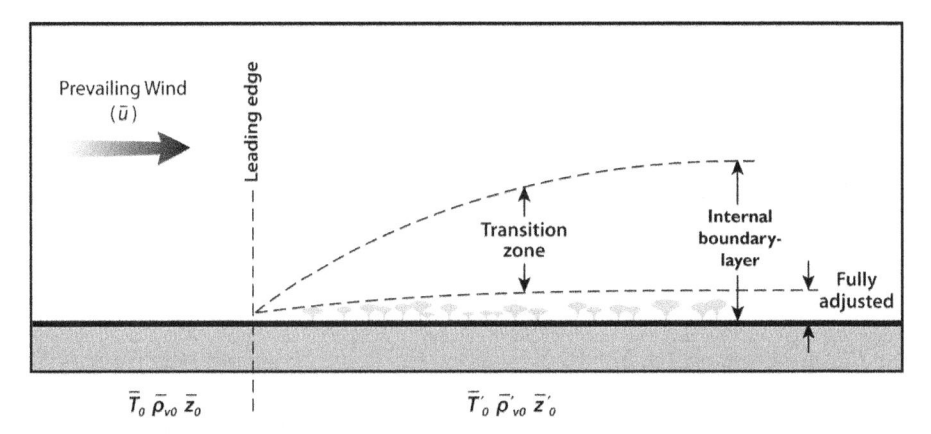

Figure 9.1 The development of an internal boundary-layer as air flows from a smooth, hot, dry, bare surface to a rougher, cooler and moister vegetated surface

rate of evaporation. If the vegetated surface is well irrigated, the *edge effect* may result in evaporation rates substantially greater than the equilibrium rate over a saturated and extensive surface. As air progresses downwind over the vegetated surfaces, its moisture content rises, gradually restricting the rate of evaporation until a new equilibrium is reached. The fetch required for the fully adjusted boundary-layer to stabilize is typically about 100 to 300m for every 1m increase in the vertical. As the distance downwind from the leading edge increases and the internal boundary-layer becomes thicker, the increase in

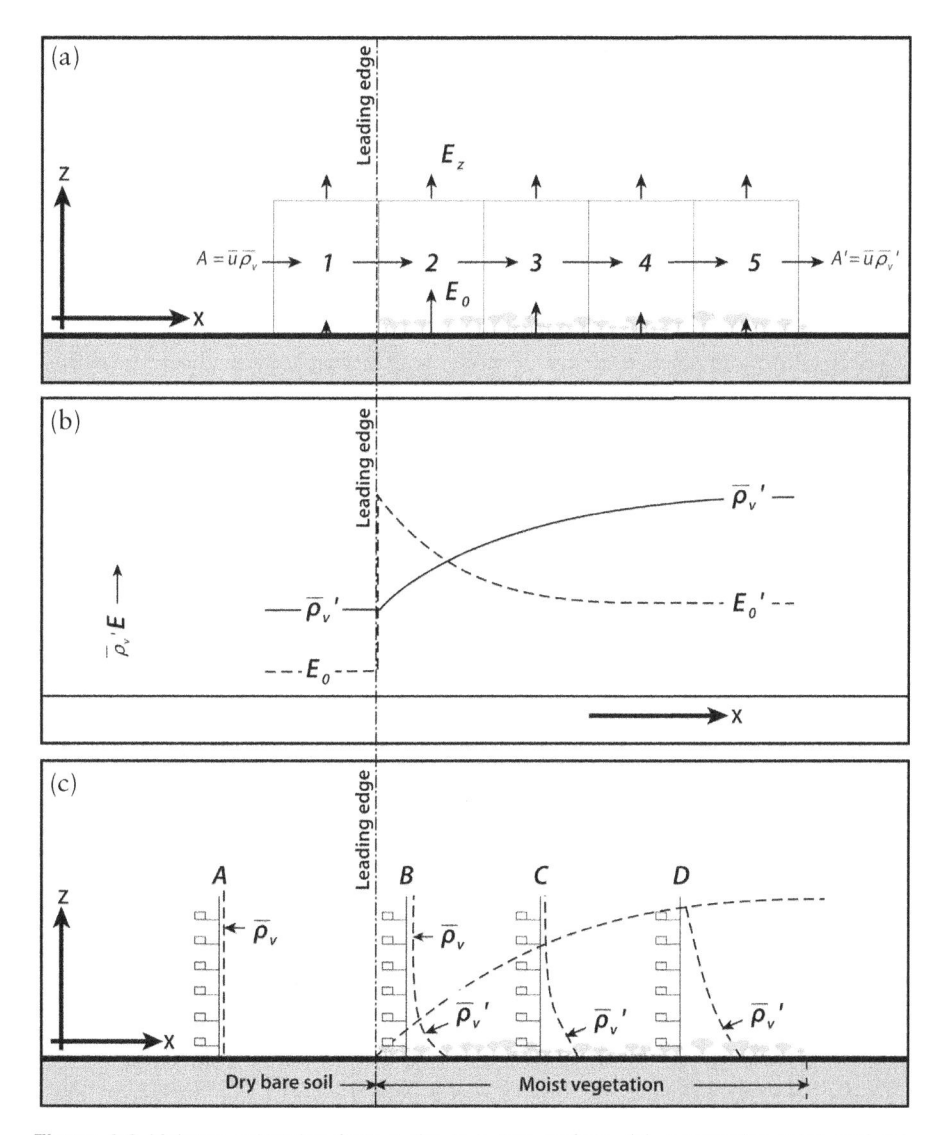

Figure 9.2 Moisture advection from a dry to a wet surface: (a) evaporation rates and the vapour balance of a surface air layer; (b) surface evaporation rate E_0, and mean water vapour concentration of the air layer; (c) vertical profile of water vapour in relation to the developing boundary-layer

Source: Redrawn from Oke (1987).

moisture content of the air is diffused to a greater height. The air above the internal boundary-layer typically experiences no increase or decrease in moisture as a result of the micro-scale changes in surface cover, and advection results in horizontal convergence or divergence only.

Increased evaporation over a vegetated surface results in an increase in the latent heat flux and in a parallel decrease in the sensible heat flux to the atmosphere (and/or storage heat flux to the soil). In extreme cases, a local surface-based inversion may be created. As the air approaches a new state of equilibrium in which evaporation is once again restricted (since the air is by now moist), the sensible heat flux will once again increase gradually, until it too reaches a new equilibrium, at a rate that is somewhat lower than over the bare, non-vegetated surface. The air cooled by evaporation near the surface is gradually diffused and the vertical temperature profile becomes more uniform compared with air over a bare surface. Finally, if the vegetated surface is also rougher than the bare, exposed soil, the vertical profile of the wind will also adapt to the increased drag.

The park cool island (PCI)

The effect of local parks in a non-homogeneous urban area has been the subject of intense study, especially once it became clear that the microclimate of built-up areas differed substantially from that of rural areas. The *park cool island* (PCI), a manifestation of the more general oasis effect, is the converse of the urban heat island. Empirical findings show that air temperatures in moderate to large parks may be substantially lower than those in surrounding built-up areas, although there are significant variations among different types of parks.

Classification of urban parks

Park cool islands may be defined by differences in surface temperature, which may be quite large, or by air temperature, where the effects of surface temperature variation are diluted by near-surface turbulent mixing and advection by wind. The distinction is very important, and is frequently forgotten by designers who assume that a park – any park – will always be cooler than the surrounding built-up area. Nonetheless, examination of the surface energy balance of various types of parks highlights differences in their thermal behaviour. During daytime, the temperature measured at a surface is affected by the presence or absence of shade, by its albedo, by water availability and by the thermal properties of the underlying soil. These properties govern the receipt of solar radiation, its absorption and the role of evaporative cooling. At night, the thermal properties of surfaces and the radiative geometry are the major controls on cooling. Urban parks vary substantially with respect to the above factors, and may be classified according to the arrangement of vegetation: grass; grass with tree border; savannah (grass with isolated trees); garden; forest; and multi-use.[1]

Park cool islands may develop either during the daytime, or at night (see Table 9.1). However, each urban park will display a regular diurnal pattern, indicating that the formation of park cool islands may be the result of a number of mutually exclusive factors.

Daytime PCIs form as a result of the combined effects of soil moisture and shading; trees shade the surface, while grass is typically cooler than most solid surfaces during the daytime, if it is well irrigated. The relative coolness of irrigated parks therefore peaks in the afternoon (forest type), or early evening (garden, savannah and multi-use types). However, trees also inhibit nocturnal long-wave radiative cooling by blocking off part of the sky, while excess moisture increases the thermal capacity of the soil and slows down surface cooling.

Night-time PCIs, on the other hand, typically form in relatively dry urban parks with a sparse tree cover. They are driven by long-wave radiative cooling (especially if the sky view factor is close to unity). Since evaporative fluxes are generally weak at night, evaporation does not play a significant role in the formation of this type of park cool island. In such parks, daytime temperatures may sometimes be higher than in neighbouring urban areas. However, there exists an edge effect that applies within distances of about 2.2 to 3.5 times the height of the park border, and which results in weaker radiative cooling where the sky view factor is reduced by obstructing features such as perimeter trees or buildings.

Table 9.1 Characterization of Park Cool Islands (PCIs)

	Daytime PCI	Night-time PCI
Type of park	Irrigated park with substantial tree cover	Dry parks with sparse tree cover
Mechanisms involved	Evaporation and shading: trees shade the surface, while grass is typically cooler than paved surfaces if it is well irrigated	Long-wave radiant cooling: sky view factor close to unity
Temporal pattern: time of maximum intensity	Afternoon (forest type) or early evening (garden, savannah and multi-use types)	Several hours after sunset
Comments		Warmer during the day than neighbouring urban areas

Additional phenomena related to urban parks

The contrast between extensively irrigated urban parks and the relatively dry surroundings creates a number of interesting phenomena.

The *oasis effect* is a local-scale phenomenon in which evaporation is enhanced as a result of mechanical subsidence of warmer regional (city) air down over the cooler park due to mass divergence within tens of metres. If water supply is not restricted, the extra downward flux of sensible heat supplements the radiative energy supply and permits abnormally high rates of evaporation. In an oasis formed as a result of agricultural land use in China, a daytime inversion layer about 8 metres thick was recorded.[2] Air temperature near the surface was about 2K lower than that at the top of the inversion layer, which was typically observed during the afternoon of fair weather days, when the wind from the surrounding desert was fairly strong.

The *thermostat effect* is a phenomenon first observed with respect to leaves, and refers to the tendency of a wet surface to maintain an almost constant temperature in an increasingly hot environment, at temperatures of 30 to 35°C or more. In principle, an extensively irrigated urban park may act like a giant leaf: as air temperature increases and approaches its daily maximum, the temperature difference between the air and the ground surface decreases, and the ground may be even be slightly cooler than the air near the time of peak heat input ($Q^* + Q_H$). However, since some of the energy required to evaporate water is sensible heat introduced from adjacent areas by advection, the process does not occur in the absence of wind, and as a result the temperature of air one metre above the surface of the park and above adjacent paved areas is very close – surface temperature differentials in excess of 15K notwithstanding.

Effects of size

The extent of vegetated area required to produce measurable effects on air temperature is of great interest to urban planners. The magnitude of the intra-urban temperature difference between parks and their urban surroundings generally increases with park size, although large differences may also be found within the parks and in the adjacent built-up areas. These may be attributed to the degree of exposure to the sky, and hence to the intensity of radiant cooling. Cool islands have been measured in clumps of vegetation less than 200m across, although the effect of vegetation in such small parks is typically limited to the planted area itself and is not felt beyond the park edge. Numerical modelling indicates that small parks of only tens of metres across may create temperature differentials of 2K or more, while the combined effect of shading and evaporation can create localized temperature differences of the same magnitude in very small courtyards, if wind speed is low and mixing of the near-surface air is limited.

Depending upon wind speed and direction, the cooling effect of a park may either decline at an exponential rate with increasing distance downwind from the border of the planted area, or it may be lost abruptly at the windward edge of the park. The horizontal gradients of air temperature may be quite large, and their spatial patterns shift constantly with wind speed and direction. This may explain apparently contradictory reports of the cooling effect of parks on their surrounding area being either negligible or extending as far away as several hundred metres.

The effect of trees on air temperature

The presence of trees in the urban matrix may affect air temperature at a range of spatial scales, from individual streets to city-scale modifications. However, the magnitude of this effect may depend on a variety of factors, because the interaction between trees and other constituents of the urban environment is so complex: trees intercept not only solar radiation, but also long-wave radiation from the ground, building surfaces and the sky. The albedo of a clump of vegetation is often lower than that of solid surfaces such as bare soil or concrete, both because of the dark leaf pigment and because sunlight penetrates the upper surface of the canopy and is then absorbed within the plant following multiple reflections among individual leaves. Even grass reflects only 20 to 22 per cent of incident sunlight, while bushes or trees may reflect as little as 12 to 15 per cent, about the same as asphalt pavement.

The dissipation of this heat load depends on the water balance and wind climate of the tree. In the presence of unrestricted water, transpiration will cause substantial cooling. However, water supply to the root system may be restricted; stomata may be physically blocked by particulates; or the heat load may be excessively high, leading to closure of the stomata. Furthermore, at night (in the absence of sunlight) there is no photosynthesis, so the stomata are closed and the tree is not cooled by transpiration. The response of trees to increased energy loading, which may occur when individual trees are planted in extensive paved areas such as parking lots, for example, will vary with species, humidity of the atmosphere and how much of the crown is exposed. Species from hot or arid habitats may be tolerant of high temperatures or able to dissipate heat with small leaves – but the evapotranspiration (ET) rates from such trees may be accordingly lower than those of broad-leaved trees, and thus have a smaller effect on air temperature in their surroundings.

Many researchers have reported that trees reduce air temperature in their vicinity, and often this is attributed directly to evapotranspiration from the leaf canopy. However, since photosynthesis occurs mainly in leaves exposed to direct sunlight, at the top of the canopy, much of the vapour transfer occurs above the tree and has little effect on the air near ground level. Furthermore, since the moisture content of air typically decreases with height above the ground (except at night, if a strong thermal inversion occurs), the latent heat flux will also tend to be directed upwards.

In most cases, therefore, the relative cooling of air under trees is primarily due to surface shading. Solar radiation that might have otherwise been absorbed at ground level, and then contributed to sensible heating of the air near the surface, is instead absorbed by the leaves near the crown of the tree. The relatively cooler ground releases less heat to the air, which more than offsets the transfer of sensible heat from the tree canopy – which because of its multi-layered structure, maintains a temperature on its underside that is not significantly warmer than the air.

Just how much cooling can trees be expected to generate? The magnitude of the cooling effect depends on several factors, including the size and type of tree, the extent of the area covered by trees, water availability, surface properties, psychrometric factors and the counteracting effects of advection. Several studies have shown that where the shaded area has a limited spatial dimension – for instance beneath a pergola or in the shade of a *liman* (a small clump of trees in an artificial flood-plain in the desert, see Figure 9.3) – the effect on air temperature at a height of one metre above the ground is negligible. Where the

Figure 9.3 The trees in this liman provide welcome relief from the desert sun, but have no measurable effect on air temperature beneath them

Photograph: Evyatar Erell.

surrounding air is dry, especially in the presence of strong sunshine, the effects of vegetation may be expected to be more noticeable, especially if the size of the vegetated area is large or if the shaded area can also be shielded from winds which would otherwise erode any local cooling very quickly. In such cases, experimental studies have found temperature reductions of 3K or more beneath trees.

The actual reduction in air temperature beneath trees has probably been overstated in many cases, due to the difficulty of measuring air temperature accurately in the presence of strong radiant loads. The contribution of trees to human thermal comfort is real enough – this is one of the reasons for the general tendency to support extensive planting of trees – but it is most likely the result of a reduction in the radiant load rather than a substantial cooling of the air.

Trees and shading – solar permeability of trees

Trees (and vines) are often employed as shading devices, both for buildings and for pedestrian space. In cold or temperate climates, many trees are deciduous, and this property is cited as being one of the main attractions of plants as shading elements: they provide shade in summer, when it is desirable, and lose their foliage in winter to allow the penetration of sunlight. However, this idealized behaviour is not always observed in practice for several reasons. Firstly, trees do not always provide shade precisely where desired. Secondly, the period in which many tree species lose their foliage may not coincide with the heating season in a given location. Thirdly, even when trees are completely bare, their branches may still create a substantial obstruction to the sun's rays (see Figure 9.4). Finally, trees cannot be manipulated to provide shading or to remove it in response to changing weather conditions, especially in the transition seasons. Each of these limitations will be discussed in turn.

Inanimate shading devices have fixed physical properties, including a precisely known geometry and solar transmissivity. Trees, however, change their dimensions and degree of opacity as they develop throughout their lifetimes. Variations among individual trees planted at the same time and in similar conditions may be considered a thing of beauty, but the planner needs to be aware of the effect of such differences on the shading pattern produced. Where shade is required from day one, it may be preferable to design a combination of artificial shading elements and trees, the contribution of the latter becoming more significant over time (see Figure 9.5).

Figure 9.4 This *Prosopis juliflora* tree loses its foliage for only several weeks each year, beginning in late February. Even when entirely bare, it still casts a substantial shadow, as seen on the wall behind it.

Photograph: Evyatar Erell.

Figure 9.5 The jacaranda trees are expected to provide most of the shade in the future

Source: Blaustein Institutes for Desert Research, Sde Boqer, Israel; photograph: Evyatar Erell (2009).

The form of a tree will determine where its shadow is cast (at a given time and location). Trees that have a broad, low-hanging canopy (horizontal ellipsoid form) will display less variable shadow patterns than tall trees with a limited horizontal section (vertical ellipsoid form). The latter cast a relatively small shadow at high solar elevation and a large but diffuse shadow when the sun is low, whereas the former cast a deep shadow when the sun is overhead: the canopy of such trees may intercept not only the direct solar radiation but also a substantial proportion of the diffuse and reflected light.

Although deciduous trees lose their foliage in autumn, there may be significant variations among different species. Figure 9.6 shows a comparison of the permeability of four species at the same location. Maximum and minimum values occur up to two months apart – indicating a possible mismatch between the actual filtering effect and the desired shading for at least some species. Little if anything can be done to modify this behaviour, but knowledge of this property for a given type of tree may assist in making a selection with the desirable microclimatic effect.

The canopy of all trees consists of branches and twigs in addition to leaves. This has important implications when considering deciduous trees. Branches and twigs are opaque to sunlight, either absorbing or reflecting practically all of the incident radiation. Leaves, on the other hand, are usually translucent to a certain degree, and allow some of the radiation through, mainly in the near infra-red part of the solar spectrum. This means that the density of the branch system matters, not only when the tree has no leaves, but also to some extent when it is in full foliage. The transmissivity of different tree species may vary from as little as 5 per cent in summer (Norway maples) to almost 90 per cent

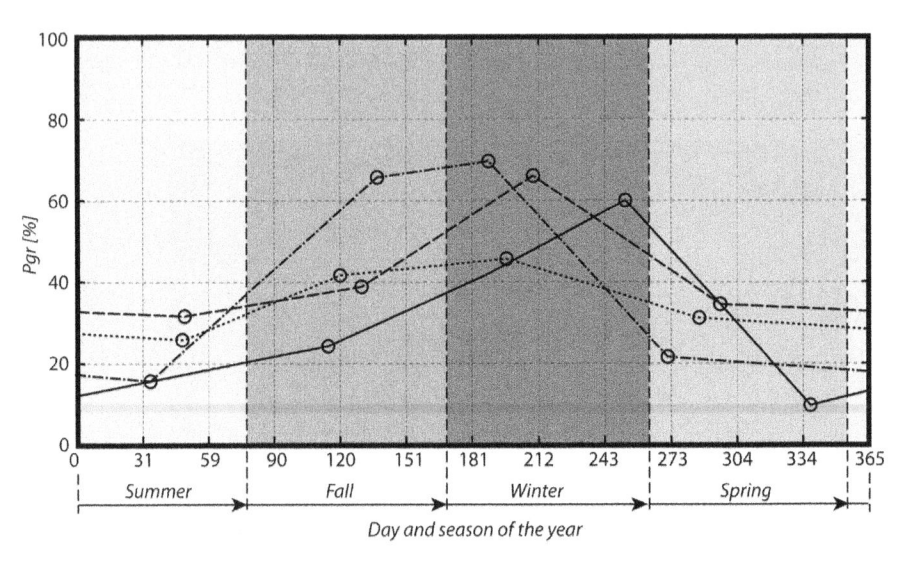

Figure 9.6 Maximum and minimum solar permeability of different tree species may vary by as much as two months

Note: Graph shows data for four tree species in Argentina, in the southern hemisphere.

Source: Redrawn from Cantón et al (1994).

in winter (American elm). Table 9.2 gives the characteristics of tree species common to North America. Designers and architects who assume that, for example, a window may be shaded by trees in summer and wholly exposed to sunlight in winter, may find that neither assumption is wholly justified.

Table 9.2 Shading effect of selected trees found in North America

Botanical name	Common name	Transmissivity range (%) summer	Transmissivity range (%) winter	Foliation	Defoliation	Max. height (m)
Acer platanoides	Norway maple	5–14	60–75	E	M	15–25
Acer rubrum	Red maple	8–22	63–82	M	E	20–35
Acer saccharinum	Silver maple	10–28	60–87	M	M	20–35
Acer saccharum	Sugar maple	16–27	60–80	M	E	20–35
Aesculus hippocatanum	Horse chestnut	8–27	73	M	L	22–30
Amelanchier canadensis	Serviceberry	20–25	57	L	M	n/a
Betula pendula	European birch	14–24	48–88	M	M–L	15–30
Carya ovata	Shagbark hickory	15–28	66	n/a	n/a	24–30
Catalpa speciosa	Western catalpa	24–30	52–83	L	n/a	18–30
Fagus sylvatica	European beech	7–15	83	L	L	18–30
Fraxinus pennsylvanica	Green ash	10–29	70–71	M–L	M	18–25
Gleditsia tricanthos inermis	Honey locust	25–50	50–85	M	E	20–30
Juglans nigra	Black walnut	9	55–72	L	E–M	23–45
Liriondron tulipifera	Tulip tree	10	69–78	M–L	M	27–45
Picea pungens	Colorado spruce	13–28	13–28	n/a	n/a	27–41
Pinus strobus	White pine	25–30	25–30	n/a	n/a	24–45
Platanus acerifolia	London plane	11–17	46–64	L	M–L	30–35
Populus deltoids	Cottonwood	10–20	68	E	M	23–30
Populus tremuloides	Trembling aspen	20–33	n/a	E	M	12–15
Quercus alba	White oak	13–38	n/a	n/a	n/a	24–30
Quercus rubra	Red oak	12–23	70–81	n/a	M	23–30
Tilia cordata	Littleaf linden	7–22	46–70	L	E	18–21
Ulmus americana	American elm	13	63–89	M	M	18–24

Note: (a) Foliation: E (Early) – before 30 April; M (Middle) – 1 to 15 May; L (Late) – after 15 May; (b) Defoliation: E (Early) – before 1 November; M (Middle) – 1 to 30 November; L (Late) – after 30 November.

Source: Reproduced from Brown and Gillespie (1995).

The effects of vegetation on building energy consumption

Landscaping and careful planting of vegetation near buildings have been credited with energy savings of up to 80 per cent in hot, dry climates. However, in spite of the fact that several studies have been carried out to quantify the effect of vegetation, especially trees, on the energy consumption of buildings, much of the evidence remains anecdotal. Furthermore, since the actual saving possible for any particular building depends upon the properties of the building and its operation, in addition to the effect of vegetation, attempts to derive a broad quantitative estimate of the effect of plants should be treated cautiously.

The mechanisms by which vegetation affects the energy exchange between buildings and the environment may be summarized as follows:

- Vegetation can reduce energy consumption in buildings in hot climates if air temperature is reduced near the buildings as a result of the planted area. However, it should be noted in this context that heat transfer through building walls is driven by differences in their surface temperature, which is affected by radiation and wind as well as by outside air temperature. Furthermore, the reduction in air temperature resulting from evapotranspiration is accompanied by an increase in the vapour content of the air. Therefore, the air-conditioning system must deal with an increased latent heat load, offsetting to some extent any gains from a lower sensible heat load.
- Plants may shade building surfaces, reducing the radiant load on the envelope. This may be beneficial in hot conditions, but detrimental in cold ones, where exposure to the sun is generally beneficial. In temperate climates with distinct heating and cooling seasons, deciduous trees are often planted, and vine-covered trellises are common in many Mediterranean areas. However, the timing of defoliation and the permeability of the bare trees vary widely from species to species and may not match the desired pattern of exposure to the sun. In the middle latitudes, cooling loads are most sensitive to shading on the roof and on the west wall, while heating loads are affected most if exposure of the south (equator-facing) and east walls is blocked. Shade may be generated by trees or by other types of vegetation, such as vines, adjacent to the wall surface: a dense growth of ivy can block radiant exchange at the wall surface almost entirely. The reduction in surface temperature resulting from the shade obviously depends upon the extent of the leaf cover, but also – perhaps less obviously – on the properties of the wall itself, such as its thermal absorptance, emittance and admittance. Thick foliage producing a full shade effect may reduce the surface temperature of a light-coloured concrete wall by as much as 10 degrees, with concomitant reductions in heat flux through the surface. Shading may not only reduce solar gains – it can limit net long-wave losses at night, since building surfaces will be exposed to relatively warm vegetation (at approximately ambient air temperature), instead of the

potentially much colder sky. The equivalent sky temperature can be as much as 20 degrees colder than air temperature in dry conditions, so the difference in outgoing flux can be substantial.

- Plants may reduce wind speed near buildings. This limits unwanted infiltration, but also restricts the potential for ventilation. It also reduces convective exchange at building surfaces. The first two mechanisms are self-explanatory, but the third has less well-known consequences. For instance, in hot climates, wind is an asset for unshaded houses because it helps remove radiant heat at the external building surfaces, reducing temperature differentials between interior and exterior. However, in poorly insulated houses, especially in cold climates, increased convective exchange at the building envelope results in increased loads on building heating or cooling systems.
- Plants in warm climates may reduce temperatures of ground surfaces by evapotranspiration (although planted surfaces may be warmer than bare soil in cold conditions) with two consequences: cooler surfaces emit less infra-red radiation, thus reducing the radiant load on building surfaces, and release less sensible heat to the adjacent air, so that buildings are exposed to cooler ambient air.
- Roof gardens (or planted roofs) are perhaps the most obvious example of the use of plants to control building energy performance, and are sometimes credited with improving the urban microclimate as well. The shading and evapotranspiration of the plants contribute to lower surface temperatures and thus to lower heat gains through the roof, which are also moderated by the large heat capacity of the soil. Experiments show that the surface temperature of an exposed roof can be reduced substantially by the addition of an irrigated lawn on a fabric matrix. Computer modelling of the complete roof–soil–vegetation system of a planted roof showed that the thermal performance of the roof depends mainly on the density of the foliage, the composition, density and thickness of the substrate, and its water content. However, unless the thermal conductivity of the soil is particularly low or the thickness of the substrate is considerable, the thermal resistance provided by the planting and substrate is usually insufficient during the cold season even in mid-latitude countries with relatively mild winters.

Computer models designed to predict the general microclimatic effect on energy consumption of augmenting urban vegetation show a fairly wide range of results. This is to be expected, given that the existing urban fabric and the climate forcing vary from city to city. Table 9.3 shows a summary of model predictions published in recent years.

Table 9.3 Summary of the results of modelling studies on the effect of increasing the vegetated area of cities

	Author (year)	Type of model	Proposed intervention	Predicted effect
1	Sailor (1998)	Mesoscale, 2 × 2km grid	Increase vegetated fraction by 0.065	Reduce cooling load by 3–5%
2	Taha et al (1997)	CSUMM (mesoscale, 200 × 200m grid)	Increase vegetated fraction by 0.03–0.04 Increase albedo by 0.03–0.05	Reduction in peak daytime temperatures. Annual energy cost in several US cities reduced by $11–55 per 100m² in offices and by $9–71 per 100m² in residential buildings
3	Krüger and Pearlmutter (2008)	OASUS (physical scaled array)	Increase vegetated fraction by 0.13	Reduction of 2–3K in peak daytime temperatures.
4	Pearlmutter et al (2009)	OASUS (physical scaled array)	Increase vegetated fraction by 0.13	Doubling of normalized latent heat flux

Effect of trees upon pollutant dispersion and air quality in city streets

Trees have been credited with the capacity to filter the air, absorbing – in addition to CO_2 – a variety of undesirable pollutants. However, the effect of trees on air quality in urban streets is not wholly beneficial. Wind tunnel studies confirm results of computer simulation showing that a row of trees planted along a city pavement interferes with the formation of the lee vortex that is one of the mechanisms for the removal of pollutants originating within the street, such as automobile exhaust.

To understand the effect of trees, it is useful to recall that the typical flow pattern in an urban canyon consists of a lee vortex in the middle of the canyon (considering its longitudinal axis) and corner eddies at the two ends of the street, where it intersects with connecting roads. (For a more detailed discussion of canyon air-flow see Chapters 4 and 8).

The presence of trees interferes with both types of air-flow, resulting in less dispersion of pollutants and consequently poorer air quality. The lee vortex is disrupted, so that the fresh air entrained at roof level flushes pollutants from the base of the windward wall only, resulting in slightly improved air quality there. However, the momentum intercepted by the trees means that there is insufficient energy to propel air from the base of the lee wall upwards, and pollutant concentrations there are substantially higher than they would have been in the absence of trees. Likewise, trees also interfere with along-canyon flow, limiting the penetration of corner eddies and thus the extent to which they may assist in providing fresh air and removing pollutants.

It is worth noting that even very porous tree crowns have a big effect on pollutant concentrations. At about 90 per cent porosity (with only 10 per cent of the volume occupied by solid material), trees begin to behave like non-porous bluff bodies. Differences among different tree species are very small in

Figure 9.7 The trees lining the broad suburban street (top) provide almost complete shade, but buildings are set back and flushing of air at street level is not a problem. In the avenue (bottom) the row of trees adjacent to the buildings on the left is too close to the facade, and when they are fully grown will cut off air-flow near the wall.

this respect. For most species, there is also little difference in their effect on air-flow between full foliage and a completely bare state: the branch and twig structure creates a substantial aerodynamic interference even in the absence of leaves.

The deleterious effects of trees on dispersal of pollutants may be mitigated, to a certain extent, by complying with the following recommendations:

- Tree crowns should not occupy large canyon volumes, in order not to suppress the ventilating canyon vortex system and the corner eddies. In particular, sufficient free space between crowns and adjacent walls should be ensured (See Figure 9.7). Otherwise, air exchange is hindered and the concentration of pollutants at street level may rise.
- The tree height should not exceed roof level, as this would result in a substantial reduction in entrained above-roof air required to ventilate the street canyon.
- Broad tree spacing creates less of an obstruction, and allows rooftop flow to generate vortices in the street.
- Trees have a smaller effect in shallow canyons (H/W<0.5) than in deeper ones. Where possible, broad avenues with two rows of trees are preferable to narrow streets with one row.

Effects of vegetation on pedestrian thermal comfort

Owing to its three-dimensional presence in an urban space, the body of a standing pedestrian is influenced in distinctly different ways by different types of vegetation. Broad trees with thick overhead foliage, for instance, create an entirely different mechanism than does an irrigated lawn – even though both of these planting types may be effective for moderating thermal stress under hot outdoor conditions.

Shade trees

The impact of trees on a pedestrian's energy balance is primarily radiative. The most obvious form this takes is direct shading of the body from incoming solar rays, neutralizing what is often the largest single source of overheating. But besides intercepting direct radiation, which is specifically directional, a wide tree canopy can reduce indirect radiative effects as well, starting with diffuse short-wave and emitted long-wave radiation from the sky vault. To the extent that the tree canopy casts shadows on surrounding surfaces such as otherwise sunlit paving and walls, it will also reduce the amount of solar radiation that is reflected from these surfaces and the amount of long-wave radiation they emit – consequently limiting the energy absorbed by a person's body.

Each of these factors is dependent on a number of properties of the tree species and the way individual trees are deployed in an urban space. The effectiveness of a tree canopy as a shading element is firstly a function of its effective opacity (i.e. the inverse of its transmissivity), which is largely determined by the density of its leaves, stems and branches. While a dense crown may transmit less than 30 per cent of incident rays at high sun angles (i.e. provide the equivalent of 70 per cent shading), this value changes with season, time of day and location for a given tree and even more so for trees that vary in structure because of their condition or particular species (see Table 9.2). When the actual solar transmission of a certain tree variety cannot be specified from direct measurements, the leaf area index (LAI) is commonly used as a surrogate measure.

Effective shading of both pedestrians and adjacent solid surfaces is also a matter of geometry, in terms of the overall form of the canopy and its position relative to the shaded object (see Figure 9.8). A single large tree with a broad, low canopy can provide a well-shaded spot at all hours, although the exact location of this spot will vary by hour and season. Trees may also be used in clusters or rows, sometimes in conjunction with other elements of the urban fabric such as building walls or shade canopies to form continuous barriers that cast shadows over a predetermined area for many hours, even at low sun angles (see Figures 9.9 and 9.10).

At the same time, trade-offs may be encountered between the effectiveness of summer shading provided by the tree due to its geometry and foliage density, and a number of other comfort-related factors. Theoretically, a dense shading canopy may itself impose a significant radiant load due to its emission of

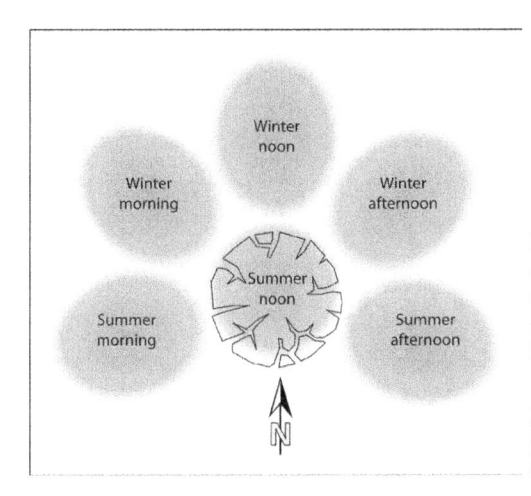

Figure 9.8 Generic location in plan view of shaded areas relative to a broad-canopy tree, by time of day and season (for mid-latitude regions in the northern hemisphere)

Note: Actual ground shading at a specific time and location can be calculated from tree dimensions, based on solar altitude and azimuth angles (see Chapter 5).

Figure 9.9 This parking lot is almost always shaded through the combined effect of the trees and the whitewashed wall

Photograph: Evyatar Erell.

Figure 9.10 Diners in this outdoor restaurant are shaded by the trees as well as by the fabric canopy

Photograph: Evyatar Erell.

long-wave radiation, though the multiple layers of leaves and branches typically ensure that the underside of the canopy maintains a surface temperature which is no higher than the surrounding air. A more prominent trade-off is the resistance to air-flow that is generated beneath the tree canopy. The latter may also be crucial to pedestrian comfort, since it is a determinant of the rate at which the body can dissipate heat by both convection and sweat evaporation.

The other important determinant of the body's convective heat loss is the temperature of the surrounding air, which according to many accounts may be significantly modified in the vicinity of transpiring shade trees. It should be stressed, however, that neither the dry bulb temperature of the air nor its vapour content (the latter of which is crucial to the body's cooling by sweat evaporation) are likely to undergo dramatic modifications due to the direct effects of a single tree. As discussed above, such air cooling is often related to the reduced temperatures of tree-shaded ground, and thus it may become significant in the middle of a large grove or heavily wooded urban park where the area of cooler ground in contact with the air-flow is considerable.

Under clear summer daytime conditions, the presence of shade trees can provide not only an incremental improvement to thermal comfort, but transform a severely stressful urban environment into a tangibly comfortable one (see Box 9.1). This is the case if (a) the air is neither extremely hot (>35°C) nor highly humid, and (b) a substantial rate of air-flow is maintained. If the tree is deciduous, a further advantage may be realized in winter – to the extent that the seasonal loss of foliage coincides with low air temperatures, and the increase in pedestrian exposure to direct sun is therefore beneficial.

Grass and vegetative ground cover

Replacing a paved surface or bare soil with a planted ground covering can moderate a pedestrian's thermal stress in several ways:

- *Low reflectance*. Typical green grass used for lawns has a relatively low albedo, with common values in the range of 0.20–0.25. This means that when compared with a concrete path or an area that is paved with light-coloured stone, a lawn will reflect considerably less short-wave radiation onto a person's body.
- *Evaporative cooling*. A well-watered lawn that is exposed to the sky can be a significant source of evaporative cooling, although the reduction in air temperature may be primarily felt close to the surface: if the mixing of air is strong and the grassy area small, then cooling may be largely limited to the lowest metre or less above the ground. The rate of evapotranspiration (i.e. the combined transpiration from grass leaves and evaporation from wetted soil) from a patch of short-cut grass will typically be 70 to 80 per cent of the evaporation from a free-water surface (such as a lake, pool or evaporation pan).
- *Low surface temperature*. Despite its low albedo and high absorption of solar radiation, a well-vegetated ground surface will tend to channel most of this absorbed energy into latent heat through evapotranspiration. Not only does this reduce the sensible heating of the adjacent air, it allows the ground to maintain a much lower surface temperature than a dry surface of a similarly dark colour (or even, in many cases, than a dry surface which is considerably brighter). The consequent reduction in emitted long-wave radiation to which a pedestrian is exposed may in fact be the main thermal contribution of a lawn, especially during summer daytime hours when outdoor thermal stress is especially pronounced (see Box 9.1).

The potential benefits of vegetative ground cover under hot conditions may be enhanced when used in combination with shade trees. Clearly, the presence of a dense canopy above the grass area can further lower ground temperatures and reduce reflected radiation on the body but it may also have indirect, symbiotic effects.

In many regions, lawn irrigation places a heavy burden on water sources which may be limited in their availability, in terms of both quantity and quality. The judicious use of shade trees or other overhead elements can significantly moderate the rate of water loss from the grass to the atmosphere, and the resulting water savings can far outweigh the irrigation requirements of the trees themselves. Achieving such a situation depends, of course, on careful selection and deployment of plant species, so that the ground cover receives sufficient daylight and other conditions needed for its maintenance.

Box 9.1 Vegetative landscape treatments and thermal stress

A controlled outdoor experiment in the hot-dry climate of the Negev desert in Israel illustrated the potential of urban vegetation for moderating thermal stress. Two identical courtyard spaces, both surrounded by single-storey buildings and oriented along a north–south axis (with a cross-sectional H/W ratio of about 0.5), were monitored using a set of different landscape treatments. One courtyard was planted with mature shade trees (mesquite and rosewood), and the other had either full exposure to the sky or was protected by a lightweight shading mesh. Both courtyards were alternately covered with a sod ground cover (Durban grass) or left with their original bare concrete paving.

When compared with the exposed bare courtyard, the grass-covered space allowed for a significant reduction in daytime thermal stress. Additional reductions were provided by the shading treatments (trees or mesh), and the maximum reductions were afforded by the combined use of overhead shading and vegetative ground cover – which produced comfortable conditions at all hours. Both the grass and the underside of the tree canopy maintained temperatures close to that of the air throughout the day.

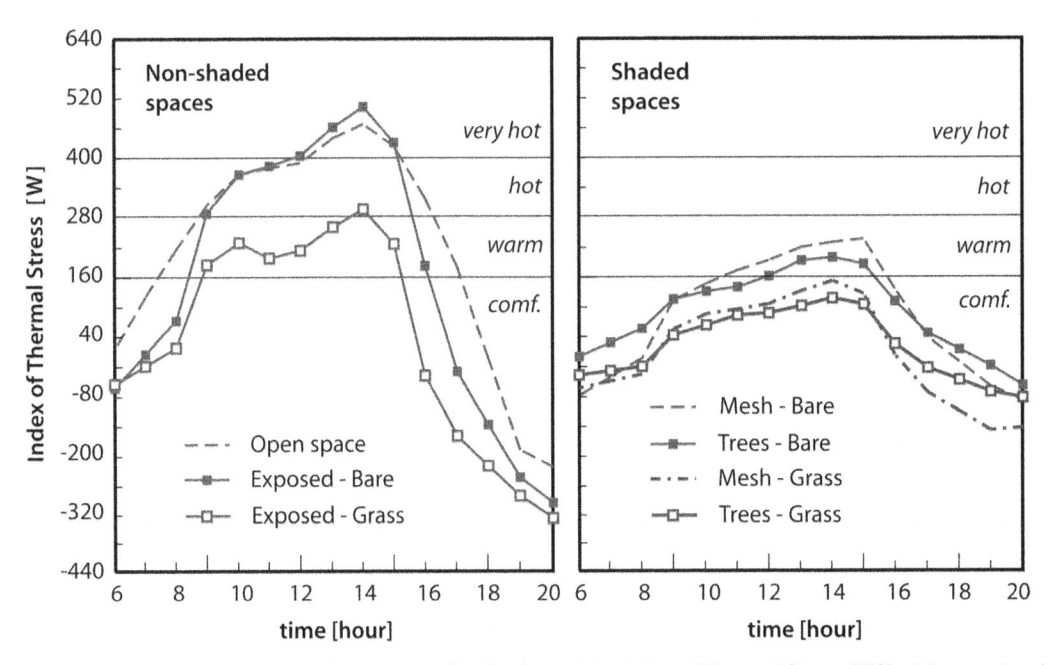

Figure 9.11 The effect of vegetation on normalized values of the Index of Thermal Stress (ITS) at the courtyard spaces during summer daytime hours (LST) with corresponding levels of subjective thermal sensation; (a) non-shaded spaces (left) and (b) courtyard configurations with overhead shading by either trees or mesh (right)

Source: Reproduced from Shashua-Bar et al (2010).

Notes

1 This classification was proposed by Spronken-Smith and Oke (1998).
2 Kai et al (1997).

References

Brown, R. and Gillespie, T. (1995) *Microclimatic Landscape Design: Creating Thermal Comfort and Energy Efficiency*, John Wiley & Sons, New York

Cantón, M. A., Cortegoso, J. L. and de Rosa, C. (1994) 'Solar permeability of urban trees in cities of western Argentina', *Energy and Buildings*, vol 20, no 3, pp219–230

Kai, K., Matsuda, M. and Sato, R. (1997) 'Oasis effect observed at Zhangye oasis in the Hexi corridor, China', *Journal of the Meteorological Society of Japan*, vol 75, no 6, pp1171–1178

Krueger E. L. and Pearlmutter, D. (2008) 'The effect of urban evaporation on building energy demand in an arid environment, *Energy and Buildings*, vol 40, no 11, pp2090–2098

Oke, T. R. (1987) *Boundary Layer Climates*, Methuen, London and New York

Pearlmutter, D., Krüger, E. L. and Berliner, P. (2009) 'The role of evaporation in the energy balance of an open-air scaled urban surface', *International Journal of Climatology*, vol 29, pp911–920

Sailor, D. J. (1998) 'Simulations of annual degree day impacts of urban vegetative augmentation', *Atmospheric Environment*, vol 32, no 1, pp43–52

Shashua-Bar L., Pearlmutter, D. and Erell, E. (2010) 'The influence of trees and grass on outdoor thermal comfort in a hot-arid environment', *International Journal of Climatology*, accepted for publication

Spronken-Smith, R. A. and Oke, T. R. (1998) 'The thermal regime of urban parks in two cities with different summer climates', *International Journal of Remote Sensing*, vol 19, no 11, pp2085–2104

Taha, H., Douglas, S. and Haney, J. (1997) 'Mesoscale meteorological and air quality impacts of increased urban albedo and vegetation', *Energy and Buildings*, vol 25, no 2, pp169–177

Additional reading

Bonan, G. B. (2000) 'The microclimates of a suburban Colorado (USA) landscape and implications for planning and design', *Landscape and Urban Planning*, vol 49, nos 3–4, pp97–114

Bruse, M. and Fleer, H. (1998) 'Simulating surface–plant–air interactions inside urban environments with a three dimensional numerical model', *Environmental Modelling and Software*, vol 13, nos 3–4, pp373–384

Ca, V. T., Asaeda, T. and Abu, E. M. (1998) 'Reductions in air conditioning energy caused by a nearby park', *Energy and Buildings*, vol 29, no 1, pp83–92

Cantón, M. A., Cortegoso, J. L., Fernandez, J. and de Rosa, C. (2001) 'Environmental and energy impact of the urban forest in arid zone cities', *Architectural Science Review*, vol 44, pp3–16

Grimmond, C. S. B., Souch, C. and Hubble, M. D. (1996) 'Influence of tree cover on summertime surface energy balance fluxes, San Gabriel Valley, Los Angeles', *Climate Research*, vol 6, no 1, pp45–57

Hoyano, A. (1988) 'Climatological uses of plants for solar control and the effects on the thermal environment of a building', *Energy and Building*, vol 11, nos 1–3, pp181–200

Huang, Y. J., Akbari, H., Taha, H. and Rosenfeld, A. H. (1987) 'The potential of vegetation in reducing summer cooling loads in residential buildings', *Journal of Climate and Applied Meteorology*, vol 26, pp1103–1116

Jauregui, E. (1990–1991a) 'Effects of revegetation and new artificial water bodies on the climate of northeast Mexico City', *Energy and Buildings*, vol 15, nos 3–4, pp447–455

Jauregui, E. (1990–1991b) 'Influence of a large urban park on temperature and convective precipitation in a tropical city', *Energy and Buildings*, vol 15, nos 3–4, pp457–463

Kanda, M. and Moriwaki, R. (1998) 'Environmental effect of Meiji-shrine forest as a sink of energy and pollutants', in S. Grimmond (ed) *Second Urban Climate Symposium*, American Meteorological Society, Boston, MA

Kjelgren, R. and Montague, T. (1998) 'Urban tree transpiration over turf and asphalt surfaces', *Atmospheric Environment*, vol 32, no 1, pp35–41

McPherson, E. G., Herrington, L. P. and Heisler, G. M. (1988) 'Impacts of vegetation on residential heating and cooling', *Energy and Buildings*, vol 12, no 1, pp41–51

Meier, A. K. (1990–1991) 'Strategic landscaping and air-conditioning savings: A literature review', *Energy and Buildings*, vol 15, nos 3–4, pp479–486

Niachou, A., Papakonstantinou, K., Santamouris, M., Tsangrassoulis, A. and Mihalakakou, G. (2001) 'Analysis of the green roof thermal properties and investigation of its energy performance', *Energy and Buildings*, vol 33, no 7, pp719–729

Oke, T. R., Crowther, J. M., McNaughton, K. G., Monteith, J. L. and Gardiner, B. (1989) 'The micrometeorology of the urban forest', *Philosophical Transactions of the Royal Society London (B)*, vol 324, no 1223, pp335–349

Onmura, S., Matsumoto, M. and Hokoi, S. (2001) 'Study on the evaporative cooling effect of roof lawn gardens', *Energy and Buildings*, vol 33, no 7, pp653–666

Palomo Del Barrio, E. (1998) 'Analysis of the green roofs cooling potential in buildings', *Energy and Buildings*, vol 27, no 2, pp179–193

Papadakis, G., Tsamis, P. and Kyritsis, S. (2001) 'An experimental investigation of the effect of shading with plants for solar control of buildings', *Energy and Buildings*, vol 33, no 8, pp831–836

Raza, S. H., Murthy, M. S. R., Lakshmi, O. B. and Shylaja, G. (1990–1991) 'Effect of vegetation on urban climate and healthy urban colonies', *Energy and Buildings*, vol 15, nos 3–4, pp487–491

Saito, I., Ishihara, O. and Katayama, T. (1990–1991) 'Study of the effect of green areas on the thermal environment in an urban area', *Energy and Buildings*, vol 15, nos 3–4, pp493–498

Schiller, G. and Karschon, R. (1974) 'Microclimate and recreational value of tree plantings in deserts', *Landscape Planning*, vol 1, pp329–337

Shashua-Bar, L. and Hoffman, M. (2000) 'Vegetation as a climatic component in the design of an urban street: An empirical model for predicting the cooling effect of urban green areas with trees', *Energy and Buildings*, vol 31, no 3, pp221–235

Shashua-Bar, L. and Hoffman, M. (2002) 'The Green CTTC model for predicting the air temperature in small urban wooded sites', *Building and Environment*, vol 37, no 12, pp1279–1288

Simpson, J. R. (2002) 'Improved estimates of tree-shade effects on residential energy use', *Energy and Buildings*, vol 34, no 10, pp1067–1076

Simpson, J. R. and McPherson, E. G. (1998) 'Simulation of tree shade impacts on residential energy use for space conditioning in Sacramento', *Atmospheric Environment*, vol 32, no 1, pp69–74

Spronken-Smith, R. A. and Oke, T. R. (1998) 'The thermal regime of urban parks in two cities with different summer climates', *International Journal of Remote Sensing*, vol 19, no 11, pp2085–2104

Spronken-Smith, R. and Oke, T. R. (1999) 'Scale modelling of nocturnal cooling in urban parks', *Boundary-Layer Meteorology*, vol 93, no 2, pp287–312

Taha, H. (1997) 'Urban climates and heat islands: Albedo, evapotranspiration and anthropogenic heat', *Energy and Buildings*, vol 25, no 2, pp99–103

Upmanis, H. and Chen, D. (1999) 'Influence of geographical factors and meteorological influences on nocturnal urban-park temperature differences – a case study of summer 1995 in Göteborg, Sweden', *Climate Research*, vol 13, pp125–139

Upmanis, H., Eliasson, I. and Lindqvist, S. (1998) 'The influence of green areas on nocturnal temperatures in a high latitude city (Göteborg, Sweden)', *International Journal of Climatology*, vol 18, no 6, pp681–700

Wong, N. H., Chen, Y., Ong, C. L. and Sia, A. (2003) 'Investigation of the thermal benefits of rooftop garden in the tropical environment', *Building and Environment*, vol 38, no 2, pp261–270

10
Linear Space

A well-defined linear space such as an urban street or pedestrian pathway is a special case in terms of urban microclimate. This type of three-dimensional arrangement, as discussed in Chapter 1, may be described as an urban canyon – which is defined geometrically by the direction of its long axis and its characteristic height-to-width (H/W), or aspect, ratio. As a model, the urban canyon has a number of distinguishing features that are of interest when thinking about climate-responsive urban design:

- The urban canyon has been the focus of numerous urban climate studies, both as a framework for describing urban canopy-layer conditions at the micro-scale, and as a building block for describing the larger urban surface at the meso-scale (see Chapter 1 for a description of these scale levels).
- Compared to more inclusive descriptions of open space, the urban canyon model makes it possible to simplify geometric relationships by reducing the description of the space to an essentially two-dimensional cross-section (assuming a semi-infinite length along which the ratio of average building height to street width is constant).
- Using simplified geometry, it is possible to clarify and highlight climatic effects that are related to fundamental issues such as urban density.

By some accounts, the aspect ratio of the street is a basic urban design descriptor that even has historical ramifications (see Figure 10.1):

> the street's dimension is defined as the ratio between the width of the street floor and the height of the vertical elements, usually comprising buildings or vegetation, or both. This ratio indicates the spatial characteristics of the street, architecturally differentiated between the narrow alleys of the medieval and the broad boulevards of the Baroque. Each architectural trend has developed its own definition of optimal street dimensions, and numerous theories give descriptions of the three-dimensional significance of the streetscape, or its 'architectural dynamics'.
> (Lillebye, 2001)

In this chapter, we will return to some of the general relationships between urban form and microclimate that were discussed in previous chapters, and examine them in the specific context of linear spaces. We will look at some of the ways in which the geometric and other attributes of a street influence radiation, air-flow and the overall thermal state of a pedestrian, and offer guidelines for responding – by design – to climate stress under different seasonal conditions.

Figure 10.1 Linear urban spaces of different aspect ratio and different character: (a) a low-rise residential street in North America; (b) a well-defined traditional European street; and (c) a pedestrian street in the dense urban fabric of a Middle-Eastern city

Photographs: David Pearlmutter

Street shading and radiant heat

Clearly, shading – or the relative lack thereof – is a prominent feature of any urban streetscape. Pedestrians may be protected from direct sun in varying degrees and circumstances by building elements such as colonnades, overhangs, awnings or trellises, as well as by trees and other vegetation. These detailed strategies, however, have their limitations:

- In many cases, built overhead elements cannot provide a reasonable continuity of shade along the pavement because of the diverse and continually changing nature of the individual buildings. Street trees, moreover, while offering numerous psychological and physical benefits that

go far beyond shading, may often be impractical to plant and maintain. (For a more in-depth discussion of shading by trees and other vegetation, see Chapter 9.)
- Even if continuous shading is achieved along a particular path at the edge of the canyon, small localized features do not necessarily provide substantial shading of the larger ground surface, leaving it as a potentially large source of reflected sunlight and/or emitted long-wave radiation (depending on the albedo and thermal properties of the paving and other types of ground cover). These indirect expressions of a lack of street shading may contribute tangibly to pedestrian thermal stress. Additionally, the practicality of installing canopies or other large shading elements over the street itself is effectively limited by the breadth of the space that needs to be covered – i.e. by the street geometry.
- Finally, shading tends to be important throughout the daytime hours, and during much of this time – including the hottest summer afternoon hours – the sun is not high overhead but at relatively low altitude angles. This means that the most effective shading elements are often vertical objects such as the buildings themselves, which can cast deep shadows that protect not only horizontal ground elements, but also vertical surfaces such as other walls, and – most importantly from the point of view of pedestrian comfort – the body itself. Shading by walls and other vertical surfaces has the added benefit of simultaneously blocking direct solar rays and leaving open the sky vault directly above the street, to which heat may dissipate through both long-wave radiation and turbulent transport (i.e. ventilation).

For these reasons, street shading is first and foremost a function of the basic canyon geometry – and can be determined quantitatively as a function of time, location and the street's geometric proportions.

Direct radiation

In Chapter 5, the shading coefficient was discussed as a key parameter in quantifying the absorption of direct solar radiation on a pedestrian's body (Equation 5.2), and in turn on their overall energy balance. This coefficient describes the proportion of the body which is exposed to the direct rays of the sun at a given point in time – ranging from a value of zero when the entire body is shaded to 1.0 when the entire body is exposed (i.e. the sun is unobstructed). In the case of a regular symmetric street canyon with a pedestrian (of height H_b) standing at the centre, the shading coefficient SC_{sv} is a simple function of the canyon's height (H) and width (W), its orientation and the appropriate solar angles (see Figure 10.2)[1]:

$$SC_{sv} = \frac{H_b - \left[H - \frac{W}{2}\left(\tan ALT_{bp}\right)\right]}{H_b} \qquad (10.1a)$$

where ALT_{bp} is the bulk plane altitude, or the effective solar elevation angle when measured in the plane of the canyon cross-section:

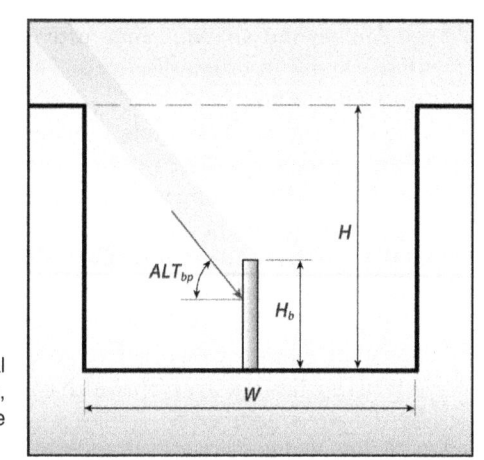

Figure 10.2 Schematic section of symmetrical urban canyon with pedestrian at its centre, showing parameters for calculation of the shading coefficient

$$\tan ALT_{bp} = \tan ALT / \cos(AZ - AZ_W) \quad (10.1b)$$

and AZ_W is the azimuth angle measured between a line normal to the shadow-casting wall and north.

Note that in a canyon with two parallel walls, only one wall will cast a shadow at any given point in time – so that during the course of a day, the relevant wall orientation AZ_W may change by 180°. For instance, in summer, in a canyon with a north–south axis, shadow will be cast in the morning by the canyon's eastern wall (i.e. facing to the west, with $AZ_W = 270°$) and in the afternoon by the wall facing east ($AZ_W = 90°$).

While the pedestrian is assumed here to be at the centre line of the canyon (at a distance from the shadow-casting wall equal to W/2), this distance could be changed to represent the shading coefficient at any other point, such as along the pavement on one side of the street or the other. Taking the mid-point, however, is useful in several ways. Even in a vehicular street (rather than a pedestrian mall, for instance), the mid-point represents an intermediate situation between the extreme cases of one sidewalk or the other, and thus indicates an average shading coefficient for a random distribution of pedestrians. Also, the number of hours during which the body at the centre point is fully exposed (SC = 1) indicates the extent to which the majority of the canyon ground surface is exposed as well.

An illustration of the way that pedestrian shading is modified by canyon geometry is shown in Figure 10.3, which compares a range of H/W ratios and axis orientations for an urban space at 30°N latitude. During mid-summer the shading from direct sun increases dramatically with steeper aspect ratios, but only when the street's long axis runs approximately north–south. In contrast, H/W proportions have a much less pronounced effect on the shading coefficient when the canyon orientation is east–west.

This distinction is a fundamental feature of the basic solar geometry, since the general summertime sun path is from east to west – with low altitude angles

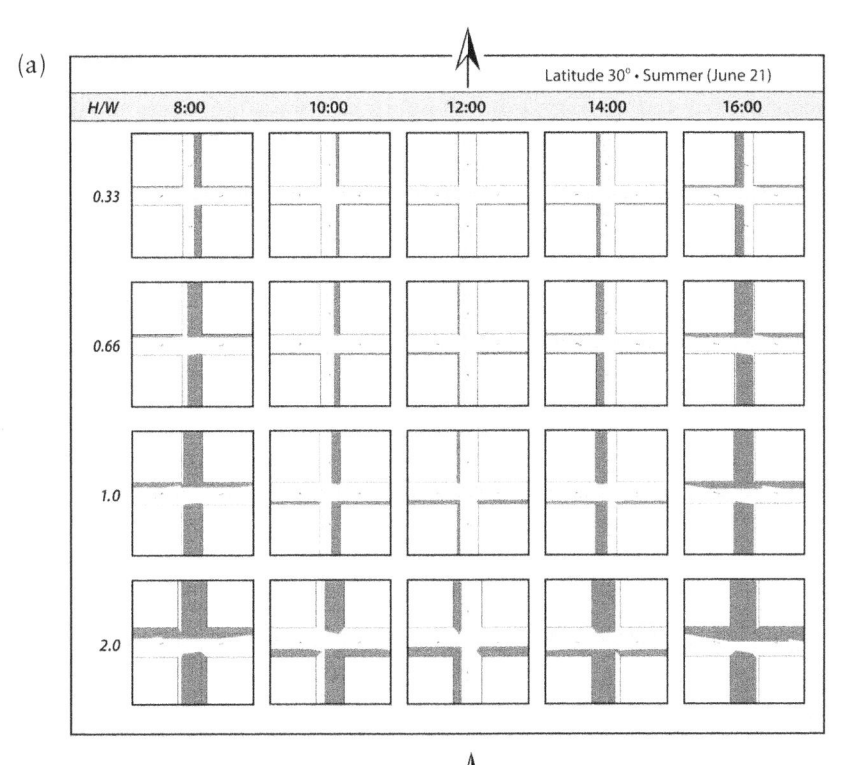

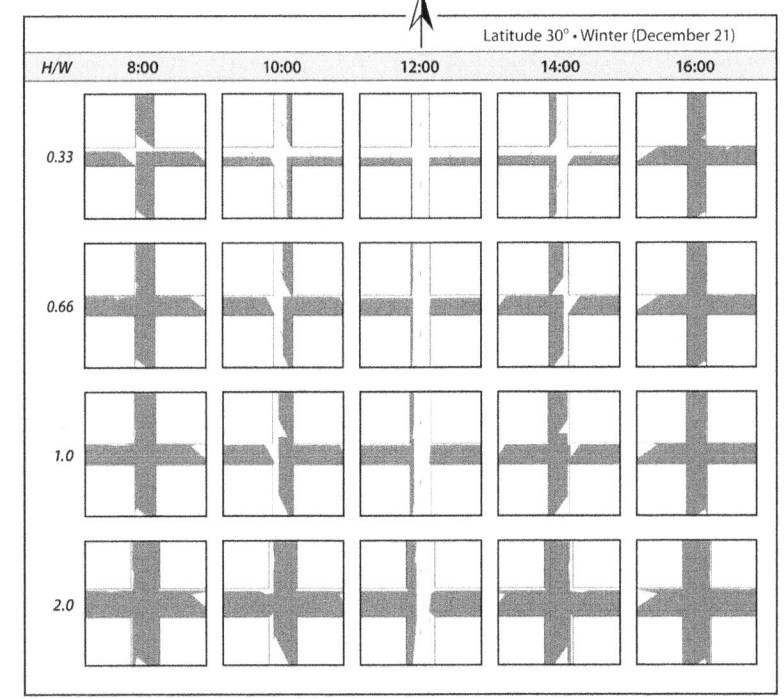

Figure 10.3 Shading patterns for street canyons of varying H/W ratio, at different hours on (a) a summer day and (b) a winter day. Shadows are calculated for a location at 30°N latitude.

in the morning hours, when azimuth angles place the sun sharply to the east, and in the afternoon hours when solar rays are directed from the west. Therefore a deep and/or narrow north–south canyon can provide shade at all but the high-noon hours, whereas the advantage of deep shading is increasingly lost as the axis is rotated towards east and west. At the same time, it should be stressed that the magnitude of this geometric selectivity depends on geographic location and specific time of year. The deviations from an east–west summer sun path increase with distance from the tropics (i.e. at latitudes which are considerably higher or lower than 15 to 30°) and with time from the summer solstice (i.e. in early May or late August in the northern hemisphere).

In winter, this pattern of canyon shading is not only modified but fundamentally transformed. In an east–west canyon, a high aspect ratio is likely to eliminate pedestrian exposure to direct sun, while in a canyon open to the south, even relatively high H/W proportions will allow solar penetration at midday. To the extent that winter daytime conditions are under-heated and pedestrian exposure to direct sun is beneficial, this winter pattern reinforces the implication that might be drawn from the summer relationships: that high aspect ratios contribute to pedestrian shading in north–south canyons, but much less so in those oriented east–west.

Indirect radiation

The significance of street shading extends beyond the exposure of a pedestrian to radiation coming directly from the sun, since the body is also exposed to *diffuse radiation* that is scattered across the sky and *reflected radiation* that arrives from the street surface and adjacent walls – depending on the attributes of the canyon space.

The critical canyon-related variable for diffuse radiation is the average sky view factor (see Chapter 5, Equation 5.5), which is estimated for a regular symmetrical canyon as:

$$\overline{SVF} = (\cos \beta)/2 \qquad (10.2)$$

Here the angle β (see Figure 10.4a) may be defined for convenience at a height of one metre on the body as:

$$\beta = \tan^{-1}[(H-1)/0.5W] \qquad (10.3)$$

Since a pedestrian's exposure to diffuse radiation is in direct relation to the SVF, it follows that a compact canyon geometry with a large H/W ratio will provide a reduction – regardless of street axis orientation – in the absorption of diffuse radiation, which is assumed to be approximately *isotropic* (evenly distributed across the sky vault). The relation between view factor and H/W ratio is shown in Figure 10.4b.

Reflected radiation, as described in Chapter 5 for horizontal and vertical surfaces (Equations 5.6 and 5.7 respectively), depends on two geometry-specific

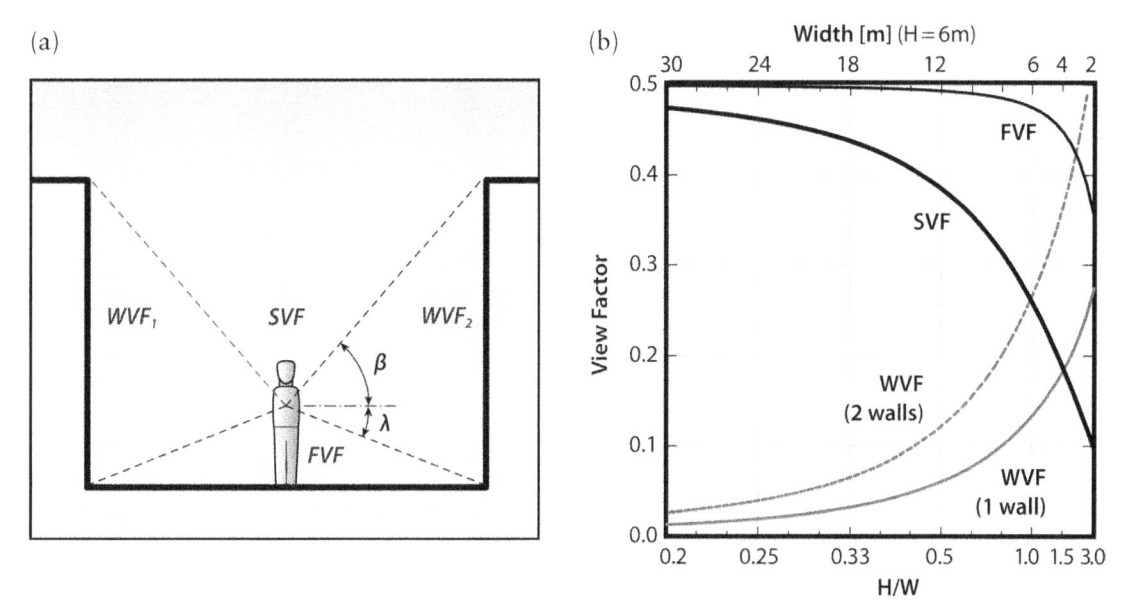

Figure 10.4 (a) Diagrammatic canyon section showing parameters for the calculation of view factors to the sky (SVF), walls (WVF) and floor (FVF) from the point of view of a pedestrian at the canyon centre; and (b) variation of these view factors, as a function of canyon H/W, for H = 6m

Note: All factors are computed from a point on the standing body at a height of one metre.

factors: the pedestrian's angle of exposure (or view factor) to the surface, and the portion of the surface area which is itself exposed to direct sun (i.e. its shading coefficient).

For the canyon's horizontal ground surface, the floor view factor is:

$$FVF = (\cos \lambda)/2 \qquad (10.4)$$

where the angle λ (Figure 10.4a) is given (once again, at a height of one metre) as:

$$\lambda = \tan^{-1}(1/0.5W) \qquad (10.5)$$

and for each of the parallel vertical surfaces (only one of which may be sunlit at any point in time), the WVF is:

$$WVF = (1 - [SVF + FVF])/2 \qquad (10.6)$$

The actual proportion of the ground surface which is exposed to (and reflects) direct radiation is given by the floor shading coefficient SC_F:

$$SC_F = \left(W - \left|H\cos(AZ - AZ_W)/\tan ALT\right|\right)/W \qquad (10.7)$$

and the proportion of sun-facing wall which is exposed to direct radiation is given by the wall shading coefficient SC_W:

$$SC_w = W/H(\tan ALT / \cos(AZ - AZ_W)) \qquad (10.8)$$

Canyon geometry has significant impacts on reflected radiation in terms of shading coefficients as well as view factors. A low H/W ratio will tend to reduce ground shading, and mutual shading of walls is only possible with relative high aspect ratios and at low sun angles. However axis orientation is crucial to this relationship as well: during early morning and late afternoon hours in summer, cross-wall shading (and thus full ground shading) is likely in compact north–south canyons, but less so as the axis turns towards east–west (see Figure 10.3). In terms of view factors, a shallow canyon will maximize the FVF and increase the pedestrian's exposure to reflected radiation from the floor, often rendering the WVF and exposure to wall-reflected radiation negligible. This is especially important at midday hours in summer, when most reflected radiation is coming from ground paving rather than from walls due to the high sun angles. The reflected radiation load from bright-coloured wall surfaces is most pronounced at intermediate aspect ratios, where the WVF is significant but the sun-facing wall is unshaded.

The interplay between canyon geometry and the reflection of radiation from various facets ultimately determines the albedo of the canyon as a system, which has important implications for the overall energy balance of the canyon. Each time solar rays strike a canyon element, only part of the incoming energy is reflected – with the remainder, the magnitude of which depends on the absorption coefficient of the material, contributing to a rise in the temperature of the surface. By multiple reflection and absorption in a compact canyon, much of the original radiant energy is absorbed, or trapped in the space – and only a small portion is ultimately reflected back to the atmosphere (see Figure 2.2, Chapter 2).

Long-wave radiation

The pedestrian-centred canyon view factors described above for diffuse and reflected short-wave radiation are also used for long-wave radiation (see Chapter 5, Equations 5.9 to 5.11). The contributions of the sky, ground and vertical elements to the total long-wave flux absorbed by a pedestrian are proportional to the product of their respective view factors (SVF, WVF and FVF) and the radiant flux emitted by each surface (which is given by the Stefan-Bolzmann equation and is a function of surface temperature and emissivity).

As with short-wave radiation, canyon proportions have a great effect on the long-wave radiant load. During the day, a deep canyon with a high aspect ratio will emit less long-wave radiation than a broader, shallower one. This is because in a narrow canyon the floor has a relatively smaller surface area (as reflected in a small FVF) and because its surface temperature is lower, due to its shading from direct sun. This can make a substantial difference in the overall energy balance, especially on sunny days when exposed ground surfaces can reach exceedingly high temperatures, making them far larger sources of radiant heating than any typical combination of vertical walls. At the same time, the restricted SVF in a deep canyon means that much of the heat absorbed during the daytime is exchanged between surfaces and (as with reflected radiation) trapped within the space, rather than being released to the sky.

Wind speed, air temperature and convection

As described in Chapter 5, the exchange of heat by convection between pedestrians and their surroundings is contingent on two variables which can be measured or otherwise estimated in an urban canyon: wind speed and air temperature. The former is embodied in a heat transfer coefficient (see Equation 5.15) and the latter in a temperature difference between the pedestrian's skin (and/or clothing) and the surrounding air. This temperature gradient typically produces a net removal of heat from the body, i.e. convective cooling. However, when the air temperature is similar to that of the skin (about 34 to 35°C), there will be little net convective exchange, and if the ambient air is warmer, convection will lead to a net addition of heat to the body.

Wind speed

Urban air-flow is discussed at length in Chapter 4, which includes a description of the three wind regimes that have been identified for flow across urban canyons. These general flow patterns, distinguished from one another by characteristic values of canyon aspect ratio (H/W), illustrate the complexity of air-flow in terms of speed, direction and turbulence. While the role of wind in modifying a person's heat loss is also subject to these complexities, the calculation of heat exchange by convection may be greatly simplified by assuming that for a standing pedestrian in the street, air movement may be expressed solely by the horizontal component of the air-flow at one point (typically at head-height in the centre of the canyon). Wind speed at this location may be averaged for any given period of time (usually between ten minutes and one hour).

Because it is often unfeasible to measure wind speed at the location in question, the ability to estimate it with relation to other measured data at a reference location (such as a meteorological station or above the roofs of buildings in the urban area) is extremely useful. In terms of time-averaged wind speed, air-flow in an urban canyon tends to be weaker than in the zone of free-flow above or outside the urban canopy – and therefore the ratio between the former and the latter is often expressed as an *attenuation* factor. The actual extent of attenuation depends on the circumstances of the site and the meteorological conditions, but it can be generalized as a function of canyon geometry.

The canyon attenuation factor is systematically linked to both the canyon's sectional proportions (H/W ratio) and its axis orientation relative to the prevailing wind (the angle of attack).

In Figure 4.6 in Chapter 4, the variation of canyon wind speed attenuation as a function of attack angle is shown for a series of aspect ratios. In general, attenuation becomes increasingly pronounced as the angle changes from parallel, along-canyon flow (0°) to cross-canyon flow (90°), but the function is not a linear one. Rather, it takes the shape of an S-curve, with relatively little variation at very high or very low angles and a sharp transition between them. Further, the magnitude of overall attenuation and steepness of the curve varies noticeably depending upon the H/W ratio. In a shallow canyon (H/W<0.33) the attenuation factor may be greater than 0.5 at low attack angles, meaning that the wind speed within the space is over half that of the free flow above. In contrast, the flow in a deep canyon (H/W>2.0) may be attenuated to less than one-third of the free flow, even at the lowest attack angles. Perhaps paradoxically, the dependence of wind attenuation on H/W ratio at sharp attack angles (i.e. cross-canyon flow) is less pronounced, because velocities are relatively low in all cases: attenuation factors are in the range of 0.2 to 0.4. Slightly higher attenuation factors may be found for intermediate aspect ratios (see H/W = 0.66 in Figure 10.4), where a *wake-interference* flow regime generates turbulent flow and significant horizontal velocities in different directions. In a *skimming* flow regime (H/W>1.0) winds blowing across the canyon may indirectly generate secondary flows deep within the canyon. In general, however, such flows are relatively weak and it may be concluded that deep canyons do tend to dampen wind speed and to impede ventilation.

Air temperature

Compared with wind speed and radiative energy components, temperatures within an urban canyon are less amenable to estimation from simple functions of quantities measured outside the space. Air temperature may be somewhat variable within the space, and its estimation is complicated by the multitude of factors (radiative, convective, evaporative and even conductive) which can affect it significantly. For this reason it is often measured on site or estimated using either physical or numerical models (see Chapter 11 for a detailed discussion of such modelling).

Despite its complexity, some degree of generalization can be applied when describing the effect of canyon geometry on air temperature. When taken in combination, several of the phenomena described above contribute to a situation in which higher air temperatures are found within compact street canyons than shallower, more open spaces. The trapping of short-wave radiation due to multiple reflection and absorption, and of long-wave radiation due to a restricted SVF, combine with the relative stagnation of air in a tightly confined canyon to increase the overall amount of heat retained in the space. This 'canyon effect' has been described extensively as one of the causes of the urban heat island, with a strong correlation having been demonstrated between heat island intensity and the H/W ratio of city-centre canyons (see Chapter 3, Figure 3.6).

An increase in air temperature will reduce the rate of heat loss from the body by convection and under very hot conditions may even lead to convective heat gain. It should by no means be concluded, however, that compact canyon geometry – even if it produces higher air temperatures – will necessarily cause an increase in a pedestrian's overall thermal stress in summer. The reason for this is that the body simultaneously exchanges energy by radiation as well as convection, and a modest degree of net convective heating can be far outweighed by a larger reduction in the net radiant load – such as may result, for example, from shading of the body.

Evaporation, thermal stress and thermal sensation

The physiological thermal stress that is imposed on a pedestrian in an urban canyon is an integral expression of the radiative and convective exchanges described above, each of which is impacted in some way by the physical properties of the canyon. In addition to these exchanges, however, an additional component must be added for the estimation of thermal stress under warm conditions: the removal of heat by evaporation.

Evaporation

The efficiency of evaporative cooling, mainly through the secretion of sweat, depends to some extent on wind speed but is mainly a function of vapour pressure, which can be calculated from air temperature and relative humidity. Humidity is the environmental factor which we have yet to account for, and it too may be modified significantly by the attributes of a street canyon. The presence of vegetation, especially irrigated ground cover such as grass or dense shrubbery, brings additional water vapour to the air in the space through evapotranspiration, or ET (the combination of transpiration from plant leaves and evaporation from the wetted ground). Bodies of water (pools, channels, fountains, etc.) may also be a major source of water vapour when used as landscape elements in canyon spaces. On the other hand, street trees, while constituting a large potential source of evaporative cooling, may contribute more humidity to the air above their transpiring leaves than below – and their shade can significantly reduce the rate of evaporation from irrigated ground beneath their canopy.

The extent to which the humidity is raised (and sweat efficiency is limited) depends firstly and most directly on the amount of vegetated area within the street, and it is most useful to gauge this vegetated fraction relative to the complete surface area of the canyon, including vertical as well as horizontal surfaces. The larger the extent of wet (evaporating and/or transpiring) surfaces relative to dry surfaces such as bare soil, paving and walls, the larger is the proportion of incoming solar energy that is converted to latent, as opposed to sensible, heat. At the same time, the increase in humidity at pedestrian head-height is ultimately limited by the mixing of humidified air with dry air from outside the canyon. This depends once again on the pattern and intensity of air-flow in the canyon, which itself is strongly affected by aspect ratio and orientation.

It should be stressed that while evapotranspiration has the effect of raising humidity and limiting sweat efficiency, a simultaneous lowering of canyon air temperature can enhance convective cooling of the body. The balance between these effects depends on the state of the ambient air, which is related not only to the urban climate but also to the climate of the region, which may vary widely, for instance between hot-arid highlands and warm-humid coastal regions. The use of vegetation in urban landscaping and its consequences for urban microclimate were discussed in greater detail in Chapter 9.

Overall thermal stress

Since a pedestrian's physiological thermal stress encompasses all of the energetic processes discussed so far in this chapter, its implications for canyon design ultimately depend on the balance between them. For instance, the consequences of urban densification (i.e. higher H/W ratios) in terms of air-flow in summer may run counter to those for direct solar shading, though they may in fact be similar to those for solar access in winter. Whether the individual processes are contradictory or reinforcing, it is their combined impact on the person's overall balance of energy exchange that dictates his or her level of thermal stress, and this balance can vary widely under the divergent conditions of climatic regions and urban settings. In cold climates, shelter from chilling winds may be the over-riding concern, while in tropical cities the issue of ventilation may be paramount.

An example of this balance is shown for a hot-arid region in Figure 10.5, which presents calculated values of the Index of Thermal Stress (see Chapter 5) over a summer daily cycle, for a range of urban canyon aspect ratios and orientations. The results are based on physical modelling with an open-air scaled urban surface, which was conducted in the Negev desert in southern Israel.[2] In this type of climate, which is characterized by clear skies, intense solar radiation, low daytime relative humidity and wide diurnal temperature swings, the dominant factor driving the ITS is shading, i.e. the extent of exposure to direct radiation. Thus in a north–south canyon (Figure 10.5a) with shadows cast by east and west walls in the respective morning and afternoon hours, daytime thermal stress is progressively reduced as the H/W ratio increases (i.e. as the canyon becomes more compact). This preferential effect is less pronounced as the canyon axis is rotated (Figures 10.5c and 10.5d), and all but disappears in an east–west canyon (Figure 10.5b) where the heat-trapping effects of steeper aspect ratios counterbalance the smaller benefits of shading.

Secondary effects are in evidence as well in this comparison. Even at midday, when solar angles approach the zenith, the pedestrian in a deep and/or narrow canyon may benefit from reduced diffuse radiation from the sky and reflected radiation from the ground plane, due to the restricted SVF and FVF. If the axis of the compact canyon is oriented north–south or close to it, then the pedestrian will also absorb minimal long-wave emission from the ground plane, both because of its relatively small view factor and because it holds less absorbed solar heat due to its shading at other hours. It should be stressed that the overall reduction in thermal stress observed in compact north–south canyons occurs in spite of the fact that air temperature in the constricted space is generally higher, and wind speed lower, than in the more open canyon of lower aspect ratio.

At night, the effect of compactness is largely reversed – with a pedestrian in a compact canyon maintaining the lowest level of net energy loss rather than energy gain. This is due to the constricted SVF of the canyon, which impedes long-wave radiant heat loss to the sky, and impaired ventilation due to the more heavily attenuated wind speed. The significance of this distinction, by which compactness creates a cooler street environment in the daytime but a warmer one at night, depends on the comfort sensations associated with these different levels of heat gain and loss, as discussed below.

Thermal sensation

Figure 10.5 also shows the levels of thermal sensation, on a scale from 'comfortable' to 'very hot', corresponding to the range of ITS values under warm conditions. While this correlation between physiological stress and perceptual comfort is clearly subject to many qualifications regarding a given pedestrian's activity and clothing as well as his or her thermal preferences, expectations and acclimatization (as discussed in Chapter 6), the broad distinctions in thermal sensation level are instructive. For example, if conditions at night are always comfortable, irrespective of canyon geometry, then the inverse relationship mentioned above between canyon H/W and the ITS during these hours is of little practical interest to the designer: it is the daytime relationship that is the critical one for thermal comfort.

The extent of thermal discomfort – or the number of hours defined by thermal sensation categories of 'warm', 'hot' and 'very hot' – is summarized in

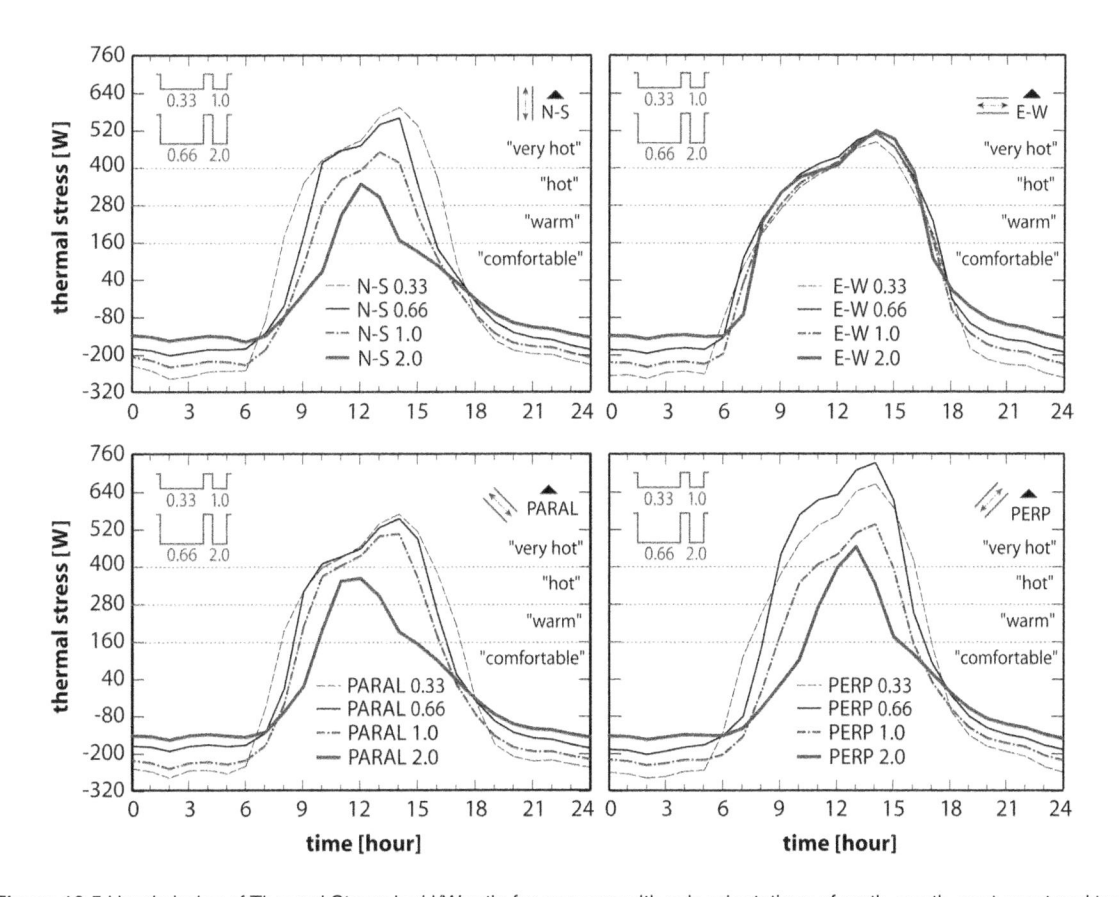

Figure 10.5 Hourly Index of Thermal Stress by H/W ratio for canyons with axis orientations of north–south, east–west and two diagonal rotations (parallel and perpendicular to the prevailing northwest wind)

Note: All values are based on outdoor modelling studies in the hot-arid Negev region under summer conditions. Also shown are corresponding levels of subject thermal sensation, based on previous correlations.

Source: Pearlmutter et al (2007a).

Figure 10.6 for the entire range of aspect ratios and orientations in the study. The upper diagram presents the sum of all such hours (i.e. total discomfort), while the lower part of the figure displays a discomfort index which accounts for both the duration of overall discomfort and its severity. In the picture that emerges, more subtle differentiations are seen between canyon geometries, such as a relative moderation of discomfort in the northwest–southeast canyon, which in this particular case is aligned parallel with the prevailing wind, relative to the canyon that is perpendicular to the flow and suffers from more severe wind speed attenuation.

The pattern that emerges from this distilled picture is fundamental to the schematic design of urban streets under hot-dry conditions. It may be briefly stated as follows: the microclimatic benefit of compactness, as expressed by a large ratio of building height to street width, is increasingly pronounced as canyon axis orientation approaches north–south.

- In a street aligned north–south, protection from solar radiation is the dominant microclimatic force differentiating one aspect ratio from another, and a sufficiently high ratio can provide this protection during nearly all daytime hours. At stake for a pedestrian is the difference between compact urban streets that are largely comfortable all day, and highly exposed spaces that are moderately to severely uncomfortable all day.
- The influence of a compact geometry is also felt in streets whose orientation deviates moderately from north–south: although this influence becomes less pronounced, it is still clear for rotations of up to 45° in one direction or the other. It is in the difference between these 'diagonal' streets that the effects of ventilation are most clearly observed, with the canyon lying most parallel to the prevailing wind (which is northwesterly under summer conditions in the Negev) benefiting from less severe discomfort. It is notable that studies in more humid areas of Israel[3] reached similar conclusions regarding north–south and east–west streets, but found that ventilation had a more pronounced effect than radiation in streets oriented at about 45° to the cardinal points of the compass.
- In a street aligned along an east–west axis, the compound effect of aspect ratio on thermal comfort is variable. Although a very compact street can provide some internal shading, the resultant overall improvement may be marginal. Therefore east–west streets hold relatively little potential for enhancing pedestrian thermal comfort through geometry alone.

The mechanism by which a compact urban geometry serves to protect pedestrians from thermal stress at critical hours may be described in terms of energy interception, storage and delay. As discussed previously, deeper canyons do indeed serve as radiation traps and increase daytime heat storage within the urban fabric. However, this increased heat intake occurs largely because solar radiation is intercepted by buildings rather than people, which on balance with other energy-exchange phenomena leads to enhanced pedestrian comfort.

The ultimate enhancement of comfort is contingent on the fact that surplus daytime energy absorbed in a compact configuration is released from storage later in the day, when ambient air is considerably cooler. The efficiency of such

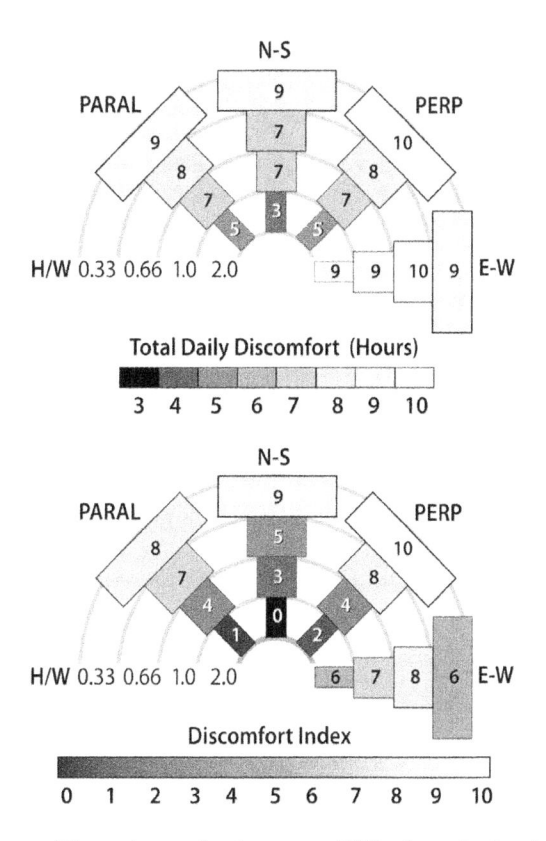

Figure 10.6 Summary of thermal sensation by canyon H/W ratio and axis orientation in terms of the total hours of discomfort on a summer day (top), and a Discomfort Index (bottom) accounting for both the duration and severity of overall discomfort

Source: Based on Pearlmutter et al (2007b).

a thermal time-lag mechanism depends on the thermal properties of the building fabric, particularly its heat storage capacity and resulting thermal inertia. Just as internal thermal mass has often been described as an essential ingredient for indoor passive climatization of buildings in arid regions, it may be reasoned that external mass is a required element in urban design strategies that seek to moderate outdoor thermal stress through compact street geometry. In practical application, building thermal mass may be provided both internally and externally through the use of a common sandwich-type wall section (combining a heavyweight inner block material, an intermediate layer of thermal insulation and an outer layer of plastered blocks or stone facing).

It should also be emphasized that in many regions, even those with considerably hot summers, conditions in winter may be harshly cold, although, as is the case in the Negev and many arid locations, low temperatures may be accompanied by a high proportion of clear days and abundant solar radiation. Additional data from the Negev studies have shown that in winter the dominant microclimatic variable affecting thermal comfort is the attenuation of chilling winds. In addition it was found that an east–west street of compact proportions can result in excessive overall pedestrian heat loss due to overshadowing, whereas this heat loss (at least at midday) is dramatically reduced in a north–south street of the same proportions, which is open to the south. A more direct argument against compact east–west streets would be the inevitable overshadowing of buildings on the north side of the street – which may benefit from solar exposure of south-facing elements for passive or active solar heating.

Street design considerations

When taken together, these findings from the summer and winter seasons highlight the potential advantages of a climatically selective urban fabric – combining relatively compact streets in most orientations, especially north–south, with less-constricted east–west streets (Figure 10.7). It is suggested that the evolution of such a pattern could, in fact, enhance pedestrian comfort as well as energy efficiency in many new or redeveloping parts of cities, particularly arid ones.

At the same time, it should be stressed that these basic relationships – and climate-related objectives in general – can only be realized within the multifaceted process of development that occurs in any real city or town.[4] Decisions concerning the compactness of a city must always be viewed in a broader context, considering the long-term sustainability of the trends (such as daily commuting and suburban sprawl) that they will undoubtedly influence.

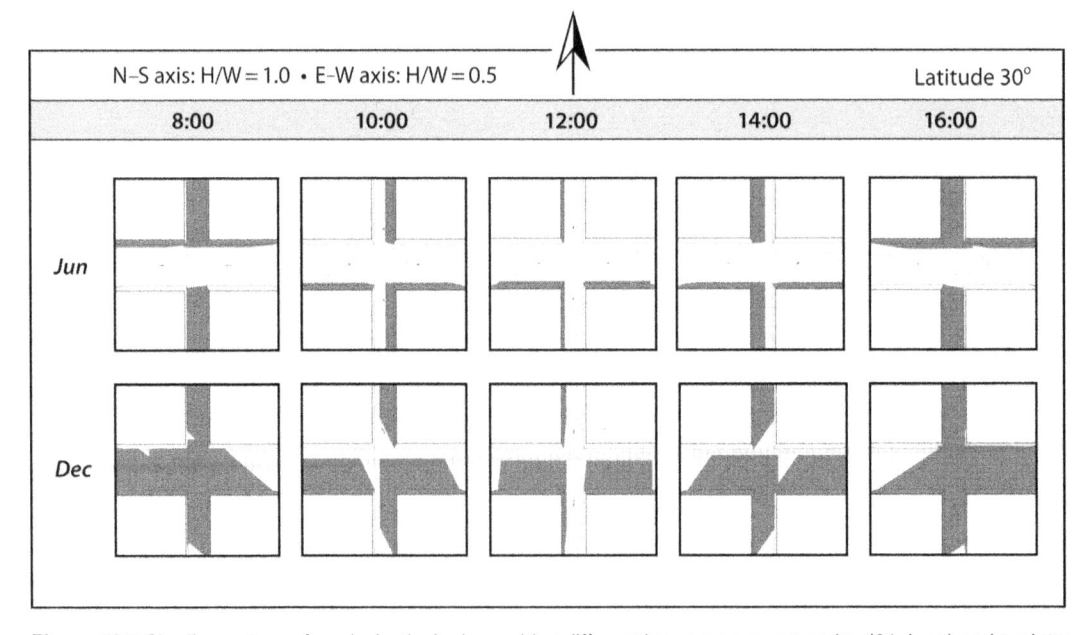

Figure 10.7 Shading patterns for a 'selective' urban grid at different hours on a summer day (21 June) and a winter day (21 Dec)

Note: The street canyon aligned on north–south axis has an aspect ratio of 1.0, and the east–west street is widened to H/W = 0.5. Shadows are calculated for a location at 30°N latitude.

The plurality of competing motivations that impinge on urban density also makes it crucial to consider a plurality of means – paying attention to the details of urban design, as well as the overall pattern.

The diagrams in Figure 10.8 offer examples of urban canyon cross-sections in which the climatic response involves detailed shading treatments as well as attention to basic geometry. These details may be integral to the building, as in the case of colonnades, arcades or overhanging balconies, or they may be separate street elements such as trees, canopies or free-standing pergolas (see examples in Figure 10.9).

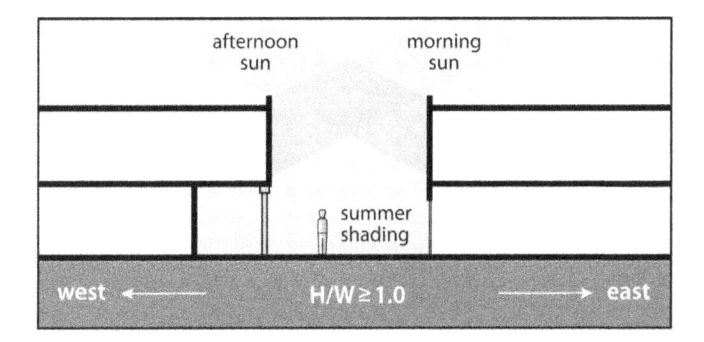

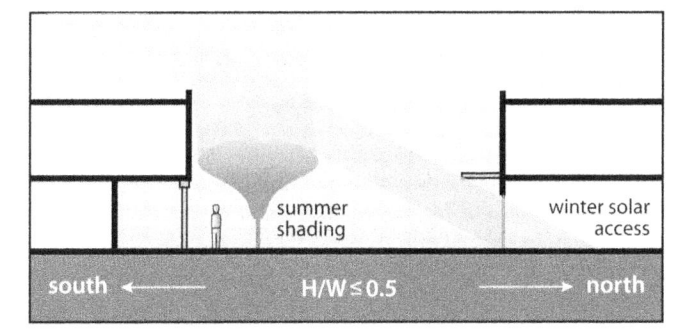

Figure 10.8 Examples of urban canyon cross-sections, looking north along a north–south axis (top) and west along an east–west axis (bottom), illustrating climatic response in terms of basic geometry and secondary shading treatments

Figure 10.9 Examples of detailed shading treatments in urban streets: (a) shade trees and building facade projections, and (b) shading canopies across the full width of a pedestrian market street

Such treatments are particularly important in streets with an east–west axis, since (as mentioned) summer shading is difficult to achieve through canyon geometry alone. The strategic placement of sufficiently large and dense shade trees on the south side of the street (i.e. adjacent to the north-facing building facades) can shade pedestrians along the pavement on at least one side of the street in summer, without impinging on solar access for south-facing building facades on the other side. More liberal use of shade trees may be made if they are deciduous and undergo a sufficient reduction in their foliage in winter, as was discussed in Chapter 9, which takes a more in-depth look at the use of vegetation in microclimatic urban design.

Notes

1   In Equation 5.2 (Chapter 5), the shading coefficient of a vertical cylinder is divided into vertical (SC_{SV}) and horizontal (SC_{SH}) components. While the computation given here is for SC_{SV} only, the value of SC_{SH} is simply equal to 1.0 when $SC_{SV} \geq 1.0$, and to zero when $SC_{SV} < 1.0$.
2   See Pearlmutter et al (2006; 2007a; 2007b).
3   Capeluto I. G., Yezioro, A. and Shaviv E. (2003) 'Climatic aspects in urban design – a case study', *Building and Environment*, vol 38, no 6, pp827–835.
4   See, for example: Mills, G. (2006) 'Progress towards sustainable settlements: A role for urban climatology', *Theoretical and Applied Climatology*, vol 38, pp43–49.

References

Lillebye, E. (2001) 'The architectural significance of the street as a functional and social arena', in C. Jefferson, J. Rowe and C. Brebbia (eds) *The Sustainable Street: Environmental, Human and Economic Aspects of Street Design and Management*, WIT Press, Southampton, pp3–44

Pearlmutter, D., Berliner P. and Shaviv, E. (2006) 'Physical modeling of pedestrian energy exchange within the urban canopy', *Building and Environment*, vol 41, no 6, pp783–795

Pearlmutter, D., Berliner, P. and Shaviv, E. (2007a) 'Integrated modeling of pedestrian energy exchange and thermal comfort in urban street canyons', *Building and Environment*, vol 42, no 6, pp2396–2409

Pearlmutter, D., Berliner, P. and Shaviv, E. (2007b) 'Urban climatology in arid regions: Current research in the Negev desert', *International Journal of Climatology*, vol 27, no 14, pp1875–1885

Additional reading

Ali-Toudert, F. and Mayer, H. (2006) 'Numerical study on the effects of aspect ratio and orientation of an urban street canyon on outdoor thermal comfort in hot and dry climate', *Building and Environment*, vol 41, no 2, pp94–108

Ali-Toudert, F. and Mayer, H. (2007) 'Thermal comfort in an east–west oriented street canyon in Freiburg (Germany) under hot summer conditions', *Theoretical and Applied Climatology*, vol 87, pp223–237

Burt J. E., O'Rourke, P. A. and Terjung, W. H. (1982) 'The relative influence of urban climates on outdoor human energy budgets and skin temperature: I. Modeling considerations', *International Journal of Biometeorology*, vol 26, no 1, pp3–23

Johansson, E. (2006) 'Influence of urban geometry on outdoor thermal comfort in a hot dry climate: A study in Fez, Morocco', *Building and Environment*, vol 41, no 10, pp1326–1338

Oke, T. R. (1988) 'Street design and urban canopy layer climate', *Energy and Buildings*, vol 11, nos 1–3, pp103–113

Pearlmutter, D., Bitan, A. and Berliner, P. (1999) 'Microclimatic analysis of "compact" urban canyons in an arid zone', *Atmospheric Environment*, vol 33, nos 24–25, pp4143–4150

11
Modelling the Urban Microclimate

The British sociologist Zygmunt Bauman has suggested that we have an ethical duty to 'visualize the future impact of all actions (undertaken or not undertaken)'. Modelling a proposed built environment project has the potential to contribute to this obligation and we might expect such means to be a normal part of responsible design decision-making. Urban climate models, both physical and mathematical, may be used to investigate urban climate factors at different scales in order to investigate the likely consequences of design proposals. This chapter provides an overview of some of the main modelling methods used in urban climatology, and illustrates potential applications of such tools in a number of detailed case studies.

Physical models

Physical scale models are used in both urban design and climate-related research, usually to study a particular environmental variable such as solar radiation or wind. Such scale models have often been employed for studies in laboratories under controlled conditions, but a number of experiments have also been conducted where scale models are exposed to the natural environment. In many cases these hardware models need to address issues of similarity and scaling, and it must be remembered that such models are inherently simplified versions of the actual built environment – and therefore are not capable of reproducing the full complexity of a particular urban site.

Radiation modelling

One of the most common applications of physical models is for studying solar shading and overshadowing. Such studies can be laboratory-based, with scale models placed beneath an artificial sky, or outdoors, where the model is exposed to natural sunlight and a heliodon is used to orientate it to simulate different times of the day and year. In recent years, computer software has become widely available for visualizing the shadows cast by buildings, trees and other urban features. Such virtual modelling offers significant advantages in terms of flexibility, and potential cost, compared with physical scale models.

At the same time, the hands-on physical model may give the designer or researcher more tangible insights into the problem at hand. For example, physical modelling has been used for studying aspects of radiation exchange which are less straightforward than direct solar shading. The outdoor modelling experiments of Aida (1982) were designed to study the influence of urban geometry on urban albedo, correlating the height and spacing of regular building blocks with the reduction in overall albedo that is caused by multiple reflection and absorption between facets. Because the short-wave radiation reflected from most built surfaces (other than mirrored glass, for instance) is diffuse and therefore multi-directional, the physical model in this case allows for quantification of a phenomenon which, if approached computationally, requires advanced statistical techniques.

A number of notable experiments have made use of hardware models to study nocturnal cooling by long-wave radiation. By placing a small-scale urban model in a cooling chamber, Oke (1981) was able to quantify the inverse relationship between radiative cooling and urban density, and this connection correlated well with observations from actual cities. Scale models have also been used to examine the rate of radiative heat loss in city parks and to study the formation of dew in urban environments, with the thermal inertia of the model enhanced to ensure surface temperature similarity with the real world. In another experiment a mock-up of an urban canyon was employed outdoors using concrete block walls of full-scale thickness, but even in this case the focus was on isolating radiative effects, and therefore no attempt was made to reproduce wind or turbulence effects in the urban atmosphere.

Wind tunnel modelling

Perhaps the most prominent use of physical modelling in building and urban climatology is the simulation and analysis of air-flow in the vicinity of built obstacles, in a boundary-layer wind tunnel. In order to allow accurate modelling of urban-scale effects, it is necessary to ensure similarity of the model and of the real environment. The first important requirement is similarity of the approach flow, dealt with by appropriate design of the upwind fetch. This is the scaled built-up terrain over which the air stream passes before reaching the point of measurement, and it must be of sufficient length to re-create boundary-layer wind profiles that are adapted to, or in equilibrium with, the characteristic surface roughness of the urban area.

The second issue is similarity between the mechanical (and in some cases thermal) features of the model and the urban area it represents. In aerodynamic terms, this requires equality of the Richardson number (which, as defined in Chapter 2, represents atmospheric stability), a zero longitudinal pressure gradient and, finally, a Reynolds number which is sufficiently large to realize Reynolds number independence. The dimensionless Reynolds number is the ratio of inertial to viscous forces, and aeronautical wind tunnel studies often require that this value be kept the same for the scale model and the full-size body it represents by scaling the velocity in the wind tunnel. However, it has been shown by several investigators that since the typical flow pattern around bluff-body buildings is fully turbulent, even wide variations in air velocity do not affect flow and pressure distribution over the surfaces. Therefore normal air velocities are commonly used when investigating building ventilation problems. Wind tunnel models have been used for analysing flows within the urban canopy, for the characterization of flow fields above the city and for identifying wind velocity profiles in the canopy based on the logarithmic profiles above.

Wind-induced environmental problems such as ground level pedestrian wind nuisance, air pollutant dispersion and wind-driven rain exposure are all issues which may be investigated in a boundary-layer wind tunnel. In some cities, for example Wellington in New Zealand (known as the 'windy city'), the city council requires all new high-rise buildings to be tested in a wind tunnel in order to assess potential wind problems. Similarly, in The Netherlands, Code NEN 8100-2006 (*Wind Comfort and Wind Danger in the Built Environment*) establishes the methodologies and performance criteria for either wind tunnel or numerical (Computational Fluid Dynamics or CFD) simulation wind comfort assessments. The code is not a legal building requirement but offers consistent procedures to incorporate wind comfort into a building design programme.

Integrated open-air models

In distinction to the scale modelling studies described up to this point, which focus largely or entirely on a single climatic process, attempts have also been made to capture the full spectrum of energy exchange by placing a scaled version of an urban arrangement outdoors and measuring the relevant variables under actual atmospheric conditions.

One of the first scale models employed to investigate the urban heat island was built near the city of Fort Wayne, Indiana[1]. A model of the city comprising 17,000 individual elements was constructed of building lathe and placed in a flat, open field. The horizontal and vertical scales of the model were not identical, a distortion deemed necessary by the roughness of the surrounding terrain (grass). The authors concluded that the model demonstrated the feasibility of using the real atmosphere as a medium in which to conduct meteorological modelling experiments. Changes in stability resulting from the model geometry were recorded, and a small heat island was measured. More recent examples of comprehensive physical models employing an open-air urban surface are the COSMO model (see Box 11.1) and the OASUS model (see Box 11.2).

The usefulness of physical models depends on their flexibility and level of detail. A highly detailed scale model may give a realistic portrayal of a particular

---

Box 11.1 The COSMO model

An extensive array of cubical scaled buildings known as COSMO[2] (Comprehensive Outdoor Scale Model Experiments for Urban Climate) was constructed near Tokyo, Japan, for the purpose of systematically analysing the full urban energy balance and providing empirical input to computational models. Originally built at a scale of 1:50, the model was able to reproduce albedo and aerodynamic drag effects satisfactorily, but was incapable of correctly reproducing the thermal inertia of the urban surface it was meant to represent. Therefore a larger array of regularly spaced concrete cubes was built at a scale of 1:5, which overcame the problem of limited heat capacity and allowed for microclimatic investigation within the scaled urban canopy.

Box 11.2 The OASUS model

Like COSMO, the OASUS (Open-Air Scaled Urban Surface) model[3] is a reduced-scale physical model which allows for the comparison of different urban building configurations under actual climatic conditions (see Figure 11.1). The model, built at Sde Boqer in the Negev desert of Israel, is composed of hollow concrete blocks arranged in rows on bare soil, and has been used to quantify urban energy exchanges at two levels: (a) between the urban surface and the atmosphere, as represented by flux measurements above regular arrays of varying density, and (b) between a pedestrian and the urban environment, as represented by climatic data measured within the urban canopy-layer in scaled street canyons of varying geometry.

The similarity of the 1:15 scale model to a full-scale urban scenario was validated in a number of ways. Firstly, the model's overall thermal inertia – as determined by overall heat capacity as well as the distribution of thermal mass between building and ground surfaces – was quantified and found to be similar to that of an actual neighbourhood studied earlier. Also ground and wall temperatures within the scaled streets were compared with full-scale measurements and found to be highly similar. In addition, similarity to actual urban sites was found in the daily pattern of surface energy fluxes. The key to establishing these patterns was the detailed measurement of the turbulent flux of sensible heat above the scale model, which required the creation (through sufficient upwind fetch) of an identifiable constant-flux surface layer with logarithmic vertical wind profiles. Both the identification of the surface layer's vertical limits and the quantification of the heat fluxes themselves was achieved with ultrafine hot-wire anemometers, which were essential to the measurements both above and within the scaled urban canopy.

Data measured both within and above the scale-modelled street array were used to develop a semi-empirical model for characterizing the thermal stress imposed on pedestrians within street canyons of given geometry, based on ambient conditions in the surface layer above. Specific correlations yielded by the scale model include wind speed attenuation as a function of canyon H/W ratio and orientation relative to wind direction (see Chapter 4, Figure 4.6), as well as estimations for air temperature and emitted long-wave radiation.

While initially used under dry conditions only, the OASUS model was subsequently employed to quantify latent heat flux as a function of the surface area available for evaporation and urban geometry. This was accomplished by placing evaporation pans of precisely measured surface area within the scaled streets of the model and quantifying the rate of water loss. Results indicated that the increase in latent heat flux with evaporating surface area was offset in approximately equal measure by decreases in storage and turbulent sensible heat flux, and the proportion of the radiant energy budget represented by evaporative heat loss increased linearly with the ratio between vegetative cover and the complete three-dimensional urban surface area. This study also analysed the impact of outdoor evaporative cooling on street canyon air temperatures and the energy demand of adjacent buildings with systematic reductions found relative to the available evaporating surface area.

(a)

Figure 11.1 (a) View of OASUS model looking north

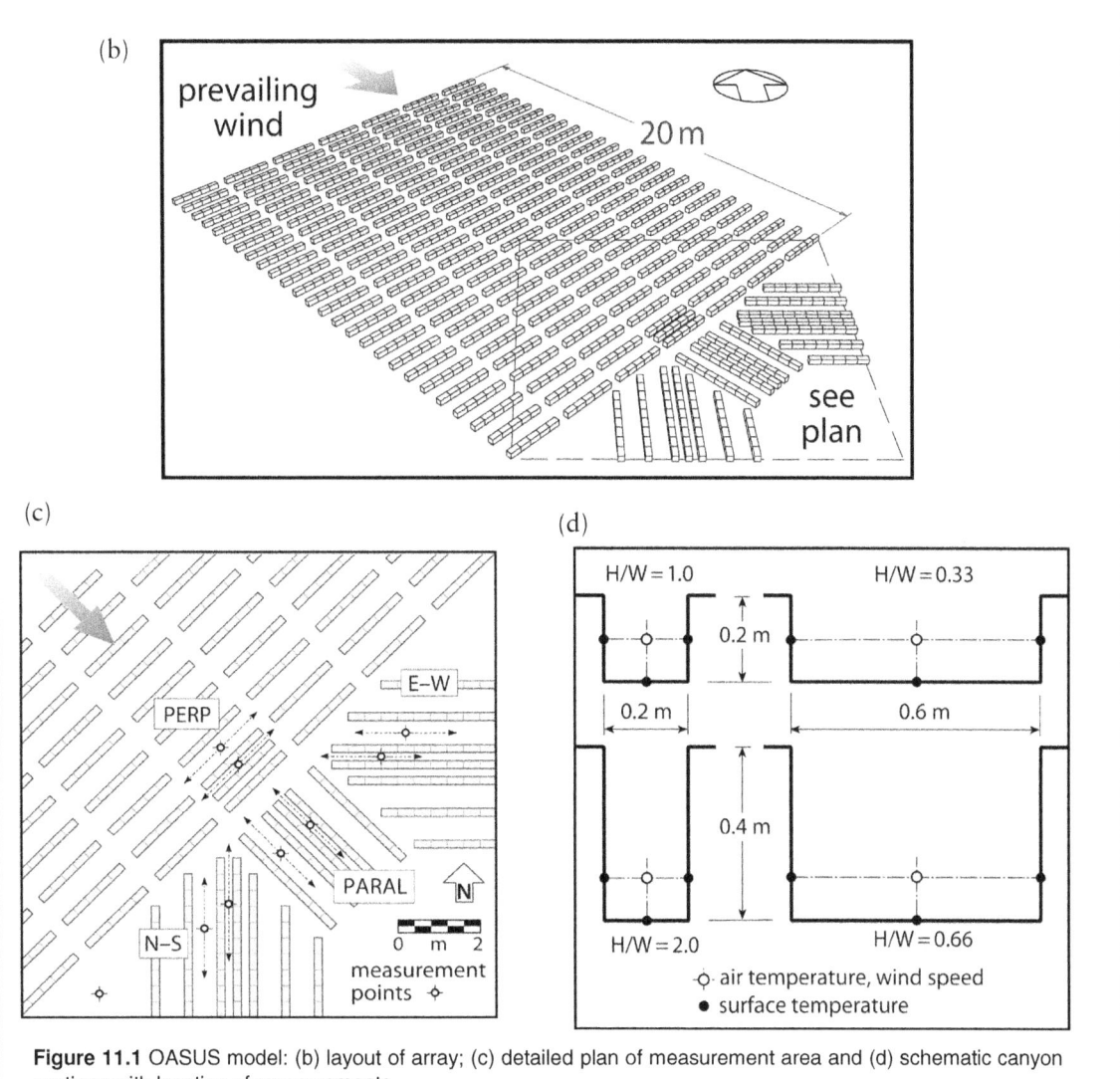

Figure 11.1 OASUS model: (b) layout of array; (c) detailed plan of measurement area and (d) schematic canyon sections with location of measurements

Source: Pearlmutter et al (2006).

urban setting, but if the model cannot be easily modified then it will be difficult to extrapolate the results to a variety of design options or conditions. In such a case, the model may have little predictive capacity for situations other than that which is defined. It is precisely these attributes of versatility and complexity, that are critical to the predictive power of mathematical models, which are increasingly central to the study of urban climatology – as they are to many other fields as well.

Mathematical models

Mathematical models are generated on the basis of analyses of the environmental processes that contribute to the microclimate in a given location. All analytical models generally require simplification of the equations describing the complex physical processes involved. Since these equations cannot be solved simultaneously, numerical techniques are used to produce approximate solutions. These generally involve convergence through a series of iterations, until predetermined criteria are met. Because mathematical models are computationally demanding they are usually implemented through a computer programme. Such programmes simulate the physical environment and produce knowledge that hopefully says something about real-world behaviour.

Mathematical models range from meso-scale models that simulate the conditions in the planetary boundary-layer (PBL) above cities, through to micro-scale models of the urban canyon. The micro-scale models may be coupled to the meso-scale ones or they may be independent. All types of models, however, require validation, and due to the shortage of well-documented high-quality data from field studies, this remains a major drawback of most urban climate models.

An important class of models of the urban microclimate deals with the surface energy balance (see Chapter 2). This in turn may be divided into the following sub-classes:

- *Slab models* represent the urban area in terms of a surface (e.g. concrete) with appropriate thermal characteristics.
- *Single layer models* represent a city by a layer of buildings, and the overall surface heat exchange is the sum of exchange on individual surfaces. This allows for more realistic representation of radiative trapping and turbulent exchange.
- *Multi-layer models* use a similar approach to single layer models, but model energy exchanges at multiple levels within the canopy, allowing for varying building height. Single and multi-layer models differ in the spatial detail of the representation of the urban morphology: one temperature and set of energy exchanges per facet versus multiple temperatures and energy exchanges per facet.

The urban surface poses great problems to the modeller, due to its inherent complexity of form and material. Of particular importance in this context is the treatment of vegetation, which behaves differently than paved or built-up surfaces. Vegetation may be incorporated in surface energy balance models as a separate type of surface, so that planted areas are treated as separate tiles that do not interact with other surface types until the first layer of the meso-scale model. Alternatively, it may be embedded into the urban area so that it affects, and is affected by, the presence of the buildings.

Computational Fluid Dynamics (CFD) is a modelling technique first developed as a tool for mechanical engineering, but which has also been employed as a tool for evaluating the indoor environment of buildings and its interaction with the building envelope, as well as for analysing aspects of the outdoor environment around buildings. CFD has been used to investigate a range of issues including air movement in and around buildings, pollution dispersal, the pedestrian wind environment, wind driven rain effects and the effects of vegetation on micro-climate. The main difficulty with CFD modelling of a built environment is the description of boundary conditions, which in a complex urban setting are often not known with sufficient accuracy. Unlike simpler methods, CFD requires that all relevant fluxes be calculated at the required scale in a full three-dimensional grid, which may be quite complex if it is to describe real buildings, as illustrated in Figure 11.2. In addition to requiring very detailed input, calculations require extensive computing resources, meaning models must be limited in space or simplified substantially. In both cases, calculation is limited to relatively short time periods, so the methodology is not applied to problems requiring time scales in excess of several days at the very most (see Box 11.3).

While computer-based simulation based on mathematical models is becoming quite well established in engineering practice for the evaluation of indoor environments, there is considerably less use for outdoor applications

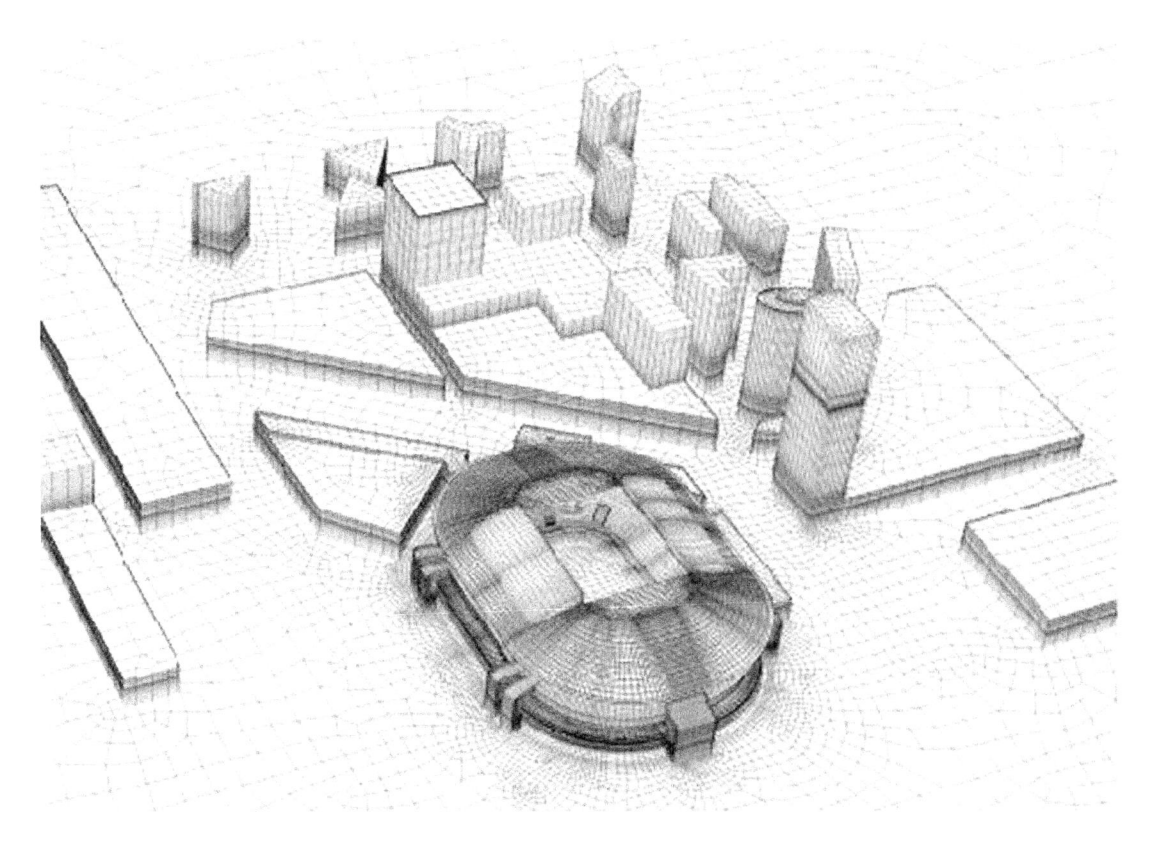

Figure 11.2 Part of geometry and computational grid for CFD study of pedestrian-level wind conditions around the Amsterdam 'ArenA' football stadium in The Netherlands

Source: Blocken and Persoon (2009).

and no evidence to suggest that at this point in time it is used as a routine means for urban climate assessments.

> ### Box 11.3 ENVI-met[4]
>
> ENVI-met is a CFD application comprising a three-dimensional computer model designed for the specific purpose of analysing the small-scale interactions between urban design and the microclimate. The model combines the calculation of fluid dynamics parameters such as wind flow or turbulence with the thermodynamic processes taking place at the ground surface, at walls and roofs or at plants. With a typical resolution between 0.5m and 10m, the model is able to simulate even complicated geometric forms such as terraces, balconies or complex quarters. ENVI-met is a prognostic model based on the fundamental laws of fluid dynamics and thermodynamics. The model includes the simulation of flow around and between buildings; exchange processes of heat and vapour at the ground surface and at walls; turbulence; exchange at vegetation and vegetation parameters; bioclimatology; and particle dispersion.

Site-specific climate data: simulating urban modification of air temperature

Site-specific climate knowledge is essential for the development of urban and building design that responds to the local environment. It is necessary for assessing the likely thermal acceptability of outdoor spaces and is essential for accurate thermal performance design of buildings (including the HVAC systems) and for the development of efficient control strategies. The following sections deal specifically with the modelling of the urban microclimate to inform building design.

Most building simulation software comes with inbuilt climate data files: either real data compiled from stations such as airports or calculated synthetic data. In each case, the climate data is assumed to be representative of the surrounding area. However, evidence of urban modification to weather indicates that the differences between city-centre locations and the typical rural reference sites used by meteorological services are often quite substantial.

The CAT model[5]

The CAT (Canyon Air Temperature) computer model was developed to predict site-specific air temperature in an urban street canyon for extended periods on the basis of data from a reference station exposed to the same meso-scale weather. Such stations are sometimes located at nearby airports or in a semi-rural location outside of the city centre. Each site is described by means of its geometry (height of buildings, if any, and street width); the albedo and thermal properties of the surfaces; moisture availability; and anthropogenic heat (energy released by human activity, such as vehicular traffic and buildings, as well as metabolic heat). In addition to the description of the two sites, CAT requires as input only time-series of meteorological parameters measured at standard weather stations and, in addition, solar radiation, typically at hourly intervals. These serve as descriptors of the constantly evolving meso-scale weather. An energy balance is then computed for each of the two sites, taking into account the effects of urban geometry on radiant exchange, the effect of moisture availability on latent heat flux, energy stored in the ground and in building surfaces, air-flow in the street based on wind above roof height and the sensible heat flux from individual surfaces and from the street canyon as a whole. By calculating site-specific modifications to air temperature resulting from the surface energy balance at each of the two sites (reference and urban), the software can predict the evolution of air temperature at the urban site based on measured meteorological parameters at the reference site, in diverse weather conditions and for extended periods.

The CAT model has been calibrated and tested using experimental data obtained in extended monitoring programmes carried out in Adelaide, South Australia, over a period of nearly a year. Field measurements were carried out at two adjacent street canyons in the urban core, running north–south and east–west respectively, and compared with data recorded at reference sites in a suburban location and at an open park.

After calibration, the model was capable of replicating measured air temperature in the urban street canyons in all weather conditions, including intense nocturnal heat islands in the city of up to 8.6K and daytime cool islands of up to 3.8K. Figure 11.3 shows a comparison of predictions made by CAT with measured air temperature in one of the Adelaide street canyons for a period of ten days, in which weather conditions varied from sunny to overcast with rain. Subsequent comparisons with measured data in Göteborg (Sweden) also show good results.

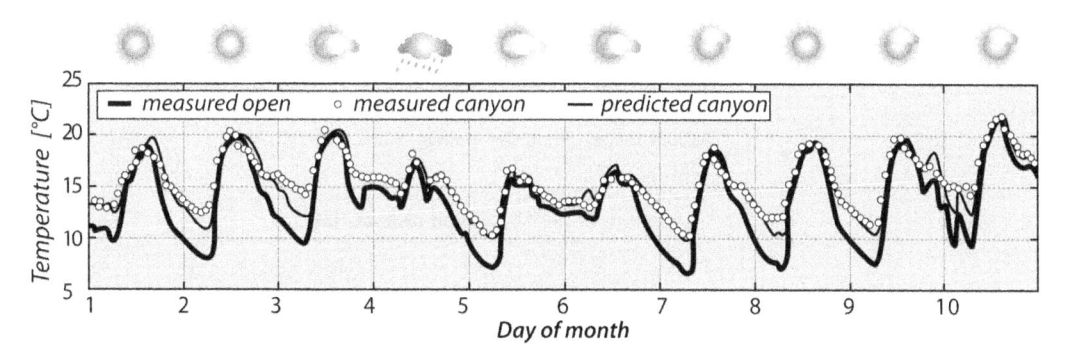

Figure 11.3 Comparison of measured air temperature at urban street canyon with temperature predicted by CAT from Bureau of Meteorology (BoM) data for a ten-day period in May 2000

Source: Redrawn from Erell and Williamson (2006).

Application of computer modelling to compare climatic regions

Intra-urban differences in air temperature are known to be affected by meteorological conditions. For example, intense heat islands are more likely to occur at night in clear-sky conditions that promote radiant cooling if wind speed is very low. The combined effect of these factors was investigated by running a series of CAT simulations using as input weather files from several study locations with different climatic characteristics: Adelaide has a Mediterranean climate with cool, humid winters and warm to hot dry summers; Glasgow has a mild to cold and damp climate, and Sde Boqer, in the desert highlands of Israel, has cool but sunny winters and hot dry summers. For each location, the simulations were carried out for a hypothetical street canyon oriented east–west and bordered by buildings with a uniform 14m height. The width of the street canyon was varied from 3.5m (representing a very narrow alley) to 56m, so that the corresponding aspect ratios (H/W) thus varied from 4 (14/3.5) to 0.25 (14/56). The properties of canyon surfaces were unchanged throughout the simulation.

Anthropogenic heat input was varied for each canyon width in an attempt to represent a realistic scenario of different development, traffic and pedestrian densities. For the narrow street canyon (H/W = 4.0) the daytime anthropogenic heat was 54W m^{-2} and for the broad street (H/W = 0.25) it was 12 Wm^{-2}. During night-time hours anthropogenic heat was reduced and fixed at a value equivalent to half the peak traffic flow.

Tables 11.1 and 11.2 show the average maximum canyon heat island and cool island, respectively, predicted by CAT on the hottest three months for each location.

As expected, the intensity of the urban effect is weakest in Glasgow: frequent extensive cloud cover and high atmospheric humidity limits nocturnal cooling in both urban and rural locations, reducing the magnitude of night-time heat islands. The effect of canyon aspect ratio on the magnitude of the intra-urban differences in temperature is discernible, but quite small. In particular, daytime cool islands are weak.

Table 11.1 Average monthly maximum canyon HEAT ISLAND (K) predicted by CAT for different canyon aspect ratios during the hottest three months of the year

Location	Canyon Aspect Ratio				
	4	2	1	0.5	0.25
Adelaide	5.9	5.5	5.2	3.7	3.1
Glasgow	4.1	3.8	3.3	2.9	2.4
Sde Boqer	4.6	4.3	3.9	3.6	2.5

Table 11.2 Average monthly maximum canyon COOL ISLAND (K) predicted by CAT for different canyon aspect ratios during the hottest three months of the year

Location	Canyon Aspect Ratio				
	4	2	1	0.5	0.25
Adelaide	1.8	1.7	1.6	1.4	1.2
Glasgow	1.1	1.0	1.2	1.1	1.1
Sde Boqer	1.3	1.0	1.0	0.8	0.6

Conditions in Adelaide are much more conducive to the formation of intense intra-urban temperature variations: the sky is frequently clear and moisture content is low, especially in summer, promoting the development of both nocturnal heat islands and daytime cool islands. There is a clear inverse correlation between canyon width and heat island intensity. The mean maximum monthly heat island intensity is 5.9K for a canyon 3.5m wide, but only 3.1K for a street 56m wide.

At Sde Boqer, one might have expected to find that conditions are even more likely to lead to the formation of intense intra-urban temperature differences. However, although the air is dry and skies are usually cloud free almost year round, wind speed is rarely low enough to allow the formation of very intense nocturnal heat islands. Low-level turbulence associated with wind induces effective mixing between near-surface and upper level air, as well as the advective transfer of sensible heat. Thus, although similar intra-urban temperature variations may be observed throughout the year – and are largest in winter – the magnitude of these differences is slightly smaller than that predicted for Adelaide.

The implications of such differences in urban modification of air temperature on the energy performance of buildings are illustrated by means of two case studies (see text boxes):

1. The effect on the potential for passive cooling by ventilation where air-conditioning is not installed, or is inoperative, using the climatic cooling potential (CCP) as a metric.
2. The effect of different urban forms on the energy consumption of fully air-conditioned buildings.

The case studies are performed for several locations representing different climate types, and this reveals substantial differences among them in the significance of urban modification. Modelling of the urban temperatures for the case studies is performed by the CAT analytical model implemented in a computer programme.

Box 11.4 Case study: The effect of urban modification of air temperature on the potential for cooling buildings by ventilation

Ventilation, especially at night, either by natural means or with mechanical assistance, is perhaps the most widespread strategy for low-energy cooling of buildings. However, it is highly sensitive to urban modification of the climate, both with respect to air temperature and to air-flow. Studies that combine extensive field measurements of urban air temperature with analysis of building ventilation requirements show that the potential for cooling might be restricted substantially, due to the reduction of wind speed and to increase in air temperature typical of many urban locations. The extent of the reduction in cooling potential depends both on the regional climate and on site-specific characteristics.

The climatic cooling potential (CCP) as a metric to assess the effectiveness of ventilation

The design of buildings that employ night-time ventilation may rely on detailed thermal performance simulation to justify their design. However, at the preliminary stages of a design the necessary detail may not be available, and the impact of climate on the thermal behaviour of a building is sometimes estimated by calculating degree-hours or degree-days for heating or cooling, relative to arbitrary reference temperatures. Such methods may be appropriate if the proposed building will be conditioned to maintain internal air temperature within a narrow range around the set point temperature. However, in the case of free-floating buildings, especially buildings with effective ventilation, internal temperature may fluctuate across much wider bands. The climatic cooling potential (CCP)[6] seeks to overcome this limitation by assuming that building temperature is allowed to oscillate harmonically in response to the diurnal cycle of external air temperature, with a time lag and decrement factor that are due to the presence of thermal mass. The CCP is defined as follows:

$$CCP = \frac{1}{N}\sum_{n=1}^{N}\sum_{h=h_i}^{h_f} m_{n,h}(T_{b,n,h} - T_{e,n,h}) \begin{cases} m = 1h \text{ if } T_{b-Te} \geq \Delta T_{crit} \\ m = 0 \text{ if } T_{b-Te} < \Delta T_{crit} \end{cases} \quad (11.1)$$

where h stands for the time of day, T_b is the building temperature and T_e is the external temperature. ΔT_{crit} is given an arbitrary value of 3K. T_b is allowed to oscillate around a predetermined temperature of 24.5°C, as follows:

$$T_{b,h} = 24.5 + 2.5\cos(2\pi\frac{h-h_i}{24}) \quad (11.2)$$

where h_i is the time at which ventilation starts, typically in the evening.

Effect of urban air temperature modification on predicted CCP

To illustrate the effect of urban modification in different climates, the CCP was used to assess the ventilation potential for different urban configurations in the three cities described above. The CAT model was then applied to modify the measured weather data to account for urban modification in hypothetical street canyons. The estimation of the CCP was subject to the following assumptions:

- Night-time ventilation may be applied, in principle, between 2000 hours and 0600 hours.
- However, it is operative in practice only when the difference between the building temperature and external ambient is greater than 3K.

The cumulative frequency distribution of the CCP was first calculated for each of the three locations, using unmodified meteorological data (Figure 11.4). Glasgow has a high CCP, because ambient air temperature is generally lower than desired indoor conditions, even in summer. At Sde Boqer, temperatures at night, though much cooler than during the daytime, are nonetheless much higher than in Glasgow (with Adelaide being in between). Therefore, it has a much lower CCP.

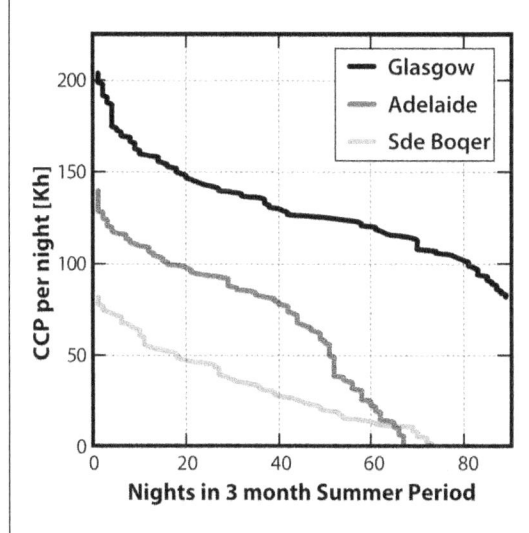

Figure 11.4 Comparison of the cumulative frequency distribution of the CCP at the reference meteorological station for Glasgow, Adelaide and Sde Boqer

The effects of urban modification of air temperature on the CCP were then calculated for each location, first without including the effects of anthropogenic heating, i.e. simulating the effects of street canyon geometry only, then with anthropogenic heat input. Integrating the CCP cumulative distribution curves gives a measure of the full ventilation potential of a particular situation. Figures 11.5 and 11.6 show the change in the CCP for urban conditions, compared with the meteorological data recorded at the reference sites in the three locations in relative terms and in absolute values, respectively. Urban effects, for a given

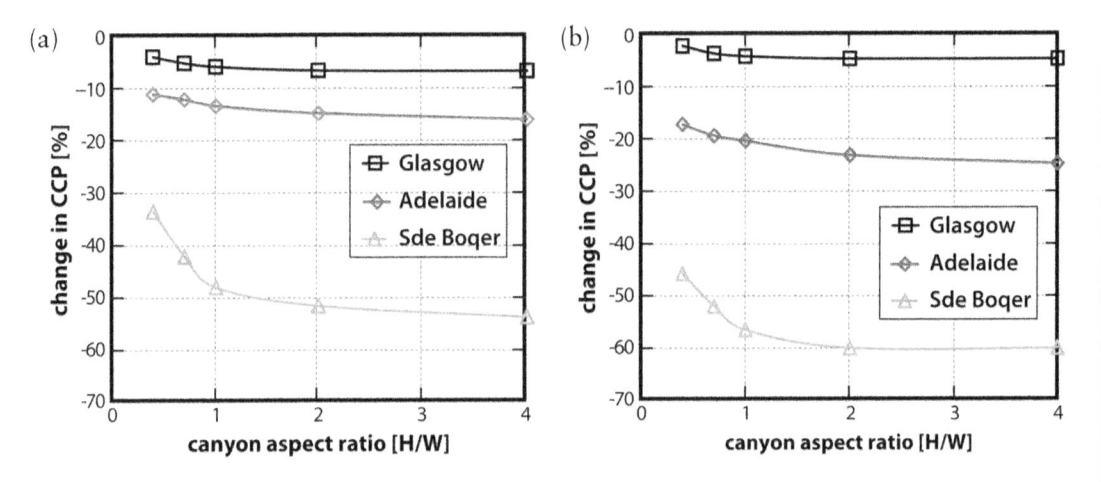

Figure 11.5 Effect of canyon aspect ratio on the *relative* change in the CCP of Glasgow, Adelaide and Sde Boqer for the three-month summer period, based on air temperature predicted by CAT with anthropogenic heat input set to zero (a) and with variable heat input (b)

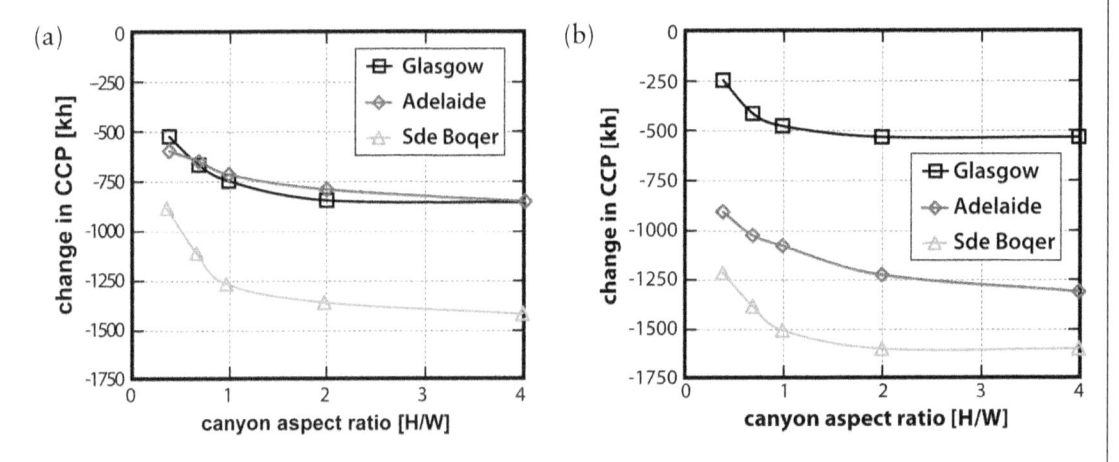

Figure 11.6 Effect of canyon aspect ratio on the *absolute* change in the CCP of Glasgow, Adelaide and Sde Boqer for the three-month summer period, based on air temperature predicted by CAT with anthropogenic heat input set to zero (a) and with variable heat input (b)

street canyon aspect ratio and anthropogenic heat input, are lowest for Glasgow and highest for Sde Boqer. The inclusion of anthropogenic heat in the simulation does not alter the qualitative conclusions of the analysis, but its effect on the magnitude of the change is not negligible, especially in the case of Glasgow.

It is worth noting that the calculated urban effect on the CCP does not correlate with the maximum intra-urban heat island (IUHI) intensity calculated for the three locations. Although the maximum intensity of the IUHI in Adelaide is greater than in Sde Boqer, the consistency of an IUHI night after night, and the persistency of the IUHI during a night, means that the average IUHI intensity is actually higher in the latter location. Overall, therefore, urban effects may cause a greater reduction in the potential for night ventilation in Sde Boqer compared with Adelaide, both in relative and in absolute terms.

Box 11.5 Case study: The effect of accounting for urban air temperature on the simulated energy performance of a fully air-conditioned office building

The effect of urban modification of air temperature on the energy performance of a test building was studied using the EnerWin whole-building energy simulation software.[7] The programme requires input of environmental data in the form of hourly records for an entire year.

A number of simulations were conducted for each situation examined. Firstly, the energy performance analysis was carried out using standard climate data. This is referred to as the reference situation. The same building was then simulated again, using modified input files with air temperature in hypothetical urban canyons representing different configurations, as predicted by CAT, in place of measured air temperature data from the standard file. The results of the simulations were then compared to assess the effect of urban modifications to air temperature (only) on the energy budget of the building. This process was then repeated, adding the effect of the shading on the study building provided by the canyon configuration.

Building description

The building used for the case study is a typical four-storey development, consisting of public spaces on the ground floor (café, etc.) and identical office-type accommodation on the upper floors (see Figure 11.7). The total floor area of the building is 1430m^2 (about 30 x 12m per floor). Some modifications are made to accommodate the context of each location; an equator-facing facade is maintained and the glass area is adjusted to reflect the expectations of the location.

Figure 11.7 Computer rendering of the case study building

Notes: The simulated building has external walls of insulated pre-cast concrete (thermal conductance U = 0.68W m^{-2} K^{-1}), a built-up concrete roof (U = 0.28 W m^{-2} K^{-1}) and concrete slab intermediate floors. Windows were taken as double-glazed low$_{-e}$ in aluminium frames (U$_{overall}$ = 2.75W m^{-2} K^{-1}). An infiltration rate of 0.6 air changes per hour was specified, along with a mechanical ventilation rate of 15 litres per second per person. Internal heat gains were calculated taking into account a detailed occupancy schedule specified in the Building Code of Australia. Lighting and equipment introduce an additional load of 15W m^{-2} on average. Thermostat settings for the simulation were: summer: 24°C when the building is occupied and 26°C when it is unoccupied; and winter: 21°C at all times.

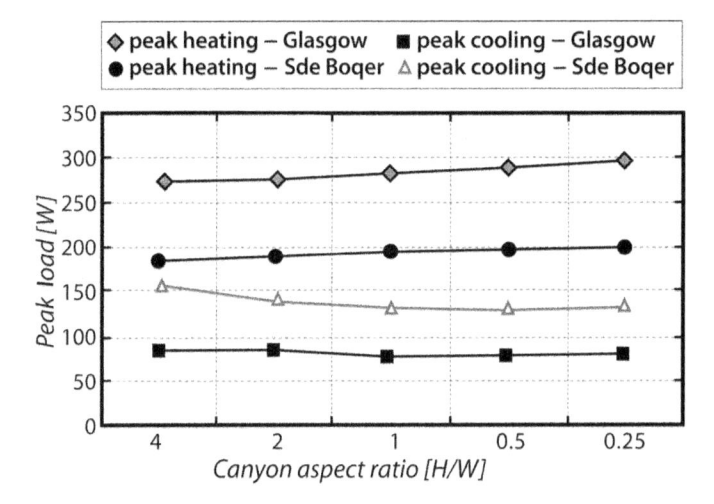

Figure 11.8 Effect of urban density on the simulated peak heating and cooling loads for Glasgow and Sde Boqer

Simulated peak loads

In general, the effect on peak loads when the air temperature is modified by increasing the density of the urban environment is to decrease the heating load and increase the cooling load. The simulated results for Glasgow and Sde Boqer shown in Figure 11.8 verify this effect, albeit the changes are relatively small.

The pattern in the peak heating load is not surprising, since the urban fabric has the effect of damping extreme diurnal variations in temperature, reflected in the nocturnal heat island. One might expect a similar effect for the cooling load, although anthropogenic heat release may often outweigh any potential cool island that might have been brought about by canyon geometry.

Of greater import is the finding that although urban effects, in particular the nocturnal heat island, might be quite substantial, they do not necessarily occur in conjunction with meteorological conditions that require the greatest heating or cooling output from the HVAC plant. Peak cooling demand typically occurs on summer afternoon hours – when the UHI is negligible. Similarly, peak heating demand may be registered on cold, windy nights (wind promotes convective heat losses at the building envelope) – but substantial heat islands rarely form in windy conditions. The implication is that urban modification of air temperature, in particular, may have less effect on the design conditions of HVAC plant than is often assumed.

Simulated energy consumption

Differences in the canyon aspect ratio affect the energy consumption of buildings in a variety of ways. For example, deep canyons restrict natural ventilation; yet they also provide mutual shading for buildings on either side of the street. The net effect of a particular canyon geometry depends on the specific design of a building: shading by adjacent buildings has little effect if it has small, well-protected windows, while the effect of differences in air temperature may be minimized by increasing thermal insulation of exterior surfaces.

Table 11.3 Annual energy budget for heating and cooling the test building in the three test locations for different street canyon configurations, using air temperature modified by CAT but assuming no mutual shading

H/W	Adelaide			Glasgow			Sde Boqer		
	heating (GJ)	cooling (GJ)	total (GJ)	heating (GJ)	cooling (GJ)	total (GJ)	heating (GJ)	cooling (GJ)	total (GJ)
4	402	558	960	1167	164	1331	314	703	1017
2	411	550	961	1181	164	1345	320	693	1013
1	423	543	965	1208	161	1369	328	685	1013
0.5	437	539	976	1241	159	1400	339	676	1015
0.25	446	538	984	1265	158	1422	343	674	1017
0	473	529	1002	1335	152	1487	360	650	1010

Note: H/W = 0 represents the reference climate file.

Table 11.3 shows the differences in heating and cooling budget calculated by EnerWin for Adelaide, Glasgow and Sde Boqer, using air temperature modified by CAT for different canyon aspect ratios but without considering the shading afforded by the canyon on the test building. This case shows the effect of the air temperature modifications only.

The effect of urban modification of air temperature on predicted energy consumption in Glasgow has the largest absolute effect, reflecting the high intensity of the urban effect when the annual average temperature is relatively low, even though in relative terms the reduction in heating demand is similar, between 12.5 per cent (Glasgow) to 15 per cent (Adelaide). This is because in Glasgow, although an increase in urban density leads to higher air temperature and thus to a substantial increase in the cooling requirement in relative terms, the increase is quite small in absolute terms, and is much smaller than the savings resulting from a reduction in the winter heating budget.

In each location, the predicted heating budget becomes progressively smaller as the street canyon becomes deeper, reflecting the increasing intensity of the nocturnal UHI. Conversely, the predicted cooling load increases.

The canyon air temperatures modelled by CAT as part of this case study are not necessarily those actually found in the respective locations. Variations in anthropogenic heat, for example, may result in significantly different heat island intensities in specific locations. However, the conditions specified for comparison of the different cities were realistic, so tentative conclusions may be drawn with respect to the effect of urban density on air temperature.

The discussion thus far has focused on the effect of urban modification of air temperature, to the exclusion of other effects of building density. However, solar access to windows may have a far greater effect on building energy consumption than air temperature, resulting in potential overheating in warm climates and in beneficial solar gains in cold regions. As Table 11.4 shows, when the effects of mutual shading by adjacent buildings are accounted for, deep street canyons resulted in a substantial increase in the heating budget of the office building in all three locations, particularly in Glasgow.

Finally, it is worth noting that in no case is the effect of the canyon aspect ratio on the predicted annual budget for heating or cooling linear. As Figure 11.9 shows, increasing the aspect ratio (H/W) beyond a value of about two (a narrow street) has only a marginal effect in all three locations. This is because the exchange of long-wave radiation with the atmosphere is affected by the sky view factor (SVF), which has a high value at this aspect ratio and increases only marginally for larger ratios.

Table 11.4 Annual energy budget for heating and cooling in the three test locations, for different street canyon configurations, as predicted by CAT – with mutual shading

H/W	Adelaide			Glasgow			Sde Boqer		
	heating (GJ)	cooling (GJ)	total (GJ)	heating (GJ)	cooling (GJ)	total (GJ)	heating (GJ)	cooling (GJ)	total (GJ)
4	1006	167	1174	1816	24	1840	864	247	1111
2	615	288	903	1411	46	1457	495	398	892
1	534	397	931	1308	89	1397	410	507	917
0.5	489	459	948	1289	116	1405	375	578	953
0.25	470	495	965	1288	131	1419	361	623	984

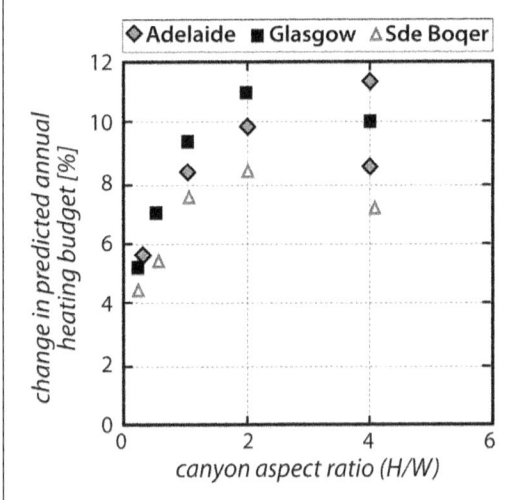

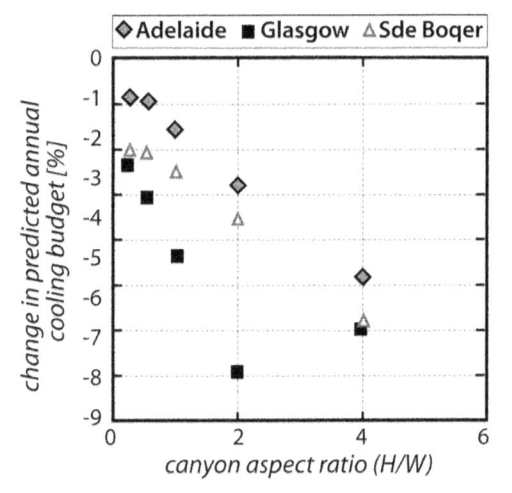

Figure 11.9 Change in annual budget for heating the generic office building (left) and cooling it (right), as a result of urban modification of air temperature and with mutual shading, as predicted by EnerWin for three locations in different climate zones

Implications for building and urban design

Urban modification of air temperature is not constant with respect to time, and the differences in temperature between a reference climate data and a particular urban location may vary according to a diurnal and seasonal pattern. Although the UHI is better known, the city may also experience lower air temperature in certain conditions and at certain times of the year (an urban cool island), as shown by the CAT simulation and as found in several field studies. As Table 11.4 shows, although there may be substantial differences in both heating and cooling budgets, the net effect of urban modification of air temperature in certain locations may be small (Glasgow shows that the largest net variation is a 10 per cent reduction). Ultimately the building energy use will depend on the relative efficiency of the heating and cooling plant. Realistic assessment of the effect of intra-urban variations in air temperature on site-specific energy consumption in buildings therefore requires dynamic building thermal simulation software that employs detailed site-specific hourly weather inputs.

Although the relationship between density and intra-urban temperature variations may be quantified with reasonable confidence, it would nonetheless be inappropriate to develop recommendations for urban form solely on this basis. As noted above, air temperature is but one factor affecting energy consumption in buildings, and may not necessarily be the most important one. A comparison of Tables 11.3 and 11.4 illustrates this point: in Glasgow, the effect of shading dwarfs that of the UHI. However, it is important that the debate on energy conservation in buildings, in the context of the global effort to reduce carbon emissions, is carried out on the basis of detailed and reliable information.

Air-conditioning loads include latent heat as well as sensible heat, and are thus affected by the moisture content of air, too. Computer models such as the CAT model are capable of predicting the effect of urban geometry and materials on the evolution of air temperature in a generic urban street canyon, but the prediction of moisture content remains less accurate.

The comparison of simulated energy consumption for street canyons of different depths and in different climate regions illustrates the capabilities of computer tools such as CAT in urban planning, in conjunction with building energy simulation software. The results are not unexpected, and highlight the roles of radiant exchange and urban thermal mass in the development of intra-urban temperature differences. Deep street canyons experience stronger nocturnal heat islands and, conversely, more prominent daytime cool islands, than shallow ones. The intra-urban temperature differences are more pronounced in dry locations, and weakest in high-latitude cities, where radiative cooling is weaker and latent heat plays a more dominant role in the surface energy budget.

While the trends illustrated by the simulation with respect to the heating and cooling requirements can also be explained in a qualitative manner, it is the quantitative nature of the results that is important. The ability to predict with confidence both peak loads on HVAC equipment and total annual heat consumption is of great value in the design of HVAC systems and in economic calculations regarding their operation and maintenance. The design of such systems is now carried out routinely using detailed whole-building energy simulation models. Failing to account for urban modifications to air temperature and radiant exchange may lead to errors that are too large to overlook. HVAC plant may be either oversized or too small, leading to unnecessary expenditure in the first instance or failure to cope adequately with loads in the latter. Optimization of life cycle costs of the equipment can only be done if the capital cost is assessed correctly and if running costs are estimated realistically. Finally, certification of the performance of the building within the framework of a building energy-rating scheme, a procedure that is now required by regulatory authorities in many countries, might be affected if local climate modifications are not accounted for. This has policy, legal and financial implications that should not be ignored.

Notes

1. David and Pearson, (1970).
2. Kanda and Moriizumi (2009).
3. Pearlmutter et al (2005).
4. www.envi-met.com (accessed 18 July 2010).
5. Erell and Williamson (2006).
6. Artmann et al (2007).
7. Degelman and Soebarto (1995).

References

Aida, A. (1982) 'Urban albedo as a function of the urban structure – a model experiment', *Boundary-Layer Meteorology*, vol 23, no 4, pp405–413

Artmann, N., Manz, H. and Heiselberg, P. (2007) 'Climatic potential for passive cooling of buildings by night-time ventilation in Europe', *Applied Energy*, vol 84, no 2, pp187–201

Blocken, B. and Persoon, J. (2009) 'Pedestrian wind comfort around a large football stadium in an urban environment: CFD simulation, validation and application of the new Dutch wind nuisance standard', *Journal of Wind Engineering and Industrial Aerodynamics*, vol 97, nos 5–6, pp255–270

Davis, M. L. and Pearson, J. E. (1970) 'Modeling urban atmospheric temperature profiles', *Atmospheric Environment*, vol 4, no 3, pp277–282

Degelman, L. O. and Soebarto, V. (1995) 'Software description for ENER-WIN: A visual interface model for hourly energy simulation in buildings', in *Building Simulation '95*, Proceedings of the 5th International IBPSA Conference, pp692–696

Erell, E. and Williamson, T. (2006) 'Simulating air temperature in an urban street canyon in all weather conditions using measured data from a reference meteorological station', *International Journal of Climatology*, vol 26, no 12, pp1671–1694

Kanda, M. and Moriizumi, T. (2009) 'Momentum and heat transfer over urban-like surfaces', *Boundary-Layer Meteorology*, vol 131, no 3, pp385–401

Oke, T. R. (1981) 'Canyon geometry and the nocturnal urban heat island: Comparison of scale model and field observations', *International Journal of Climatology*, vol 1, no 3, pp237–254

Pearlmutter, D., Berliner, P. and Shaviv, E. (2005) 'Evaluation of urban surface energy fluxes using an open-air scale model', *Journal of Applied Meteorology*, vol 44, no 4, pp532–545

Pearlmutter, D., Berliner, P. and Shaviv, E. (2006) 'Physical modeling of pedestrian energy exchange within the urban canopy', *Building and Environment*, vol 41, no 6, pp783–795

Additional reading

Arnfield, A. J. (2000) 'A simple model of urban canyon energy budget and its validation', *Physical Geography*, vol 21, pp305–326

Barlow, J. F. and Belcher, S. E. (2002) 'A wind tunnel model for quantifying fluxes in the urban boundary layer', *Boundary-Layer Meteorology*, vol 104, no 1, pp131–150

Best, M. J. (2005) 'Representing urban areas within operational numerical weather prediction models', *Boundary-Layer Meteorology*, vol 114, no 1, pp91–109

Best, M. J., Grimmond, C. S. B. and Villani, M. G. (2006) 'Evaluation of the urban tile in MOSES using surface energy balance observations', *Boundary-Layer Meteorology*, vol 118, no 3, pp503–525

Bonacquisti, V., Casale, G. R., Palmieri, S. and Siani, A. M. (2006) 'A canopy layer model and its application to Rome', *Science of the Total Environment*, vol 364, nos 1–3, pp1–13

Bruse, M. and Fleer, H. (1998) 'Simulating surface–plant–air interactions inside urban environments with a three dimensional numerical model', *Environmental Modelling and Software*, vol 13, nos 3–4, pp373–384

Clarke, J. A. (1985) *Energy Simulation in Building Design*, Adam Hilger, Bristol

Cermak, J. E. (1995) 'Physical modelling of flow and dispersion over urban areas', in J. E. Cermak, A. G. Davenport, E. J. Plate and D. X. Viegas (eds) *Wind Climate in Cities*, Kluwer Academic Publishers, Dordrecht

Dandou, A., Tombrou, M., Akylas, E., Soulakellis N. and Bossioli, E. (2005) 'Development and evaluation of an urban parameterization scheme in the Penn State/NCAR mesoscale model (MM5)', *Journal of Geophysical Research*, vol 110, D10102

Dupont, S. and Mestayer, P. G. (2006) 'Parameterisation of the urban energy budget with the submesoscale soil model', *Journal of Applied Meteorology and Climatology*, vol 45, pp1744–1765

Erell, E., Soebarto, V. and Williamson, T. (2007) 'Accounting for urban microclimate in computer simulation of building energy performance', in S. Wittkopf and B. K. Tan (eds) *Sun, Wind and Architecture*, Proceedings of PLEA 2007, 24th International Conference on Passive and Low Energy Architecture, Singapore, pp593–600

Fortuniak, K., Offerle, B. and Grimmond, C. S. B. (2004) 'Slab surface energy balance scheme and its application to parameterisation of the energy fluxes on urban areas', NATO Advanced Study Institute: 'Flow and Transport Processes in Complex Obstructed Geometries', Kiev, Ukraine, 4–15 May 2004, pp82–83, www.met.rdg.ac.uk/urb_met/NATO_ASI/talks.html, accessed 27 June 2010

Grimmond, C. S. B. and Oke, T. R. (1991) 'An evaporation-interception model for urban areas', *Water Resources Research*, vol 27, pp1739–1755

Grimmond, C. S. B. and Oke, T. R. (2002) 'Turbulent heat fluxes in urban areas: Observations and local-scale urban meteorological parameterization scheme (LUMPS)', *Journal of Applied Meteorology*, vol 41, pp792–810

Harman, I. N. and Belcher, S. E. (2006) 'The surface energy balance and boundary layer over urban street canyons', *Quarterly Journal of the Royal Meteorological Society*, vol 132, no 621B, pp2749–2768

Kanda, M., Kawai, T., Kanega, M., Moriwaki, R., Narita, K. and Hagishima, A. (2005) 'A simple energy balance model for regular building arrays', *Boundary-Layer Meteorology*, vol 116, no 3, pp423–443

Kanda, M., Kawai, T., Moriwaki, R., Narita, K., Hagishima, A. and Sugawara, H. (2006) 'Comprehensive Outdoor Scale Model Experiments for Urban Climate (COSMO)', *Proceedings of the 6th International Conference on Urban Climate*, Göteborg, Sweden, pp270–273

Kastner-Klein, P. and Plate, E. J. (1999) 'Wind-tunnel study of concentration fields in street canyons', *Atmospheric Environment*, vol 33, nos 24–25, pp3973–3979

Kondo, H., Genchi, Y., Kikegawa, Y., Ohashi, Y., Yoshikado, H. and Komiyama, H. (2005) 'Development of a multi-layer urban canopy model for the analysis of energy consumption in a big city: Structure of the urban canopy model and its basic performance', *Boundary-Layer Meteorology*, vol 116, no 3, pp395–421

Krayenhoff, E. S. and Voogt, J. A. (2007) 'A microscale three-dimensional urban energy balance model for studying surface temperatures', *Boundary-Layer Meteorology*, vol 123, no 3, pp433–461

Krüger, E. L. and Pearlmutter, D. (2008) 'The effect of urban evaporation on building energy demand in an arid environment', *Energy and Buildings*, vol 40, no 11, pp2090–2098

Kusaka, H., Kondo, H., Kikegawa, Y. and Kimura, F. (2001) 'A simple single-layer urban canopy model for atmospheric models: Comparison with multi-layer and slab models', *Boundary-Layer Meteorology*, vol 101, no 3, pp329–358

Lee, S. H. and Park, S. U. (2008) 'A vegetated urban canopy model for meteorological and environmental modelling', *Boundary-Layer Meteorology*, vol 126, no 1, pp73–102

Lemonsu, A., Grimmond, C. S. B. and Masson, V. (2004) 'Modeling the surface energy balance of the core of an old Mediterranean city: Marseille', *Journal of Applied Meteorology*, vol 43, pp312–327

Martilli, A., Clappier, A. and Rotach, M. W. (2002) 'An urban surface exchange parameterisation for mesoscale models', *Boundary-Layer Meteorology*, vol 104, pp261–304

Masson, V. (2000) 'A physically-based scheme for the urban energy budget in atmospheric models', *Boundary-Layer Meteorology*, vol 94, no 3, pp357–397

Masson, V. (2006) 'Urban surface modeling and the meso-scale impact of cities', *Theoretical and Applied Climatology*, vol 84, nos 1–3, pp35–45

Masson, V., Grimmond, C. S. B. and Oke, T. R. (2002) 'Evaluation of the town energy balance (TEB) scheme with direct measurements from dry districts in two cities', *Journal of Applied Meteorology*, vol 41, pp1011–1026

Mills, G. (1997) 'An urban canopy-layer climate model', *Theoretical and Applied Climatology*, vol 57, pp229–244

Oke, T. R. (1981) 'Canyon geometry and the nocturnal urban heat island: Comparison of scale model and field observations', *International Journal of Climatology*, vol 1, no 3, pp237–254

Pearlmutter, D., Berliner, P. and Shaviv, E. (2007a) 'Integrated modeling of pedestrian energy exchange and thermal comfort in urban street canyons', *Building and Environment*, vol 42, no 6, pp2396–2409

Pearlmutter, D., Berliner, P. and Shaviv, E. (2007b) 'Urban climatology in arid regions: Current research in the Negev desert', *International Journal of Climatology*, vol 27, no 14, pp1875–1885

Pearlmutter, D., Krüger, E. L. and Berliner, P. (2009) 'The role of evaporation in the energy balance of an open-air scaled urban surface', *International Journal of Climatology*, vol 29, no 6, pp911–920

Richards, K. (2002) 'A review of scaling theory for hardware models and application to an urban dew model', *Physical Geography*, vol 23, no 3, pp212–232

Richards, K. and Oke, T. R. (2002) 'Validation and results of a scale model of dew deposition in urban environments', *International Journal of Climatology*, vol 22, no 15, pp1915–1933

Sakakibara, Y. (1996) 'A numerical study of the effect of urban geometry upon the surface energy budget', *Atmospheric Environment*, vol 30, no 3, pp487–496

Spronken-Smith, R. and Oke, T. R. (1999) 'Scale modelling of nocturnal cooling in urban parks', *Boundary-Layer Meteorology*, vol 93, no 2, pp287–312

Taha, H. (1999) 'Modifying a mesoscale meteorological model to better incorporate urban heat storage: A bulk parameterization approach', *Journal of Applied Meteorology*, vol 38, pp466–473

Tanimoto, J., Hagishima, A. and Chimklai, P. (2004) 'An approach for coupled simulation of building thermal effects and urban climatology', *Energy and Buildings*, vol 36, no 8, pp781–793

Voogt, J. A. and Oke, T. R. (1991) 'Validation of an urban canyon radiation model for nocturnal long-wave fluxes', *Boundary-Layer Meteorology*, vol 54, no 4, pp347–361

Williamson, T. and Erell, E. (2008) 'The Implications for building ventilation of the spatial and temporal variability of air temperature in the urban canopy layer', *International Journal of Ventilation*, vol 7, no 1, pp23–35

Williamson, T., Erell, E. and Soebarto, V. (2009) 'Assessing the error from failure to account for urban microclimate in computer simulation of building energy performance', in P. Strachan and N. Kelly (eds) *Building Simulation 2009, Proceedings of the 11th International IBPSA Conference*, Glasgow, pp497–504

12

Case Study 1: Neve Zin

The Neve Zin neighbourhood of Sde Boqer in the Negev desert of Israel comprises a total of 79 private, single-family detached houses. Notwithstanding its small size, its significance lies in its unique master plan and building regulations, which were aimed specifically at promoting (though not mandating) energy-conscious building design and creating an outdoor environment that responds to the local climate. Buildings in the neighbourhood were designed by independent architects commissioned by building owners. The role of the master plan was therefore limited to the creation of a framework within which the architects could operate, rather than the creation of a design complete in every detail.

The planning of the neighbourhood was commissioned in 1984, and the first buildings were occupied in 1990. This allows a certain perspective from which to evaluate the success of the design, in terms of its stated objectives as well as in other respects. However, this case study will deal only with those elements of the design that are related directly to microclimate and the environment.

Analysis of local climate

Sde Boqer is located in the arid Negev Highlands region of southern Israel (30.8°N latitude, 475m altitude). The region is characterized by hot dry summers and cool but sunny winters, with wide diurnal fluctuations (Figures 12.1 and 12.2). With clear skies most of the year, solar radiation is substantial and especially intense in summer, when daily global radiation on a horizontal surface averages over 7.5kWh m^{-2}. Prevailing winds from the northwest are strong in the summer afternoon and evening hours, often carrying considerable amounts of airborne dust. Although daytime temperature in winter is relatively comfortable, cold nights lead to an annual heating requirement of approximately 1100 heating degree days (18.3°C base). Average annual precipitation is about 85mm, but potential evapotranspiration (PET) is extremely high – about 2045mm, creating an annual water deficit of almost 2000mm (Figure 12.3). The air is typically dry, with a vapour pressure deficit of at least 5g/kg: daytime relative humidity in summer is low, averaging about 30 per cent in the early afternoon, although strong nocturnal cooling results in frequent dew. Figure 12.4 shows a bioclimatic chart summarizing the environmental conditions with respect to a human 'thermal comfort bubble'.

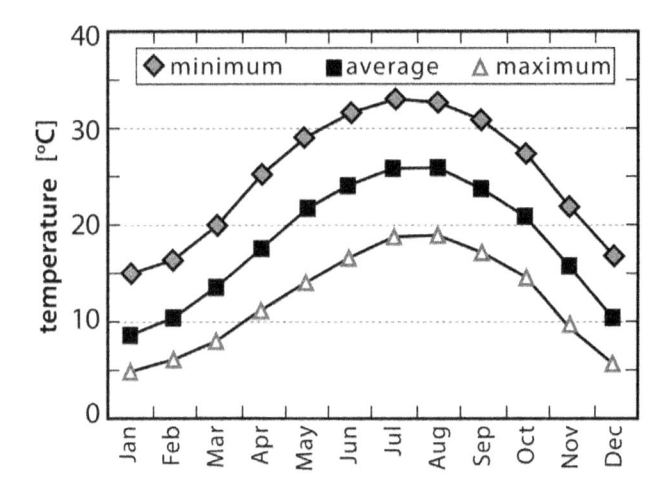

Figure 12.1 Monthly average values of air temperature at Sde Boqer

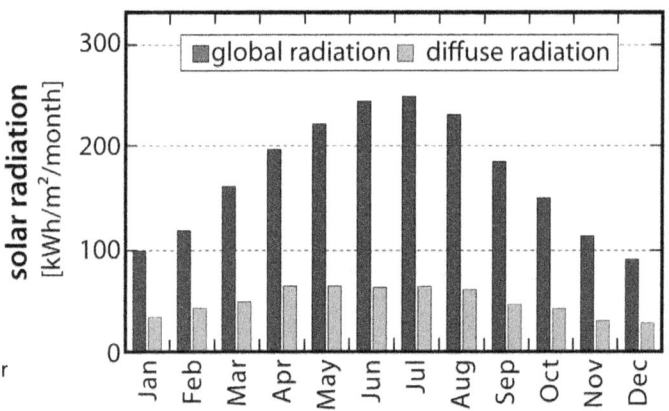

Figure 12.2 Total monthly insolation at Sde Boqer

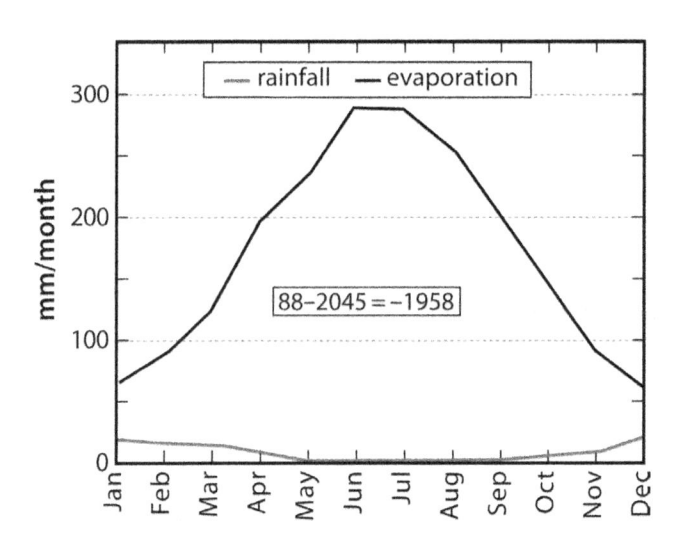

Figure 12.3 Monthly water balance for Sde Boqer, showing difference between precipitation and potential evapotranspiration (PET)

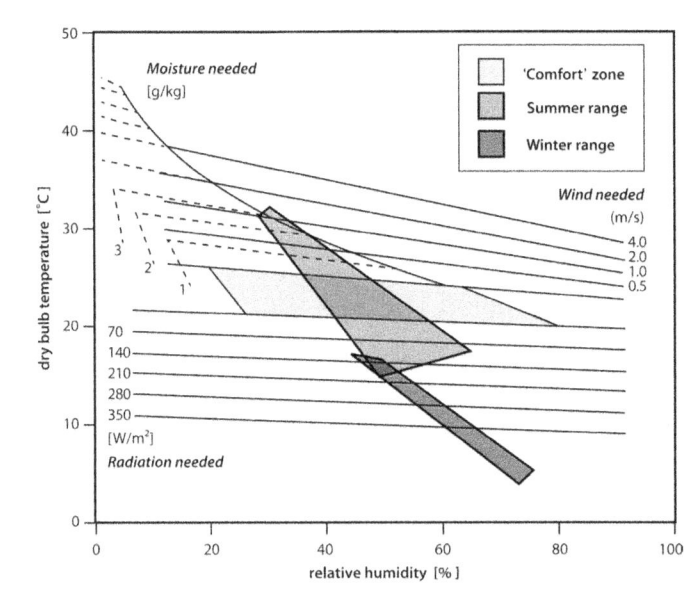

Figure 12.4 Thermal comfort analysis for Sde Boqer

Note: The winter range was constructed from average monthly minimum and maximum temperatures for the months of December and January, and the corresponding relative humidity values. The summer range represents similar data for the months of June and July.

Design goals

The overall goal of the design was to 'create a modern desert neighbourhood that will be responsive to the harsh conditions of the environment and at the same time will provide dwellers with all modern facilities'.[1] This was to be achieved by strategies that deal with a variety of issues, including building thermal performance and pedestrian comfort in outdoor spaces.

Objectives related to building thermal performance

Since Sde Boqer has cool but sunny winters, buildings can benefit from substantial energy savings through passive solar heating – provided that solar access is preserved. One of the primary goals of the design was therefore to guarantee unobstructed solar access to all buildings in the neighbourhood.

In summer hot days are typically followed by relatively cool nights, so buildings may benefit from effective night ventilation to remove excess energy absorbed during the daytime. Accordingly, the design sought to create breezeways that promote air-flow through the neighbourhood.

Objectives related to pedestrian comfort in outdoor spaces

Pedestrian thermal comfort in outdoor spaces is affected by several factors, such as net radiant exchange, air temperature, humidity and the degree of exposure to wind. The neighbourhood plan for Neve Zin sought to promote comfort all year round through the design of pedestrian areas – paths and public squares – where the natural environmental conditions are modified through man-made construction.

In addition to thermal comfort, people staying outdoors in desert areas are exposed to airborne dust, which is often a major source of discomfort. The neighbourhood plan therefore sought to minimize exposure to dust.

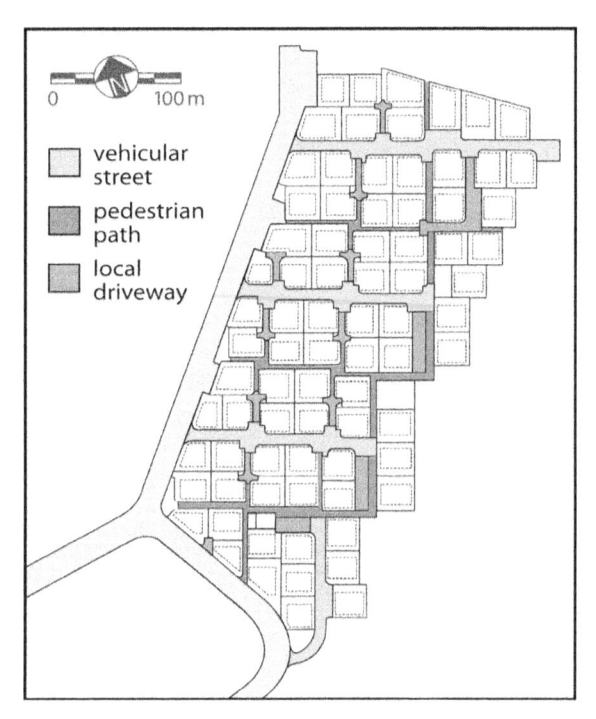

Figure 12.5 Two circulation systems at Neve Zin

Climate-related response

The planning of Neve Zin sought to address both of the aforementioned goals in a comprehensive and integrated manner. In order to do so a number of unconventional features were incorporated in the neighbourhood master plan.

Circulation

Neve Zin has two separate circulation networks: pedestrian-only paths, and 'woonerfs' providing combined access to motor vehicles and to pedestrians. The planning of the two networks was influenced by climatic considerations related both to the microclimate of the respective outdoor spaces and to the exposure of buildings in the neighbourhood to the sun and wind.

The neighbourhood is bounded on the west by a peripheral road, from which vehicles may enter three woonerfs whose main axis is approximately east–west (Figure 12.5). These streets have no sidewalks, and pedestrians share the primary circulation space with cars. Travelling speed throughout the neighbourhood is restricted to less than 25km/h by means of various landscaping elements (Figure 12.6), ensuring a very safe environment. The woonerfs are about 8m wide – a distance large enough to ensure that two-storey buildings on the south side of the road do not

Figure 12.6 Driving speed in the woonerfs is restricted by the landscaping

Photograph: David Pearlmutter.

Figure 12.7 North–south alleys with pergolas provide shade and protection from wind and dust

Photograph: David Pearlmutter.

shade the buildings on its north side in winter, when passive solar heating demands full exposure to the sun. Each of the woonerfs provides vehicular access not only to buildings bordering it on either side, but also to buildings in a second row that are connected to them by means of short and narrow driveways. This arrangement is more compact than the traditional one, in which each building is accessed directly from the street.

A secondary, pedestrian-only circulation network consists mainly of narrow alleys oriented north–south (Figure 12.7). These alleys, only 2.5m wide and about 50m long, are bounded on both sides by masonry walls up to 2m high which are required by the neighbourhood master plan. The walls, in conjunction with pergolas constructed above the alley at strategic locations, create a shaded and protected environment in both summer, when the main concern is shading, and in winter, when the primary concern is to reduce exposure to cold winds. Additional protection is provided by adjacent buildings, which the plan specifies must be built close to the alley (see following paragraph for more details).

Building clusters

The precise location of buildings in each plot (with respect to the plot lines) is restricted. Rather than the conventional approach of locating buildings in the middle of each plot, often creating both a front yard and a back yard with relatively little space between adjacent buildings, the Neve Zin plan created clusters of four plots each, in which the buildings are placed at the outside corners of the cluster (Figure 12.8). Since the plans of individual buildings were not known in advance, this was achieved by stipulating that the external envelope of the building in question must overlie the intersection of the two setback lines farthest from the centre of each cluster, a point marked on the plan as the 'P-point'. This had several benefits:

- Adjacent buildings arranged north–south in the same cluster are separated as far as possible, reducing the obstruction of direct sunlight and thus contributing to the strategy of solar rights protection.

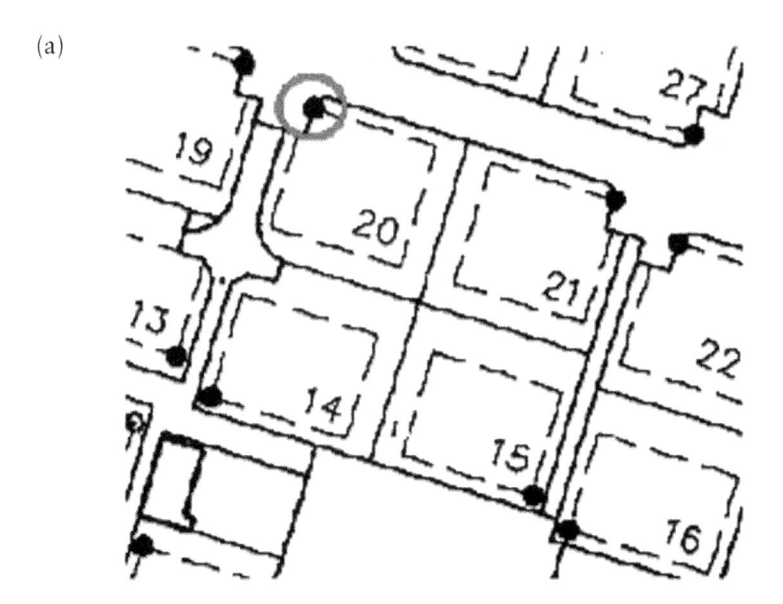

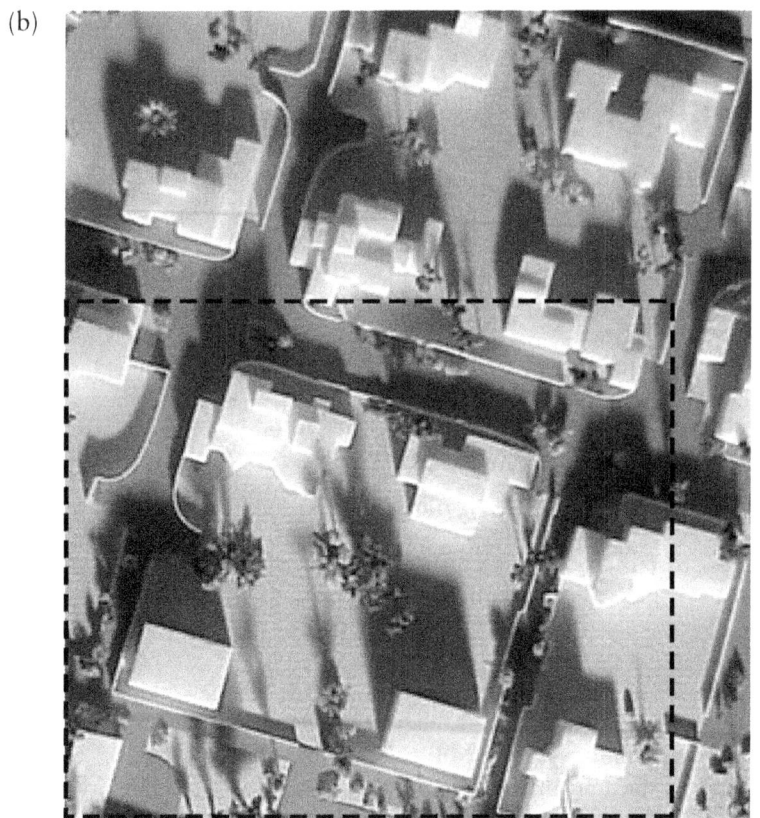

Figure 12.8 Building lots at the Neve Zin neighbourhood are clustered in groups of four. Building envelopes must overlie a 'P-point' at the extremity of the cluster. Drawing (a) shows location of P-points in two neighbouring clusters, while photo (b) shows a model of actual buildings constructed in the respective lots. Shadows in photo correspond to 9.00am on the winter solstice.

- The east- or west-facing walls of buildings adjacent to the outer extremes of each cluster are placed close to narrow north–south alleys running between the buildings, shading them and providing protection from wind.
- North-facing walls adjacent to the outer extremes of each cluster are placed close to the main east–west roads, helping to shade them.

Setback lines

Setback lines were established with two aims in mind:

- To establish the perimeter of the portion of each site to which solar access was guaranteed.
- To help in creating well-defined, shaded outdoor spaces, especially narrow pedestrian alleys.

Solar envelope

Solar access to all buildings was promoted through several features of the neighbourhood plan, including street orientation, restrictions on building location within each plot (applied by means of setback lines and the P-point) and an absolute height limit of 8m. In addition, solar access was specifically protected by means of a mandatory solar envelope, which defined the maximum height of any part of a building with respect to its location on the site. The solar envelope was presented in the form of an imaginary plane intersecting the southernmost setback line of a plot at an angle of 26.5 degrees to the horizon (see Figure 8.2, Chapter 8), limiting the height of an adjacent building to the south. The limiting angle was calculated to allow the south facade of each building full exposure to the sun between 0830 and 1430 hours (local time) on the winter solstice, thus guaranteeing solar access throughout winter in the main sunshine hours.

Public landscaping

Exposed soil in the desert often becomes a source of dust, which may be entrained by even light breezes and thus contributes to discomfort in outdoor spaces. While planting helps to reduce potential dust sources, in the arid climate of Sde Boqer all landscape vegetation requires irrigation, so that vegetative ground cover – especially in the form of lawns – is an expensive option which is quite possibly unsustainable. Therefore most public open space in the neighbourhood is covered with brick paving, while spaces that are landscaped with vegetative ground cover are confined to small areas and protected by shade trees and adjacent buildings. The compact nature of the public spaces – whether they are part of the circulation network, playgrounds or general landscaping – has reduced the extent of space that must be maintained and ensured that islands of more intensive greenery are concentrated in spots where they will be used to maximum benefit.

Critique

Any examination of the Neve Zin neighbourhood must begin by recognizing that the design brief called for low-rise, single-family houses in individual lots. This arrangement, although widespread in many countries, including the United States and Australia, is less common in Europe as well as in Israel, where multi-family apartment houses are the norm. Such developments provide much higher density (in terms of number of residents per unit area) and are typically medium- or high-rise. A low-rise development such as Neve Zin has much greater flexibility in terms of providing for solar access. Conversely, its low density also restricts the capacity to implement strategies that require compact spaces or low sky view factors to affect microclimate.

Neighbourhood planning for optimum building performance may sometimes result in strategies that are at conflict with an attempt to achieve comfortable outdoor spaces for pedestrians. In the case of the Neve Zin neighbourhood, the planners sought to maximize solar access for passive heating of buildings while providing shaded pedestrian zones. The first of these goals necessitated unobstructed roads with an east–west axis: the woonerfs therefore have no trees (in the public realm), and pedestrians may find shade cast by buildings and walls only in a very narrow strip adjacent to the south side of the street. Furthermore, since the pavement is almost wholly exposed to direct sunlight for most of the day, these streets are characterized by high radiant temperature during the daytime. To conserve water and minimize the cost of maintaining the public landscaping, vegetation is restricted to small 'islands' surrounded by paving blocks. Thus there is no scope for plants to moderate the environment of these spaces through shading or evaporative cooling. An alternative approach, whereby a row of trees would have been planted along the south side of each road, could have provided a continuous strip of shade for pedestrians. However, to preserve solar access to buildings on the north side of the street, its overall width would have had to be substantially larger.

The narrow north–south alleys are shaded throughout much of the day, as intended, even where pergolas, specified in the master plan, were not constructed. These spaces would have benefited from the growth of vines on the trellises, as intended by the planners – but their geometry ensured that even without them, pedestrians enjoy protection from the sun.

Note

1   Etzion, Y. (1990) 'A desert solar neighborhood in Sde Boqer, Israel', *Architectural Science Review*, vol 33, pp105–111.

13
Case Study 2: Clarke Quay

Lying near the mouth of the Singapore River, the site of Clarke Quay was the centre of commerce in the city during the late 19th century. It was named after Sir Andrew Clarke, Singapore's second Governor and Governor of the Straits Settlements from 1873 to 1875, who played a key role in positioning Singapore as the main port for the neighbouring Malay states. The development of a new commercial centre for Singapore led to gradual decline and decay of this district. In 1993, a major conservation project was launched by the government, in which a five-block section of the river-front, Clarke Quay Festival Village, was the focal point.

In 2006, further development of the area was undertaken, resulting in a weather protected and comfortable environment that can promote greater use of indoor and outdoor space throughout the year. The 21,428m^2 site comprises five blocks of buildings of warehouses and shop-houses that retain their original 19th century style. The project was aimed at transforming the buildings and at regenerating the riverside area in Singapore. In the renovated heritage buildings, the existing air-conditioning system has been replaced with a newer (conventional) one and new services have been provided throughout. However, the objective of this case study is to describe the design strategies adopted for outdoor spaces.

Analysis of local climate

Singapore lies just north of the equator (latitude 1.5°N). Its climate is classified as equatorial (Köppen climate classification *Af*). It has no true distinct seasons, although there are some differences between the northeast monsoon and the southwest monsoon seasons, which are separated by two relatively short inter-monsoon periods. Owing to its geographical location and maritime exposure, its climate is characterized by almost uniform temperature all year round, high atmospheric humidity and abundant rainfall (see Figures 13.1–13.3). Air temperature has a daily minimum of about 24°C and an average maximum of 31°C. Relative humidity is high all year round, averaging 87 per cent. The average annual rainfall is approximately 2,150mm.

Pedestrians exposed to the environment in Singapore are likely to feel some level of discomfort at nearly all times (see Figure 13.4), due to the combination of high humidity and warm temperature. Under these conditions, thermal comfort in outdoor spaces can be significantly improved only if air-flow is enhanced – provided that during the daytime radiant gains are also reduced.

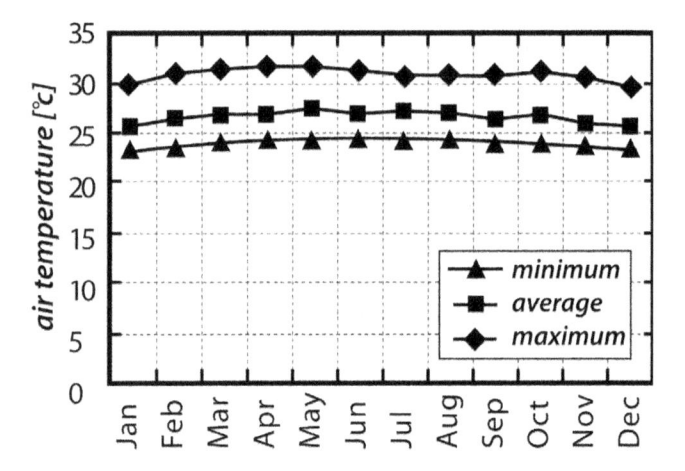

Figure 13.1 Monthly average values of air temperature at Singapore

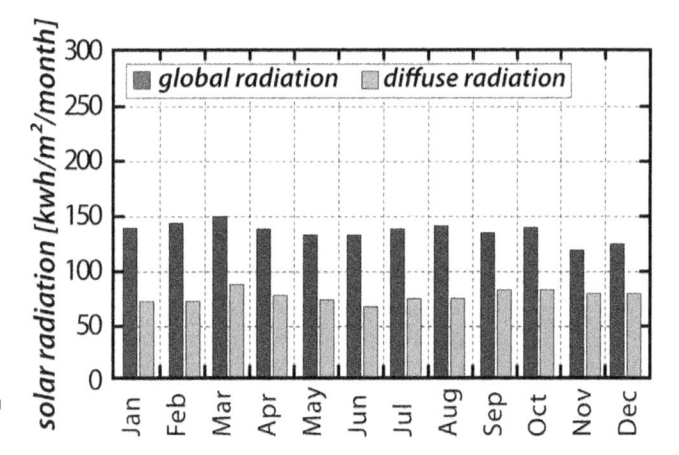

Figure 13.2 Total monthly insolation at Singapore

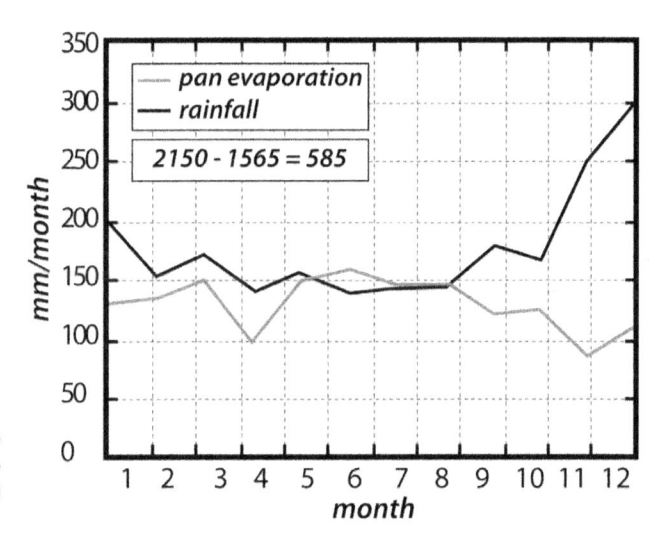

Figure 13.3 Monthly water balance for Singapore, showing difference between precipitation and potential evapotranspiration (PET)

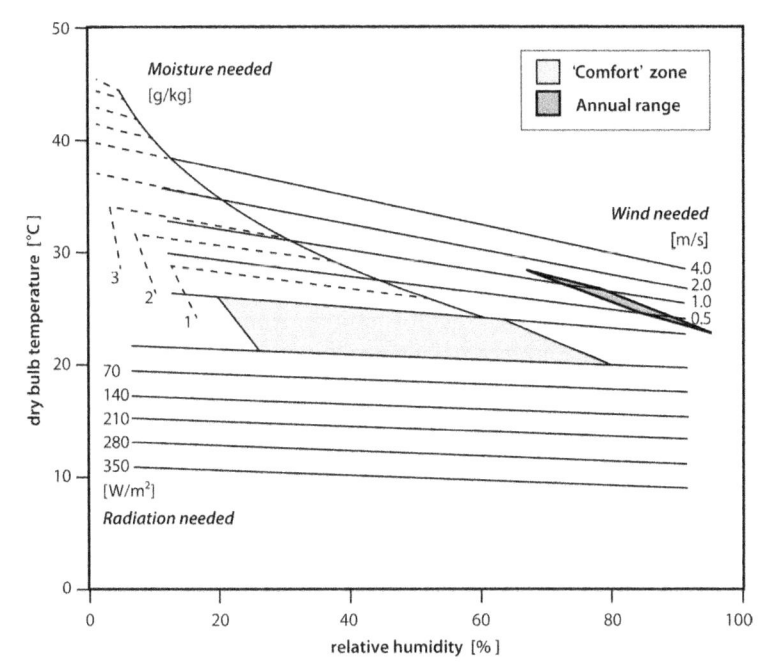

Figure 13.4 Thermal comfort analysis for Singapore

Note: The small shaded polygon indicates the annual temperature range, constructed from average monthly minimum and maximum temperatures for the months of July and December, which are the warmest and coolest months respectively, and the corresponding relative humidity values.

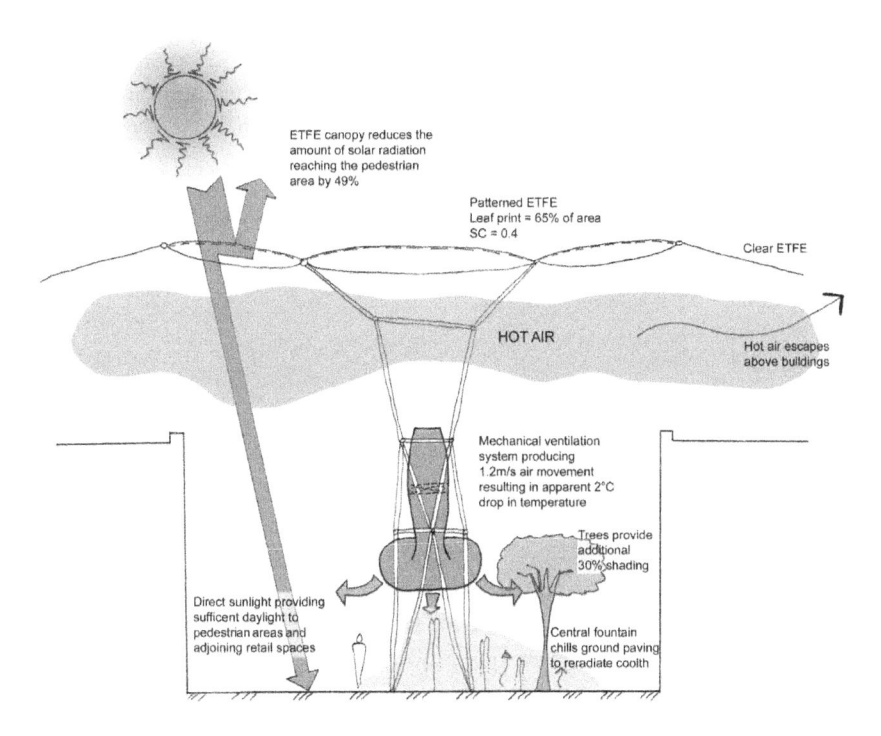

Figure 13.5 Overall conceptual approach to microclimate modification at Clarke Quay

Source: The Singapore Tropical Building Submission (STBS) for the ASEAN Energy Efficiency Awards (2006).

Design goals

The redevelopment of Clarke Quay into Singapore's only riverside festival village combining dining, shopping and entertainment posed several challenges. The complex was to retain the heritage buildings, provide occupants with comfort and protection from the elements, and be inherently low energy. The first option was to cover and air-condition the street areas, creating one large building. However, this would not have met the challenge of energy efficiency. Instead the design team sought to modify the microclimate of the streets and squares within the village to improve human thermal comfort and to promote activity in these spaces – without resorting to conventional air-conditioning of the space.

Climate-related response

The overall concept of the design, combining both shade and ventilation, is summarized in Figure 13.5. An artificial canopy acts as an urban forest, balancing daylight, shading, view and breeze. It optimizes these elements to improve comfort under humid tropical conditions.

Shading

The existing street design limited the opportunities to optimize the response to orientation and was a major constraint that the design team needed to address. Their primary response was to introduce artificial shading elements, which are supported independently of the buildings. These elements, in the form of individual canopies (Figure 13.6), cover almost the entire cross-section of the main streets within the development (Figure 13.7).

The canopy consists of a two-layer ethylene tetrafluoroethylene (ETFE) canopy with patterned sections in the middle and clear edges, providing an overall shading coefficient of 0.51 with 65 per cent printing on the external surface of the patterned sections.

Ventilation

In the tropics the benefits of cooling breezes should be maximized. The canopy projects above roof-top height to allow breezes from the river to permeate the urban streets (see Figure 13.8). This breeze is augmented by air blowers that increase the air movement to generate the feeling of a light breeze. The structural frame of the canopies, in addition to providing support for the shading elements, also combines fans that were included in the canopy frame design to provide a low-energy method of increasing the air velocity in the street (see Figure 13.9). These have been designed to provide a flow rate of $4.12 m^3/s$ per fan, achieving an average of $1.2 m/s$ along the streets.

Vegetation

Trees were added to complement the shade canopies and to provide cooling by evapotranspiration (Figure 13.10). The trees will grow to have over 30 per cent

Figure 13.6 Shade canopies in the Clarke Quay development

Photograph: Evyatar Erell.

coverage providing shade and enhancing the aesthetics of the environment. The light transmission of the canopy was specifically determined to ensure good plant growth while limiting excessive heat gain. The placement and size of trees was designed and modelled so as to maximize shade while not impeding the air-flow from the fans. Pruning and maintenance will be required to ensure that these branch heights are achieved.

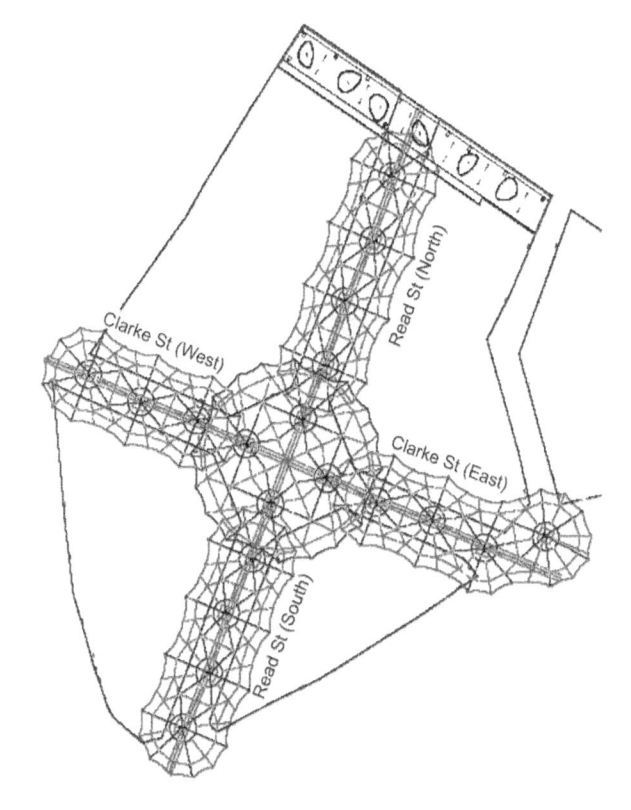

Figure 13.7 Plan view showing arrangement of the canopies in the Clarke Quay development

Source: STBS (2006).

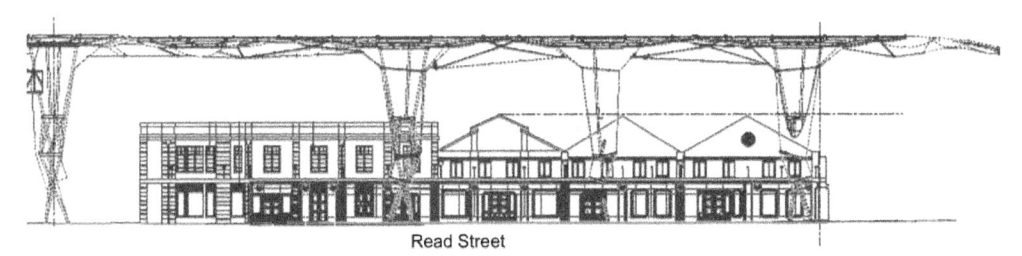

Figure 13.8 Section through street showing shade canopies projecting above roof height

Source: STBS (2006).

Evaporative cooling

The four main pedestrian streets converge on a central courtyard which is the focus of the development. A fountain has been designed here not only for the enjoyment of the users of the space but also to provide evaporative cooling (Figure 13.11): the water in the fountain is chilled by evaporation to between 15 and 20°C. Although operation of the jets is intermittent, water flows over the paving slabs before being collected into a gully around the fountain. This prolongs the cooling effect, since the thermal mass of the cooled pavement absorbs excess heat even when the water is not running.

CASE STUDY 2: CLARKE QUAY 245

Figure 13.9 View of air vents and ventilation fans installed to supplement natural air-flow at street level by mechanical means

Photograph: Evyatar Erell.

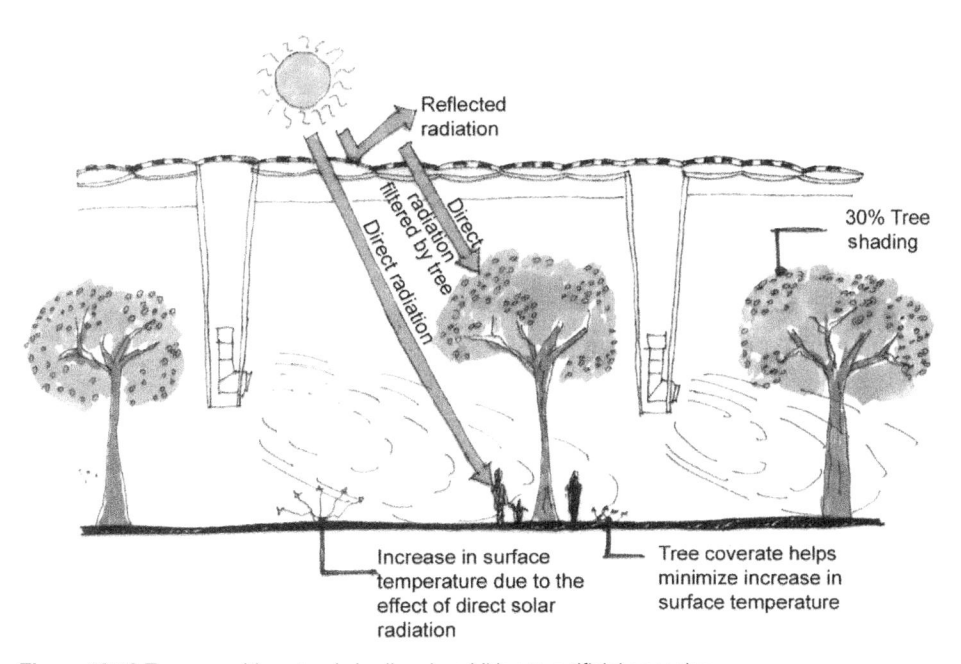

Figure 13.10 Trees provide natural shading, in addition to artificial canopies

Source: STBS (2006).

Figure 13.11 View of central plaza with sprayers operating

Photograph: Evyatar Erell.

Performance indicators

Three major criteria have been optimized in the design of the canopy and fans: pedestrian thermal comfort, air movement and daylighting. Each of these will be discussed in brief in the following paragraphs.

Pedestrian thermal comfort

Human thermal comfort in the renovated area was evaluated using the Equatorial Comfort Index (ECI)[1]. The ECI, developed in 1959 as a method of quantifying comfort in tropical environments, uses air temperature, humidity, mean radiant temperature and air velocity to categorize the sensation felt by a test sample of people. Compared to the existing uncovered street condition which serves as a base case, there is a significant improvement under the canopy – with, as mentioned, an average air velocity of 1.2m/s throughout the streets. The canopy and fans result in an increase in the hours that are considered to be in the most comfortable bands, from 41 per cent to 80 per cent (Figure 13.12). Both conditions were verified with on-site testing before and after construction.

The benefit of the fountain cooling was evaluated by measuring the mean radiant temperature (MRT) at standing height in and around the fountain. In the area around the fountain the MRT was reduced by 1.5 to 2K with the fountain running.

According to the project consultants, the combined effect of the design strategies is to create a street with an apparent drop in temperature of 3 to 4K,

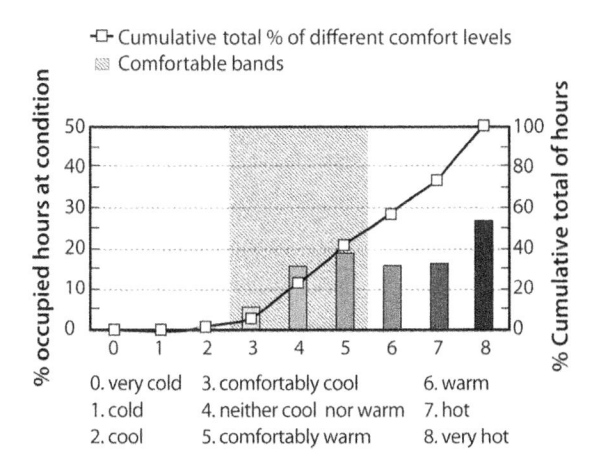

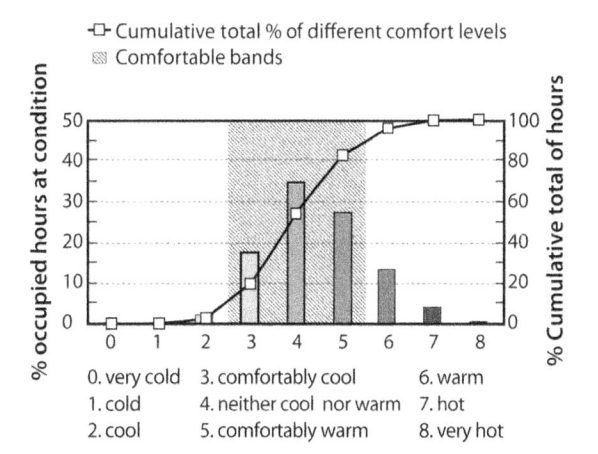

Figure 13.12 Predicted thermal comfort results for street level: with no canopy or fans (left); with shade canopy installed and assisted ventilation (right)

Source: STBS (2006).

significantly improving occupant comfort. The measured comfort levels are similar to those experienced in an air-conditioned, glass covered atrium. The space in Clarke Quay is estimated to be nearly ten times more energy efficient than an equivalent air-conditioned atrium space.

Air movement

The fans have been designed to work with the prevailing southerly wind to create a constant light breeze in the street areas. In tropical conditions, a wind speed of 1–1.5m/s creates a cooling effect that is equivalent to a 2K drop in temperature, thus improving the thermal comfort of the street users. This air velocity is also low enough not to cause problems with excessive movement of debris. Computational Fluid Dynamics (CFD) simulation was used in the design process to aid in the design of the fans and their location. The fans have been tested on site following the completion of the works, and an average air speed of 1.2m/s was achieved along each of the streets tested.

Daylighting

Although a reduction of radiant loads was a central feature of the pedestrian comfort strategy, it was decided that introduction of shading from the canopy and trees would nevertheless allow natural daylighting of the main public outdoor spaces. A computer package (RADIANCE)[2] was used to carry out a daylighting analysis of the design. The simulation study demonstrated that the canopies provide ample light for people at street level, that visual comfort should be acceptable under most conditions and that an appropriate level of light is also provided for the trees within the streetscape. The daylight levels are also sufficient to reduce the need for artificial lighting in the shop-front retail outlets.

Other environmental impacts

In addition to its beneficial contribution to pedestrian comfort, the canopy also reduces thermal loads upon the buildings adjacent to the streets. The reduction in air temperature in the streets is small, but the canopies reduce the solar load on the building facades facing the street by about 50 per cent, thus reducing the amount of energy required to air-condition the buildings.

One of the main aims of the Clarke Quay redevelopment was to complete the project in an environmentally friendly manner, considering the environmental impacts of all aspects of the design. The following areas have been addressed with a view to reducing or eliminating the negative environmental impacts and maximizing the positive contribution:

- *Waste management.* By refurbishing the existing buildings and maintaining the heritage of the riverside area rather than demolishing and building a new complex, large amounts of construction waste were avoided.
- *Air pollution.* The low-energy design means that carbon emissions for the site are lower, reducing the impact of the project on global climate.
- *Noise pollution.* As the site has been pedestrianized (i.e., vehicle access is restricted), the most common cause of noise pollution has been removed from the centre of the site. In addition, the soft surfaces of trees and water elements limit the extent of noise propagation. By using an open canopy instead of a closed glass atrium to cover the street, noise reflection and amplification have been avoided. The cooling towers for the site have also been installed in a location where the noise cannot be detected by the building users or people passing by.

Critique

The Clarke Quay restoration project demonstrates the application of engineering techniques to modify the microclimate of open public space. Due to their considerable expense, the solutions adopted in this project are unlikely to be applied on a larger scale. However, the primary features of the solution – shading and enhancement of air-flow – may be achieved by other means that are more suitable for city-wide application.

Disclaimer

The views expressed in the project critique represent the opinion of the authors of this book only.

Acknowledgement

The chapter draws extensively on the Singapore Tropical Building Submission for ASEAN Energy Efficiency and Conservation (EE&C) Best Practice Competition in Buildings, ASEAN Energy Awards (2006). Material from this presentation was provided by Ms. Heather Clement of Arup Singapore, consultants for the design team on building physics.

Notes

1   Webb (1959).
2   RADIANCE is an open source synthetic imaging system developed at the Lawrence Berkeley National Laboratory, CA: http://radsite.lbl.gov/radiance/HOME.html, accessed 28 June 2010.

References

Singapore Tropical Building Submission for ASEAN Energy Efficiency and Conservation (EE&C) Best Practice Competition in Buildings, ASEAN Energy Awards – 2006.

Webb, G. C. (1959) 'An analysis of some observations of thermal comfort in an equatorial climate', *British Journal of Industrial Medicine*, vol 16, pp297–310

Glossary

Absorptivity – the tendency of a material to absorb incident radiation. It depends on the incidence angle of the beam and upon its wavelength. Typically given as a decimal fraction, having a value between '0' and '1'. The absorptivity and *emissivity* of an object are equal for any given angle of incidence, wavelength and temperature.

Adiabatic process – a thermodynamic process in which the system experiences no net change in enthalpy.

Advection – transport of a substance or a conserved property in a fluid due to its bulk motion in a particular direction. The term is also used to distinguish horizontal flow from vertical transport of a scalar such as energy or moisture, termed convection.

Albedo – the proportion of incident solar radiation reflected by a surface. Typically given as a decimal fraction, having a value between '0' and '1'.

Anthropogenic heat – heat generated by human activity, including heat dissipated from buildings, heat given off by vehicles and the metabolic heat of people themselves.

Aspect ratio (H/W) – the ratio between the average height (H) of adjacent vertical elements (such as building facades) and the average width (W) of the space (i.e. the wall-to-wall distance across the street).

Attenuation factor (wind) – the extent to which wind speed is reduced at a given point in the urban canopy, such as at the centre of an urban canyon, relative to the wind speed at a given point above the canopy.

Black body – a (hypothetical) body that absorbs all the radiant energy incident upon its surface. Black bodies not only have an absorptivity of '1' but also are perfect emitters.

Boundary-layer – the layer of a fluid, such as air, that is adjacent to a solid surface.

Bowen ratio – the ratio between sensible heat flux and latent heat flux in a given location ($\beta = Q_H/Q_E$).

Canyon geometry – the urban canyon is typically described by means of its aspect ratio, which is the ratio of the average height of the adjacent buildings (H) to the width of the space (W). It is assumed to be much longer than it is wide (i.e. semi-infinite in length), but if the distance between adjacent intersections is small, the ratio of its length (L) to its cross-sectional width (W) affects the characteristics of flow in the space.

Canyon orientation (axis) – the angle between a line running north–south and the main axis running the length of the street or other linear space, measured in a clockwise direction.

Comfort zone (thermal) – a combination of environmental factors in which the majority of people may be expected to experience thermal comfort. The zone is sometimes depicted on a chart with dry bulb temperature and relative humidity as the axes, but other representations are possible.

Computational fluid dynamics (CFD) – a branch of fluid mechanics that uses numerical methods and algorithms to solve and analyse problems that involve fluid flows.

Conduction – the transfer of thermal energy between neighbouring molecules in a substance due to a temperature gradient. Conduction does not require bulk motion of matter.

Constant flux layer (also: inertial sub-layer) – part of the boundary-layer found above the roughness sub-layer in which the blending effect of turbulent mixing erases the significance of individual roughness elements so that vertical fluxes of scalars such as energy or moisture are spatially uniform within the layer.

Convection – bulk movement of molecules within fluids resulting in transfer of heat and mass. Convection is the sum of diffusion and advection in a fluid.

Cool island – a region, such as an urban park, that is cooler than its surrounding urban area.

Diffuse radiation – solar radiation that is scattered by the atmosphere and thus arrives from the entire vault of the sky.

Direct beam radiation – solar rays arriving directly from the direction of the sun. Beam radiation is measured on a plane normal to the direction of the beams.

Displacement height (zero-plane displacement) – the height above the ground at which the mean bulk drag of the surface appears to act; the base level from which the roughness length is measured. The sum of zero-plane displacement and roughness length indicates the height at which a logarithmic wind speed profile extrapolates to zero.

Eddy covariance – a technique to measure and calculate vertical turbulent fluxes within atmospheric boundary-layers. It requires accurate measurement of the 3D wind and another variable (such as the CO_2 concentration), which are decomposed into mean and fluctuating components. The flux of this property is proportional to the covariance between its fluctuating component and the fluctuating component of the vertical wind.

Effective temperature – the temperature at which motionless saturated air would induce the same sensation of comfort as that induced by the actual conditions of temperature, humidity and air movement.

Emissivity – the tendency of a surface to emit radiant energy, compared to a black body at the same temperature. Expressed as a decimal fraction between '0' and '1'.

Energy balance – the difference between the total incoming and total outgoing energy of a physical system. If this balance is positive, warming occurs; if it is negative, cooling occurs.

Evaporation – the physical process by which a liquid is converted to its gaseous state.

Evapotranspiration (ET) – the total process of water transfer into the atmosphere from vegetated land surfaces, comprising the sum of evaporation and transpiration.

Fetch – distance measured in the upwind direction.

Friction velocity – a measure of the shear stress of the wind above a surface, defined by the relation $u_* = \sqrt{(|\tau/\rho|)}$, where τ is the Reynolds stress, ρ the density and u_* the friction velocity.

Frontal area density – a three-dimensional measure of urban density, defined as the ratio between the vertical surface area of all building facades facing the prevailing wind direction and the overall horizontal plan area.

Geographic Information System (GIS) – an information system that integrates, stores, edits, analyses, shares and displays geographic information in a form suitable for a variety of applications such as remote sensing or land surveying.

Globe temperature – the temperature measured inside a globe thermometer, typically consisting of a black copper globe of 100 or 150mm diameter, or a 40mm ping-pong ball. It is affected by the balance between the radiant gain at the surface of the globe and the energy loss by convection.

Grey body – a body with constant surface emissivity over all wavelengths and temperatures that is less than '1' (a black body has a surface emissivity of '1' over all wavelengths and temperatures).

Heat capacity (volumetric) – the amount of energy required to produce a unit increase in the temperature of a unit volume of a material. It may be calculated as the product of the specific heat and the density of the material.

HVAC – Heating, Ventilation and Air-Conditioning systems in a building.

Isotropic radiation – an approximation that assumes that diffuse solar radiation has a uniform distribution across the whole sky dome.

Latent heat – the amount of energy released or absorbed by a substance during a change of phase (e.g. from solid to liquid) that occurs without changing its temperature.

Latent heat of vaporization – the amount of energy required to evaporate a unit mass of a liquid.

Leaf Area Index – the ratio of the total surface area of the leaves of a tree (single-sided in broad leaf species and projected area in needle canopies) to the area of the canopy projected on the ground.

Liman – a small clump of trees planted behind a levee constructed across an intermittent desert stream.

Long-wave radiation – electromagnetic radiation in the infra-red range with wavelengths of about 3 to 100μm.

Mean radiant temperature – the area-weighted mean temperature of the surfaces surrounding an object.

Microclimate – the climate of a very small space, which differs from that of the surrounding area. Microclimatic conditions such as air temperature, wind flow and the radiation balance within an area that may range in size from a few centimetres to several kilometres are influenced by the physical nature of the immediate surroundings as well as by the climate of the surrounding region.

Mixed layer (urban) – part of the boundary-layer which lies above the inertial sub-layer, where the atmosphere is influenced by the presence of the urban surface, but is not fully adapted to it. It comprises the bulk of the urban boundary-layer.

New effective temperature (ET*) – the temperature of a (hypothetical) standard environment (here defined as an environment in which air temperature is equal to the mean radiant temperature, relative humidity is 50 per cent and airspeed is less than 0.15ms^{-1}) in which a subject would experience the same skin wettedness and mean skin temperature as in the actual environment.

Nusselt number – the ratio of convective to conductive heat transfer across (normal to) the boundary between a solid and a fluid adjacent to it.

Oasis effect – a local-scale phenomenon in which evaporation is enhanced as a result of mechanical subsidence of warm air over a relatively cool surface due to mass divergence within tens of metres. If water supply is not restricted, the extra downward flux of sensible heat supplements the radiative energy supply and results in abnormally high rates of evaporation.

Park cool island – an area within a city where the presence of vegetation results in lower temperature than in the surrounding built-up areas.

Physiological equivalent temperature (PET) – the air temperature at which, in a typical indoor setting (without wind and solar radiation), the heat budget of the human body is balanced with the same core and skin temperature as under the complex outdoor conditions to be assessed. It is based on the Munich Energy-balance Model for Individuals (MEMI), which models the thermal conditions of the human body in a physiologically relevant way.

Plan area density – the density of building coverage on the ground expressed as the simple ratio between horizontal area of buildings and the total horizontal area.

Prandtl number – the ratio between viscous diffusion (measured by the kinematic viscosity) and thermal diffusion (measured by thermal diffusivity) in a fluid. The Prandtl number depends only upon the properties of the fluid itself (which may be affected by temperature but which are independent of a length scale).

Reflected (solar) radiation – solar radiation reflected from the ground or building surfaces.

Reflectivity – the tendency of a surface to reflect incident radiation. Reflectivity depends on the angle between the incoming radiation and the surface, and is usually measured at normal incidence. Expressed as a decimal fraction between '0' and '1'.

Reynolds number – a dimensionless number that gives a measure of the ratio of inertial forces to viscous forces in a fluid and consequently quantifies the relative importance of these two types of forces for given flow conditions. The Reynolds number is used to characterize flow as laminar or turbulent.

Richardson number (Ri) – a dimensionless number based on the ratio between buoyancy forces and inertial forces in the air, whose value determines whether convection is free or forced.

Roughness elements – features of the land surface or objects upon it that create greater drag and generate increased turbulence in the air flowing adjacent to it.

Roughness length – a measure of the aerodynamic drag of a surface, which results from the size and density of the individual roughness elements.

Roughness sub-layer – the layer adjacent to the surface, wherein the flow and turbulence are influenced by individual roughness elements.

Sensible heat – heat that results in a temperature change in a substance.

Sherwood number – the ratio of convective to diffusive mass transport in a fluid.

Short-wave radiation – solar radiation, comprising the radiant energy in the near-ultraviolet visible, and near infrared wavelengths, between about 0.2–3µm.

Sky emissivity – the emissivity that would need to be assigned to a hypothetical layer of air with a temperature equal to the ambient dry bulb temperature near the ground so that it would radiate the same amount of energy as that received from the actual sky by a horizontal radiator.

Sky temperature – the temperature a black body would have in order to radiate the same amount of energy as that received in practice from the sky by a horizontal radiator.

Sky view factor (SVF) – the proportion of the sky dome that is 'seen' by a surface, either from a particular point on that surface or integrated over its entire area.

Sol-air temperature – the equivalent outdoor temperature which will cause the same rate of heat flow at a surface and the same temperature distribution throughout the material as results from the actual outdoor air temperature and net radiation exchange between the surface and its environment.

Solar envelope – the maximum volume of an object, typically a building, such that it will not cast a shadow upon a given space at predetermined periods of the day and of the year. Solar envelopes are used as a tool in urban planning to ensure solar access.

Solar geometry – the relative position of the sun in the sky at a particular time and location.

Solar rights (of a building or of an urban space) – a legal guarantee of exposure to direct sunlight in a predetermined period, typically several hours each day during winter.

Standard effective temperature (SET*) – the dry bulb temperature of a hypothetical environment at 50 per cent relative humidity for subjects wearing clothing that would be standard for the given activity in the real environment.

Storage heat flux – the residual of the net radiant, sensible and latent heat fluxes at a surface, in the form of energy absorbed or given off by a solid such as the ground or built structure.

Sublimation – the transition of a substance from the solid phase to the gas phase without undergoing intermediate liquefaction.

Thermal admittance – the ability of a surface to accept or reject heat, expressed as the change in its temperature produced by a given change in heat flux. It may be calculated as the square root of the product of the material's thermal conductivity and volumetric heat capacity.

Thermal conductivity[1] – a measure of the ability of a material to conduct heat. It is measured as the quantity of heat flowing through a unit cross-sectional area of the material per unit time, if perpendicular to it there is a temperature gradient of one degree per unit thickness.

Thermal diffusivity – the simple ratio between the thermal conductivity (k) and the volumetric heat capacity (C) of a material.

Thermal inertia – the tendency of a material to resist rapid change in its temperature. Thermal inertia is affected by a material's thermal conductivity and by its heat capacity.

Thermostat effect – the tendency of a wet surface (such as a leaf or a planted area in an urban park) to maintain an almost constant temperature in an increasingly hot environment. Since some of the energy required to evaporate water is sensible heat introduced from adjacent areas by advection, the effect is not observed in the absence of wind.

Transmissivity – the fraction of incident light at a specified wavelength that passes through a material. Expressed as a decimal fraction between '0' and '1'.

Transpiration – a process whereby water is absorbed by plants (mostly though the roots), transported to the leaves and lost to the atmosphere through small openings in the leaves called stomata.

Troposphere – the lowest portion of the Earth's atmosphere, in which most weather phenomena take place, and which is generally characterized by appreciable water content and a decrease in temperature with increasing height above the ground. The thickness of the troposphere varies between about 10 and 20kms.

Turbulence – random chaotic disruptions to the flow of a fluid that result in rapid variations of pressure and velocity in space and time.

Turbulent flux – transport of a quantity such as energy or water vapour by quasi-random eddies in the atmosphere.

Urban boundary-layer (UBL) – part of the planetary *boundary-layer* that is affected by the presence of an urban surface. It typically begins at ground level, a short distance upwind of the city, and may extend a substantial distance downwind at higher elevations.

Urban canyon – a simplified representation of the complex 3D urban surface in the form of a semi-infinite street whose cross-section is defined by two geometrical parameters: the average height of buildings along the street (H) and the street width (W). The urban canyon is the basic unit used in many studies of the urban microclimate.

Urban heat island (UHI) – a difference in temperature observed between a city and its surrounding rural areas, whereby if isotherms are drawn for the area in question, the city is apparent as a series of concentric, closed lines of increasing temperature towards the centre.

Vapour pressure (of water) – a measure of the moisture content of air, based on the partial pressure exerted by water molecules in the air. Typical values near the surface are less than 4kPa (compared to total atmospheric pressure at sea level of about 100kPa).

Vegetated fraction – a measure of green space in the city, quantifying the ratio of horizontal area covered by vegetation to total horizontal area.

Ventilation – desirable air movement between the outside and inside of a building, which may occur naturally (natural ventilation) or by means of mechanical equipment (controlled ventilation).

Note

1. Thermal properties characteristic of a substance or material are denoted by the suffix 'ity', e.g. conductivity, transmissivity. The thermal behaviour of a material in situ, which depends not only on the characteristics of the substance but also upon its thickness or alignment, is denoted by the suffix 'ance', e.g. conductance, transmittance.

Index

3D urban models 22–23
absorption
    solar radiation 29–32, 79, 115
    see also thermal storage
acceptable conditions 135–137
adaptation 131
adaptive model of comfort 129–130
Adelaide, South Australia 76, 78, 136
    modelling building energy
        performance 225–226
    modelling climatic region
        comparisons 218–219, 221–222
    monitoring of CAT model 217
advection 51, 59–60, 166
    canyon air-flow 93–94
    urban heat islands 73, 105
aerosols 153, 158
air-conditioning 56, 75, 77, 125, 176
    modelling building energy
        performance 223–227
air-flow
    around buildings 86–88
    canyon wind flow regimes 88–90,
        197, 199
    canyon wind speed
        attenuation 90–91, 197–198
    controlling 150–153
    detailed patterns in an urban
        canyon 91–94
    effect of atmospheric stability
        on 104
    near the ground 85
    over obstacles 85–86, 89, 158
    and pedestrian thermal comfort 182
    urban-scale wind 105
    wind modification in the urban
        boundary-layer 95–103
    see also ventilation of urban streets;
        wind speed
air pollution *see* air quality
air quality 75, 153
    effect on radiant exchange 36–37
    effect of trees 178–180
    measuring 153
    planning for improvement 158–159
    urban geometry and diffusion of
        vehicle emissions 153–158
air speed *see* wind speed
air temperature
    and choice of building
        materials 159–161
    effects of parks and trees on
        168–172
    implications of urban modification for
        design 226–227
    modelling urban modification
        of 216, 218–226
    urban canyons 40, 197–199
    see also surface energy balance
        (SEB); thermal comfort;
        urban cool islands; urban
        heat islands (UHI)
albedo 29–30, 72
    building and paving materials 79,
        114, 160–161
    effect of urban geometry upon 30–33,
        196
    grass 183
    modelling 210
    skin 115
    soils 74
    vegetation 171
altitude, long-wave radiation 35
American Society of Heating,
    Refrigerating and Air-Conditioning
    Engineers (ASHRAE) 130
anthropogenic heat flux 49, 51, 54–55,
    60
    effect on heat islands 75, 78
    magnitude 56–57
    spatial variability 57
    temporal variability 58–59
architecture 6, 12*n*
    and microclimate 17–18
    and street dimensions 189
aspect ratios (H/W ratio) 7, 19–20,
    53–54, 189
    and air-flow 88–93, 197–198
    direct radiation 192–194
    effect on energy consumption of
        buildings 224–226
    reflected radiation 196
    thermal comfort 201–204
asphalt 160

atmosphere 15–18
　water vapour *see* evaporation;
　　evapotranspiration (ET)
atmospheric emissivity 35–36, 116
atmospheric stability 104
Australia
　distinction between urban and
　　rural 3–5
　see also Adelaide, South Australia
axis orientation 20
　air-flow 88, 90–93, 197–198
　direct radiation 191–192, 194
　effect upon albedo 31
　reflected radiation 196
　thermal comfort 201–204
　thermal stress 200–201

biogenic hydrocarbon emissions 79
Bosselmann, P. 2
boundary-layer heat islands (BLHI) 69
Bowen ratio 46–47
building and paving materials
　albedo 79, 114, 160–161
　surface temperature 48–51, 117,
　　159–161
　urban heat islands (UHI) 74, 159–160
buildings
　air-flow around 86–88
　anthropogenic heat from 54–58
　applications of microclimatology 142
　cooling through ventilation 220–222
　density and heat island
　　formation 72–73
　direct solar radiation 115
　effect of height upon albedo 31
　energy consumption 137, 176–178,
　　223–226
　relationship to shelterbelts 152–153
　solar rights for 145–148
　thermal storage 48–50, 202–203
　see also urban canyons

canopy-layer heat islands (CLHI) 69
carbon dioxide (CO_2) emissions 75, 80
CAT (Canyon Air Temperature)
　computer model 216–219, 221–222,
　　225, 227
CCP (climatic cooling potential)
　219–222
CFD (Computational Fluid Dynamics)
　214–216, 247
CIB Committee W60 (Performance
　Concept in Building) 10

circulation networks, vehicle and
　pedestrian 234–235
Clarke Quay case study 239
　analysis of local climate 239–241
　climate-related response 242–246
　design goals 242
　other environmental impacts 248
　performance indicators 246–248
climate 5, 203–204
　application of knowledge to
　　design 8–11, 141–144
　impact of buildings on
　　atmosphere 15–17
　impact on indoor environment 6,
　　109–110
　impact of thermal properties of urban
　　surfaces 161
　scales of study 17–18
　studies in urban areas 6–7
climatic cooling potential (CCP)
　219–222
climatic determinism 8
climatic region comparisons 218–219
clothing 115, 117
　and environmental comfort indices
　　128–129
clouds 35–36, 74–75, 114, 116
complexity of microclimate issues
　143–144
compound environmental
　indicators 130–131
comprehensive approach to problem
　solving 144
Computational Fluid Dynamics (CFD)
　214–216, 247
conduction, human energy balance 109
constant flux layer 16
convection, human energy balance
　117–120, 197–199
convective sensible heat flux 37–42
cool coatings 161
COSMO model 211
courtyards 170, 184, 244
　sky view factor 21–22

deciduous trees 172–176
desertification 158–159
design
　applications of science 8–11
　climatic determinism 8
　definition of 2
　see also urban design
dew 45, 210

diffuse radiation   111, 113, 115, 194, 200
direct solar radiation   111–113, 115, 191–194
diurnal patterns of change
　advection   60
　anthropogenic heat flux   58–59
　parks   168–169
　thermal storage   51–53
　urban heat and cool islands   68–71, 76–78
drag   95, 97
dust from arid regions   153, 158–159, 237
dynamic thermal equilibrium   128

economic considerations   143
eddies   42, 87–89
　corner   154, 159
eddy covariance   42
effective temperature scale   126
energy consumption
　air-conditioned buildings   223–226
　Clarke Quay case study   247–248
　implications of urban modification of air temperature   226–227
　influenced by outside spaces   137
　influenced by vegetation   176–178
　low-energy cooling of buildings   220–222
　Neve Zin case study   233, 238
energy weighted albedo (EWA)   32
EnerWin whole building energy simulation   223–226
ENVI-met   216
environmental comfort indices   125–129
environmental sustainability   7–8, 143
　Clarke Quay case study   248
Equatorial Comfort Index (ECI)   246
evaporation   43, 45–46, 73, 79
　fountains for cooling   244
　human energy balance   120–122
　urban canyons   199
　vegetated surfaces   167–170, 183
evapotranspiration (ET)   43–46, 48
　cooling   171, 177, 183, 199

Fanger, P.O.   128
fieldwork-based assessments of urban spaces   131–132
First Law of Thermodynamics   27
fish-eye lens photography   22–23
Fort Wayne, Indiana   211

fountains   244, 246
frictional drag due to roughness   95–96
friction velocity   95–97
frontal area density   24, 99–100

Gehl, Jan   1
geometric descriptors of the urban fabric   18–24
Glasgow, UK   218–219, 221–222, 224–227
glazed surfaces   115, 122n
　and solar radiation   32
global warming and urban heat islands (UHI)   68, 80
globe thermometers   119, 130–131
grass   45, 169, 171, 183
greenhouse effect   75, 80

heat capacity   50
heat transfer coefficients   37–40, 197
human activity
　applications of microclimatology   142
　see also anthropogenic heat flux
human adaptability   129–130
human energy use see anthropogenic heat flux
human metabolism   55, 58, 120–121, 128–129
human rights   7
humidity   46, 199

incoming sky radiation   34–35
Index of Thermal Stress (ITS)   120–122, 200–201
indigenous architecture   6
indoor environment
　impact of climate   6, 109–110
　impact of outside spaces on   137
industry, anthropogenic heat from   55, 58
inertial sub-layer   16, 41
internal boundary-layers (IBL)   166–168
intra-urban thermal breeze (IUTB)   105
inversion layers, oasis effect   169–170
irrigation
　effect on surface energy balance   45–46, 48, 167
　grass   79, 183–184
　parks   169–170
ISO 7243:1989, Hot Environments   131
ISO 7730 Moderate Thermal Environments   128, 136

isolated obstacles to air-flow   85–86, 89, 158
isolated roughness air-flow   88–90

Kirchoff's Law   34
Kuwait City   70

landscaped areas
    Neve Zin case study   237
    see also vegetation
latent heat flux   43–49, 212
    vegetated areas   168, 171
leaf area index (LAI)   180
logarithmic wind profiles   102–104
London   6
long-wave radiation   31, 33–36, 196–197
    asphalt   160
    effect of air pollution   37
    effect of vegetation   165, 169, 176–177, 180
    and human energy balance   110–111, 116–117
    modelling nocturnal cooling   210
Los Angeles   161

mathematical models   214–216
mean radiant temperature   117, 119
meteorological weather stations   6, 35, 80, 101, 142, 216
Mexico City   37, 47, 68
microclimate and architecture   17–18
    applications in urban planning   141–144
    Clarke Quay case study   239–248
    Neve Zin case study   231–238
micro-scale convection   37–40
Millennium Development Goals   7
models see urban climate models
Monin-Obukhov similarity theory (MOST)   106n
morphometric models   98–99

nadir view albedo (NVA)   32
Negev desert, Israel   120–122, 184, 200–201, 203–204
    see also Neve Zin case study; Sde Boqer, Israel
neutral temperature   129, 138n
Neve Zin case study   231
    analysis of local climate   231–233
    climate-related response   234–237

critique   238
design goals   233
New Effective Temperature   126–128
nocturnal cooling
    modelling   210
    and trees   79, 169
    urban and rural   75
non-canyon urban spaces   21–23

oasis effect   169–170
OASUS model   212–213
objective hysteresis model (OHM)   52–53
obstruction angles   146–147
Obukhov length   104
Olgyay Bioclimatic Chart   126–127
OUT-SET   128
ozone levels   79

parametric analysis   137
park cool islands (PCI)   168–170
parks   105, 165, 168–170
paving see building and paving materials
pedestrians
    controlling solar access for   148–150
    effect of wind   150–151
    Neve Zin case study   234–235
    see also thermal comfort
pervious and impervious surfaces   45, 73
physiological equivalent temperature (PET)   117, 128–129
physiological heat exchange   120–122
plan area density   24, 100
    effect upon albedo   30
plan area index   99
Planck's Law   33
plazas, sky view factor   21
pollution see air quality
population density
    urban growth   7, 80
    urban/rural indicator   4–5
power law relationship   95
power law wind profiles   101–102
precipitation   45, 73
predicted mean vote (PMV)   128, 131
predicted percentage dissatisfied (PPD)   128

RADIANCE   247
radiation   29
    effect of vegetation   73, 165

and the human energy balance 109–117
modelling 209–210
and thermal storage 48, 51–53
see also long-wave radiation; solar radiation
reflection of solar radiation 29–32, 111, 194–196
axis orientation 196, 200
surface materials 113–115, 160
vegetation 171
research, field studies versus laboratory-based 126, 129–130, 136–137
Reynolds number 38, 210
Richardson number 104, 210
roof gardens 177
roofing materials 32, 159–161
roughness
estimating parameters 97–101
and frictional drag 95–97
roughness length 96–97
rural and urban environments 3–5
albedo 30, 32
dew formation 45
effect of air pollution on radiation 37
effect of precipitation 73
thermal storage 50–51
urban heat islands 67, 71–72, 74–75, 159–160
vegetation 43
RUROS project 131–132

Sacramento, California 161
Sde Boqer, Israel
modelling building energy performance 224–226
modelling climatic region comparisons 218–219, 221–222
Neve Zin case study 231–238
OASUS model 212–213
solar envelopes 147
SEB *see* surface energy balance (SEB)
shade *see* solar shading
shear stress 95–97
shelterbelts 151–153
Singapore *see* Clarke Quay case study
site-specific climate data 216–217
skimming air-flow 88–90, 92, 100, 198
skin 115, 117
sky view factor (SVF) 19–20, 200, 225
diffuse radiation 113, 194
non-canyon urban spaces 21–23

parks 169
urban heat islands 72–73
soils
surface properties 50–51, 74
thermal capacity 169
sol-air temperature 117–118
solar envelopes 146–147, 150
Neve Zin case study 237
solar power 145–146
solar radiation 29–33, 41, 72, 76–77, 191–196
controlling pedestrian exposure 148–150, 190–191, 202–204
effect of air pollution 36–37
effect of vegetation 165
and human energy balance 110–115
reducing absorption 79, 160
rights to access to 145–148
solar shading 20, 76–77, 112–114, 225
Clarke Quay case study 242–245, 247
design for 148–150, 190–194, 205–206
parks 169
trees 171–176, 180–184
source area for air-flow 95, 98
Standard Effective Temperature 127–128
standard environments 126, 128
standards for thermal comfort 128, 130
Stefan-Boltzmann Law 33, 36, 196
storage heat flux 48–54, 212
street aspect ratio *see* aspect ratios (H/W ratio)
street obstructions 85–86, 89, 158
subsidiarity 143, 149
surface energy balance (SEB) 27–29
advection 59–60
anthropogenic heat 54–59
convective sensible heat flux 37–42
latent heat flux 43–48
modelling 214
radiation 29–37
thermal storage 48–54
urban heat islands 70
vegetation 73–74, 165–168, 176–177
surface heat islands (SHI) 69–70, 74
surface layer 15–16, 41
surface temperature
effects on heat transfer coefficients 40

properties of materials   48–51, 117, 159–161
surface water run-off   165
surplus incoming energy   45
sustainable planning   7–8, 143
SVF *see* sky view factor (SVF)
sweat   109, 117, 120–121, 182
    efficiency   199
system boundaries   27–28

temporal variability
    anthropogenic heat flux   58–59
    thermal storage   51–53
    vegetation   74
thermal admittance   50–51
thermal comfort   109–110, 125
    adaptive approach   129–130
    convection   117–120
    effects of grass and ground-cover planting on   183–184
    effect of trees on   172, 180–183
    environmental comfort indices   125–129
    fieldwork-based assessments of urban spaces   131–132
    long-wave radiation   116–117
    Neve Zin case study   233, 238
    solar radiation   110–115
    thermal preferences   134–137
    urban canyons   201–204
    see also Clarke Quay case study; thermal sensation models; thermal stress
thermal differentials and canyon air-flow   93–94
thermal diffusivity   51
thermal inertia   50, 203
thermal preferences   134–137
thermal sensation models   120, 122, 126–128, 132
    compared with thermal preferences   134
thermal storage   48–54, 60, 78, 202–203
thermal stress   111, 120–122
    measuring compound environmental indicators   130–131
    urban canyons   198–201
    vegetative landscape treatments and   184
thermal time-lag   202–203
thermostat effect   170

trees
    Clarke Quay case study   242–243, 245
    effect on air quality   178–180
    effect on air temperature   170–172
    effect on humidity   199
    and pedestrian thermal comfort   180–183, 205–206
    shelterbelts   151–153
    solar permeability   172–175
turbulent sensible heat flux   41–42, 212

UHI *see* urban heat islands (UHI)
universal design criteria   10–11
urban areas, definition of   2–5
urban boundary-layer (UBL)   15–17, 27
    air-flow and disturbance   85
    boundary-layer heat islands (BLHI)   69
    wind modification   95–103
    wind tunnel modelling   210–211
urban canopy-layer (UCL)   16–17
    canopy-layer heat islands (CLHI)   69
    solar radiation   29
    wind speed and direction   88
urban canyons   19–20, 189–190
    air temperature   40, 197–199, 220–222, 227
    albedo   31–32
    anthropogenic heat flux   56–57
    cool islands   76–77
    detailed air-flow patterns   91–94
    effect on energy consumption of buildings   224–227
    evaporation   199
    heat island development   72–73
    pollutant dispersal   154–158, 178–180
    street design   200, 204–206
    street shading and radiant heat   190–197
    thermal comfort   201–204
    thermal storage patterns   53–54
    thermal stress   198, 200
    wind flow regimes   88–90, 197
    wind speed attenuation   90–91, 197–198
    see also CAT (Canyon Air Temperature) computer model
urban climate models
    3D urban models   22–23
    adaptive model of comfort   129–130

CAT (Canyon Air Temperature)
    computer model 216–219,
    221–222, 225, 227
  integrated open-air models 211–213
  mathematical 214–216
  morphometric models 98–99
  objective hysteresis model
    (OHM) 52–53
  physical scale models 209–211
  see also thermal sensation models
urban cool islands 75–77
  computer modelling 218–219
  factors affecting intensity 77–79
  park cool islands (PCI) 168–170
urban design
  definition of 2, 5
  definitions of ends in 10–11,
    132–133
  impact on indoor environment 137
  means 133–134
  mismatch between theory and
    practice 11
  Neve Zin case study 231, 233–238
  for pedestrian thermal comfort
    134–137, 148–150, 204–206
  requirements 132–133
  solar rights for buildings 145–148
  thermal environment 132
  see also Clarke Quay case study
urban growth 7
urban heat islands (UHI) 6, 9, 67–69,
    142
  and air pollution 37
  building density 72–73, 198
  and changes in rural environment
    51
  computer modelling 218–219, 222
  effect on cooling demand 224
  formation 69–71, 75
  geographic location 75
  and global warming 68, 80
  human activity 75
  mitigation 79
  modelling 211
  properties of urban materials 73–74,
    159–161
  thermal breezes 105
  types 69
  urban form 71–72
  vegetation 73–74
  weather 74–75
  see also urban cool islands

urban planning
  applications of microclimatology
    141–142
  for better air quality 158–159
  guidelines for considering urban
    microclimate issues 142–144
  for pedestrian thermal comfort
    159–161, 200, 202–205
  to moderate city climates 161
  see also urban design
urban-scale wind 105

vegetated fraction 24, 48, 199
vegetation 79, 165
  Clarke Quay case study 242–243,
    245
  effects on building energy
    consumption 176–178
  effects on pedestrian thermal
    comfort 172, 180–184
  effect on surface energy
    balance 73–74, 165–168
  effect of trees on air
    temperature 170–172
  mathematical modelling 214
  parks 105, 165, 168–170
  shelterbelts 151–153
  size of area 170
  solar permeability of trees 172–175
  street trees and air quality 178–180
  see also evapotranspiration (ET)
vehicular traffic 54, 58–59
  air pollution 75, 153–158
  Neve Zin case study 234–235
ventilation of urban streets 153–158, 198
  Clarke Quay case study 242, 245, 247
  effect of trees 178–180
  guidelines for 159, 202
  modelling potential for cooling
    buildings 220–222
vortices 89, 91–94, 154–155
  effect of trees on 178
  solid barriers 151

wake interference air-flow 88–90, 198
water balance 43–47
water bodies 45–46, 199
  fountains 244, 246
weather 17, 58
  effect on urban heat islands 74–75
wet bulb globe temperature (WBGT)
    130–131

wicked problems   11–13*n*
Wien's Displacement Law   33
windbreaks   151–153
wind modification in the urban
   boundary-layer   95–103
windows   115
window-to-wall ratio   32
wind regimes   20, 75
wind speed   95–97, 197
   around buildings   86–88
   attenuation   90–91, 197–198
   effect of solid objects on   158
   effect of vegetation   165, 177
   and heat transfer coefficients   38–40, 117, 119
   porosity of barriers   151–153
   transforming data   101–103
   turbulence   41–42
   urban heat islands   72–73
wind tunnel models   88, 90, 100, 158, 210–211
World Meteorological Organization   7

zero-plane displacement   96–97